STATIUS' *SILVAE* AND THE POETICS OF EMPIRE

Statius' *Silvae*, written late in the reign of Domitian (AD 81–96), are a new kind of poetry that confronts the challenge of imperial majesty or private wealth using new poetic strategies and forms. As poems of praise, they delight in poetic excess whether they honour the emperor or the poet's friends. Yet extravagant speech is also capacious speech. It functions as a strategy for conveying the wealth and grandeur of villas, statues and precious works of art as well as the complex emotions aroused by the material and political culture of Empire. The *Silvae* are the product of a divided, self-fashioning voice: Statius was born in Naples of non-aristocratic parents, and his position as outsider to the culture he celebrates gives him a unique perspective on it. The *Silvae* are poems of anxiety as well as praise, expressive of the tensions within the later period of Domitian's reign.

CAROLE NEWLANDS is Professor of Classics at the University of Wisconsin–Madison. She has published *Playing with Time: Ovid and the Fasti* (1995).

STATIUS' *SILVAE* AND THE POETICS OF EMPIRE

CAROLE E. NEWLANDS

PUBLISHED BY THE PRESS SYNDICATE OF THE UNIVERSITY OF CAMBRIDGE
The Pitt Building, Trumpington Street, Cambridge, United Kingdom

CAMBRIDGE UNIVERSITY PRESS
The Edinburgh Building, Cambridge CB2 2RU, UK
40 West 20th Street, New York, NY 10011-4211, USA
477 Williamstown Road, Port Melbourne, VIC 3207, Australia
Ruiz de Alarcón 13, 28014 Madrid, Spain
Dock House, The Waterfront, Cape Town 8001, South Africa

http://www.cambridge.org

First published 2002

Printed in the United Kingdom at the University Press, Cambridge

Typeface Baskerville Monotype 11/12.5 pt.   *System* LATEX 2ε   [TB]

A catalogue record for this book is available from the British Library.

Library of Congress Cataloguing in Publication data

Newlands, Carole Elizabeth.
Statius' Silvae and the poetics of Empire / Carole E. Newlands
p.   cm.
ISBN 0 521 80891 X (hardback)
1. Statius, P. Papinus (Publius Papinius). Silvae. 2. Occasional verse, Latin – History and criticism.
3. Laudatory poetry, Latin – History and criticism.
4. Rome – History – Domitian, 81-96. 5. Imperialism in literature. 6. Emperors in literature.
7. Rome – In literature. I. Title.
PA6698. N38 2002
871'.01–dc21   2001037762

ISBN 0 521 80891 x hardback

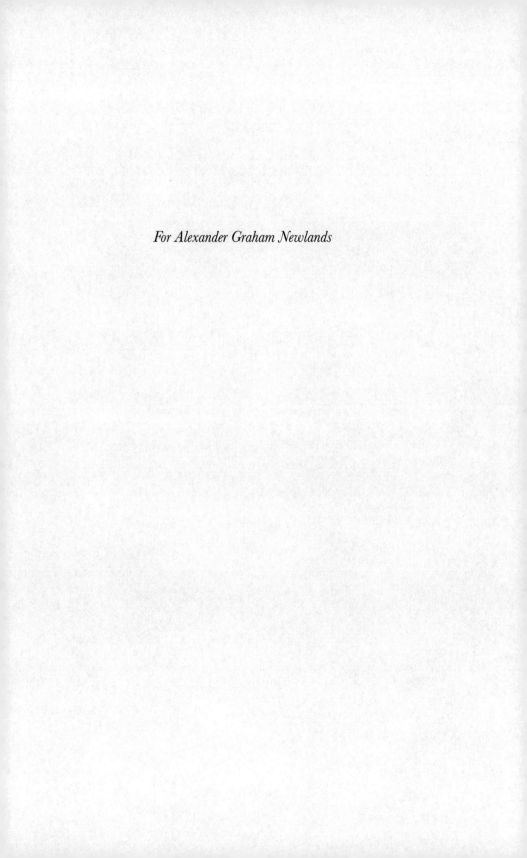

For Alexander Graham Newlands

Contents

Acknowledgments

I am grateful to the many people who have generously provided their time and support as I thought and wrote about Statius' *Silvae*. This book received its impetus from the sponsorship of the Virgilian Society, which invited me to take part in a panel on Flavian culture at the APA in 1996 and a conference at Cumae in 1997. That same summer the University of Tübingen allowed me to try out my fledgling ideas under the astute and kindly aegis of Professor Ernst Schmidt. The 'Statius workshop' organised by Kathleen Coleman at Trinity College Dublin in March 1998, provided a wonderful opportunity to engage with a wide community of scholars working in the field of imperial literature and culture; many of them have generously shared their time and interests with me. A grant from the National Endowment from the Humanities allowed me to spend the academic year 1997–8 in Cambridge, England, where a fellowship at Clare Hall provided me with my own 'locus amoenus'. Lectures given at the University of Cambridge and the University of Exeter that year helped me direct my own research in a more productive fashion. Thanks also are due to UCLA for supporting sabbatical leave and for annual faculty research grants, and to the University of Wisconsin–Madison for leave to complete the book. I would like to thank in particular Susanna Braund, Sven Lorenz, and Diana Spencer for reading and commenting on chapters of my work in draft. I am also very grateful to my students at UCLA for encouraging my interest in the *Silvae*, especially Charles McNelis and Jessamyn Lewis. My reviewers at Cambridge University Press were immensely patient and helpful. Above all, my thanks to John Henderson, for taking the time to set me on the road.*

* A shortened version of chapter 7 appears in W. Dominik and A. J. Boyle (eds.), *Flavian Rome* (Leiden, 2002).

CHAPTER I

Introduction

> To the Reader
> With the same leave, the ancients called that kind of body *sylva*,
> or 'ὕλη, in which there were works of diverse nature and matter
> congested, as the multitude call timber-trees, promiscuously grow-
> ing, a wood or forest; so am I bold to entitle these lesser poems of
> later growth by this of *Underwood*, out of the analogy they hold to
> *The Forest* in my former book, and no otherwise.
>
> Ben Jonson, preface to *Underwood*

This book about Statius' *Silvae,* a diverse collection of poems of praise,
sets out to make large claims about Statius' 'lesser poems of later growth'.
Written as his epic poem the *Thebaid* was reaching completion, and published in two sets late in the reign of the emperor Domitian in AD 93
and 95, the *Silvae* have been often dismissed as 'occasional' and therefore
trivial verse.[1] The subject matter of the *Silvae* – banquets, the emperor's
new statue, a new road – have been taken as evidence of the political
and literary decadence of an age that no longer had anything important to say.[2] Despite important work that has recently been done on
the *Silvae,* they continue to be branded with this derogatory stereotype.[3]
Yet, as Gunn points out, 'all poetry is occasional: whether the occasion
is an external event like a birthday or a declaration of war, whether
it is an occasion of the imagination, or whether it is in some sort of
combination of the two ... The occasion in all cases – literal or imaginary – is the starting point, only, of a poem'. Indeed, what matters are
the 'adventures' that the poet draws out from the occasion, 'adventures

[1] On the dating of the *Silvae* see Coleman (1988) xvi–xx.
[2] Thus Conte's (1994) history of Latin literature describes Statius' *Silvae* as exploiting the noble
inheritance of the Augustan poets Virgil, Horace, Propertius and Ovid 'in order to highlight
everyday kitsch (which includes the emperor and his worship)' (483). See however the more
balanced assessment of Fantham (1996) 170–82.
[3] See for instance White (1974), (1975), (1978); Hardie (1983); Ahl (1984a); Malamud (1995);
Henderson (1998); Hinds (forthcoming); Myers (2000).

that consist of the experience of writing'.[4] Statius' *Silvae* are a bold
new adventure in the writing of poetry in the age of Domitian. Taking as their starting-point a visit to a friend's estate in the country or to
the emperor's palace on the Palatine, for instance, they transform the
original occasion into a dynamic exploration of cultural values in an
age of enormous wealth and prosperity and rapid social and political
change.

Few might agree now with the enthusiastic declaration of Crusius in
his seventeenth-century edition of the *Silvae* that Statius is second only
to Virgil or even equal to him.[5] Yet even a brief study of the reception
of the *Silvae*, which it is not my task to delve into here, suggests the
shifting prejudices of different ages towards imperial power and private
wealth. In 1978 Williams famously described the period in which Statius
wrote the *Silvae* as an age of cultural and political decline.[6] But from the
point of view of many earlier scholars and writers, including importantly
Ben Jonson, Statius was an innovative poet, not a deficient imitator of
Virgil.

Indeed, along with the epigrams of Martial, Statius' *Silvae* are our
only contemporary poetic witnesses to the age of Domitian.[7] Since they
describe its monuments, its entertainments, its households, its country estates, and its court, they are important social as well as literary
productions. While they celebrate the magnificent villas of friends living in retirement as well as the majestic monuments of the emperor,
they also suggest alternative systems of value than the cultivation of
wealth alone. They provide a far more nuanced approach to Domitian's
Rome than is found in the later, hostile works of Pliny, Suetonius and
Tacitus. For the *Silvae* celebrate and explore in all its variety and ambiguity a flourishing literary and artistic culture which the condemnation
of Domitian's memory after his assassination has largely suppressed.
The *Silvae* deserve consideration therefore for what they reveal about
the role of poetry in imperial society as well as about imperial art and
architecture.

In order to express the public grandeur of the emperor and the
private magnificence of friends, Statius developed a new poetics in
the *Silvae*, what I have called here the 'poetics of Empire'. The *Silvae*

---

[4] Gunn (1982) 106–7.
[5] On the discovery of Statius' *Silvae* and their subsequent transmission see Reynolds (1983) 397–9.
[6] G. Williams (1978) 6–51.
[7] Although we do not know the relationship between Martial and Statius, since neither mentions
the other, they were clearly working in institutional proximity. See White (1975) 291–3.

are poems of praise. Whether they honour the emperor or the poet's friends, they delight in poetic excess with their extravagant language, elaborate metaphors and similes, elevated patronymics, and other special features. Poetic excess has been recognised as a feature of the *Thebaid* and crucial to the poem's overall epic effect.[8] In the *Silvae*, poetic excess exists in creative tension with the polished refinement and often playful wit characteristic of the small-scale poem. The poetics of the *Silvae* are fashioned to address the many facets of Empire, among them the new possibilities for acquiring political power, wealth, social status, and different forms of cultured leisure. Yet the extravagant language of the *Silvae* not only expresses the poet's intense appreciation for his object of praise; it also admits doubts and reservations and draws attention to the wider cultural significance of the original occasion. For praise, as recent work on panegyric has demonstrated, can encompass advice, admonition, criticism, even anxiety, as well as celebration.[9] Extravagant speech is also capacious speech; it functions as a strategy for conveying the wealth, the grandeur and the majesty of Empire as well as the complex emotions that such enormous power aroused.

All the same, the disjunction in the *Silvae* between small-scale form and expansive style has led to another powerful stereotype of the *Silvae* as 'mannerist' works that exalt artifice over sense. The epithet 'mannerist', an art-historical term uneasily applied to literary texts, bears with it strong associations of artistic decline.[10] Yet perhaps, as Melchiori has suggested, we should think of 'mannerism' not as a style of decadence or of transition between periods of greatness but rather as the expression of a certain type of adventurous and incisive sensibility.[11]

The hyperbolic praise of the emperor and friends that is characteristic of the *Silvae* was a new phenomenon in Latin literature. For the Augustan poets the *recusatio* had provided a polite way of acknowledging the ruler's greatness, while promulgating their own Callimachean abhorrence of the

---

[8] See the discussion of Hershkowitz (1998) 249.

[9] See for instance Whitby (1998) 1.

[10] Vessey (1973) 8, describing the style of the *Silvae*, defined what he termed their 'mannerism' as 'a disease of classicism'. Drawing upon Curtius's exposition of 'mannerism', Vessey, 7–14, promoted the view of Statius as a writer who prioritises art over sense, the unnatural over the natural. See Curtius (1973) 273–301. See also Vessey (1986), who argues that the *Silvae* accurately reflect the stifling world of court society: 'boys and parrots, like villas and "objets de luxe," were baubles in a gilded world' (2785). However, Vessey does not take into account the different positions from which Statius speaks; for instance, none of the villas that are described in the *Silvae* belong to members of the court. See also Cancik (1965) 38–43.

[11] Melchiori (1956) 26.

grandiose.[12] The contrast between small-scale form and often exuberant style in the *Silvae* allows Statius, who claims to have spent twelve years upon his epic *Thebaid* (*Theb.* 12. 811–12), to play with epic motifs in a new and dynamic fashion.[13] The *Silvae* confront the challenge of imperial majesty or, indeed, of a friend's enormous wealth and prestige by new poetic strategies that provocatively accommodate Callimachean topoi of exclusivity and refinement to the celebration of grandeur. The *Silvae* are self-reflexive poems that constantly draw the reader's attention to the diversity of their sources and inspiration. True poems of Empire, they reshape their varied poetic plunder into new poetic forms.

In the *Silvae*, linguistic extravagance is closely associated with artistic extravagance, with the emperor's daring new monuments and friends' avant-garde villas. For this was an age of innovative art and architecture. Domitian expressed the power and pre-eminence of the imperial city by rebuilding Rome in his own image as no emperor had before him apart from Augustus; he thus also strengthened his own dynastic authority.[14] Flavian civic architecture was characterised by a new concern with height and space, in particular with the creation of interior space on a large scale.[15] The Colosseum provides an obvious, familiar example. In domestic architecture too, painting of the so-called Fourth Style, which decorated the walls of the villas of Pompeii, showed a preference for unrest and sparkling light as well as for elaborate, fantastic architectural structures that created a sense of space and distance.[16] Statius' *Silvae* share in this aesthetic of grandeur and extravagance, particularly in those poems that deal with works of art and monuments. Linguistic extravagance functions in part as a response to the architectural and technological audacity of the imperial age.

Pliny's books on the history of art (*HN* 34–6), written at the start of the Flavian period under the emperor Vespasian, testify to the flourishing material culture of Empire. Vast economic and mineral resources fostered the production and display of great works of art as well as luxury

---

[12] See Fowler (1995a) 253–5, who comments on the political import of the Augustan poets' abhorrence of the grandiose.

[13] See the preface to Book 1 where Statius argues that epic poets have historically been allowed 'to play with a more relaxed style' (*remissiore stilo praeluserit, praef.* 1. 9).

[14] See Sablayrolles (1994). Although many of Domitian's buildings and works of art were destroyed, Sablayrolles (113) notes that the large number of *fistulae plumbeae* (lead water pipes) bearing Domitian's name testify in themselves to the great extent of the emperor's public works in Rome.

[15] Macdonald (1982) 72–4.

[16] See for instance the description of the Fourth Style of painting in Andreae (1977) 154.

goods for both public and private consumption.[17] New wealth, combined with relative social mobility, made possible the social diffusion of taste. The paintings of villas on the walls of relatively modest homes in Pompeii, for example, testify to the importance of social emulation in the downward spread of aristocratic values.[18] As Goldthwaite has argued, social emulation gives particular vitality to the development of culture as its values are perpetuated, generated, and transformed by the possession of wealth and luxury goods.[19]

Pavlovskis has pointed out that the *Silvae* are the first poetry in Latin literature to celebrate openly the amenities made possible by the Empire's abundant wealth: 'Statius may well have been the first to devote whole poems to the praise of technological progress, as well as the delights of a life spent in a setting not natural but improved by man's skill.'[20] Yet wealth presents a moral challenge. This flourishing material culture was also accompanied by anxieties about the moral costs of technological progress and the dangers of limitless expansion.[21] Pliny's *Natural History* is a case in point. Pliny presents the history of art as a narrative of technological progress and moral regress.[22] Art, after all, is shaped from the materials of the natural world; these materials, however, can be used for perverted purposes to foster human greed and unnatural desires. For Pliny, art can become as corrupted as the natural world. As Barkan points out, 'insofar as art is at the nexus of nature and public power, it may come into conflict with them'.[23] Thus after the assassination of Domitian, Pliny the Younger in his *Panegyricus* (50–2) attacked Domitian's building programme as gaudily excessive, vehemently opposing that emperor's architectural extravagance to Trajan's architectural restraint. Modern critics have followed ancient critics in seeing Flavian art and architecture as symptomatic of the moral decline of the age.[24]

Yet in the *Silvae* Statius participates in and helps propel a shift in attitudes towards luxury. His poetry reflects a new confidence in wealth and

---

[17] See Beagon (1992) who argues for the importance of the *Natural History* to an understanding of first-century attitudes.

[18] Zanker (1998) 23.   [19] Goldthwaite (1993) 3.   [20] Pavlovskis (1973) 1.

[21] On the moralising tradition against luxurious building see Edwards (1993) 250–72; on fears over geographical expansion see Romm (1992), especially 121–71.

[22] On Pliny's pessimistic views on art and technology in his own age see in particular Barkan (1999) 66–88. On the social anxiety that underpins Pliny's views see Wallace-Hadrill (1990). See also Beagon (1992) 55–63, 75–9.

[23] Barkan (1999) 69.

[24] See for instance Newmyer (1984) who argues that Flavian art and literature is the embodiment of excess.

the freedom to use it for private purposes as well as for civic good. And as extravagantly ornamented poetry written for patrons and friends, these poems too participate in the material economy of Empire, creating what Connors has called 'a literature of leisure'.[25] An interesting precedent is provided here by Pindaric poetry, which, as Kurke has argued, openly celebrated the architectural display and magnificence of the poet's patrons. Yet there luxury was validated by the community when it was linked to munificence and concern for the public good.[26] Pindar was an influential poet for Statius. The private poems to Statius' patrons, however, acknowledge a departure from the former public-spirited idea of the uses of wealth. Still, as Connors points out, leisure too is a cultural artefact. A reader's freedom to enjoy luxurious works such as the *Silvae* assists in the self-definition of the imperial élite.[27] Moreover, as Goldthwaite has commented of a similar shift in attitudes towards luxury in Renaissance Italy, the possession of expensive material goods was important in the creation of cultural identity. A gorgeous house, an expensive work of art provided pleasure, to be sure, but these things also helped create the owner's image in a community and establish a social network of friends and acquaintances.[28]

Luxury in the *Silvae* is closely implicated with ideas about social status and artistic patronage. Furthermore, as we shall see, in these poems luxury is presented as the enabler of virtue. Through the celebration of luxury Statius proposes a provocative new concept of nobility to which economic, moral and artistic values rather than hereditary qualifications are essential. Indeed, in the *Silvae* private patrons are represented as the guardians of traditional morality as well as art; the imperial court, on the other hand, fosters the novel and the exotic. In *Carm.* 2. 15 Horace famously deplored private luxury and endorsed public magnificence. The poems of the *Silvae*, however, portray a society where traditional civic values are now largely nurtured in the private sphere. Indeed, as we shall see, private magnificence implicitly provides a critique of the public realm. While the *Silvae*, then, challenge conventional morality about luxury, their enthusiasm for wealth and 'technological progress' is not unreflective; indeed, particularly in the poems to the emperor, Statius exploits ancient ambivalence about technology as part of a larger meditation about the nature and limits of imperial power.

---

[25] See Connors (2000); also Hinds (forthcoming).   [26] Kurke (1991) especially 163–94.
[27] Connors (2000) 492–3.   [28] Goldthwaite (1993) 204–12, especially 208.

The *Silvae* therefore are intimately engaged with the reshaping of artistic and literary traditions. In particular, the relationship of the *Silvae* to the moralising traditions embedded in earlier literature is not unimaginative but, to borrow a term from Greene, 'heuristic'.[29] The heuristic text uses the confrontation with the specificity and alterity of prior texts to develop a new modern voice and idiom, and by calling given codes into question it goes on to produce a fresher, more hospitable code for the modern age. The *Silvae* boldly contest and reshape Greek and Roman poetic tradition and their related systems of values in order to express the new grandeur and complexity of imperial society. They embrace then a semiotic programme of resistance to the literary traditions in which they are inscribed. Exulting in extravagance of thought and expression, they represent an ambitious attempt to reformulate cultural values and explore new means of expression for the cosmopolitan culture of Empire.

In this book then I reject the idea of decline. Indeed, as Hinds has commented, the concept of 'decline' can in any event be an enabling trope.[30] I wish in particular to call attention instead to the ways in which Statius' *Silvae* are pioneers of new literary forms and modes of expression. In their exploration of different social, political and literary relationships they are audacious, experimental poems – true poetry of Empire as they mark out new poetic terrain. The *Silvae* are not exercises unimaginatively derivative of the Augustan 'masters' but new poetry which, through its negotiation with previous literature, displays the poet's provocative attempts to find an appropriate voice and idiom for the Flavian age.

This book on Statius' *Silvae* will focus on the poems that describe both private and public works of art or monuments. Descriptions of works of art bring into play important issues involving patronage and the relationship of the state to the artist: art after all is an important index of culture. My aim is to provide a revisionist view of the *Silvae* as sophisticated and extravagant poetry concerned both with the workings of imperial power and with the social function and status of poetry in the later period of Domitian's rule. This was a difficult time politically and intellectually, as I shall explain shortly. Domitian, it seems, carefully controlled artistic and literary production through state-sponsored festivals. At the same time, this period also seems to have offered expanded opportunities for

---

[29] For a discussion and definition of 'heuristic' see Greene (1982) 40–3.

[30] Hinds (1998) 83–98. Earlier he notes that imperial poets can in fact emphasise their 'secondariness', in particular in relation to the Augustan poets. As readers however we should try to resist interpreting poets according to their own self-interested terms (55–6).

leisure, social mobility, and the acquisition and enjoyment of wealth. By surveying Domitian's Rome from a variety of social and geographical situations and points of view, the *Silvae* register some of the variety of popular feelings about society and government in a period of great prosperity and continuing social and political change. They significantly give voice to the hopes, joys, desires, and concerns of Romans at the end of the first century of the imperial system. They are poems then of anxiety as well as praise.

DOMITIAN AND HIS MONUMENTS

Our views of the reign of Domitian have been generally influenced by the partisan writings of Pliny and Tacitus, who represent Domitian as a cruel despot. Suetonius too associates the latter part of Domitian's rule, the very period in which the *Silvae* were written, with a 'reign of terror' during which many senators were executed.[31] Recent accounts of Domitian's reign by Jones and Southern have attempted to re-evaluate the character and achievements of this emperor and to call attention to the senatorial bias of those writers opposed to his rule.[32] It is significant that, according to Suetonius, who reports the public reception of Domitian's assassination, the people were indifferent, the military were outraged, and only the senators were glad.[33] But since much material evidence for Domitian's reign was destroyed after his assassination, the task of re-evaluation is of course difficult. Part of the problem too resides in the fact that Domitian was the last of his line; he had no successors to protect his memory.

It seems clear, however, that Domitian's reign was in some trouble in the period in which Statius was writing the *Silvae*. In AD 89, Rome

---

[31] See for instance Suet. *Dom.* 10; for a revision of Suetonius' view that the latter part of Domitian's reign was one of terror see Syme (1988). Coleman (1998) rejects the notion that there was any substantial political crisis in AD 93, the year of the majority of Domitian's senatorial executions as well as of the expulsion of the philosophers in Rome. The broad spectrum of political opinion in Rome, she argues, would not have been unsettled by the removal of aristocratic dissidents (354). Yet the aristocrats could still influence and shape public opinion in various ways, and several of them were important writers and intellectuals.

[32] Jones (1992); Southern (1997); also the collection of essays in Pailler and Sablayrolles (1994). Gsell's biography of Domitian (1894) was innovatory, as it attempted to move away from a purely negative interpretation of the emperor. Gsell concluded that although Domitian was a good administrator, he was a bad financier and a mediocre general; his chief fault lay in his execrable character! On Gsell's work see Lengrand (1994) 57–67. A whitewash of Domitian that provides a strong corrective to uniformly negative readings of the sources is offered by Waters (1964).

[33] Suet. *Dom.* 23. On this passage see the commentary of Jones (1996) 152–7.

had again been faced with the possibility of civil war as the legions, on the anniversary of Vitellius' insurrection in AD 69, mutinied under Saturninus on the Rhine.[34] Suetonius dates the 'reign of terror' from this event as Domitian, increasingly suspicious of senatorial dissent, executed prominent senators and intellectuals.[35] Senatorial sources represent AD 93, the year of the publication of the first collection of the *Silvae* (Books 1–3) as a particularly terrible year for intellectuals and senators. Domitian expelled philosophers from Rome, and he brought seven important accusations of *maiestas* against senators, resulting in three executions and four sentences of exile.[36] Among those executed were writers who, according to senatorial sources, were punished for what Domitian perceived as political insults: Helvidius Priscus the Younger for ridiculing Domitian in a mime (Suet. *Dom.* 10. 4); Herennius Senecio for praising the elder Helvidius Priscus (Tac. *Agr.* 2. 1) and for writing his biography (Dio Cass. 67. 13. 2; Plin. *Ep.* 7. 19. 5); Q. Arulenus Rusticus for praising Thrasea Paetus (Tac. *Agr.* 2. 1; Suet. *Dom.* 3; Dio Cass. 67. 13. 2). But were they executed for their writings or for other offences? It is at least significant that all these men were intellectuals and writers.[37]

Syme, however, has claimed that Rome in the early nineties enjoyed relative peace and prosperity, since active war was at an end for Rome by AD 92. Yet military and economic stability was surely not all. The expulsion of the philosophers and the executions of senatorial writers must have been unsettling at the very least to the intellectual community of which Statius was a part. Indeed, Syme does admit that this period – the time of composition of the *Silvae* – was a time of dynastic instability as Domitian increasingly isolated himself from family and supporters and failed, after twenty years of marriage, to produce or adopt an heir to carry on the dynasty.[38] His own brother's premature death too must have created anxiety among the populace of Rome who would not have forgotten the carnage of the last crisis over succession in AD 68–9. As

---

[34] See Jones (1992) 144–9.

[35] Suet. *Dom.* 10. 1; Tac. *Agr.* 45. Jones (1992) sees no clear evidence for a change in Domitian's policy after this uprising but admits that it may have exacerbated Domitian's 'suspicious nature' (149).

[36] Suet. *Dom.* 10. 4. On the date and sources see Jones (1996) 93.

[37] Waters (1964) 76 endorses the view of Rogers (1960) that a number of the charges against the writers and philosophers were genuine and politically motivated, not based solely on their literary compositions. See Coleman (1998) 346 for a list of the senatorial executions and exiles. She notes (347, n. 42) that none of the three offenders executed was condemned for a philosophical work *per se*, but finds it significant that all were senatorial and therefore representative of a tradition devoted to intellectual and autonomous pursuits.

[38] Syme (1988) 259–62.

Vinson comments, 'Domitian's only real crime was to be the last Flavian; it is this political failure on his part which constitutes the only historical reality of any moment for the literary tradition; it is this which must be justified and explained; this, which serves as the distorting mirror through which his imperial career as whole is viewed.'[39]

Senatorial sources describe Domitian as an isolated, paranoid, and secretive ruler. Yet the ruler's isolation, enhanced by his failure to build a future dynasty, was in some ways also the inevitable result of his cultivation of a new divine ideology that set him above and beyond mortal limits and experience. These divine ambitions of Domitian were reflected in his physical dominance in the urban context. As Elsner notes, 'there has always been a symbiosis between the will to power and monumental display'.[40] Domitian took Augustus seriously as a model and transformed the face of Rome with magnificent new or restored buildings and works of art that proclaimed Rome's status as the political and cultural capital of the world and the emperor its divinely appointed ruler.[41] Indeed, next to the first emperor, Domitian was the most important builder of the imperial city.[42] The city that tourists visit today is in large part a Flavian, not an Augustan city. In particular, Domitian's cultivation of the divinity of his family and of his own proximity to the gods is seen early on in his reign in the Arch of Titus, which provides us with the first artistic representation of a ruler's apotheosis.[43] Other monuments stressing the divinity of his family followed, including a temple to the Flavian family on the site of Domitian's place of birth that commemorated both the present ruler and the deceased members of his family who had been made gods.[44]

To understand the ideas about the emperor that were encoded in Flavian monuments, let us pause for a little from the *Silvae* to consider in particular two imperial works of art that are crucial for an understanding of the imperial ideology of Statius' poetry: the obelisk currently in the Piazza Navona, and the Cancellaria reliefs.

---

[39] Vinson (1989) 449. Note too that the epitome of Dio Cassius comments that Titus' satisfactory record as emperor may in part at least be due to the brevity of his reign (Dio Cass. 66. 8. 3–5).

[40] Elsner (1996b) 32.

[41] Jones (1996) 49–50 notes that Suetonius in *Dom.* 5 significantly underplays Domitian's public works out of hostility to the emperor. Thus Suetonius fails to list among Domitian's architectural achievements the enormous palace complex on the Palatine. For a more generous account of Domitian's restorations and buildings see Gsell (1894) 90–119; D'Ambra (1993) 19–46; Darwall-Smith (1996) 102–252.

[42] On Domitian's emulation of Augustus see Sablayrolles (1994).

[43] See Richmond (1969) 218–23. Richmond dates the Arch of Titus to the early 80s (219). See also Darwall-Smith (1996) 168–71.

[44] D'Ambra (1993) 33–5; Darwall-Smith (1996) 159–65.

In the centre of the Piazza Navona, the former site of Domitian's grand stadium, an obelisk today towers up from Bernini's 'Four Rivers' fountain. This is not the obelisk's original location, which is not known for certain.[45] Domitian erected the obelisk, of Aswan granite and over sixteen metres high, probably at the start of his reign. It is inscribed with hieroglyphs that were cut by Roman, not Egyptian, stonecutters, and the hieroglyphic inscriptions were probably commissioned by Domitian himself.[46] The obelisk is a striking amalgam of Egyptian traditions used to express imperial realities.[47]

The obelisk survived the destruction of images and inscriptions of Domitian after his assassination, undoubtedly saved by the fact that the hieroglyphs were incomprehensible to the majority of the population. Its inscriptions therefore are important for a rare understanding of Domitianic ideology. According to Grénier, who has undertaken a thorough study of them, they constitute a hymn of praise to Domitian and the Flavian dynasty, despite the Pharaonic formulaic language in which they are couched.[48] They proclaim Domitian a king and divine ruler like the ancient Pharaohs; they ascribe to him the virtues traditional in the Egyptian cult of the ruler such as military prowess, worldwide glory, and divine birth. The divinisation of Vespasian and Titus is also proclaimed on the obelisk. While this proclamation is in accordance with Roman imperial procedure for deceased emperors, it also reflects the comprehensive approach to dynasty adopted by the Hellenistic cult of the ruler.[49] The obelisk then served as a covert instrument of imperial propaganda and had particular relevance to Domitian's reign.

The concept of deification was essential to Flavian imperial politics as it had been to those of the Julio-Claudians. Julius Caesar's deification, for example, had been a crucial element of Augustan ideology that

---

[45] We do not know the date, either, but Grénier (1987) 939 speculates a date early in Domitian's reign. This article provides a thorough interpretation of the hieroglyphic inscriptions, relating them specifically to the imperial ideology of Domitian. Historiographical tradition situates the obelisk in the space between the Iseum Campense and the Serapeum. Grénier (1996) 357–8 argues that the complex on the Quirinal, vowed by Domitian to the sacralisation of his family and of his own birth there, may be a location more in keeping with the nature of the inscriptions. For a detailed discussion of the obelisk and its inscriptions see also Darwall-Smith (1996) 145–50.

[46] Grénier (1987) 961.   [47] Grénier (1987) 959.

[48] Grénier (1996) 357. Note that Darwall-Smith (1996) 148–9 expresses scepticism about Grénier's ideological interpretations; he argues that they are simply in conformity with Egyptian standards and styles for inscriptions. Yet they are provocative in their concept of a ruler's divinity set within a Roman context.

[49] Rose (1997) 5 argues that Ptolemy IV established a significant precedent when he added to the dynastic cult all the previous Ptolemies who had been earlier omitted, so that the cult stretched uninterruptedly from Alexander to the present rulers.

legitimated Augustus' own right to rule.[50] Unlike the Julio-Claudians, however, the Flavians had no long aristocratic heritage on which to draw. Domitian was from an upstart family. According to Suetonius, Domitian's father Vespasian was the son of a tax-collector.[51] He came to power through the support of the military in a civil war many of whose significant events were brutally fought out in Rome itself. His need to advertise to the general populace the legitimacy of his rule was particularly urgent. Thus, Suetonius comments that although Vespasian lacked *auctoritas* ('authority') and *maiestas* ('majesty'), he quickly set about acquiring them.[52] Lacking aristocratic credentials, he found legitimation for the new dynasty through claiming the protection of the gods, in particular the Egyptian god Serapis. While in Alexandria worshipping the god in his temple, Vespasian is said to have had a striking vision that was linked to the collapse of the Vitellian resistance in Rome; in the temple too he displayed sudden healing powers.[53] Both miracles confirmed the special protection of Serapis and Vespasian's divine right to rule. Domitian developed the ties of the Flavians with Egyptian cult by rebuilding, for instance, the Alexandrian sanctuary to Isis in the Campus Martius, and by the carving of the obelisk, a monument to Domitian's divine aspirations.[54]

Hannestad has argued that in art, coinage, and literature, Domitian was associated with the gods to a greater degree than any of his predecessors.[55] On the obelisk, through the imperial appropriation of the overt language of Egyptian ruler-cult, the hieroglyphs emphasise the legitimacy of the Flavians as a new dynasty in Rome both through the sanction of the gods and the claims that the family has earned the right of deification. Such claims thus assert Domitian's predestined right to rule.[56] Yet the additional claim on the obelisk for Domitian's divine birth is startling, for this implies that Domitian is a living god. Such a claim represents a bold intensification of the dynastic politics that provided the impetus for this monument. The hieroglyphs represent a sort

[50] On the dynastic need for Augustus to be divine see Barchiesi (1989) 91–7 (discussing Ov. *Met.* 15. 745–51).

[51] See Suet. *Vesp.* 1–2; *Dom.* 1. Jones (1992) 1–3 argues that claims of Flavian poverty were a myth, but that Vespasian's father was the first to give the family any kind of eminent standing.

[52] Suet. *Vesp.* 7. 2.   [53] Suet. *Vesp.* 7.

[54] On the close ties between the Flavian dynasty and Egyptian cult see Malaise (1972) 407–17.

[55] Hannestad (1988) 140–1.

[56] Grénier (1987) 952 argues that predestination was an important aspect of Flavian ideology for Vespasian and Titus as well.

of personal code for the emperor, a private language through which he could speak what he did not perhaps dare to proclaim openly in words: his aspirations to divinity and absolutist monarchy. They suggest that Domitian was attempting a tacit revolution in the image of the emperor that was in line with Egyptian and Hellenistic ideas of kingship and far distant from the Augustan concept of the emperor as *princeps*, first citizen.

Augustus' famous obelisk, erected in the Campus Martius as part of a symbolic complex with the Ara Pacis and the Mausoleum, served as an elaborate form of sundial that marked the passing of the hours, days, and seasons. Along with its claims to supreme social and political authority, the Augustan obelisk conveyed the idea of the emperor as the benefactor of the people, both controller and provider of time.[57] Domitian's obelisk, on the other hand, reveals the dominant dynastic preoccupations of his regime. Although most Romans would not have understood the meaning of the hieroglyphs, a pyramidion on top of the obelisk would have given them some idea of the monument's message. This pyramidion was carved with reliefs showing the Egyptian gods themselves making obeisance to Domitian; it visually represented the divinity and indeed sacred superiority of Domitian.[58] Besides, the Roman populace would have recognised the Egyptian obelisk as a traditional monument of regal and divine power. Obelisks were first erected by kings in Egypt; a prophetic dream, according to Pliny, commanded the first king to do so.[59] In its new site in the capital, an obelisk was also a sign of Rome's military and economic dominance. Pliny tells us that the transportation of an obelisk to Rome was an extremely challenging, expensive undertaking.[60] Domitian's obelisk, then, expressed the idea of Empire, of a power that could not only dominate other important nations but also transcend ordinary human limitations. Even without providing comprehension of its script, the obelisk was a prominent symbol of imperial authority that approximated the divine. Indeed, the very arcane nature of the script signified the emperor's separation from ordinary mortals and the sacred, inscrutable nature of his power.

The obelisk represents in hieroglyphic code what is visually implied by the Cancellaria reliefs, the impetus to legitimate the new dynasty

---

[57] On Augustus' obelisk see Buchner (1982).
[58] Darwall-Smith (1996) 149.   [59] Plin. *HN* 36. 14. 64.
[60] Plin. *HN* 36. 14. 70. The achievement of bringing obelisks by sea to Rome is described by Pliny as a 'miracle'.

through close association with the gods.[61] These beautifully sculpted reliefs were found in 1937–9, not in their original location, but stored in a sort of builder's yard under the Cancellaria Apostolaria. They provide significant evidence of the importance of the themes of apotheosis and military triumph to Domitian's promotion of the new dynasty.[62] Their date is controversial, though the prevailing argument seems now to be that these are sculptures from late in Domitian's reign, around AD 92.[63] Such a date coincides with the period in which Statius was writing the *Silvae*. Although the events depicted on these reliefs have been variously interpreted, it seems clear that both reliefs – known as A and B – stress the authority and indeed the validity of the new dynasty now headed by Domitian; they are companion pieces to one another.[64]

The basis of support for the Flavian dynasty was the army, which had brought Vespasian to power in civil war. Yet this unsettling reality of Roman imperial politics had to be occluded by the cultivation of the imperial fiction that the gods sanctioned the Flavian inheritance of the imperial mantle. Relief B has been generally interpreted as providing a retrospective view of Vespasian's *adventus* into Rome in AD 70 at the end of the civil war, when Domitian handed over his temporary power in the city to his father. According to Dio, this was an occasion for rebuke, as Domitian had been behaving out of line.[65] This relief, however, provides a picture of 'mutual trust' between Domitian and his father Vespasian.[66] Here the gods surround father and son in a framework of divine authorisation. Vespasian and Domitian stand side by side with arms outstretched to one another, poses that suggest a transfer of power; above Vespasian's head are traces of a flying Victory holding a triumphal crown. The Geniuses of the people and of the senate surround them, while Roma, in military garb, is throned on the left of Domitian along with the Vestals. The event, as Simon has argued, represents Vespasian's return to Rome as Domitian *wanted* it to be known.[67] Domitian thus has the commanding position on the relief. An epigram of Martial commemorates this event, commenting however that Domitian deferred to his elder brother

---

[61] For helpful discussion of the disputed Cancellaria reliefs see Richmond (1969) 223–8; Kleiner(1992), 191–2; Darwall-Smith (1996) 172–7.

[62] D'Ambra (1993) 34.   [63] Kleiner (1992) 191; Darwall-Smith (1996) 175.

[64] Thus Simon (1960), who also discusses the conflicting opinions on the meaning of the reliefs. She argues that relief B demonstrates the *pietas* of the emperor, relief A the *virtus*.

[65] Dio Cass. 65. 9. 3–10. 1.

[66] Richmond (1969) 224. Richmond argues that this relief was 'intended' to kill such negative stories about Domitian's behaviour.

[67] Simon (1960) 151.

Titus by giving up his temporary authority in Rome and consenting to be the 'third' in power.[68] But Titus is not represented on the Cancellaria relief. Vespasian's assumption of Roman *imperium* is mediated through his younger son in the 'hour of birth of the Flavian dynasty', which is sanctioned in a solemn ceremony by the gods and sacred personifications of the Roman state.[69] The representation of Domitian with Vespasian, surrounded by gods, lictors, Vestals, and vividly portrayed abstractions, endows the new dynasty with an *auctoritas* and *maiestas* that is expressed through both religious and military iconography. This relief, then, provides a review and re-evaluation of Domitian's first period in power.[70] The prominence of Domitian fits in with what we know of his later memorialising practices: when he restored older buildings, he erased all mention of the former builders and the dedicatory inscriptions bore his name alone.[71]

About relief A there has been less agreement. Domitian (his head resculpted after his assassination to resemble Nerva, the emperor who succeeded him) is in military dress and is engaged in a formal ceremony that has been interpreted as either a military *profectio* or an *adventus*.[72] Victory, Mars, and Domitian's divine patroness Minerva lead Domitian; Geniuses of the Senate and People salute him, and soldiers form his retinue along with lictors. Both reliefs suggest that Domitian's right to rule is sanctioned by the gods, by his father, and by his people, including, significantly, the army. As Hannestad has argued, the Flavians strongly associated their dynasty with the concept of victory.[73] Thus, despite the different occasions represented on these reliefs, Victory is common to both. Through personification monumentalised in stone, the reality of military supremacy can be given a religious, quasi-divine authority. Political praxis and moral and religious authority are harmoniously combined on these reliefs. Indeed, both reliefs provide a significant perspective upon the development of dynastic ideology in Domitian's later years.

---

[68] Mart. 9. 101.

[69] Simon (1960) 154. Waters (1964) 56–7 discounts suggestions that relations between Domitian and Vespasian were strained at this time. Last (1948) 9–14 argues that relief A makes a pointed response to relief B, proving Domitian's fitness to rule and to engage in military affairs.

[70] Thus Hannestad (1988) 135.

[71] Hannestad (1988) 139.

[72] Kleiner (1992) 191–2, argues that relief A specifically represents Domitian's *profectio* for the Sarmatian War of AD 92–3. See also Darwall-Smith (1996) 174–5 who argues that it more generally represents a *profectio*.

[73] Hannestad (1988) 139.

The classicism of the Cancellaria reliefs challenges the previously entrenched conception of the art of this period as 'Flavian Baroque'.[74] As Richmond comments, the contrast between these reliefs and those on the Arch of Titus, with its dense crowding of figures and rich elaboration of planes, could hardly be greater.[75] Indeed, the classicising style of the Cancellaria reliefs evokes comparison with the restrained dignity of the friezes of Augustus' Ara Pacis. But the ideological strategies of the Ara Pacis and the Cancellaria reliefs are very different. Rose has argued that the Ara Pacis represented a radical break with Republican commemorative tradition. Family portraits had traditionally been retrospective. The Ara Pacis however prospectively presents contemporary families; it thus demonstrates the new importance in this era of women and children on public monuments and the careful dynastic groupings that supported and legitimised the first imperial dynasty.[76] On the Ara Pacis relief Augustus moves within a procession of family and priests. The gods are kept entirely separate, represented on separate sides of the altar where they do not mingle with humans.

The Cancellaria reliefs represent another radical departure in imperial iconography. Here gods mingle with humans, priests with soldiers, and there are no women and children. Personifications too are intermingled, making concrete abstract notions of imperial authority in a development that is paralleled in literature in Statius' *Thebaid*, where a major innovation lies in the impact that personifications have upon human beings.[77] This is a bold new expression of imperial power as sustained by the reality of military support on the one hand, and by the myth of the emperor's proximity to the gods on the other. Indeed, the complicity of the army with the emperor is represented as part of the divine, normative ordering of the Roman universe under Domitian.

Moreover, the Cancellaria reliefs validate Domitian's dynasty in a more abstract way than the Ara Pacis reliefs and with more concentrated focus on the emperor. Gods and personifications replace the family – women and children – that mingle with the senators and priests on the Ara Pacis and that suggest the fertility and prosperity of the Julio-Claudians. The personifications – the genius of the people, the genius of the senate, Roma, and Victoria – conceptualise and

---

[74] Hannestad (1988) 133–4.
[75] Richmond (1969) especially 225–8.   [76] Rose (1997) 15–16.
[77] See Feeney (1993) 364–91. Richmond (1969) 223 notes the novel intermingling of minor deities and personifications on the Arch of Titus.

elevate the broad base of political and indeed military support on which the emperor's authority rests; the presence of the gods authorises that support as a function of the divine will. The Cancellaria reliefs suggest the importance to Domitian of a dynastic ideology sustained by the twin props of military success and the divinely sanctioned right to rule.

Significantly, I believe, the Cancellaria reliefs lack the theme of fertility that is so prominent on the Ara Pacis. The prospective ideology of the Augustan monument is expressed on the Cancellaria reliefs through the theme of divinity, not fertility. Family members, apart from Vespasian on relief B, are absent. The Flavian dynasty was a family affair, yet Domitian had no direct heir, his only child having died in infancy while Vespasian was still emperor.[78] According to Tacitus, Vespasian was able to claim the throne because, unlike his competitors in the civil war of AD 68–9, he had two sons on whom to build a dynasty, a stable line of succession.[79] But by the time of these reliefs – and of the composition of the *Silvae* – the peace and order of the imperial state had come to depend upon a single person. Hence, in order to assert the continuing legitimacy of the new Flavian dynasty and his right to rule, Domitian had a particularly pressing need, perhaps, to advertise both the divinity of posthumous family members and his own close relations with the gods.

Statius' poems of imperial praise in the *Silvae* interpret and scrutinise the myths upon which such monuments of Domitian were based, investigating the new militaristic and monarchical expressions of imperial power and the relocation of that power within a court modelled upon that of Hellenistic rulers. The *Silvae* are important contemporary witnesses to the development of the ruler-cult in Rome and to the thoughts and feelings aroused by such a development. In particular, as I shall argue in this book, as poetry of praise they encompass anxiety as well as celebration. In them, as Tacitus' account of the rise of the Flavians to power in the *Histories* has also shown, the question of how to achieve dynastic stability is an integral theme that lacks any certain or comforting resolution.[80] The *Silvae* too reveal in various ways anxiety about the stability of the Flavian dynasty that, late in Domitian's reign, rested on the fiction of divine invincibility rather than upon the real presence of living heirs.

---

[78] On Domitian's lack of an heir see Scott (1936) 72–5.
[79] Tac. *Hist.* 2. 77.   [80] Ash (1999) 136–46.

POETRY OF PRAISE

The *Silvae* are worth careful investigation for the insight they offer into the conditions of speech under imperial autocracy. In particular, the poems that address public figures are a key witness to the political ideology of Flavian Rome and to the poet's complex relationship with imperial power. Coleman has shown that there is sound evidence that portrays Domitian as an active patron of the arts and literature; for instance, he instituted Greek-style competitive festivals, the Capitoline and the Alban games.[81] Yet although he clearly encouraged the arts in a highly public way, Domitian seems to have actively suppressed speech that could be construed as dissident.[82] As a writer Tacitus publicised the senatorial opposition to Domitian, and his remarks have to be treated with caution. Yet his comment at the start of the *Agricola* that the most dangerous kind of literature in Domitian's Rome was panegyric, suggests, at the very least, the enormous artistic challenge posed by the project of praise and the changed political conditions governing speech.[83]

Encomiastic poetry traditionally fell under the rubric of epideictic, the branch of literature concerned with display, with the pleasure of the audience, and often associated therefore with false embellishment.[84] Thus poetry of praise has often been dismissed as mere flattery, particularly among imperial poets themselves.[85] Today the *Silvae* have provoked sharply opposing reactions, particularly as regards the poems concerning Domitian and his entourage. They have been considered either as court propaganda or as a form of 'doublespeak' that mocks and subverts a hated tyrant.[86] According to Vessey, Statius' poems to the emperor 'mirror faithfully an ideology developed, self-protectively, by Domitian'.[87]

---

[81] Coleman (1986) offers the fullest revisionary discussion of Domitian's patronage of the arts. Quint. *Inst.* 10. 1. 91–2 praises Domitian as a fine poet, whose imperial duties have taken him from the Muses. Suet. *Dom.* 20 says that Domitian had no time for reading apart from official documents of Tiberius.

[82] Coleman (1986) 3115 concludes that although Domitian did encourage literary activity, he could not tolerate writings with a political stance.

[83] Tac. *Agr.* 1.

[84] On the relationship between the *Silvae* and the prescriptions of epideictic rhetoric, see Hardie (1983) 91–102. The suspicion of epideictic oratory goes a long way back. See for instance Pl. *Symp.* 198d-9; Cic. *Orat.* 65; and the discussion of Levene (1997) 96–9. For a helpful definition of the terms 'panegyric', 'encomium', and 'epideictic' see Russell (1998) 20–1, who however notes that the genres of prose literature are ill-defined.

[85] For instance, Persius' *Prologue* to his *Satires* denounces the florid art of the Silver poet whose greed dictates the debased art of imperial adulation.

[86] For the term and notion of 'doublespeak' see Bartsch (1994) 98–147, applied, however, not to the *Silvae* but to Tacitus' *Dialogus* and Juvenal's *Satire* 7.

[87] Vessey (1986) 2798.

Alternatively, according to Ahl, they are subversive poems that use panegyric to mock and deride Domitian in a covert fashion. In his important article 'The Art of Safe Criticism', Ahl demonstrates that the Romans made a distinction between speech that was understood *aperte*, openly, without secondary meaning, and speech that was understood *palam*, meaning one thing on the surface but implying another, quite different meaning.[88] This second kind of speech, which Ahl calls 'figured', was particularly useful for addressing autocratic rulers in the presence of an attentive audience trained to analyse rhetorical argument. Ahl grants autonomy to the writer of imperial praise. Addressing the emperor becomes a subversive activity, a clever encoding of oppositional points of view.[89] Ahl views Statius as a master of irony and ambiguity, features he sees as essential to panegyric.

Yet if we accept Ahl's view of the *Silvae* as cleverly coded documents of subversion, we must also accept Tacitus' and Pliny's assessment of Domitian as a psychopathic monster who could only be properly addressed by covert means. And this also means acceptance of the hierarchy of genres that accords more weight to the opinion of the historian than to the writer of 'occasional' verse. Taking a different approach, Dewar has argued that in any discussion of imperial panegyric the question of the truth or falsehood of praise is irrelevant. Imperial panegyric was based on fantasy, and this was a convention fully understood by an audience who knew not to accept hyperbolic praise literally.[90] Fantasy is an important feature of the imperial *Silvae*, yet acknowledgment of its presence should not obscure the important work that panegyric can perform. Fantasy invites the reader to engage with a wide range of ideas through symbol, simile, and metaphor. Indeed, the figured speech of panegyric, to which Ahl rightly draws attention, serves more complex purposes than either fantastic flattery or mockery, as ancient thinking about panegyric demonstrates.

In his discussion of the epideictic genre in oratory, Quintilian points out that although panegyrics are classified as epideictic in that they involve display, at the same time, however, they are necessarily advisory and involve national interests.[91] Indeed, for Quintilian, there is no strict demarcation between the three branches of oratory – the forensic,

---

[88] Ahl (1984b).

[89] See Levene (1997) 97, n. 110 for a brief discussion of Ahl (1984b). He suggests that the accounts of 'figured speech' in classical rhetoricians may be governed less by the reality of speech under tyranny than by the necessity of defending panegyrical rhetoric itself.

[90] See especially Dewar (1994) 209.   [91] Quint. *Inst.* 3. 4. 1–16.

the deliberative, and the epideictic – for he locates epideictic 'in practical matters as well as in display', *tum in negotiis tum in ostentatione.*[92]
Aristotle divorced epideictic from the practical side of oratory and reserved it solely for the pleasure of the audience. Quintilian does not
acknowledge this strict separation: *sed mos Romanus etiam negotiis hoc munus
inseruit* ('but Roman practice has made this class too a part of practical affairs').[93] Panegyrical oratory has a place at the law court, on state
occasions, or at funerals, for instance.[94] Thus, although Quintilian acknowledges that the purpose of epideictic speech is to embellish and
praise, he does not entirely divorce such praise from an admonitory
or advisory function. Important to Quintilian are not only the immediate subject of praise but also the audience, which learns from the
panegyric to test character and judge moral worth.[95] Indeed, Quintilian
likens the epideictic genre to *suasoriae* on the grounds that the same
features used to persuade are often used to praise. Thus Quintilian acknowledges the public function of epideictic in Roman society, yet, as
Russell notes, he gives little in the way of practical advice such as how
a consul might thank an emperor.[96] Indeed, the surviving 'textbooks'
that deal with panegyric are late works and limited in their range and
application.[97] Russell cautions that we must not think that panegyrical literature was derived from textbook prescriptions. Instead it dipped
deep into a rich literary culture, and this is certainly the case with Statius'
Silvae.[98]

As Braund has shown, Quintilian's discussion is borne out by the
marked protreptic element in Latin panegyric.[99] For instance, Pliny's
Panegyricus, delivered at the start of the emperor Trajan's reign, provides
an important example in prose for thinking about Statius' poems of
imperial praise.[100] Pliny explains the function of panegyrical speech as
advisory as well as celebratory. Panegyric provides a way of helping
good rulers recognise the value of their deeds and bad ones recognise

[92] Quint. *Inst.* 3. 4. 14.   [93] Quint. *Inst.* 3. 7. 2.
[94] Some critics have sought the origin of the Latin panegyric in the *laudatio funebris.* Our extant
   panegyrics differ from the *laudatio* in being in praise of the living, not the dead. A strong case has
   been made for the political uses of the *laudatio funebris*, including its influence on the subversive
   vitae of the early Empire and Tacitus' *Agricola.* See Durry (1950) xvii–xxiv.
[95] Quint. *Inst.* 3. 7. 14–16.   [96] Russell (1998) 28.   [97] Russell (1998) 24–33.
[98] Russell (1998) 40.   [99] Braund (1998) 58–68.
[100] This speech was delivered before the Senate and Trajan on 1 September AD 100 – not long
   after the publication of Book 4 of the *Silvae* in AD 95 – and was subsequently expanded for
   publication. It takes the form of a *gratiarum actio*, the formal offering of thanks made by a consul
   on the assumption of his office. See Durry (1938) 5–8. Date of publication was not long after
   delivery, either in 101, or at the latest 103. On the expansion for publication see Plin. *Ep.* 3. 13
   and 3. 18. 1–2. See Coleman (1988) xix on Dio Cass. 67. 14. 1.

what their deeds should be (*Pan.* 4. 1). Pliny here uses the formal vote of thanks, traditionally delivered by the consul at the start of the year, as an occasion to set down the rules of good government for the new emperor. Thus he emphasises that the purpose of his speech is in part protreptic, to warn by example all future rulers against the evil model set by Domitian (*Pan.* 53. 5); he thus set about protecting the interests of his own senatorial class.[101] Since the speech was delivered at the start of Trajan's reign, the advice subtly and tactfully encompasses the present emperor, encouraging him to persist in his good beginnings.[102] Braund points out that the extensive contrast that Pliny draws between Domitian and Trajan (*Pan.* 46–55) provides an important means by which Pliny can tactfully recommend or 'even prescribe a programme of behaviour to the new emperor'.[103] To praise is also to encourage, to advise, and sometimes to admonish.[104]

Panegyric has a further and related function. Once published – and read therefore at different times in an emperor's reign – panegyric becomes a means by which an emperor can be judged. It invites the reader to measure the extent to which the emperor has lived up to the model of the good prince presented to him; it becomes a vehicle by which fears and doubts as well as adulation and respect can be expressed. This is particularly true of panegyric written or read later in an emperor's reign, such as Statius' poems of imperial praise.[105] Indeed, as Nixon and Rogers have argued in their study of the later Latin panegyrics, 'panegyrics can be most illuminating in providing alternative points of view; they bring out matters of central political importance and voice specific concerns of the populace'.[106]

Thus the writing of poetry of praise was a more challenging enterprise than has perhaps been generally acknowledged. Indeed, in a collection of poems that addresses a range of persons, some of them public figures, some private, there was always the risk that praise of a friend might offend the emperor, or vice versa. Tacitus' hostility to Domitian undoubtedly

[101] Durry (1938) 23–4 argues that Pliny wrote with the interests of the Senate at heart, desiring that under Trajan their interests and rights, limited as they were, should be protected.

[102] See Durry (1938) 9–15.

[103] Braund (1998) 66. As Nixon and Rogers (1994) 25 note, it became conventional in later panegyric to treat of 'rivals' to the emperor in only the most derogatory terms. Cf. also Plin. *Pan.* 53. 2, where Pliny states that it is the primary duty of pious citizens to praise a good emperor by attacking those unlike him.

[104] See also Whitby (1998) 1.

[105] MacCormack (1981) 13 sees the function of late imperial panegyric as in part a form of 'stock-taking', as panegyrics often responded to times of great change and movement.

[106] Nixon and Rogers (1994) 35.

led him to exaggerate the oppressiveness of the literary climate of that emperor's reign. On the other hand, it is clear that the writing of imperial praise, whether as speech or as poem, posed a new challenge for the writers of the first century AD, not just for those of the reign of Domitian. As White observes of the reign of Augustus, the founding of a dynasty confronted poets with a new and difficult challenge for which they had no familiar style of discourse.[107] Faced with a fluid and evolving form of imperial government, writers had to explore new literary forms and modes of expression for a period of emergent monarchy where freedom of speech was circumscribed but the limits were not clearly drawn. The Flavians, as a new and upstart dynasty, provided writers with a new set of challenges. In turn, as we see in the *Panegyricus*, Pliny displays his need to articulate for Trajan a new rhetoric of sincerity, a new decorum of praise.[108]

As the first poems in Latin literature to deal extensively with the relationship between the poet and a court circle, the *Silvae* attempt various strategies of praise to articulate the poet's relationship to the emperor as well as to a range of acquaintances and friends. The essence of panegyric is amplification, *amplificare et ornare*, in Quintilian's words of prescription for orators (*Inst.* 3. 7. 6).[109] As Russell points out, almost all surviving panegyrical speeches are by writers of note. Since they aim to confer immortality on the person or object of praise, they represent high culture and set their subject in a worldwide context through such elaborate means as poetic allusion and comparisons with history and myth.[110] But poets could be even more lavish in amplification than orators, for as far back as Isocrates it was recognised that poets could praise in a more elaborate style than prose writers, having more ornaments at their disposal.[111] Thus grandiloquence in the *Silvae* offers an appropriate strategy for celebrating the outstanding wealth and virtue of friends or of an emperor.

Indeed, Domitian posed a particular challenge for the imperial poet, for he developed the notion of divine leadership well beyond that of

---

[107] White (1993) 201.

[108] Bartsch (1994) 148–87. Bartsch approaches the *Panegyricus* as a 'late' reader of this text, arguing that Pliny's protestations of sincerity in fact provide proof of the lack of sincerity, of the loss of significant meaning to important moral terms and imperial virtues. She denies therefore the authority of Pliny's expressions of hope at the start of Trajan's reign.

[109] Most of the surviving Latin panegyrics are late prose panegyrics. For an overview of the Greek and rhetorical sources for panegyric see Russell (1998), and for an insightful discussion of early Roman imperial panegyric see Braund (1998). See Nixon and Rogers (1994) and Whitby (1998). For the links between the *Silvae* and panegyrical tradition see Coleman (1988) 62–5.

[110] Russell (1998) 49.   [111] Isoc. *Evagoras* 8–11. See Russell (1998) 24.

his predecessors.[112] Drawing upon Hellenistic ideas of divine rulership, Domitian decisively advanced the emperor's position, as Hannestad has put it, 'another rung up the ladder to the stars'.[113] The *Silvae* explore the implications for the poet and society of an emperor who conceived of himself as no longer 'first citizen' (*princeps*) but as closer to the gods than to his subjects and therefore above human law.[114] The well-being of the state therefore depended to a large extent on the moral conduct of its ruler. The *Silvae* invite scrutiny of the manipulation of imperial power in ways that are perhaps more complex and certainly more direct than those found in the *Thebaid*.[115] Yet the inevitable comparisons between the emperor and the gods create, as Feeney has remarked, slippery terrain.[116] For grandiloquent speech is also capacious speech, capable of rich and varying construction. In particular, the terms of comparison between man and god cannot be easily controlled.

The *Silvae*, then, approach Domitian and his court circle from a variety of positions that incorporate praise and criticism, wonder and anxiety. The capacious, extravagant speech of the *Silvae* is indeed 'figured' speech in its mythological and allusive complexity, yet it is employed here to negotiate and express the complexities of Flavian society, including the delicate relationship between the poet and the remote, god-like emperor. The *Silvae*, for instance, typically fashion access to the emperor through an opulent rhetoric in which the poet himself is often displaced by a plurality of 'voices' as other characters are introduced to articulate the song of praise. Statius' poems of imperial praise are not monologic; they can be seen as interrogative rather than subversive, monitory rather than simply adulatory. Figured speech conveys a range of feelings about the emperor and his aspirations to divinity; it also invites reflection upon the role of the imperial poet within imperial culture and literary tradition. For the *Silvae* are engaged in the imperialist project of rewriting and even overturning long-standing criteria of poetic excellence and decorum. The *Silvae* test the limits of panegyric as the emperor tested the limits of his power.

To refer to the points of friction, disjunctions, and oddities that occur within the discourse of praise, I prefer to borrow the term 'faultline' from Sinfield. Faultlines, unlike the notion of fantasy, are taken seriously.

---

[112] On this development within the principate see Millar (1977) 3 and Hannestad (1988) 140–2.

[113] Hannestad (1988) 142.

[114] See Wirszubski (1950) 130–6, on the development of absolutism in the concept of the emperor in the first century AD. The emperor was not exempted from all laws, but effective means of enforcement were lacking.

[115] Feeney (1993) 359.   [116] Feeney (1993) 220.

Faultlines run deep below the ground, some forty or fifty miles perhaps. The people who live near major faultlines build their homes, their offices, their bridges, and their highways over these nearly invisible lines of friction, constructing an edifice of illusory stability over permeable ground. Occasional tremors from the faultlines disturb human complacency, exposing the contradiction on which people have built their lives, yet, barring a major earthquake, most continue to be complicit with the widely accepted myth of permanence and stability. With this notion of 'faultline' Sinfield disengages the literary text from an antithetical mode of interpretation.[117] He applies the term 'faultline' fruitfully, I believe, to refer to the alternative stories or possibilities that from beneath the surface of a text help invite a critical perspective upon it.[118] For Sinfield, 'all stories comprise within themselves the ghosts of the alternative stories they are trying to repress'.[119] These 'ghosts' do not subvert, but they disturb, creating faultlines that can provoke anxiety and analysis on the part of the reader. 'Faultline stories' insistently address the awkward and unresolved issues that are situated within every dominant discourse; they 'distress the prevailing conditions of plausibility'.[120]

I use this term advisedly, for I write from a somewhat different perspective from Sinfield, who is broadly concerned to produce from the study of texts and their social and political roles a general theory of dissidence involving class, race, and gender. My attention in this book on the *Silvae* remains focussed upon the specificity of these texts and their complex function as poetry of praise in the Flavian era. I wish to reclaim the value of Statius' poems as both literary and social productions, the term 'literary' being broadly understood to refer to the qualities of a body of writing in which aesthetic, social, cultural, and political values are intertwined. All the same, 'faultline' provides a fruitful image for Statius' *Silvae*. The capacious verse of this collection, particularly in the poems of imperial praise, enthusiastically celebrates the splendours of Empire and yet allows for other possible, competing themes or stories that unsettle the dominant discourse of praise. What have often been regarded as ridiculous or infelicitous comparisons, for instance, open the text to the possibility of different interpretations that can suggest the unsettling gap between the fictions and practices of imperial power. The term 'faultline' connotes the discontinuity that we find in Statius' *Silvae*; in addition, it

---

[117] Sinfield is heavily influenced by Williams's (1981) argument for the coexistence of residual and emergent cultural forces in varying relations of negotiation, incorporation and resistance with the dominant system.
[118] Sinfield (1992) 38–47.   [119] Sinfield (1992) 21.   [120] Sinfield (1992) 47.

provides an appropriate metaphor for the anxiety that is part of Statius' poetry of praise, anxiety related to the matter of the emperor's power and that of his patrons as well as to the author's own social and literary status. Faultlines do not undermine the dominant discourse of praise but they disturb it. Different voices and positions come into play within the text, providing significant points of inquiry and indeed resistance to the universalising claims of a dominant culture.

As poetry of praise in the imperial era, the *Silvae* address perhaps the most awkward issue of all, the problem of honouring the emperor without detriment to other powerful interests or to Statius' own place within the Roman world as an eminent poet. Thus the *Silvae* are riddled with faultlines, inconsistencies and incoherences that arise from an extravagant and capacious rhetoric and that create fissures within the text without destroying its overall plausibility as a discourse of praise and celebration. Viewed thus, the *Silvae*, as I shall discuss more fully in the next chapter, are neither works of flattery nor subversion but rather poems of anxiety as well as celebration written late in Domitian's reign, a time of increasing dynastic difficulty. Indeed, panegyrics in general are particularly associated with periods of political instability.[121] As Whitby claims, despite their often common topoi and themes, they 'construct a meaningful and individual message' for their times.[122]

In my thinking about the *Silvae* I have found helpful recent work on Elizabethan court poetry. There are broad similarities between Elizabethan and Flavian society. For instance, both were dominated by an autocratic ruler who was both vulnerable and highly visible; both were marked by a well-educated, intelligent élite that chafed at absolutist power; in both regimes literature could be a matter of life and death. At the same time, Elizabethan England, like imperial Rome, lacked the technological and material means to enforce acceptance of its royal fictions. Indeed, despite the ability of the emperor to stamp his monumental image upon his capital city, we must not assume for Rome, as Montrose cautions with reference to sixteenth-century England, 'an absolute and totalistic structure of royal power, cynically and successfully recuperating every contestatory gesture'.[123]

Like Sinfield, Montrose sheds helpful light on what he calls the 'containment/subversion debate'. By this phrase he refers to the opposition between those critics on the one hand who argue for the capacity of monarchs to contain subversion and for the complicity of writers

---

[121] Whitby (1998) 7–10.   [122] Whitby (1998) 13.   [123] Montrose (1986) 330–1.

with the powers of the state – we might put Vessey on this side of the divide – and those who argue for the effective agency of individuals and subjects against various forms of domination – where we might locate Ahl.[124] Montrose attempts to break down this division by arguing that the monarch is not the simple product of a craftily promoted self-image. Rather, Montrose argues for a notion of ideology as 'a dynamic, agonistic and temporal process'.[125] Ideological dominance is qualified and contested by the writers, the readers, and the medium through which that dominance is conveyed and appropriated. In poetry of praise the relationship between state and subject is both constructed and contested. As the ruler shapes the poet's discourse, so the poet's discourse also shapes the representation of the emperor through his choice and synthesis of materials and the particular emphasis given to them.

Like Elizabethan ideology, Roman imperial ideology was not static, but rather was a dynamic process that was shaped significantly both by the emperor and by the writer. Rather than passively reproducing an ideology imposed from above, the *Silvae* subject to constant scrutiny the complex relationship between the poet and holders of power within the imperial system and the new hierarchical society of the court. In the *Silvae* the relationship negotiated between the poet and his patrons, including the emperor, is an implicitly competitive one that acknowledges the patron's authority but also asserts the poet's control over his own medium and its independent nexus of values. Indeed, Statius' claim to literary authority, his carving out of his own literary space, grants him an important voice in the analysis of the social and political order.

The *Silvae* then are self-reflexive poems, highly conscious that they are breaking new poetic ground, in which Statius reflects upon and interrogates the social function of poetry in the Flavian age. To this end he presents himself as an innovative poet engaged in an ongoing exploration of different strategies and situations of poetic praise. Like the emperor and the men and women of wealth and influence whom he celebrates, Statius, as the premier poet of his age, attempts in the *Silvae* to impose his own mark on the national culture and thus take a major place in literary history.

The *Silvae* are exuberant poems that form, moreover, a counterpart to the *Thebaid*. The *Thebaid* has been recently read as an exploration through myth of the contemporary realities of Rome.[126] In my view, the

---

[124] Montrose (1996) 7–16.   [125] Montrose (1996) 13.

[126] For the relevance of the Theban myth to contemporary Rome see especially Dominik (1990) and (1994), especially 130–80; also Ahl (1986) and Henderson (1991 and 1993). Hardie (1993a)

epic has a protreptic function; it acts as a 'mirror for princes' in its provision of a cautionary narrative of dynastic failure and corrupt monarchy. Written as the epic poem was nearing completion, and when the threat of fraternal competition had been removed with Titus' death, the *Silvae* broadly speaking construct an alternative story for Flavian society that, if we ignore the faultlines which disturb the tenor of praise, runs as follows. Instead of two warring brothers, there is firm control by one man (who is too isolated, perhaps); instead of relationships severed by war or by envy, there are strong, enduring marriages (including one with a eunuch); instead of lament there is consolation; instead of ruined palaces and homes, there are magnificent villas and mansions and a prosperous city; instead of war, there is peace, with a cultured aristocracy devoted to poetry and philosophy rather than civil strife. To some critics, the *Silvae* reflect a flattering and highly distorted view of Rome designed to please Domitian and to protect Statius himself from charges of disloyalty – a sort of 'insurance' against the incisiveness of the *Thebaid*.[127] Yet is the Theban myth of Rome any more 'real' than the Silvan myth? Rather than employing tragic myth, as the *Thebaid* does, the *Silvae*, with exuberance and wit, draw upon contemporary social and political occasions to explore the foundations and limits of imperial power and assert the enduring importance of the poet to the state. Like the *Thebaid*, they reveal an intense concern with the issue of succession and the foundations of dynasty. Indeed, the *Silvae*, more directly than the *Thebaid*, are key texts to an understanding of the mechanisms of imperial ideology and to the various means by which imperial dominance was celebrated, scrutinised, and contested.

PATRONAGE AND PUBLICATION

Perhaps surprisingly, however, poems honouring the emperor or major public figures do not constitute the major category in the *Silvae*. In the first three books, which were published late in Domitian's reign, there are only two poems (out of a total of eighteen) that directly deal with achievements of Domitian, both in Book 1 (*Silv.* 1. 1 and 1. 6). Book 4 reverses that trend to some extent with three poems concerning the emperor arranged sequentially at the beginning. Poems honouring friends and acquaintances are far more common. These poems provided Statius

---

88–119 sees Statius' *Thebaid*, in common with imperial epic, as concerned with the problems of political succession in an exemplary way. See also McGuire (1997).
[127] Thus Dominik (1990) 76.

with a different kind of challenge from that posed by imperial authority, since in several cases his friends had decisively turned their backs
on political life and on Rome. Despite the social and political obscurity
of several of Statius' friends, private buildings and civic buildings are
praised in almost equally extravagant terms. As a result, a critical dialogue is established in the *Silvae* between the relative merits of withdrawal
from public affairs and engagement with them. Through this creative
dynamic the *Silvae* explore effective means of scrutinising the often competing ideologies of a friend or of an emperor; indeed, the private realm
can provide a protreptic model for the public realm.

Although I will use the term 'patron' in general of the people whom
Statius addresses in his poems, it should be recognised, as White has
shown, that this is an anachronistic term.[128] There is no evidence to suggest that literary patronage in imperial Rome involved material benefits
that were in any way different from those received by other 'friends' of a
great man. In fact, Statius' relationships with his patrons are often based
on shared intellectual interests that seem to erase distinctions of rank.
The *Silvae* suggest that Statius' patrons, or friends of varying degrees of
intimacy, helped promote the poet's work in several ways, ranging from
the provision of intellectual companionship to the acceptance of a literary dedication.[129] Yet as Goldhill has observed, 'the patron as audience
is also implicated in demarcating the praise he is offered by the poet'.[130]
The relationship between poet and patron as well as that between poet
and emperor is inevitably an ambiguous one. In the *Silvae* Statius negotiates a delicate balance between himself and his patrons. The poet's
self-assertiveness can be contained by the rhetoric of self-depreciation.[131]
He walks a fine line between satisfying his patrons and demonstrating to
posterity his poetic worth.

White has noted that the majority of the people to whom Statius
addresses his poems are not major public figures.[132] Few of them were
from traditional aristocratic families. Instead, they reflect a variety of
social positions – rich men who have turned their backs on public life,
Neapolitans, freedmen; Books 2 and 3 end respectively with poems to
Lucan's wife and Statius' own wife. Apart from the emperor himself,
of all the people honoured with a poem in the *Silvae* only the urban
prefect Rutilius Gallicus held a top political position in Rome, and his

---

[128] White (1978) 78.
[129] As White (1978) 86 argues, 'writers depended on the good offices of prominent citizens to
prepare a favorable reception of their work among people of fashion'.
[130] Goldhill (1991) 119.   [131] See Goldhill (1991) 121.   [132] White (1975) 265.

poem (*Silv.* 1. 4) was published after his death. Many different areas of
human experience find expression in the *Silvae*, offering far from universal
confirmation of patriarchal ideas.[133]

Habinek has argued that Roman literature serves the élite sector of
a traditional aristocratic empire.[134] He relies here upon a generalised
concept of the aristocracy that does not take account of the competing social groups within Roman society in Statius' day and the mobile
overlap of classes, roles, and aspirations.[135] The *Silvae* offer a view of society in which the traditional Roman aristocracy was being displaced by
provincial families, by freedmen, and by a new class of bureaucrats who
supplanted or threatened senatorial power. Significantly then, Statius'
private poems provide a new view of cultural identity in which virtue,
rather than high birth, is central to nobility. In this regard, among others, Statius is unlike Horace. Statius' poetry promotes relatively obscure
people on the basis of virtue, learning, and wealth, rather than on birth:
there are no Maecenases in Statius' Silvan world.

Statius was in a different social situation from Horace. He was not, it
seems, supported by particularly powerful or influential friends. Horace
writes, moreover, of imperial patronage with some disdain. As Oliensis
comments, Horace, addressing Augustus in *Epistles* 2. 1, endeavours 'to
keep his poetry out of the imperial sun'.[136] Horace, an established, well-
supported poet, could afford to adopt this attitude. The conditions for
patronage were different in Flavian Rome. As Hardie has pointed out,
Domitian developed an institutional form of patronage by establishing
the Alban and Capitoline games, two artistic festivals modelled on the
great competitions of the Greek world, though associated with archaic
Roman ritual.[137] Success at these contests seems to have mattered greatly;
in *Silv.* 3. 5 Statius, having lost at the Capitoline games, decides to leave
Rome, complaining that Domitian has acted unfairly towards him.[138]
The influence and favour of the emperor was extremely important, it
seems, in the making of a poet. All the same, the emperor's literary
interests were limited.[139] The social range of the people to whom Statius

---

[133] Social relationships are often quite complex. *Silv.* 2. 1, for instance, consoles and honours Atedius
Melior through praise of the deceased Glaucias, a beloved young freedman and servant whom
he had adopted.
[134] Habinek (1998) 3.
[135] See Garnsey and Saller (1987) 107–25.   [136] Oliensis (1998) 192.
[137] Hardie (1983) 45–7; Coleman (1986) 3097–100; Darwall-Smith (1996) 223–6.
[138] On Statius' loss in the Capitoline games see *Silv.* 3. 5. 31–3; on his success at the Alban games
see *Silv.* 4. 2 65–7.
[139] Coleman (1986) 3097–100.

writes attests to the continuing importance of patronage outside the court in nurturing and maintaining a diversified literary culture.[140]

Statius needed patrons, for significantly he himself was neither a member of the élite nor a native of the city of Rome. His family was probably not even of equestrian status.[141] He was born in Naples (*Silv.* 3. 5. 12–13) and raised by a father who, as professional poet and *grammaticus*, gave Statius a thorough and even recondite training in Greek literature (*Silv.* 5. 3. 148–61). In the first century AD Naples was a magnet for wealthy Romans, for it offered a version of Hellenism that was accommodated to Roman tastes. As Lomas has argued, the major Neapolitan festival, the Sebasta, founded by Augustus and maintained through imperial patronage, had the complex purpose of reaffirming the Greek identity of the region while mediating that identity in a way that would attract Roman patronage.[142] The strength of Naples lay in its culture, for politically it was marginalised.[143] We know of only three or possibly four senatorial families that came from Naples.[144]

As an outsider, Statius occupies a unique position among imperial poets. His family was distinguished by intellectual achievements, not by birth; his father had won the important contests in the Greek literary world.[145] The loyalties of Statius as poet lay with Greek culture as much as with Roman. Indeed, in the *Silvae* he provocatively fashions Naples as a kind of counter-world to Domitianic Rome. Undoubtedly, then, there is a degree of self-interest in Statius' new concept of nobility; through virtue and learning he too can gain access to sources of privilege, patronage, and power. But as Habinek has argued, friendship between social unequals did not necessarily involve a tradition of flattery; rather, it often permitted

---

[140] See Wallace-Hadrill (1989), who argues that patronage was a form of social control, essential in the Empire for the emperor could not operate a network of loyalties alone. He contests Millar's (1977) view of the emperor as 'a solitary spider at the centre of the web' (84).

[141] Coleman (1988) xv–xx provides a useful survey of Statius' career. She argues that the family had lost equestrian status (xv).

[142] Lomas (1993) notes that the patronage of the region by emperors such as Nero and Domitian, and their promotion of the Neapolitan games founded by Augustus, encouraged the prominence of Naples: 'For the Romans, they [the games] were a means of legitimating Roman rule by adopting local traditions, and of coming to terms with the ambiguities inherent in Greek culture in the Roman world, by adopting a form of Hellenism which was distinctively Italian' (141).

[143] Leiwo (1994) 41 (commenting on Statius, *Silv.* 3. 5, an epistle urging his wife to return with him to Naples): 'The question arises, therefore, what really represented Hellenism or "Greekness" to the Romans? I believe that for the Romans the positive side of it was the culture: literature and arts, but also architecture.'

[144] Leiwo (1994) 208–11.

[145] On the achievements of Statius' father at the poetic festivals of Greece see Clinton (1972) and Hardie (1983) 2–14. Also *Silv.* 5. 3. 113, 141–5.

friends of unequal status to act as counsellors.[146] Thus Statius' poetry of praise can often be considered protreptic. Moreover, Statius was no ordinary friend: he was a distinguished poet, famous for his *Thebaid*; he had his own source of literary authority and the potential to confer immortality through his verse. Moreover, as an outsider he could also offer a unique perspective on Roman society and its imperial ambitions. In the *Silvae*, his Greek training is meaningfully deployed both in the expansion of a new language of praise and in his articulation of new concepts of Roman identity for the socially fluid, cosmopolitan culture of the imperial state.

Significant in this regard is the influence of Pindar upon the *Silvae*. In *Silv.* 4. 7 Statius invokes Pindar to inspire his new type of poetry (5–12).[147] But it is not in this one poem alone that Pindar's influence is felt. The *Silvae* as a whole have a Pindaric sweep that, though accommodated to the social circumstances of Rome of the late first century AD, powerfully elevates the occasions and topics of their verse through a rhetoric of luxury and magnificence. Moreover, the *Silvae* evoke a context of performance. Statius claims that the *Silvae* originated as extempore productions, often performed on the spot at informal occasions before friends, such as a dinner party. Since his father had been a professional poet, performing at the great literary festivals of the Roman and Greek world, Statius had received his poetic education in part within a culture of virtuoso literary performance: he himself performed at the public games that Domitian had instituted.[148]

Of course Statius, operating under the constraints of imperial autocracy and different relationships of patronage, sought to find an authoritative voice through the private sponsorship of friends, many of whom conducted their lives apart from the public community at large. Performance here was adapted to the imperial institution of the *recitatio* or recital, which allowed the writer not only to advertise his work but also to test it orally in front of friends and critics before publication in a fixed form.[149] Pindaric grandeur, then, was freshly attuned to the new social and political realities of the Flavian age, including a culture of friendship and literary patronage that valued both refinement and luxury. Yet, in

---

[146] Habinek (1990).

[147] Thomas (1983) 94–6, claims that Roman poets as a whole show little interest in Pindaric poetry. But Statius' Greek background and training as well as his request for Pindaric inspiration in *Silv.* 4. 7 should not be dismissed lightly. The lines of influence, besides, are rarely monolithic.

[148] On Statius' literary background in the Greek culture of performative praise poetry see Hardie (1983) 15–36.

[149] See Markus (2000).

the composition of poetry of praise, Statius shares with Pindar the search
for an authoritative voice that interweaves the honour of the patron with
that of the poet who commemorates the patron's deeds. Of course, apart
from the emperor, Statius' patrons on the whole lacked the political and
social status of the rulers that Pindar addressed. The very evocation
of Pindar reveals the gap between the position of the archaic and the
Flavian poet. All the same, the opulent rhetoric of the *Silvae* asserts the
central importance of poetry to the state even as it draws attention to
the circumscription of the poet's voice and status. For the *Silvae* have none
of the familiarity of Horace's *Epistles*: they are focussed not on the poet's
private musings and interest in personal development, but are directed
outwards to the object of praise. Certainly, in the private poems Statius
is often at his most playful with epic motifs, tempering their connotations
of grandeur with Callimachean polish and wit. Yet at the same time the
elevation of his richly textured verse places new, important value upon
the virtues of friendship and intellectual companionship within Roman
society.

The importance of the relationship between Statius and patrons in
the production and circulation of his poetry is indicated by a unique
feature of the *Silvae* – the dedicatory preface attached to the start of
each book. None of them is dedicated to the emperor. The friends to
whom the *Silvae* are dedicated then function as guides to the reception of
the poetry of praise. As Genette has shown, the functions of a preface in
general are several: it honours the dedicatee; it provides unity to a diverse
collection as well as a table of contents; it suggests an order of reading; it
provides a means of garnering the reader's favour, *captatio benevolentiae*.[150]
Genette insists that the overall function of the preface is not merely
homage to a patron; rather it provides a discreet authorial discourse
of valorisation and thus forms an attempt to assure a 'good reading'.
A preface is addressed not only to the patron – a highly cultured, well-
educated individual, well-disposed to the poet – but to the implied reader
whom, along with the patron, the preface guides and at the same time
jointly constructs as the ideal reader.[151] The patron who is honoured by
the dedication imposes a stamp of quality upon the work; his willing act
of reception guarantees the poetry's worth – the strong possibility of a
good reading – and validates it through his own marks of distinction.
These marks of distinction are above all literary, for of the four men to
whom Statius dedicates his poetry books, only two held political office:

---

[150] Genette (1987) 182–218.   [151] Genette (1987) 197.

Arruntius Stella of Book 1 and Vitorius Marcellus of Book 4. Atedius Melior of Book 2 and Pollius Felix of Book 3 were both elderly and retired from public affairs. All four, however, are represented as sharing with Statius keenly discriminating interests in poetry.

Although Statius claims to have composed and performed many of his *Silvae* on the spot for his patrons, we must also then take into account the fact of their publication, by means of which they came into circulation bearing the patrons' seal of approval. These patrons provided a wider, more diverse readership with initial assurance both of the collection's worth and of how, in a sense, the poetry should be received.

Moreover, Statius' prose prefaces provide us with his self-reflexive comments on the nature of his new poetry. He adopts here a rhetoric of self-depreciation, apologising for the improvisational nature of his poems and claiming that they are hasty, unrevised compositions, written in the heat of the moment – *hos libellos, qui mihi subito calore et quadam festinandi voluptate fluxerunt* ('these little books, which flowed from me in sudden heat and with a certain pleasure in the haste', *praef.* 1. 3–4). 'None of them took more than two days to write, some poured out in only one day' (*nullum enim ex illis biduo longius tractum, quaedam et in singulis diebus effusa, praef.* 1. 13–14). His *Thebaid*, on the other hand, took twelve years to write (*Theb.* 12. 811–12).

We should know better than to take such disclaimers at face value. In the first preface to the *Silvae* Statius is defining his new poetry through dramatic distinction with his former work: the *Silvae* are produced at speed, the *Thebaid* with lengthy labour. They are extemporaneous productions that subtly evoke a context of inspired performance. Moreover, Statius' protestations in his prefaces that his poems are impromptu productions are fully in line with prefatory convention, for authorial valorisation, Genette insists, is normally discreet. The words 'talent' and 'genius' are taboo.[152] Statius' insistence on the hastiness of his work falls into the same category as Catullus' apologies in his first poem for his *nugae*, his 'trifles'.[153] White assumes that when Statius talks of *libellos* (*praef.* 1. 3), he means that the book which he is presenting to his friend Stella is a rough draft.[154] With *libellus*, I believe, Statius compresses two stages in the production of his poetry: first the recital at which his poems were evaluated, then the revision for publication. Significantly, like Statius in his first preface, Catullus refers to his poetry book as *libellum* and *libelli*.[155] The more elaborate nature of Statius' apologies is a function of the formal

---

[152] Genette (1987) 184. [153] Catull. 1. 4. [154] White (1974) 44–5. [155] Catull. 1. 1 and 8.

conventions of the prose dedication, not only of the novelty of his enterprise. Statius' *libellus* therefore places him in an honoured tradition of
self-depreciatory rhetoric that Jonson continues with his witty reference
to his 'lesser poems of later growth'. Such apologies in fact draw attention
to the excellence of a work in a circumspect way that does not occlude
the importance of the patron.

And indeed, as in Catullus' first poem, there is a certain ambiguity in
Statius' choice of expression. *Fluxerunt* (*praef.* 1. 4) for instance suggests not
just haste but smoothness and beauty of style. As Statius' contemporary
Quintilian prescribes, good speech should ideally 'flow'.[156] Juxtaposed
with *voluptate*, *fluxerunt* suggests pleasure on the part of both author and
reader. Thus Statius' prefaces serve discreetly as an authorial valorisation of the text and its poetics, a valorisation supported by the patron.
Like Catullus' reference to his poetry as *nugae*, Statius' disclaimers draw
attention to the unique quality of his achievement.

At the same time, however, the anxiety that lies behind the prefatory disclaimers is clearly palpable. Statius was attempting new literary
forms and modes of expression in the *Silvae*. His preface alerts the reader
not only to the quality of his verse but also to the novelty of his poetic
project.[157] In addition, this anxiety, I believe, has a political dimension.
Statius was attempting one of the most challenging of poetic genres:
poetry of praise. As Goldhill points out, 'to praise a patron requires a
complex rhetorical awareness of the limitations and distinctions of flattery and glorification; so, too, self-praise is fenced here with a (defensive)
rhetoric of self-depreciation'.[158] Statius' collection of *Silvae* represents a
skilful negotiation among the competing needs of patrons and emperor.
Statius' disclaimers in his prefaces can be read not simply in terms of a
literary-historical discourse but as politic devices that protect the writer
within the complex lines of exchange established between the poet and
his patrons.

The prose prefaces alert the reader to the fact that the *Silvae* as we
possess them now are part of a collection. They are no longer poems
written for the moment and tested in recital but are published for a
past occasion and, as the prefaces suggest, consciously and artfully arranged. The first collection of the *Silvae*, published in AD 93, consisted of
three books, each one dedicated to a separate patron. These poems are
therefore intended not just to be read by the patron, to whom, White has
argued, they were first individually sent, but also by a far wider and more

---

[156] Quint. *Inst.* 9. 4. 112.   [157] See Szelest (1966).   [158] Goldhill (1991) 121.

diverse readership.[159] Statius may have written the poems quickly, but he clearly took his time over publication and collection, as he suggests at the beginning of the work as a whole with a significant opening gambit drawn from the start of Cicero's dialogue *Orator*: *diu multumque dubitavi* ('I have hesitated a lot and for a long time', *praef.* 1. 1).[160] In the *Orator* this opening marks the start of a serious investigation into the nature of the ideal orator, set within the context of personal friendship. Likewise, the prefaces of Statius' *Silvae* draw on the rhetoric of friendship to introduce a personal investigation into the conditions of speech in the Empire.

As Patterson says of Jonson's *Underwood*, a collection of court poetry clearly indebted to Statius' *Silvae* on the basis of its title alone, 'collection . . . is also recollection'.[161] Generally the *Silvae* have been read in isolation, as separate, improvisational texts. However, their original occasion is only one of the conditions of their selection and placement in their book. The poems are part of a carefully crafted ensemble that reflects the poet's processes of afterthought. Thus the poems in part render their full range of meaning only from their arrangement and from their interaction with one another in ways that could not have been foreseen when they were first composed. Indeed, social and political critique exists as much in the dynamic between poems within the collection as within the individual poems themselves. The dialectical nature of the collection opens the poems up to a wider cultural discourse concerning the social function of poetry and the nature and limits of fame in the dazzling but uncertain society of Domitian's Rome. But collection not only creates new relationships among texts; in addition, new meanings accrue to the poems through the effects of time and history. Thus what Patterson calls 'extratextual reverberations' – such as the death of the person to whom the poem was addressed – may have accrued to the text since its original composition, thereby creating new conditions of meaning.[162] The prefaces to the *Silvae* suggest that Statius paid careful attention to the selection

---

[159] White (1974) 43–5, 60. Comparing the dedicatory prefaces of the *Silvae* to those of Martial's *Epigrams* he concludes that 'Statius wrote these prefaces as much for the eye of the ordinary reader as for the announced recipient of the letter.'

[160] Cic. *Orat.* 1. 1: *diu multumque, Brute, dubitavi.*

[161] Patterson (1984) 127.

[162] Patterson (1984) 127. One of her examples concerns a poem written to accompany the publication of Sir Walter Raleigh's *History of the World*, 'The Mind of the Frontispiece to a Booke.' Patterson argues (127–31) that the poem, not published until after Raleigh's execution in 1618, serves as a ghostly vindication of Raleigh as well as an ironic critique upon court politics. We can compare Statius' poem on Rutilius Gallicus, *Silv.* 1. 4. Gallicus was dead by the time of publication, having failed to make the recovery from illness predicted in Statius' poem. See chapter 6 below, 223–4.

and arrangement of the poems in each book. As an ensemble, these poems are carefully crafted and are placed within their books so that they create a stimulating dialogue with one another over the relative merits of private versus public life, poetry of withdrawal versus poetry of engagement, Rome versus Naples. The poems interrogate one another.[163]

A NEW VERSION OF PASTORAL

As a collection, the *Silvae* are constructed on a cultural dynamic between poems on private and public occasions. Such a dynamic, I suggest, can be seen as typical of a new kind of pastoral, reformulated for the social circumstances of the Flavian age. Indeed, the title *Silvae* situates Statius within a poetic genealogy that extends from Lucan, who wrote ten books of *Silvae* – unfortunately not extant – to Virgil, who expanded the possibilities of Theocritean pastoral by introducing public, national figures and themes to his *Eclogues*.[164] As is characteristic of this richly allusive poetry, the title of Statius' work has of course multiple associations.[165] It links Statius' collection with Hellenistic poetry, particularly epigram and the custom for naming poetry collections by terms suggesting growth in nature such as flowers and meadows.[166] Thus Statius' *Silvae* contain a variety of poems – 'a variety in unity' as Hardie puts it – just as a wood encompasses a variety of trees.[167] The title is also associated in the singular with the literary metaphor *silva*, which connotes a certain randomness and lack of literary refinement.[168] The title *Silvae* can in addition bear the more refined sense of the material of a literary predecessor that the allusive poet metaphorically 'invades' in his allusive reworking.[169] Most

---

[163] The importance of reading the poems as a part of a collection emerges also from recent studies of Greek and Latin epigram. See Gutzwiller (1998); Lorenz (1997).

[164] Statius refers to his collected poems as *Silvae* in the preface to Book 3. 7 and the preface to Book 4. 25. Oddly he does not mention Lucan's *Silvae* in his poetic tribute to Lucan in *Silv.* 2. 7. Only a late biographer attests to Lucan's *Silvae*, and we know nothing of their style or content. See Bright (1980) 37.

[165] See Bright (1980) 20–49 for the most extensive discussions of the meaning of the title.

[166] Tertullian in *De anim.* 2. 6 testifies to the application of *silvae* to mean a collection of poetry. On the naming of collections of poetry after groupings in the natural world see Bright (1980) 40–2. On expansion as a feature cultivated by Hellenistic epigram see Bing (1995).

[167] Hardie (1983) 76.

[168] Servius, for instance, defines *silva* as an uncultivated grove: *nemus composita multitudo arborum, silva est defusa et inculta* (Serv. *Auct.* in *Aen* 1. 310). Cic. *Orat.* 3. 12 seems to derive from this definition the metaphorical meaning of 'raw material' to be used by orators; Quint. *Inst.* 10. 3. 17 extends this definition to literary work composed at speed and unrevised. Hardie (1983) 76 remains unconvinced that the meaning of the singular *silva* has any bearing on the plural title.

[169] Thus Hinds (1998) 12–14 demonstrates how Virgil at *Aen.* 6. 179, *itur in antiquam silvam*, uses the term *silva* to metaphorise (and problematise) his engagement with Ennius, his literary predecessor here. See also Masters (1992) 25–9.

importantly, perhaps, the title advertises its connection with the new, politicised version of pastoral introduced to Roman poetry by Virgil. At the start of *Eclogue* 4 Virgil uses *silvae* to designate his pastoral poetry when he programmatically announces that he will sing of 'woods worthy of a consul' (*silvae consule dignae, Ecl.* 4. 3) and thus introduces panegyric to pastoral. Statius takes up this mandate in the *Silvae*, I believe, and furthers its implications to focus upon contemporary social and political issues.[170]

As we shall see, the title *Silvae*, far from indicating trivial, light verse, offers a new version of pastoral for the Flavian age in its recurring dialectic within the collection between city and country, court and villa, withdrawal and engagement. The title *Silvae* thus in fact conflates two of the major meanings of *silva* / *silvae*: Virgilian pastoral seen from the perspective of the late first century AD as material to be reworked, revised, and contested. The title, I believe, is characteristically and wittily ambiguous, suggesting both the experimental and the sophisticated.

This pastoral dialectic is facilitated by the situation of the poet himself, who, as a native of the region of Naples, represents himself in his poetry as to some extent an outsider to the culture that he celebrates. The *Silvae* are fashioned both by and against the project of public, imperial service. They look to both Naples and Rome for their definition. The third book of the *Silvae* is exemplary in this regard. *Silv.* 3. 1, the poem celebrating the dedication of Pollius' temple to Hercules on the Bay of Naples, introduces a series of three poems concerning three men in service to the imperial court (3. 2, 3. 3, and 3. 4). But Book 3 ends with an epistolary poem to Statius' wife, announcing the poet's decision to return from the capital to Naples to live, for Statius claims that he has failed to gain the imperial recognition that he craved (28–33). The poem concludes with a eulogy of Naples as an alternative Rome, equally cultured but free from the uncertainties of political life (81–112). In its longing for a city that is *other* than Rome *Silv.* 3. 5 reverses the poetic stance of Ovid in the *Tristia*.[171] By ending Book 3 and the first collection of *Silvae* with a poem that announces his decision to return to Naples, Statius suggests the importance of Greek poetry and culture to his own self-definition as a poet (a definition that he will continue to question and refine in Book 4). But in addition, the opening and concluding poems of Book 3 provide vantage points from which the glories and vagaries of a career at Rome can be evaluated. They also further Statius'

---

[170] See Tanner (1986) 3042: 'the proper commentary on this choice of title for the whole collection may therefore be Virgil, ecloga 4, 1–3'.

[171] On links between *Silv.* 3. 5 and the exile poetry of Ovid see Laguna (1992) 342.

meditation on his poetic allegiances and place within literary tradition. As the structure of Book 3 suggests, therefore, Rome and Naples form a cultural axis within the *Silvae* along which the poet's own social and literary situation remains subject to continuous negotiation.

This dialectic plays a key role in Statius' exploration of a poetics of Empire and his own role within imperial culture. Constructed as a dialogue between public and private splendour, the poetics of Empire bring into question the social function of poetry in the Flavian age. From what position should a poet speak? From the heart of Empire or its margins? And can or should the margins be redrawn as the centre? Should art be therapeutic, a safe art devoted to soothing the passions and creating pleasure, or should it actively engage in public life, voicing political and social concerns? The structure of Book 3, for instance, invites the reader to engage in the poet's continuing exploration of the constraints and possibilities operating upon poetry that both provides pleasure and engages with serious issues of patronage, social and political advancement, national identity, and the stability of the Flavian dynasty itself.

Taken as a whole, the *Silvae* offer insight into the values and sentiments of a society where a powerful autocracy was creating new possibilities for both career advancement and withdrawal. They provocatively challenge some of the values traditionally tied up with Roman cultural identity and offer a more expansive vision of what it meant to be a subject of Empire in the first century AD. Statius positions himself in his poetry as caught between the competing claims of two different cultures and ways of life, between Naples and Rome. In important ways, the *Silvae* are the product of a divided voice. The pastoral dialectic on which the collection of *Silvae* is founded is embodied not only in the tension between public and personal virtues, national and regional identities, but in the single figure of the poet, who values peace but longs for fame.

ECPHRASIS

Statius makes a major innovation in the *Silvae* by devoting entire, full-length poems to the description of works of art and buildings; he was the first Roman poet to do so.[172] One factor that unifies my discussion of the *Silvae* is my focus upon individual poems of praise that describe

---

[172] See Szelest (1966) 186–8, who argues that Statius is original in expanding the role of ecphrasis found in epigram while detaching it from its narrative context in epic.

works of art, estates, houses, and similar creations. The main part of my book examines the first collection of the *Silvae*, Books 1–3. The last two chapters deal exclusively with poems from Book 4, which was published separately in AD 95.[173] I do not deal with Book 5, which was published posthumously and was not collected by Statius.[174] In separate chapters I discuss in turn the equestrian statue of Domitian and the miniature statue of Hercules (chapter 2), a townhouse in Rome and the imperial palace (chapter 3), a villa at Tibur (chapter 4), a villa on the Bay of Naples (chapter 5), private baths (chapter 6), the imperial amphitheatre (chapter 7), the imperial palace on the Palatine (chapter 8), and the Via Domitiana (chapter 9). Statius' *Silvae* describe some of the most striking artistic features of imperial culture, in particular the highly visible, lofty monuments of the emperor and the strikingly opulent villas of the cultured élite. The importance of the work of art to the collection is signalled by the opening poem, a dazzling, encomiastic description of Domitian's colossal equestrian statue. The erection of a statue, like the building of a house, is an important means by which a person can express status, wealth, power, and a system of beliefs. Indeed, such works of art or architecture are complex signs that express in visual language powerful social and political myths. Ecphrasis therefore provides a significant strategy for the poet of praise, for the exploration of a complex sign can invite interpretation and interrogation of its underlying mythology.

The roots of ecphrasis lie far back in classical poetry, beginning with Homer's extended description of the shield of Achilles.[175] Ecphrasis functioned as an important descriptive pause in classical epic, or later served as the brief topic of epigram.[176] To Horace, ecphrasis was associated with decoration and florid embroidery, an influential judgment that has often led to a general devaluation of ecphrastic writing as excessively mannered.[177] For instance, as Scott remarks, it is often the case that 'ekphrasis falls firmly on the side of excess and error' in its transgression of poetic decorum.[178] Since concepts of decorum may differ from age to age and from genre to genre, however, and since the art of description is such an essential aspect of Statius' poetic achievement, I prefer to use the term without prejudice.

---

[173] Coleman (1988) xvi–xx on the dating of the publication of Books 1–3 and Book 4.
[174] Coleman (1988) xxxi–xxxii.
[175] See the important historical survey of Friedländer (1912) 1–103.
[176] On the importance of ecphrasis to the thought and meaning of Virgil's *Aeneid* see Putnam (1998).
[177] Hor. *Ars P.* 14–19.   [178] Scott (1991) 304.

Ecphrasis is generally employed now in modern criticism to refer exclusively to a literary description of a work of art.[179] As Webb has pointed out, however, in the ancient definition of ecphrasis works of art are of peripheral interest; what matters is the quality of *enargeia* in description, that is, the quality that can bring the subject matter vividly before the reader's eyes.[180] That subject matter itself was varied. According to the rhetorical handbooks which provided guidelines for the exercises known as *progymnasmata*, ecphrasis in ancient literature was broadly concerned with places, persons, times, and events, and could be used in various types of composition.[181] Works of art as the subject of ecphrasis are not mentioned in the rhetorical tradition until the fifth century AD.[182] Subject-matter then, Webb argues, is of secondary importance in ancient thinking about ecphrasis, which was defined 'in terms of its impact on an audience'.[183]

Ecphrasis is thus an appropriate term to use of those poems of the *Silvae* that, often within a performative context, describe works of art and buildings – villas, baths, the amphitheatre – and the events that take place within them. Crucial to these poems is the viewer, and the effect that his perceptions have on his audience and reader.[184] Ecphrasis draws the reader into the text, at the same time inviting the reader's critical evaluation; it invites the reader not just to 'see' but also to think. The work of art or monument thereby becomes the vehicle for broader critical reflection on the social function of art and literature. Ecphrasis therefore provided Statius with an appropriate tool for engaging the reader in his celebration and exploration of the extravagance of Flavian culture and his own poetic art.

Descriptions of works of art or buildings in Roman poetry generally concern fictitious objects: the shields of Achilles and Aeneas or the cloak of Jason, for instance. This type of ecphrasis is what Hollander calls 'notional'.[185] The *Silvae*, however, describe purportedly real works

---

[179] Becker (1995) 2, n. 1 provides a useful bibliography on the ancient and modern uses of the term *ecphrasis*. See also Webb (1999).

[180] On *enargeia* see Webb (1999) 11–15. Cf. also Webb and James (1991) 9: 'an ekphrasis aims to recreate for the listener the effect of its subject on the viewer, who is the speaker'.

[181] Webb and James (1991) 4–7 provide an excellent overview of the four extant rhetorical handbooks dating from the first to fifth centuries AD that deal with ecphrasis. See also Becker (1992) 8–14 for a survey of the rhetorical criticism of ecphrasis, and Becker (1995) 23–40.

[182] Webb and James (1991) 6 point out that works of art are not mentioned as a subject of ecphrasis until the fifth-century writer Nikolas Rhetor, and then only 'as an afterthought'.

[183] Webb (1999) 12.

[184] On the importance of the act of viewing in ecphrasis see Laird (1996) 82–4, 96–7; also Geyssen (1996) 137–40.

[185] Hollander (1995) 7–29. Hollander (1988) 209 puts the case succinctly with his statement that

of art and buildings. They are based on the highly visible, present signs of imperial culture and are thus intimately linked with encomium. As Macrides and Magdalino point out, to define ecphrasis merely as 'description' is problematic, since the function of ecphrasis is in most cases celebration.[186] Moreover, the observer of a villa or a temple, unlike the observer of a painting, is part of the landscape in which the building is set, part of the architectural context. He or she is also a participant in its chronological narrative, for spatial observation is often linked to the time of the visit. In *Silv.* 3. 1, for instance, Statius assumes the role of celebrant and sacrificer as he views the new temple of his friend Pollius, his poem itself forming his offering.[187] As both an observer of the temple and a participant in its landscape and ceremonies, the poet has an intimate relationship with the object of his description. His position as viewer is compromised by the obligations of friendship and social occasion. Thus, in the *Silvae* ecphrasis is fused with encomium, as the wonders of the owner's opulent possessions are made to reflect upon his virtuous character.[188]

This fusion of encomium, ecphrasis, and the presence of the poet as observer has implications that go well beyond the immediate context of praise. For description of a work of visual art can often be a competitive, literary exercise in which word is matched against image, writer against architect or painter. As Rosand has commented in his discussion of ecphrasis and painting, 'in the sibling rivalry of the arts the fame of the painter echoes through the centuries thanks to the writer'.[189] Ecphrasis turns on the contest between verbal and visual representation. The relationship of Statius to the works of art or buildings that he describes is duplicated in his relationship with his patron, for the poet's linguistic powers compete with the ocular image and with the maker of that image. The relationship between the poet and his patron is a complex one that acknowledges the patron's power but also asserts the poet's control over his own medium of language and its independent nexus of values. Seen thus, ecphrasis provides an important means by which faultlines are created in a text.

'the earliest ekphrastic poetry describes what doesn't exist, save in the poetry's own fiction'. He cites as classical examples the shields of Achilles and Hercules, the ivory cup of Theocritus' first *Idyll*; the armour of Aeneas and the paintings in the temple of Juno.

[186] Thus Macrides and Magdalino (1988) 50: 'the root of the problem lies in defining ekphrasis as description, when the function of most ekphraseis we possess was clearly to *celebrate* what they were describing'.

[187] Thus in the preface to Book 3 he says that he 'worshipped the god's temple in verse as soon as he saw it', *statim ut videram, his versibus adoravi* (*praef.* 3. 10).

[188] Newmyer (1979) 40.   [189] Rosand (1990) 65.

Thus, although ecphrasis praises a patron through a work of art or architecture, it is also a reflexive process.[190] Heffernan defines ecphrasis as 'a verbal representation of visual representation'.[191] This is a useful definition for the *Silvae*, for it invites attention to the sophisticated function of ecphrasis as an interpreter of cultural attitudes and poetics. Ecphrasis tells us not so much about the appearance of a work of art as about ways in which it was perceived in a specific society. Similarly, buildings or works of art are not themselves neutral objects. The works that Statius describes are culturally specific forms that visually express an architectural language of power and authority. Indeed, the colossal equestrian statue in the Roman forum, the massive bulk of the Palatine palace, and the villas poised on rugged cliffs test the limits of architecture in their defiance of nature. Appropriately in this connection the Latin word *monumentum* has a dual meaning as visual object and as written record.[192] So too in the *Silvae* Statius tests the limits of language as he strives for new means to interpret and describe the monuments of Roman audacity.

As the first poems in Latin literature to use ecphrasis as their central organising principle, Statius' *Silvae* fully exploit the possibilities the work of art or architecture offers as a complex symbol of social and political status and artistic power. Hardie has argued that Horace's reluctance to evoke the wealth of the contemporary arts in his poetry is connected to the persona worn by Horace, who disapproves of luxury and external signs of wealth.[193] Statius on the other hand enthusiastically describes extravagant buildings and works of art. Yet, simultaneously, he explores, like Horace, the idea of the poem as itself a monument. Oliensis has argued that in his poetry Horace presents in particular two 'faces', one of authority, the other of deference.[194] To some extent this is also true of Statius in the *Silvae*, except that, given the constraints imposed by patronage and praise, his expressions of authority are generally and necessarily oblique. Statius' close engagement with architectural and artistic monuments in the *Silvae* permits him, nonetheless, to sustain throughout his descriptive poems a self-reflexive exploration of his own poetics and to draw subtle attention to their literary worth. Ecphrasis

[190] See Putnam (1998) on Virgil's *Aeneid*, who argues that ecphrasis serves as a commentary on the poem as whole; also Barchiesi (1997), especially 271–6. Laird (1996) 86 comments that 'no ekphrasis is innocent of reflexivity'.
[191] Heffernan (1993) 3.
[192] On *monumentum* as both written record and building see Kraus (1994) 86 on Livy 6. 1. 2; Fowler (2000) 197–8.
[193] Hardie (1993b) 121–2.   [194] Oliensis (1998) 3–4.

inevitably draws attention to the writer as well as to the work of art and its owner. It thus forms an excellent strategy for the Flavian writer concerned, despite social and political constraints, to impose the marks of his own subjectivity upon his text and to fashion his own poems as worthy of memory beyond their occasion.

Thus, although I will use 'ecphrasis' and 'description' interchangeably in my discussion of the *Silvae*, it should be understood that my use of either term implies not the objective conveying of a visual reality but a verbal, interpretive response on the part of both poet and reader to the ideas and feelings expressed in and through a work of art or building. Indeed, in the *Silvae* this response involves not only the work of art and its owner but also the poetics of representation. As we shall see, in the *Silvae* ecphrasis as a mode that is both partial and selective provides an ideal medium for the oblique assertion of the poet's own worth.

The preceding remarks will be clarified, I believe, through a brief look at one of Statius' most self-reflexive poems, *Silv.* 2. 7. This poem is not about works of art, but about art itself, for it honours one of Rome's most outspoken public poets, Lucan. Written for the occasion of the dead poet's birthday at the request of his widow Polla, *Silv.* 2. 7 provides a poetic 'monument' to Lucan's career. At the same time, however, the poem uses the commemorative occasion to define Statius' poetics as well as Lucan's own.

Silv. 2. 7 acts as a 'seal' poem for Book 2 and serves as a reminder that Statius places himself in the tradition of Lucan as well as of the Augustan poets and Callimachus. As Malamud has shown in her brilliant analysis of this poem, Statius engages here in an implicit contest with Lucan, particularly in his role as epic poet.[195] Its competitive mode forms a counterpart to the ecphrastic poem. Instead of competing with a builder, Statius here competes on his own terms with a dead poet, an important literary predecessor. Statius' engagement with his youthful predecessor demonstrates his ability not only to surpass him in literary prowess but also to pursue different paths of poetic excellence. The important place given to this poem about Lucan suggests, I believe, Statius' interest in the poetry of political engagement, as well as his own struggle to find an effective voice within an autocratic society.

Lucan offered a model of speech that was politically and openly defiant and that ended in personal and political disaster with his suicide. Using the metaphor of drawing a sword from its sheath, Calliope tells the infant

---

[195] Malamud (1995). As Statius somewhat misleadingly tells us in the preface to Book 2, he writes in hendecasyllables, as he does not dare adopt Lucan's epic metre (*praef.* 2. 24–6).

Lucan in prediction that 'you will unsheathe a Roman song' ('*carmen...* *exseres togatum*', 53); in other words, Lucan will engage in the particularly Roman practice of making war, though with words. In foretelling Lucan's death, Calliope expresses her opinion that it was both wrongful and untimely: '*(o dirum scelus! o scelus!) tacebis!*' ('oh dreadful crime! Oh crime!) You will be silent!' (*Silv.* 2. 7. 104). By falling foul of Nero, Lucan's brilliant poetic career was cut short; his suicide is described as the silencing of his poetic voice. Malamud argues that in the *Thebaid* Statius found 'another way of writing the past, a different way of writing the dead'.[196] The contrapuntal voices of lamenting women in the *Thebaid* constantly interrupt the public, commemorative voice of epic and invite scrutiny of normative assumptions about militarism and the heroic ethos.

In the *Silvae* too Statius explores new, safer ways of writing the present as well as the past. Juvenal, who abandons epic and myth in his *Satires* for social and political criticism of everyday life, dares to speak only of the dead.[197] But Statius in the *Silvae* draws upon the rich, expansive rhetoric of praise to celebrate contemporary Flavian culture and also interrogate it, subtly and allusively and with fantasy and wit. In the *Silvae*, as well as in the *Thebaid*, yet in an entirely different way, Statius attempts to avoid silence, the fate of Lucan. He establishes and maintains his poetic authority through a 'poetics of Empire' that constitutes the art of obliquity practised in extravagant and stylish ways.

Thus it is in the *Silvae*, late poems of Domitian's reign, rather than in the *Thebaid*, that Statius engages most fully with contemporary issues and indeed examines his own role as a poet within Flavian society. Here Statius experiments with different poetic voices to suit his various topics. The descriptive poems of the *Silvae*, in particular, provide a challenging format in which relationships with the emperor as well as with friends can be negotiated and defined. Ecphrasis, then, provides a richly evocative, diplomatic strategy by which the poet can construct and manipulate his own literary genealogy and its political affiliations while honouring his patrons. Writing within a varied collection of verse about contemporary social and political life, in particular its splendid public and private buildings and works of art, permits Statius fully to explore the conditions of speech within imperial society.

The epigraph to this chapter, Jonson's emphatic understatement that the title *Underwood* has only one meaning and 'no otherwise', subtly draws attention to the fact that his readers expected, on the contrary, a richly

---

[196] Malamud (1995) 189.   [197] Juv. *Sat.* 1. 170–1.

evocative rhetoric of praise capable of manifold meaning. Profoundly different cultural attitudes about decorum and the role of praise within society stand today between contemporary readers and the readers of Statius and Jonson. Yet if we can overcome the novelties of tone and style, we can recognise that the *Silvae* provide important criticism of literature and society. The 'poetics of Empire' lavishly fashion a bold and complex celebration of Rome at the height of its power. Indeed, these are true poems of an Empire at a high level of technological and cultural achievement, exulting in world domination. Swift poems, supposedly dashed off in the heat of the moment, are part of a culture of wonder, of an Empire that tried to sustain the myth that any obstacles to its dominion could be swiftly and easily overcome. These poems have an excitement, an aggression as, under the cover of rich and capacious speech, they embark on the adventure of conquering new and contested poetic terrain.

At the same time, these poems are also true products of Empire in that they rest on a stressed dualism that encompasses praise and critique, joy and awe, excess and refinement. Meditating on the turn of the twentieth century in a editorial for the *Guardian Weekly*, Collini wrote that 'standing at the end of the 20th century, looking nervously over the edge, we are more acutely aware than ever of the dialectic of social optimism and cultural pessimism, of confidence and anxiety, of progress and nostalgia'.[198] This perception of our own situation in time is in many ways applicable to the situation of Rome at the end of the age of Domitian. All was not glitter in Statius' Rome. Extravagance brought with it anxiety as well as delight. The *Silvae* alert the reader to the competing voices within imperialism itself.

---

[198] Collini (2000) 11.

CHAPTER 2

Embodying the statue: Silvae *1. 1 and 4. 6*

> Comely and calm, he rides
> Hard by his own Whitehall;
> Only the nightwind glides;
> No crowds, no rebels, brawl.
> Gone too, his Court; and yet,
> The stars his courtiers are;
> Stars in their stations set;
> And every wandering star.
>
> Lionel Johnson, *By the Statue of King Charles at Charing Cross*

> But heaven this lasting monument has wrought,
> That mortals may eternally be taught
> Rebellion, though successful, is but vain,
> And kings so killed rise conqueror again.
>
> Edmund Waller, *On the Statue of King Charles I, at Charing Cross*

The *Silvae* open with a poem on a public monument that traditionally expresses a ruler's military might and majesty, the equestrian statue. The statue in question – a colossal equestrian statue of Domitian in bronze, which stood in the Roman Forum in honour of his German victories – no longer exists. But aside from Statius' poem we have a likely image of it on a sestertius minted at the end of Domitian's reign in AD 95–6, which depicts on the reverse an equestrian statue.[1] Text and image coincide in showing the emperor in triumphal pose, dressed in armour, right hand prominently outstretched; the horse is checked from galloping off by its rider, who thus reveals his supreme control; a figure, which Statius tells us is an allegorical representation of the Rhine, crouches subjugated beneath the horse's hoof (50–1). The statue reveals the close association between the Flavian dynasty and military victory. Indeed, the self-fashioning of Domitian as

---

[1] Hannestad (1988) 139. Carradice (1983) 123 and pl. XI, 1.

successful military leader was an important means of legitimating his rule.[2]

What the coin cannot represent, of course, is the grand scale of the equestrian statue. The vast size of many Flavian monuments has been frequently derided as a sign of the tasteless excesses of that particular dynasty.[3] Yet the recent find of a gigantic equestrian statue at the naval base of Misenum, the front of the head of Domitian recarved to represent Nerva, gives us some idea of the continuing importance and monumentality of this type of sculpture as a public expression of imperial power.[4] The perpetuation of this gigantic, public image of imperial authority and majesty suggests, in a sense anyway, that, as Waller says, 'kings so killed rise conqueror again'. The Flavian dynasty set the artistic pattern for the new language of Empire.[5] At the same time, the 'recycling' of the imperial image suggests that this was also a public art form particularly vulnerable to desecration – a point that underlies Statius' poem on the equestrian statue.

Statius' poem particularly emphasises the enormous size and weight of the statue. The head of its rider, for instance, he claims was wreathed in the upper air of heaven (32). Thus this first poem of the *Silvae* has been at the centre of a controversy on how to read imperial panegyric. For Ahl, the poem is subversive of Domitian's power and authority.[6] Ahl argues that the extravagance of Statius' praise represents either mannerism gone mad, or Statius' attempt to ridicule Domitian for future generations.[7] Ahl favours the latter view. He thus attempts to rehabilitate Statius as a master of irony and ambiguity, features he sees as essential to panegyric. For Vessey on the other hand, the *Silvae* accurately mirror imperial ideology in all its extravagance.[8] In his study of *Silv.* 1. 1 Geyssen has followed Vessey in seeing Statius in his first poem as the passive reproducer of Flavian ideology.[9] For Geyssen, *Silv.* 1. 1 uses the statue to celebrate unequivocally the emperor's achievements.

---

[2] Hannestad (1988) 139; Strobel (1994) 365–8; Jones (1992) 126–7 notes that Domitian was the first Roman emperor to spend substantial time outside Rome on military ventures. Mattingly (1926) 151–2 notes that Domitian's coinage shows a preponderance of military imagery.

[3] E.g. Newmyer (1984); Hannestad (1988) 132–3 makes the important argument that the Flavian period was one of change and cannot be classified according to one set of stylistic criteria.

[4] Kleiner (1992) 201; Varner (2000b) 12.

[5] See Darwall-Smith (1996) 227–33 on the form and situation of the equestrian statue. He makes the point (230–1) that the statue conformed to other representations of imperial power. However, it is hard to tell whether, as Statius' poem suggests, Flavian equestrian statues were on a far larger scale than earlier ones. See also Guiliani (1995).

[6] Ahl (1984a) 91–102.   [7] Ahl (1984a) 91.   [8] Vessey (1986) 2798.   [9] Geyssen (1996).

Militating further against the appreciation of this poem today is the controversial place that sculpture occupies in contemporary public life. In his fine book on the role of sculpture within modern poetry, North suggests that modern discomfort with the public monument derives from the common perception that commemoration of national heroes or historical events is an embarrassment, since the mythologies and the conventions that sustain them have been discredited.[10] Particularly for classicists, the fascist remodelling of Rome has perhaps caused a particular aversion to public monuments that are ostentatious and executed on the grand scale.[11] Little wonder then that *Silv.* 1. 1 has proved alien to the modern reader and that to enliven it and bring it to some prominence it has to be deconstructed in Ahl's brilliantly subversive reading.

I would like to try to move beyond these two positions by suggesting that the subject of the poem, the equestrian statue, is itself ambiguous and invites a variety of interpretive responses. Public monuments today certainly evoke mixed reactions in their viewers, and the same is true to some extent, North has argued, for the past. We should not oversimplify the place that statues have held in public mythology, for, as he argues, 'sculpture has held a public place in the past partly by virtue of its ambiguity, not because it is the simplest of the arts, but because it is able to satisfy conflicting desires'.[12] The recent reception of *Silv.* 1. 1 has precisely indicated the ability of this poem about a statue to satisfy conflicting desires, on the one hand for mockery and subversion of a tyrannical emperor, on the other hand for devoted, unequivocal celebration. Each critical response is to some extent valid but partial. The poem's ambiguity derives from the ambiguity of the sculpture itself, an ambiguity central to ancient descriptions of art, as Gordon has argued. For the legacy of Daedalus, legendary maker of statues that move, prompts the antitheses that register the ambiguous status of sculpture and painted figures: they deny and assert life, and they constantly play with the boundaries between the permissible and the forbidden.[13] *Silv.* 1. 1 explores the meaning of Domitian through a work of art that by its very nature is unstable and invites conflicting responses to it.

[10] North (1985) 17. North has argued that according to the 'myth' we have constructed for ancient sculpture, it clearly possessed three attributes: it commemorated a person or event; it was didactic; it embodied public agreement in style and message. Highly influential in contemporary perception of the role of monuments in public life have been the ideas of Mumford (1938), who persuasively argued in the thirties that modernism meant change and forward movement, whereas the public monument was obsolete and represented 'a petrified immortality' (434).
[11] On the remodelling of Rome under Mussolini see Elsner (1996b) 32–5.
[12] North (1985) 18–19.   [13] Gordon (1979) 6–10, especially 7.

Moreover, as Rose has argued, the production of the imperial image 'was not controlled by the Imperial court but was rather shaped by a multiplicity of factors' in which the donor's perception of the emperor's role played a significant part.[14] We are told in *Silv.* 1. 1 that the equestrian statue of Domitian is a gift of the Senate and people (99). The statue is therefore not a monolithic expression of imperial power. As a gift, it embodies the ideas, hopes and anxieties of the people and Senate about the emperor. In addition, a statue of a national hero or monarch in particular, by virtue of its public nature and situation and the heroic myth it inculcates, is open to a variety of public responses. Pliny the Elder, for instance, testifies to the ambiguous status of ancient sculpture in its popular appeal. In Book 36 of the *Natural History* he notes that people would travel great distances to see a famous monument or sculpture; such works of art endowed a city with enormous prestige.[15] Yet he also notes that sculpture could arouse vilification; in particular, the monuments of kings were prone not just to natural deterioration but also to defacement and destruction through change of taste, political opinion or sheer neglect.[16] Thus even as an object of veneration, the public monument is subject to political pressures – as the fate of most of Domitian's monuments testifies.

Silv. 1. 1 therefore deals with a subject that is capable of rich and varying construction. The norm for monuments in literature, Fowler has claimed, is 'a multiplicity of readings'.[17] Praise itself is a capacious concept and should not be equated with mere adulation. I wish to argue in this chapter first of all that *Silv.* 1. 1 has a protreptic or advisory function as well as a celebratory one. The viewer as poet is crucial to the construction of the statue's meaning. Ecphrasis provides a critical response to a visual image. Here it is used to convey and interpret some of the range of feelings that the statue as the gift of the Senate and the people represents. Certainly, in many ways the description of the statue is over the top, but that is part of the fun of the poem, a way of suggesting delight and confidence in an Empire that seems to promise limitless possibilities. But, as I wish to argue, *Silv.* 1. 1 is a poem of anxiety as well as celebration. In particular, *Silv.* 1. 1 uses the monument to channel concerns about the future and stability of the Flavian dynasty.

Furthermore, the poem concerns poetics as well as politics. Through the innovative use of ecphrasis, Statius explores his own new poetic

---

[14] Rose (1997) 51.   [15] Plin. *HN* 36. 4. 21.   [16] Plin. *HN* 36. 4. 11–12; 27–29.
[17] Fowler (2000) 207.

enterprise in the *Silvae*. The first poem of the *Silvae* intimately concerns literary as well as sculptural power, for not only is the statue a novelty, so too is this poem. There is no literary precedent for ecphrasis forming the subject of an entire, full-length poem in Latin literature, self-contained and divorced from any narrative context. *Silv.* 1. 1 is a startlingly innovative poem. In this first poem of the *Silvae*, and the first of the poems of imperial praise, Statius draws attention to his bold experiment with a completely new form of poetic expression. Ecphrasis of a monument here provides a particularly powerful literary strategy for investigating the nature and purpose both of imperial power and of imperial panegyric, for it is an artistically reflexive mode.[18] The occasion of imperial praise, of course, placed considerable constraints on the Flavian poet's own self-promotion. Hence the advantage of ecphrasis, which provides an ideal, safe medium both for the expression of anxiety and for the oblique assertion of the poet's own worth.

Indeed, the notion that poetry competes with monumental sculpture in the commemoration of famous people underlies *Silv.* 1. 1 and shapes the poet's response to the statue as a form to be inscribed with his own poetic values.[19] As Fowler reminds us, the word *monumentum*, monument, is 'crucially ambiguous', as it can refer both to the visual and to the written record, to image or to text.[20] In praising the emperor through his monument, Statius here continually blurs the boundaries between text and image. In particular, in this first poem of the *Silvae*, he plays subtly upon the metaphor developed in Augustan poetry of the poem itself as monument, and a more enduring means of memorialisation than stone.

But *Silv.* 1. 1 represents only one aspect of the complex poetics of the *Silvae*. In the conclusion of this chapter I shall consider a poem about a sculpture that stands at the opposite end of the scale from the equestrian statue. *Silv.* 4. 6 charts the poet's response to the miniature statue of Hercules, the property of a friend. The contrasting aesthetics of the colossal and the miniature dramatises the differing ideologies associated with public and private poetry. The cultural dialogue that runs throughout the *Silvae* is here expressed in the dialectical relationship between the two statues. The statue in the *Silvae* functions as a text for the inscription of different moral, political, and literary ideologies.

---

[18] See chapter 1 above, 38–43.
[19] On the identification of poet and monument in *Silv.* 1. 1 see Geyssen (1996) 141–4.
[20] See chapter 1 above, n. 192.

THE EQUESTRIAN STATUE

The statue, according to North, has often been ambiguous in three particular areas: its status as referential object; its relationship to the past and the future; its relationship to the public.[21] I propose in my discussion of *Silv.* 1. 1 to look at each of these three areas in turn in an attempt to appreciate the complex strategies that Statius employs in response to the new language of power embodied in Domitian's monuments. For not only is Statius responding to a new, expanded concept of the imperial office, he is also in the *Silvae* exploring a new form of artistic expression.

I shall begin then with the statue's vexed status as referential object. In his study of Pushkin's use of the statue in his writings, Jakobson has observed that through its three-dimensionality a statue, unlike a painting, problematises the relationship between the inert material and the subject of representation. The duality of this sign is subject to pressure and collapse as the boundaries between stone and human become blurred, particularly when its aesthetic criterion rests on a 'realism' that gives the impression of life and motion. Jakobson argues that poetry most effectively captures the basic opposition in the statue between immobility and rest.[22] So too Johnson's lines quoted at the start of this chapter point up the contradiction between the living appearance of the statue, which 'rides', and the immobility of its stone – 'Only the nightwind glides' – a contrast that in this case plays upon the ultimate futility of monuments and the transcendent serenity of the monarch.

A similar antinomy between movement and rest is vividly expressed in Statius' opening lines (1–7):[23]

> Quae superimposito moles geminata colosso
> stat Latium complexa forum? caelone peractum
> fluxit opus? Siculis an conformata caminis
> effigies lassum Steropen Brontenque reliquit?
> an te Palladiae talem, Germanice, nobis
> effinxere manus, qualem modo frena tenentem
> Rhenus et attoniti vidit domus ardua Daci?

What enormous mass, doubled by the colossus that surmounts it, stands embracing the Roman forum? Has the work flowed down from heaven completed? Or has the shaping of the image in the Sicilian workshops left Brontes and Steropes exhausted? Or have Minerva's hands fashioned you for us, Germanicus, portraying you in the same guise as when the Rhine and the mountainous

---

[21] North (1985) 18.   [22] Jakobson (1987), especially 352–6.
[23] The text used throughout this book is that of Courtney (1992).

fastness of the awe-struck Dacian lately saw you, curbing your horse with the reins?

The opening barrage of questions begins the poem in dazzling fashion: repetition, apostrophe, chiasmus, personification, mythical allusion and elaborate epithets create an opulence of style that matches the grandeur and exotic nature of the statue. Language here tries to gain a sense of spatial form, physical presence, and iconic representation. However, the contrast between *stat* (2) and *fluxit* (3) aroused Ahl's ire, for how could a statue so inert and heavy 'flow' from the sky?[24] Yet this opening verbal antithesis immediately points to the ambiguity of the statue itself. Its immobility is expressed in the first verb *stat* along with the other dominant words of weight and mass that fill the sentence, whereas the possibility of motion is expressed in the second verb *fluxit* (3) with its short sentence. Statius explores this ambiguity between mobility and immobility in the rest of the poem. It is summed up perhaps most succinctly and vividly in the later, terse description of the horse, its mane rigid like stone, its body surging with life-like motion: *cui rigidis stant colla iubis vivusque per armos | impetus* ('its neck and mane stand stiff, a lively urge for movement surges through its shoulders', 47–8).

The initial focus of the poem falls upon the art of the statue – its physical medium, its possible creators, and its method of creation. The emperor is not identified as the subject of the sculpture until line 5, *Germanice*. 'Holding the reins' the emperor provides a picture of control and ordered governance. The title Germanicus, granted for Domitian's victory over the Chatti in AD 83, presents him as a civiliser who has van-quished the barbarians of the North.[25] The control of the rider is linked here with his maintenance and protection of the Empire's boundaries. Yet his honorary 'cognomen' is linked with the speculation that the hands of his patron, Minerva, fashioned his statue. The size of the statue along with its possible divine and mythical creators removes it from the merely human realm and implies the godlike stature of its rider. Indeed, extrav-agance in the statue and in the poem with its grandiloquent opening becomes a means of response to an emperor whose self-representation approximated the divine. Hariman has argued that courtly politics dif-fers from other political cultures by its emphasis on the body of the monarch. In this symbolic system the body is further divided into 'parts mortal and mystic', thereby providing 'material and transcendental axes

---

[24] Cf. Ahl (1984a) 92, who sees mockery here in the opposition of *stat* and *fluxit*.
[25] Vollmer (1898) 44–6; Strobel (1994) 367.

for royal power'.[26] The equestrian statue of Domitian, poised between immobility and movement, makes manifest this symbolic system as the body of the emperor, along with that of his horse, is metaphorically preserved in lustrous bronze and yet surges with life. The statue thus suggests both the physical presence of the emperor and his transcendent nature.

In these opening lines, attention is drawn also to the innovatory nature of Statius' poem by the allusion at line 4 to the ecphrasis of the shield of Aeneas in *Aeneid* 8, for Brontes and Steropes were two of its craftsmen.[27] The Cyclopes too, along with Vulcan, fashioned the fatal necklace of Argia in Statius' *Thebaid*.[28] Both these ecphraseis were incorporated into their epic narratives. The allusion to these passages in *Silv.* 1. 1 underscores Statius' originality. An ecphrasis about a symbol of Rome's national identity – in the *Aeneid* a shield figured with symbols of Rome's future glory, here an equestrian statue – is entirely independent of a narrative context and constitutes a free-standing poem. Moreover, by exhausting the epic labours of Steropes and Brontes, the statue, so it is implied, has outdone the most epic of endeavours and clearly then poses an enormous new challenge for the poet of the *Thebaid* to encompass in a new kind of verse. The opening questions throw down the poetic gauntlet. Here is a new poetic strategy and a new poetic topic – a way of addressing the emperor and singing of his deeds outside formal epic. The novelty of the statue and the wonder of its effects function as a cue to the reader to wonder too at the novelty of Statius' poetry. The emotion of wonder draws attention to the judgment of the poet and to the fact that he exists in a relationship not just with the statue but with his readers.

The preface to Book 1 indicates the introductory poem's importance with the statement that the collection begins with Jupiter, *a Iove principium* (*praef.* 1. 17). Here Statius conflates politics and poetics. Statius compliments the emperor by alluding to the emperor's cultivation of his association with Jupiter.[29] Moreover, by identifying Domitian with Jupiter, Statius uses this particular feature of imperial ideology to his own advantage. Jupiter, the supreme divine authority, endows the new poetry book of Rome's premier poet with the seal of inviolable authority. Furthermore, by calling the emperor a sacrosanct witness to his first poetry book, *sacrosanctum testem* (*praef.* 1. 16), the poet appropriates the emperor's authority as proof of the value of his new collection. Thus, as

---

[26] Hariman (1995) 58.   [27] *Aen.* 8. 425. See Vollmer (1898) 216.
[28] *Theb.* 2. 269–305. On the necklace as a poetic programme for the entire poem see McNelis (2000) chapter 2.
[29] On Domitian's cultivation of analogies with Jupiter see Fears (1981).

he makes tribute to Domitian, he does so in a way that acknowledges the writer's authority in the manipulation of the symbols of imperial power.

Moreover, Statius acknowledges the emperor through the special filter of his own allusive art. The phrase *a Iove principium* makes direct allusion to Theocritus' *Idyll* 17 and Virgil's *Eclogue* 3; the grand style that Roman imperial extravagance demands is accommodated to other poetic influences, here Hellenistic court poetry and pastoral.[30] Indeed, by claiming that his poetry book begins with Jupiter, Statius makes a further allusion here to Callimachus' first *Hymn*, which begins with Zeus. As Haslam has noted, Callimachus' *Hymn to Zeus* is surprisingly short for a hymn dedicated to the highest god; through the structure of his first poem Callimachus wittily encodes a programmatic statement about the importance of the short, refined poem.[31] The poem on the equestrian statue, *Silv.* 1. 1, is likewise comparatively short; in the first book only *Silv.* 1. 5 is shorter. In this poem, then, Statius explores the tension between the colossal size and weight of the statue and the sophisticated aesthetics of the poet, between the contemporary realities of imperial politics and the varied literary traditions that shape his representation of the statue.

The statue's ambiguous status between rest and movement is related then to the new, ambitious poetics of the *Silvae*, which involve constant interplay between the grandeur in style and conception traditionally associated with encomiastic themes, and the refinement associated with Callimachean poetics.[32] The poem plays upon the paradox involved in the encompassing of such an enormous, weighty subject within the confines of a short poem. Indeed, like the statue itself, which has perhaps flowed from the sky (*caelone peractum* | *fluxit opus?* 2–3), this poem has flowed swiftly from the poet's stylus (*fluxerunt, praef.* 1. 3–4). In a re-evaluation of the apologetic poetics of the preface, speed and fluency it seems can be virtues. The opening antithetical set of questions then – 'does the statue stand / did it flow?' – gives voice to a new, innovative poetics that transgresses generic decorum in search of a new form of public expression that incorporates stateliness and facility of expression, dignity and wit.

In *Silv.* 1. 1, the antinomy between immobility and mobility is also specifically related to the concepts of peace and war, both of which are embodied in the statue. The statue stands in the Roman Forum, the civic centre of Rome, yet while its right hand 'forbids war' (37), its left hand

---

[30] Theoc. *Id.* 17. 1; Verg. *Ecl.* 3. 60.   [31] Haslam (1993) 115–16.   [32] Cameron (1995) 463–71.

holds a statue of Minerva clutching the Gorgon's severed head (37–8).
With his adoption of Minerva as his special patron – a goddess who
was both warrior and guardian of domestic institutions – Domitian gave
divine sanction to the idea of the emperor as military hero as well as
civic benefactor.[33] Minerva's temple, built by Domitian as the centrepiece of his Forum Transitorium, was flanked on one side by Vespasian's
Temple of Peace, on the other by the Temple of Mars Ultor in Augustus'
Forum; in its topographical situation, the temple symbolically expressed
the imperial idea of peace as a function of military strength at home and
abroad.[34] Thus the poet's response to the emperor's image as seeming
to promise both peace and war agrees with Flavian ideology according
to which peace and war were not opposing concepts but were mutually
dependent. The *Silvae* therefore put a new valuation on war from that explored in the *Thebaid*. War brings military glory to the victor and peace to
his subjects. In *Silv.* 1. 1 Statius rewrites epic, putting a new positive interpretation on motifs traditionally associated with war's most tragic aspect.

Yet, as the poet grapples for adequate means of expression to describe
the equestrian statue, he does not always resolve the tension between
the statue's antinomies; there is often some slippage in interpretation.
The enormous size of the statue creates a particular area of ambiguity
between the mortality and the divinity of the emperor, his dependence
on his people's good will and his otherness. As Gordon notes, the Greeks
(and we might add the Romans) registered the otherness of the gods
by playing upon size with their colossal statues.[35] The colossal size of
Domitian's equestrian statue aligns him therefore with divinity; he was
not yet, however, a god. Statius' poem raises the question of how far an
emperor can usurp the privileges of divinity. The statue, as two particular mythical comparisons in the poem suggest, conveys a sense both of
majesty and of transgressive power.

The opening image of the ruler's self-control, for instance, is disturbed
first of all by the comparison of the equestrian statue of Domitian to the
Trojan horse (8–16):

> nunc age fama prior notum per saecula nomen
> Dardanii miretur equi cui vertice sacro
> Dindymon et caesis decrevit frondibus Ide:
> hunc neque discissis cepissent Pergama muris

[33] See *tuae...Minervae* here at 1. 22. On the close connection between Domitian and Minerva see
Scott (1936) 166–89; D'Ambra (1993) 73–4.
[34] On the layout of the Forum Transitorium see Coleman (1988) 69–71.
[35] Gordon (1979) 14.

> nec grege permixto pueri innuptaeque puellae
> ipse nec Aeneas nec magnus duceret Hector.
> adde quod ille nocens saevosque amplexus Achivos,
> hunc mitis commendat eques: iuvat ora tueri
> mixta notis, bellum placidamque gerentia pacem.

Well then, let the legend of former days admire the immortal fame of the Trojan horse, for whose making Dindymon's sacred summit was laid bare and Ida's leaves were shorn. Pergamum could not have admitted this [sc. Domitian's] horse, even though its walls were breached; boys and unmarried girls mingling in a crowd could not have led in this horse, neither Aeneas himself nor great Hector. In addition, the Trojan horse was harmful and harboured savage Greeks; a gentle rider recommends this horse. It is pleasant to look at his face, which is mixed in its signs, and wages both war and placid peace.

This particular comparison is not mandated by ruler cult or by imperial ideology but is the result of the poet's own artistic choice. It is therefore one of the most controversial passages of the poem. For Geyssen, the Trojan horse should be read as a beneficent sign for Rome, signifying the new city that will rise from the ashes of Troy. Without the Trojan horse, indeed, Domitian's Rome would not exist.[36] Basing his argument upon his concept of figured speech, Ahl on the other hand sees the comparison between the Trojan horse and Domitian's statue as highly ambivalent. In his view, the equestrian statue gives artistic expression to the threat that Domitian, a psychopathic monster, represents for Rome.[37] Can we negotiate between these two positions?

Hunter has put forward the idea of selective reading as a method for approaching imperial panegyric.[38] Indeed this passage, Statius suggests, should be read selectively by the reader, screening out the negatives. He makes a point of claiming, for instance, that though both statues were enormous in size, Domitian's equestrian statue is different in that it poses no threat to Rome (11–16). Indeed, the emperor's horse is not harmful, for it has a gentle rider (*mitis, Silv.* 1. 1. 15), on whom it is pleasing to look (*iuvat ora tueri | mixta notis, bellum placidamque gerentia pacem,* 15–16). *Iuvat* ('it is pleasing') interprets the act of viewing as one that brings delight. Thus Statius invites his readers to discard the negative associations which the Trojan horse bears and to recognise the wonderful qualities of this new horse and its rider, who is equally adept in the acts of peace and

---

[36] Geyssen (1996) 48–53.   [37] Ahl (1984a) 92.

[38] See Hunter (1996) 163–6. Hunter argues that Theocritus' celebration of Helen in *Id.* 18 is in accordance with Ptolemaic ideology, which expected the audience to retain the complimentary associations of the comparison and screen out the negatives.

war. The triumphal garb of the rider and the subjugation of 'captive Rhine' (50–1) beneath the horse's feet establish the close connection between military might and imperial authority and control that we see expressed on the Cancellaria reliefs. Statius thus draws attention here to the necessity of making choices in interpretation. As in Pliny's *Panegyricus*, a negative example – here the Trojan horse, not Domitian – serves to recommend and reinforce a positive model of leadership, not just for the emperor, but for the wider readership of Statius' poetry which, as Quintilian remarks, valued the exemplary nature of panegyric.[39]

Yet the comparison is not simply a function of Statius' humour and exuberance. At the same time the comparison is phrased in a way that invites the reader to consider just how well it works. The presence of the negative example of the Trojan horse (8–14) – on which, incidentally, the emphasis falls (seven lines as opposed to two) – functions also as a cautionary device, an implied protreptic to the emperor to be benevolent and also an invitation to the reader to assess the true nature of the power that Domitian yields. The rider 'wages both war and placid peace' (*bellum placidamque gerentia pacem*, 16), a striking image whose conceptual balance between peace and war is shifted towards the latter by *gerentia*. *Gerentia* blurs the conventional antithesis between peace and war, between the calmness suggested by *placidam* and the action of *gerentia*; in an apparent paradox, Domitian 'wages' peace. The ambiguity in the statue then between stillness and movement conveys the idea of the emperor's vigilance on behalf of the Empire; this is a figure always ready to go to the defence of the realm and maintain its boundaries. But it also latently suggests the possibility of exploding those boundaries. The statue thus conveys the ambiguity of imperial power itself, poised (how securely?) between the gentle rider and the Gorgon's head.[40]

In particular, the poet's concluding remark that it is pleasing to look on the rider's face blurs the distinction between emperor and statue and presents Domitian as a text that is to be deciphered, a combination of signs: *iuvat ora tueri | mixta notis* ('it is pleasing to look at a face mixed in its signs', 15–16). The head after all is the most important part of the statue, the detachable sign of the rider's identity.[41] This important 'text', however, provides mixed 'signs' for the reader. The simile of the

---

[39] Quint. *Inst.* 3. 7. 13–14, 23–4.
[40] Jupiter is introduced with similar ambiguity in the *Thebaid*, when he is described as 'shaking all things with peaceful expression' (*placido quatiens tamen omnia vultu, Theb.* 1. 202). The juxtaposition of *placido* and *quatiens* neatly suggests the paradoxical nature of autocratic power.
[41] Stewart (1999) 165.

Trojan horse with its concluding image of the emperor's inscrutable face invites reflection upon contemporary leadership, not just adulation of it. We are moving here towards the image of the emperor cultivated in late imperial art in which the imperial face, disengaged from the earthly viewer, suggests the ruler's approximation to a god.[42] The question of course always remains, what type of god?

In a further mythological comparison, the poet confronts the reader with another set of mixed signs through reference to the astral figure of Orion (43–5):

> it tergo demissa chlamys, latus ense quieto
> securum, magnus quanto mucrone minatur
> noctibus hibernis et sidera terret Orion.

A military cloak flows down its back, its side is protected by its sheathed sword, its point as big as that with which the giant Orion threatens and terrifies the stars on winter nights.

Here the poem lyrically expresses the contrast between the magnificent stillness of the rider, a paragon of control, and the magnificent life contained in the horse that the rider nonetheless contains. The rider's sword is safe, sheathed in quiet, but at the same time the verbs *minatur* (the latter picked up in the straining motion of the horse, who threatens to run, *cursumque minatur*, 47) and *terret* place the emphasis on the figure's capacity to act and threaten and terrify. Vollmer urges a selective reading here, arguing that the comparison between the emperor and Orion hinges purely on size.[43] But the choice of the giant Orion is wittily apt, and not just in terms of size, for the comparison suggests that the viewer of the statue, like the viewer of the constellation of Orion, has to look upwards towards the sky to see the statue. Thus while it conveys the colossal scale and dazzling brightness of the statue, it also subtly plays upon the notion that Domitian in his afterlife will become a star through apotheosis.

At the same time, however, the comparison also surely conveys a sense of menace. With the comparison to the Trojan horse, Statius emphasises difference; here he emphasises similarity. Given also the presence of the verbs *minatur* and *terret,* the threatening aspects of Orion cannot be completely discarded. Orion was a giant who was punished for thinking that his extraordinary size and strength gave him the liberty to violate the

---

[42] On the development of the imperial image in Late Antiquity see MacCormack (1981) 42–5. A particularly interesting description of the impassive, divinely inspired face of Constantius is found in Amm. Marc. 16. 10.

[43] Vollmer (1898) 224.

gods.[44] In the *Aeneid*, Virgil compares Mezentius when he is on his mur-
derous rampage to Orion, described here, as in our Statius passage, as
magnus Orion (Aen. 10. 763). The comparison in the *Aeneid* rests not only
upon enormous size but also upon destructive power.[45] The mythological
comparison in *Silv.* 1. 1 thus has a complex function. The poem's initial
representation of the rider 'holding the reins' (6) and thus checking the
horse provides an image of containment and self-control that suggests
well-ordered governance. But the comparison with Orion associates the
emperor not only with military prowess and success over barbarians, a
means of securing *pax Romana,* but also with ideas of excess and transgression that threaten the stability of that peace. In *Silv.* 1. 1, the statue's ex-
ceeding of normal physical boundaries is associated, through the mighty
but impious Orion, with the potential overstepping of moral and political boundaries. The comparison has therefore a protreptic function as
a reminder of the dangers inhererent in such extraordinary powers as
Domitian was arrogating to himself. As the boundaries between life and
stone are blurred, so too are those between war and peace, between war
moreover as a function of social control and war as a function of social
disruption.

Thus, the comparison of the Trojan horse, along with the later one
of Orion, creates a 'faultline', a fissure that reveals a gap between the
noble myth of military success and containment and the lurking threat
of indiscriminate power and violence. Despite the poet's protestations,
there lurks beneath the dominant discourse of praise an uncertainty
about the meaning of Domitian's statue and the concept of power it
embodies.[46] The equestrian statue monumentalises military strength and
success. But is it indeed a purely benevolent image of power and military
triumph? The statue above all means excess, from the massive weight
of its pedestal upon the ground (56–60) to the gigantic tip of its sword.
Indeed does excess – the enormous size of the statue, the ambitions it
expresses – suggest, in addition to the idea of imperial majesty, the threat
to the stability of the state from one who has constructed himself as
above human law? In exploiting the ambiguity inherent in the public

[44] There were two independent myths of Orion's translation to the stars. In the one he tried to
violate Diana, who killed him (e.g. Hor. *Carm.* 3. 4. 70–2; Stat. *Theb.* 7. 255–8), in the other
he made an outrageous boast about his hunting prowess that offended the gods (eg. Ov. *Fast.*
5. 537–4). In either case he is a grotesque figure, outsize in appearance and behaviour. See
Fontenrose (1981) 5–32.
[45] Verg. *Aen.* 10. 763–8. Mezentius is described as 'shaking his spear' and tempestuous, *turbidus,* as
he strides over the battlefield (762–3).
[46] On Sinfield's (1992) notion of 'faultline' see chapter 1 above, 23–5.

monument, Statius' text highlights the fine line an autocratic ruler of necessity walks between admiration and fear, benevolence and menace.

As a referential object, then, the statue is ambiguous in its blurring of the boundaries between movement and rest, life and stone. And such a blurring of boundaries is related to the blurring of boundaries in the political praxis of Domitian himself, an emperor whose expansive concept of imperial power evokes awe and admiration but also anxiety, even fear. The basic antinomy between rest and movement in *Silv.* 1. 1 then is directly related to a concept of the emperor's rule as fundamentally ambiguous. This, Millar has argued, is in any case the quintessential condition of imperial power, 'that arbitrary exercise of power and favour on the one side, and that ever-present fear and uncertainty on the other'.[47] But in reaching for the stars Domitian, more than his predecessors, had cultivated his dissociation from ordinary people as well as family members and close associates.[48] Pagán has argued that a major preoccupation of Tacitus' *Annales*, and indeed of imperial politics, is the threat posed to the idea of a well-ordered Principate by geographical, political, and moral transgression.[49] The statue embodies the might yet ultimate unknowability of the power of an emperor set so far above his subjects in inhuman remoteness that the stability of the state could be placed in jeopardy.

Let me now turn to a second area of ambiguity mentioned by North, the statue's relationship to the past and to the future. In *Silv.* 1. 1 the statue is addressed by the early Roman hero Mettius Curtius, who draws a link between Rome's venerable institutions and its dynastic future (66–83). The visionary speech by a dead hero is a standard motif of epic poetry. Indeed, the practice of ascribing an encomiastic speech to a mythological character is characteristic of Statius' poems of imperial praise.[50] The poet's response to the statue then is mediated not just by his own voice but by that of another. This practice of ascribing a speech of praise to a hero or god has been generally interpreted as a strategy whereby flattery, through displacement to a fictitious speaker, can be made less

---

[47] Millar (1977) 10.   [48] See Syme (1988); Strobel (1994).   [49] Pagán (1999), especially 315.

[50] *Silv.* 1. 1. 74–83 (Curtius praises Domitian); 3. 4. 32–45 (Venus praises Earinus) and 3. 4. 95–7 (Cupid praises Earinus); 4. 1. 17–43 (Janus praises Domitian); 4. 3. 72–94 (the river Volturnus praises Domitian) and 4. 3. 124–63 (the Cumaean Sibyl praises Domitian). A speech of praise by mythological characters is a particular feature of Statius' imperial poems. It occurs only twice in the 'private' poems, both of which play upon the elevated, quasi-imperial role of the person being honoured. In *Silv.* 2. 7. 41–104 Calliope laments and praises Lucan, who is honoured as a god (note *adoret* at the poem's end, 135); in *Silv.* 3. 1. 91–116 and 166–83 Hercules praises Pollius, who has taken on imperial powers of building. See Coleman (1999).

blatant.[51] Yet the point of view of the eulogiser cannot be assumed to be the same as that of the poet who represents the speech, or indeed of the multiple readership that receives it. Characteristic of focalised speech is a restricted perspective. As Genette cautions, we should not confuse the information given by a focalised speech with the interpretation that the reader is guided to make.[52] In Statius' poems of imperial praise, the issue of focalisation is crucial.[53] Like comparison, such speeches encourage openness to different lines of thought and meaning and diversify the fabric of encomiastic verse.

With Curtius' speech, Statius here varies the dazzling fabric of his encomiastic verse. He treats Curtius, as we shall see, in the style of Hellenistic court poetry, with a combination of seriousness and droll sophistication, historicity and fantasy. Curtius, a 'ghost', addresses the statue as if it were Domitian himself; his speech yet again blurs the boundaries between the physical body of the emperor and its symbolic representation, between historical 'reality' and myth. Curtius makes a dramatic and comic appearance in *Silv.* 1. 1, raising from the Lacus Curtius in the Roman Forum his head 'venerable with decay' and crowned with the badge of honourable civic service, the oak wreath (69–70).[54] The poem here plays with the idea of the distant past. Curtius is so old that he is well on the way to decay. Then again, he reverses the normal relations between the dead and the living by being terrified by the sight of the statue (*expavit*, 72, *trepidans*, 73); three times he dips his head back in his lake before plucking up courage to speak.

Is he therefore an odd figure to voice an encomium? Again, it is characteristic of the *Silvae* to blur the boundaries of decorum; humour, as I have said, is not exclusive of encomiastic intent. At the same time, as Coleman has suggested, the timid reaction of Curtius, who was renowned for his courage, makes Domitian's magnetism all the more forceful.[55] Indeed, the oddly comic figure of Curtius points to the difference between Rome's ancient past and glorious imperial present; his shabby figure conjures up a striking contrast with the new, gleaming icon of imperial supremacy before him. Moreover, this unconventional eulogiser invites an ironic distance between the poet and the encomiastic voice here, a dramatic reminder that Statius and Curtius are not to be identified. Curtius disturbs the illusion of authenticity. He draws attention to the

[51] Coleman (1988) 65.   [52] Genette (1980) 197.
[53] Genette (1980) 189–211; see also Genette (1988) 64.
[54] On the site see Coleman (1999) 67–8.   [55] Coleman (1999) 68–9.

poet as not simply viewer standing agape in front of the statue, but as an artist involved in the skilful representation of the imperial image.

There were three possible historical models for the 'Curtius' of Statius' poem.[56] There was the Mettius Curtius who saved his country by plunging into the ravine; there was also the Sabine enemy who showed his bravery by escaping through the lake; finally there was the Republican consul in whose term of office the chasm was struck by lightning. Since the identity of 'Curtius' in *Silv.* 1. 1 is not secured until the middle of the speech when he refers to himself as *semel auctor ego inventorque salutis | Romuleae* ('I was responsible for finding a way to save Romulus' people', 78–9), Curtius raises at first in mild form the question of Barthes: *qui parle?*[57] Curtius then is almost a composite figure who brings the combined weight of the past to the evaluation of the statue, thereby acknowledging its traditional affiliations with time-honoured Roman concepts of patriotic and religious duty and military prowess, concepts that are also important on the Cancellaria reliefs. The statue then is validated by Rome's distant past, a past construed primarily in terms of service to the state. At the same time, Curtius' surprise and wonder at the statue mark Domitian as a new kind of leader compared to the heroes of old. Curtius' speech ends by remarking that Domitian would be more daring than Curtius (81–3) if given the chance. Domitian is thus celebrated as both a hero in the ancient Roman mould and as a new, bold figure of the Roman Empire whose statue and deeds exceed mortal limits.

But more troublingly, Curtius' speech itself also deals with the recent past as it cites Domitian's military achievements (79–83):

> tu bella Iovis, tu proelia Rheni,
> tu civile nefas, tu tardum in foedera montem
> longo Marte domas. quods(i te) nostra tulissent
> saecula, temptasses me non audente profundo
> ire lacu, sed Roma tuas tenuisset habenas.

You win Jove's wars, you win the battles of the Rhine, you win the evil of civil conflict, you win in lengthy war the mountainous region reluctant to come to terms. But if you had been born in my age, you would have tried to plunge in the depths of the lake even though I did not dare, but Rome would have held back your reins.

---

[56] See Livy 7. 1–6 for the self-sacrificing soldier; Livy, 1. 12–13 for the Sabine soldier; Varro *Ling.* 5. 14 for the pious consul.

[57] As Barthes (1992) 41 claims, 'the more indeterminate the origin of the statement, the more plural the text'.

Curtius' speech strikingly intermingles references to civil war with references to long drawn-out German campaigns, *longo Marte* (81). With *bella Iovis* (79) Curtius refers specifically to the civil war of AD 68–9 which culminated in the burning of the Capitol; with *civile nefas*, placed emphatically in the same metrical position in the following line, he probably refers to the more recent uprising of Saturninus in AD 89.[58] Indeed, as Hardie notes, this poem was probably written in the aftermath of that revolt, a difficult period for Domitian when there were other challenges to his power such as a false Nero in Parthia and unrest in Dacia.[59] The equestrian statue here is given expanded meaning. The triumphal pose suggests not just victory over foreign tribes but also victory over rebels of the state who seek to overturn the prevailing order. Curtius' speech praises Domitian's triumphs over his enemies at home and abroad; nonetheless, his speech with its two references to internal insurrection raises the spectre of civil conflict.

Moreover, the place from which Curtius speaks, the Lacus Curtius, did not simply commemorate a venerable and heroic past. It was the site of one of the most horrific acts of butchery and impiety in the conflict over the succession after Nero's death. Tacitus and Suetonius tell us that it was here that the emperor Galba, an old man and unarmed, was treacherously murdered by Roman soldiers newly in Otho's pay.[60] Galba's body was mutilated, his head decapitated and impaled for public display; later it was given back to the body and buried in a humble tomb. Vespasian, it seems, vetoed a senatorial decree that there be a statue to Galba on the spot that Domitian's equestrian statue now occupied.[61] The Lacus Curtius therefore was imprinted in recent memory with the stain of civil war.

The figure of Curtius as encomiast activates the several dissonant associations of the statue's site. It is not just the distant past of patriotic service that Curtius recalls but also the recent notorious past of internecine strife and changing emperors. The lake forms a silent, if powerful, memorial to dynastic instability. Curtius' speech then contains the 'ghosts of alternate stories', of antagonistic positions taken to Flavian supremacy.[62] They serve as an unsettling reminder of the possibility of opposition and of violent strife, of the horrors that can ensue when an emperor dies without an heir. Nor is foreign victory described as the easy

---

[58] See Vollmer (1898) 227–8; Jones (1992) 144–9.   [59] Hardie (1983) 189.
[60] Tac. *Hist.* 1. 40–1, 49; Suet. *Galb.* 20. 2.   [61] Suet. *Galb.* 23.
[62] For the idea that 'all stories contain within themselves the ghosts of the alternative stories they are trying to repress', see Sinfield (1992) 21.

matter that the superhuman rider and horse suggest: victory comes from long drawn-out war (81). As a veteran of Rome's military past Curtius' speech uncomfortably probes at the historical reality behind the statue's image of invincibility. The statue stands literally and metaphorically on unstable ground.

Adding to the plurality of this encomiastic speech is the ghost of another story, that of the *Thebaid*, a striking mythical instance of conflict that is long and drawn out. In the preface to this epic Statius announces that he cannot yet sing of *bella Iovis* (*Theb.* 1. 22) – the same phrase that Curtius uses in *Silv.* 1. 1. 79 to refer to the burning of the Capitol in the civil wars of AD 68–9. Appropriately, then, in the first poem of the *Silvae* the challenging subject of the 'wars of Jupiter' is incorporated into Curtius' speech, not the poet's own. Ahl has suggested that Mettius Curtius, in his committal of himself to a chasm, is a Roman, voluntary version of Amphiaraus, the seer of the *Thebaid*.[63] The arousal of Curtius from the Underworld suggests, moreover, that the statue disturbs the boundaries between earth and the Underworld which are so permeable in the *Thebaid*. Indeed, *Silv.* 1. 1 elsewhere plays off the *Thebaid* with the comparison of the horse to Arion, the famous steed of the Argive king Adrastus (52–5).[64]

Yet, rather than put a negative interpretation upon these allusions to the *Thebaid*, we can see them, perhaps, as marking the contrast between that mythical world and the world of Domitian. Curtius' leap into the chasm is a self-sacrificing act which Domitian would not be allowed to replicate (81–3), presumably because that would entail too great a loss to Rome. Curtius himself, unlike Amphiaraus, returns from the Underworld to celebrate and authorise a new regime. The horse, unlike Arion who flees in panic when Polynices attempts to ride him, is harmoniously matched with his imperial rider and is captured and controlled in bronze. In asserting that the contemporary world of Rome operates by different laws and modes of restraint, Curtius' speech has a metapoetic frame of reference: here is a new and different way of treating warfare from that explored by Statius within the *Thebaid*. This is warfare within the glorious context of Empire, sanctioned therefore by Rome's heroes and gods. Such warfare can be the inspirer of an ambitious new poetics. Nonetheless, the distinction between the *Thebaid* and the *Silvae* is not entirely clear-cut; war in the *Silvae* too encompasses civil strife. As

[63] Ahl (1984a) 97; *Theb.* 7. 688–823.
[64] *Theb.* 6. 301–25; on Arion and Polynices, *Theb.* 6. 424–517.

Silv. 1. 1 shows, Statius constructs his own mythical world within the political and artistic circumstances of Domitian's Rome, thereby permitting a good deal of latitude in the imaginative discourse of praise. Allusions to recent insurrection and civil strife as well as to the *Thebaid* disturb the hegemonic discourse of the noble rider whose perfect control of his steed allegorises his position as head of the Roman world. Through the very celebration of military might in the *Silvae*, Statius invites reservations about the imperial fiction of invincibility.

Following Curtius' speech, the statue, in the concluding portion of the poem (84–107), is employed as a focus for anxieties about the stability of Domitian's rule and indeed of the Flavian dynasty, for the future of emperor and monument is specifically addressed in the clear antinomy between the durability and the transience of monuments that emerges at the poem's end. Public monuments, like rulers, are subject to decay. Statues are destroyed or changed in various ways, by fire or by the cutting off of the head, or by defacement, sometimes combined with substitution of the face by another portrait type. As we have seen, this was the fate of the head of Domitian on the Cancellaria reliefs and on the equestrian statue found at Misenum.[65] Indeed, even if a statue endured, its original identity could be lost, as was the case with the equestrian statue of Marcus Aurelius whom a later period identified as 'Constantine'.[66] Stewart has shown that the practice of destroying statues of disgraced rulers was a common one in Roman society from the first century BCE to the end of the fourth century AD and was generally associated with, or substituted for, the mutilation of the ruler's body.[67] Before Nero's death, for instance, the angry public made threats against him through desecration of his statues; a Roman standard-bearer provided the impetus for the murder and decapitation of Galba by removing the emperor's image from his standard and dashing it to the ground.[68] For the statue symbolically represented the physical person of the ruler himself; it thus gave the public immediate access for acts of either worship or violation.

The conclusion of *Silv.* 1. 1 falls into three parts. In the first section (84–90), Domitian's equestrian statue is favourably compared to the equestrian statue of Julius Caesar that stands nearby.[69] But this

---

[65] See Plin. *Pan.* 52 for an evocative description of the smashing and melting down of public statues after Domitian's assassination; Rose (1997) 9–10 on the vulnerability of the imperial image; also Stewart (1999) and Varner (2000).

[66] North (1985) 27; Hannestad (1988) 219–21.   [67] Stewart (1999) 161–9.

[68] Suet. *Ner.* 45. 2; Tac. *Hist.* 1. 41.   [69] Plin. *HN* 8. 64. 155.

earlier statue, too, provides a tacit warning of the mutability of the public monument (84–87):

> cedat equus Latiae qui contra templa Diones
> Caesarei stat sede fori, quem traderis ausus
> Pellaeo, Lysippe, duci (mox Caesaris ora
> mirata cervice tulit)

Let the horse which stands in Caesar's forum opposite the temple of Venus Genetrix give place to you – the one which people say you, Lysippus, daringly made for the leader from Pella (and which soon bore Caesar's countenance to the amazement of its neck)

The comparison is complimentary, to be sure.[70] A statue made by Lysippus, one of the most famous sculptors of Greece – the only sculptor Alexander permitted to sculpt his image – is surpassed by Domitian's equestrian statue, which is presumably, then, an even more daring project (*ausus*, 85). The formulaic introduction of this passage with *cedat* ('let it give place') acknowledges the superiority of this new work of art and therefore, by implication, of the poem about it, especially since Statius too characterises his poetry as produced boldly (*audacter, praef.* 1. 22).[71] But at the same time the compliment also underscores the transience of the monument and the earthly power it represents, for we are told that the equestrian statue of Julius Caesar was once, before the change of head, the statue of Alexander. Statius represents the change through humorous personification. The neck is amazed at the change, *mirata cervice*. Wonder is a frequent response to superb works of art. Here, however, wonder is directed towards the swiftness of the change; soon (*mox*) we are told, this change happened. Alexander's fame did not prevent the quick erasure and change of the rider's identity. The equestrian statue therefore has an admonitory as well as honorary function.

The poem however insists that Domitian's statue will stand apart from the temporality to which rulers and their monuments have fallen victim. A fresh exhortation thus begins which asserts the ability of this statue to survive the ravages of weather and of time, its permanence assured by the essential fact of its divinity (91–8):

---

[70] In his discussion of this poem Hardie (1983) 189–91 however notes the unusual comparisons between Julius Caesar and Domitian at lines 22–4 and here. These references conjure up again the reminder of civil war; both the Julio-Claudian and the Flavian dynasties were founded on civil conflict. In addition, as Hardie empasises, the novel reference to Julius Caesar reasserts the principle of dynastic succession.

[71] Cf. also *Silv. praef.* 3. 4 where Statius refers to his 'boldness of pen' (*audaciam stili*).

non hoc imbriferas hiemes opus aut Iovis ignem
tergeminum, Aeolii non agmina carceris horret
annorumve moras; stabit, dum terra polusque,
dum Romana dies. hoc et sub nocte silenti,
cum superis terrena placent, tua turba relicto
labetur caelo miscebitque oscula iuxta.
ibit in amplexus natus fraterque paterque
et soror; una locum cervix dabit omnibus astris.

This work does not dread the winter rains or the forked lightning of Jupiter, the battalions of winds from the Aeolian prison or the slow passing of years; it will stand, as long as earth and sky, as long as the Roman day will endure. In the silent night, when earthly matters please the gods, your family will leave heaven and glide down to exchange kisses with you. Your son, brother, father, and sister will come to your embrace; your neck alone will provide a place for all these stars.

In this evocative passage, Statius imagines the statue in majestic isolation at night. Situated in the hub of the Forum, the statue is now deserted by the crowd, but encircled instead by its own crowd (*turba*), the deified relatives. This is a striking image. It conveys the divine majesty of the statue, standing in proud isolation from ordinary mortals despite the public nature of the space. Here, in evoking the magnificent isolation of the statue, the text, like Johnson's later poem, evokes the essential isolation of the holder of power who exists far above his subjects, an isolation that Domitian himself seems to have encouraged in his aspirations to divinity.

   Although such isolation is an aspect of Domitian's imperial majesty, it is also presented as a matter of public anxiety. The poem was directly inspired, we are told, by the ceremony of dedication of the statue, and was given to the emperor on the following day (*praef.* 1. 18–19). But Statius does not evoke the crowds who come to admire the statue, himself presumably among them. Despite the public nature of the event at which the statue was dedicated, and despite its situation in a public space, we see the statue only in its confrontation with the dead: Mettius Curtius and the deified relatives, including Domitian's son. The Cancellaria reliefs promoted a new concept of dynastic authority based on the emperor's proximity to the gods and his removal from the ordinary human realm. But in *Silv.* 1. 1 the intermingling of family members with the statue, along with the prospective wish at the poem's end for grandchildren (106–7), creates a disjunction with the emperor's childlessness.

   Augustus and other of the Julio-Claudians had pursued a vigorous policy of dynastic marriages and adoptions in order to strengthen their

dynasty; not so Domitian.[72] The existence of an heir was an essential
founding stone of the Flavian dynasty.[73] But Domitian's only child, a
son, had died in infancy some twenty years earlier.[74] The importance
of that child nonetheless is reflected in his deification.[75] Carradice has
noted that coins minted early in Domitian's reign and showing the deified
infant son of Domitian attest to the importance of dynastic continuity
to the security of the new emperor.[76] Later in the reign an epigram of
Martial, ascribed to AD 90, expresses a pious and urgent hope for an
heir for Domitian, but no child was born.[77] The epigram may well have
been protreptic in intent, the product of anxiety over a dynastic situation
that, by the time Statius was writing the *Silvae*, remained troublingly
unresolved.

The physical isolation of the emperor's statue vividly evokes the
majesty but also the vulnerability of an emperor whose basis of authority
was constructed in part upon the myth of the divinity of a family that
had no living heirs. Domitian promoted that myth by deifying Vespasian,
Titus, his niece Julia, and his infant son and placing probably all of their
ashes in the special family shrine he constructed on the Quirinal, the
Templum Gentis Flaviae; this made him the son, brother, uncle and father of *divi*.[78] The evocative loneliness of the statue in the night square,
addressed only by the figure of Curtius aroused from the dead, is then
matched by the physical isolation of the emperor from the living. *Idyll* 17
of Theocritus celebrates the fertility of Ptolemy and his wife; the poem
concludes with an emphatic portrait of the happy, prosperous royal couple together. In Statius' poem, however, Domitian is shown consorting
only with the dead, including his son who should have been his heir.

Thus, the visitation of the deified relatives inserts the statue into the
troubling dynastic situation of the 90s as well as into the more general
context of earthly transience. In a striking image, the deified family of

[72] On Domitian's one known abortive attempt to adopt an heir see chapter 9 below, 317–18.
[73] Tac. *Hist.* 2. 77. 4–6 makes the claim that in the civil wars of AD 68–9 Vespasian is the preferred
claimant to the throne because he has two sons as heirs.
[74] Some time between AD 74 and 80. See Southern (1997) 28.
[75] Silius Italicus, *Pun.* 3. 629, concludes Jupiter's prophecy to Venus with the picture of Domitian's
deified son. Mart. 4. 3 imagines Domitian's deified son's playing with snow in the *aether*. Mattingly
(1926) 151 notes that coinage represents the infant Caesar seated on the globe like an infant
Jupiter and playing with the stars. See also Mannspergo (1974) 965–6.
[76] Carradice (1983) 20–1.
[77] Mart. 6. 3. Cf. ll. 2–3: *nascere, magne puer |cui pater aeternas post saecula tradat habenas* ('be born,
great child, so that in ages to come your father might hand you over the eternal reins'). For
the rebuttal of the theory that this epigram refers to a pregnancy of Domitia that ended with a
miscarriage see Southern (1997) 29; Jones (1992) 37.
[78] Sablayrolles (1994) 134.

Domitian encircle the neck of his statue as stars ('your son, brother, father, and sister will come to your embrace; your neck alone will make a place for all these stars', 97–8). But the neck is the most vulnerable point of the statue, the key in a sense to its stable identity.[79] The change of head from Alexander to Julius Caesar is marked by the neck, *mirata cervice*, 87. The *cervix*, the place in the statue at which its identity could be changed, becomes the symbolic juncture of both memorialisation and obliteration.

Furthermore, at the same time as the passage elaborates on the notion of the statue's permanence, the opening lines here strikingly allude to the ending of Ovid's *Metamorphoses*, which itself reformulates Horace's famous boast in *Carm.* 3. 30 that he has constructed a verbal monument more enduring than brass, that poetry therefore is more important than visual memorials. Ovid furthers the comparison between visual and verbal modes of representation by claiming that he has finished a work that will outlast the anger of Jupiter and fire: *iamque opus exegi, quod nec Iovis ira nec ignes | nec poterit ferrum nec edax abolere vetustas* ('and now I have fashioned a work, which neither the anger of Jupiter nor fires nor iron nor corrosive age will be able to abolish', *Met.* 15. 871–2). Ovid's *opus* of course is his masterpiece, the *Metamorphoses*. At the end of his great epic poem, Ovid claims immunity not only to time but also to the anger of his particular Jupiter, Augustus.[80] In a deferential gesture, Statius turns the referent of *opus* back to the statue, thus suggesting a new delicacy and anxiety in imperial address.[81] Yet the allusion nonetheless subtly provides a discreet reminder of the emperor's dependence on a poet, even more than on an artist, to preserve his memory, for statues have been shown to be vulnerable.

In the peroration of *Silv.* 1. 1, the statue is inserted into a competitive discourse concerning the uncertainty of fame (99–104):

> utere perpetuum populi magnique senatus
> munere. Apelleae cuperent te scribere cerae
> optassetque novo similem te ponere templo
> Atticus Elei senior Iovis, et tua mitis
> ora Tarans, tua sidereas imitantia flammas
> lumina contempto mallet Rhodos aspera Phoebo.

[79] As Stewart (1999) 165 points out, decapitation served the erasure of an emperor's identity best.

[80] Fowler (2000) 196 observes on this passage that the Empire-wide booktrade ensures Ovid's victory over Augustus' attempts at suppression.

[81] Habinek (1998) 110–14 claims that in *Carm.* 3. 30 Horace attempts to erase the distinction between paper and stone. Yet Statius uses this allusion subtly to assert the superiority of the written medium.

Enjoy forever the gift of the people and the mighty senate. The waxes of Apelles would have wished to depict you, and the old Athenian master [sc. Phidias] would have liked to place your statue in the new temple of Elean Jupiter, and mild Tarentum would have preferred the likeness of your face, rocky Rhodes, scorning its Phoebus, the starlike fire of your eyes.

As Fowler comments, 'the relationship between old and new can be agonistic, with the latest monuments ever attempting to efface those of earlier times'.[82] Here at the end of *Silv.* 1. 1 the emperor and his statue are placed in temporal succession. For the compliment to the emperor also encompasses acknowledgment of the fickleness of cities which honour their leaders but abandon them when they have outlasted their usefulness. Tarentum boasts a famous colossal statue of Zeus, Rhodes a colossal statue of Apollo, yet they would rather have the equestrian statue of Domitian. The concluding lines can be understood then as subversive of their own exhortation. Statues are vulnerable to changing tastes and events, for cities are selective in the memorialisation of their dead. Ironically too, Pliny the Elder tells us that the famous colossal statue at Rhodes had fallen due to an earthquake sixty-six years after its erection. No longer an object of divine veneration, it was still admired as it lay on the ground as a curiosity (*miraculo*) that the people could now freely touch and measure.[83]

And this brings me to the third area of ambiguity, the statue's relation to its public. The statue, we are told, is a gift of the Senate and the people (99). We are reminded here, as Rose puts it, that 'imperial statues formed part of a political system of exchange' whereby the donors hoped to acquire prestige and increase their political capital at the imperial court.[84] In such a system of reciprocity, a gift is never free but carries with it the obligation of benefaction in return. With this gift, then, the emperor is quietly placed under an obligation to earn his fame, his place in history, and his continuing memorialisation in bronze. The enormous power that the emperor wields and that is embodied in his statue is modified here in the recognition of the emperor's dependence on the goodwill of the people and the Senate, of his need to repay his debt to his subjects and prove worthy of the gift. The magnificence of the statue with its colossal scale testifies to the wealth and grandeur of a world empire and the prosperity of the imperial subjects who can afford such a gift. At the same time, however, the colossal size of the statue suggests the emperor's distance from the very people who have donated it, producing

---

[82] Fowler (2000) 203.   [83] Plin. *HN* 34. 18. 4.   [84] Rose (1997) 10.

a troubling gap between the realities of power and the fictions necessary to sustain it. The statue thus functions as a vehicle for the expression of concerns about the expansion of imperial power to a point remote from the people's concerns.

The ambiguity in the public perception of the statue is perhaps suggested by Curtius' initial reaction to it. Gazing at the colossal statue, he reacts with both fear and pleasure, *trepidans, laetus* (73).[85] Curtius' reaction suggests that the statue disturbs boundaries and transgresses well beyond human norms, for it has finally roused him from his chasm, penetrating the physical boundaries of the lake and the spiritual boundaries between the living and the dead.[86] The statue thus arouses admiration for its artistic virtuosity and majesty and concurrently anxiety over its colossal mass and scale – signs of exorbitant pretensions that could endanger the state.

The statue embodies the two major aspects of Domitian's self-fashioning as god and triumphant general. Yet these two aspects are not smoothly fused within the poem. The divine aloofness of the rider suggests the emperor's remoteness from his people and from the laws that govern human conduct, while the displacement of the emperor's body onto the material form of the statue carries a reminder of the mortal limitations of his power. Indeed, the vulnerability of his person is expressed through the physical vulnerability of such statues.

The poet's identity has been essentially occluded in this poem. The place from which he speaks is never made clear. The opening barrage of questions suggests initially that he recalls standing as one of the crowd in the Forum admiring the new statue. He thus conveys some idea of the public reception of the statue and the idea of the emperor it represents. But in his interpretive stance he also stands apart from the people and the Senate who donated the sculpture, for, as the maker of this innovative poem, he is a separate donor. Indeed, by inserting the equestrian monument at the poem's end into a competitive discourse concerning the famous statues of the past, he draws attention to the importance of his own poetic enterprise. Addressing Domitian in the end directly in person, not through his statue, Statius comments that Apelles, the court painter of Alexander, would have liked to represent (*scribere*, 100) Domitian. This is a compliment to the emperor that also glorifies the poet.[87] For with

---

[85] Ahl (1984a) 98 interprets *laetus* as dissimulation.

[86] Foucault (1978) makes the important argument that transgression can take place only when limits have been clearly established.

[87] On Apelles see Plin. *HN* 35. 36. 79–87.

scribere Statius puts his own special art of writing poetry in competition
with the plastic and painterly arts; indeed, in writing this poem he is taking an opportunity that was denied the most famous painter of the past.
Thus at the poem's end Statius makes a subtle allusion to the challenging
and innovative poetics with which he too can manipulate the imperial
image. As North observes, 'the monument without a text is weak and
defenceless, no more proof against time than an ordinary stone'.[88] In
writing on papyrus, not on metal, with the stylus rather than with wax,
it is implied, the poet finds a different, more enduring way to memorialise the emperor and remove him from the cycle of temporal succession
and the incursions of time. For the poem, unlike the statue, is endlessly
reproducible.

In *Silv.* 1. 1, with Domitian's equestrian statue, Statius takes a richly
evocative, ambiguous text and subjects it to his virtuoso and controlling
gaze. He uses the image of the statue in the first place to explore in an
oblique, yet persistent way, the strengths and limits of imperial power.
Like the Cancellaria reliefs, the poem legitimates Domitian's dynastic
ambitions through a sculpture that suggests his military strength and
his divine right to rule. Yet such legitimisation does not conceal anxiety.
Even as it celebrates the artistic expression of imperial majesty, the poem
raises through the statue concerns about the scope of imperial power
and the stability of the Flavian dynasty under Domitian.

The anxieties that run like faultlines through this poem do not then
hint at the sinister activities of a dissimulating monster but rather focus
upon durability and stability of rule. Here, we are indeed far from the
negative image of Domitian that we find in the later writings of Tacitus
and Pliny. Rather, through the strategy of extended ecphrasis, the poem
explores the ambiguity of the statue as a complex image of the body
of the emperor – majestic, remote, and also vulnerable. The statue is a
symbol of permanence and impermanence, of divine transcendence and
mortality. Prophetically perhaps, the poem about Domitian's equestrian
statue in the Roman Forum expresses anxiety about the very fate that
Domitian's monuments were to encounter.

The two poems about Charles I that head this chapter use an equestrian statue to problematise the relation of a discredited monarch to his
future public. Waller attempts to recuperate the reputation of the king
through the didactic message he imposes upon the statue; yet the immobility of the statue and its subjection to the passing of time conflict

---

[88] North (1985) 27.

today, perhaps, with his claims for royalty's continuing vitality. Johnson develops the issue of the statue's irrelevance to the present. His poem emphasises the magnificent isolation of the statue, a symbol of majesty divorced from any meaningful contemporary referent. His poem, like Statius', blurs the distinction between ruler and sign. Isolation here is a function of desertion, both by a viewing public and by courtiers. Both these poems deal with a monument that has endured but has been essentially emptied of its royal significance. The equestrian statue, once a proud symbol of monarchical control and grandeur, has become for the future a blank text on which the poets attempt to impose their own politicised meanings.

But in *Silv.* 1. 1, playing upon the confusion of text and image, Statius also uses the statue as a medium through which he can express his own poetic programme. Unlike Horace, who directly compares his poem to a monument at the start of *Carm.* 3. 30 and asserts the former's superiority (*exegi monumentum aere perennius*, 'I have constructed a monument more enduring than bronze'), Statius is more circumspect in his assertion of the poet's worth. At the same time, he goes further than Horace, who avoids description of the visual arts in his poetry.[89] In *Silv.* 1. 1, Statius celebrates both the monument *and* his poetic art. Although he does not openly claim, as does Horace at the start of *Carm.* 3. 30, that his own poem is superior to the work of art, in a sense he appropriates the statue by shaping it within the confines of his own innovative verse and by imprinting it with his own poetic values. As the statue tests the limits of imperial art with its colossal scale, so the poet here tests the limits of imperial panegyric with a bold new poetic form that ambitiously expands the concept and function of ecphrasis and rewrites epic for the contemporary age.

THE STATUE OF HERCULES

A different aesthetic and a different relationship between poet and statue are explored in *Silv.* 4. 6, a poem that in many ways forms a complement to *Silv.* 1. 1. Both poems describe a statue. The statue of *Silv.* 4. 6, however, is a miniature of the god Hercules, and is the prize piece in the private collection of Statius' friend Novius Vindex, a figure unknown outside the poems of Martial and Statius.[90] Humour and wit are prominent elements of this poem, along with sophisticated learning – hallmarks of a refined

[89] See Hardie (1993b), especially 121–3.   [90] Coleman (1988) 173.

Callimacheanism. The poem playfully explores antinomies between the economic and aesthetic value of the statue and its size as well as between the epic stature of the god, *fortissime divum* (96), and his diminutive form.

Coleman has suggested that Statius, as dinner guest, was possibly 'ordered' by Vindex to write this poem.[91] But the idea of such a commission is alien to the idealised representation of the relaxed and genial relations within Vindex's house. Moreover, this poem is more than a playful compliment to a patron. It intimately concerns Statius' own poetic art and the values it can promote. As we shall see, the statue of Hercules is closely identified with Statius' own work; he makes the statue in important ways his own. Indeed, since the statue was formerly owned by Alexander the Great, Hannibal, and Sulla, this poem raises the larger question of patronage within Flavian Rome, specifically the matter of who owns and controls its artistic culture.

The topic of this poem, the ecphrasis of a marvellous work of art, is a familiar theme of epigram; Vindex's statue is indeed the topic of two epigrams of Martial, *Epigram* 9. 43 and 44. But Statius takes the short poem to new lengths and cultivates the paradox of a long short poem on the subject of the miniature statue of a god famed for his strength and size. Hercules too was a god associated with imperial cult; Martial tells us of a temple to Hercules on the Appian Way whose cult statue bore the features of Domitian.[92] *Silv.* 4. 6 is the longest of the poems in Book 4, longer than the first three poems that celebrate the emperor. By thus developing the 'short' poem, Statius gives its private themes a political frame of reference.

Although at the opposite end of the scale in size from the equestrian statue, working in miniature presents a comparable artistic challenge to working upon a colossal form, either in sculpture or in literature.[93] Economic value provides a metaphorical link between the two forms of sculpture. The statue of Hercules that Statius describes is a very specialised item sculpted by Lysippus (37), court sculptor of Alexander and one of the finest artists of Greece: he alone, Pliny tells us, was allowed to sculpt Alexander's portrait.[94] Indeed, this statue was once the possession of Alexander. Lysippus, so we are told in *Silv.* 1. 1. 85–6, also sculpted the equestrian statue of Alexander that was eventually to bear the head of Julius Caesar in Rome. By drawing upon the political genealogy of the statue, *Silv.* 4. 6 therefore relates the physical contrast between grandeur

[91] Coleman (1988) 178.
[92] Mart. 9. 64, 65, and 101. See Darwall-Smith (1996) 133–6.
[93] Plin. *HN* 36. 4. 43.   [94] Plin. *HN* 7. 37. 125.

and smallness to a moral contrast between public and private virtue. As the public statue of the emperor expresses an elevated idea of governance, so the private statue of Hercules expresses an elevated idea of friendship. In *Silv.* 4. 6 Statius develops the rich semiotic possibilities of a visual sign whose dual status as god and precious work of art situates it within both the ethical and the artistic world. Indeed, through the miniature statue, *Silv.* 4. 6 provides an exemplary aesthetic for the private poem.

Whereas *Silv.* 1. 1 begins with a dramatic outburst of questions, the opening of *Silv.* 4. 6 suggests quiet informality with its first word *forte* ('by chance'). This opening, a witty reprise of the start of Horace's *Sat.* 1. 9 in which Horace has an unfortunate encounter with a bore, establishes an intimate relationship between the poet and his readers that is an extension of his relationship with his host.[95] Statius situates himself at the poem's opening in the Saepta Iulia, one of the busiest public spaces in Rome, like the Roman Forum in which the equestrian statue was situated.[96] Unlike Horace, however, Statius does not linger there. Rather, he makes a decisive departure from this public space when, we are told, a sudden dinner invitation from Vindex snatched (*rapuit*, 3) him away to a private world of refined discourse and appreciation of art.

The choice of opening site marks the rupture between Horace's times and Statius' own. As Connors points out, electoral assemblies used to take place in the Saepta Iulia; by Statius' day, however, it had become the site for upmarket shopping. The shift in topographical meaning of the Saepta Iulia from Republic to Empire replicates the shift in the statue's fortunes from public to private ownership.[97] The rupture does not trivialise the statue or its owner, however. Indeed, the poem uses the realm of connoisseurship to address the important questions of governance and patronage within imperial culture.

Although Vindex's home is not a humble dwelling, the meal is simple (5–11), a metaphorical positioning of the host and his guests as neo-Callimacheans as much as it suggests the denial of vulgar luxury.[98] Vindex spends his wealth not on indulging bodily needs but on cultivating aesthetic sensibilities. His good taste is demonstrated in his possession of an outstanding collection of art that demands in poetic representation a correspondingly refined and rich, complex aesthetics. At the same time, too, Vindex's connoisseurship provides an index to his character

[95] On the relationship with *Sat.* 1. 9 see Coleman (1988) 176.
[96] On the Saepta Iulia see Coleman (1988) 177.   [97] Connors (2000) 515.
[98] On the culinary basis of literary metaphors and the association between simple fare and Callimacheanism see Gowers (1993) 121–30.

that in turn, as we shall see, invites an investigation of the qualities that constitute true leadership and virtue.

Since Cicero brought public shame to Verres, the collecting of works of art has been seen, perhaps, as a particularly Roman and exploitative practice. The expansion and wealth of the Roman Empire made possible the collecting of works of art for private as well as for public use. Pliny reports with disgust the story of a statue by Lysippus that Tiberius removed from public display for his own private delight, until he was forced by an angry mob to restore it.[99] But collecting should not be dismissed as simply a matter of ostentatious expenditure and selfish pleasure. As Goldthwaite has argued, collecting can reflect an owner's artistic tastes and philosophical and scientific interests; it can have an educational and moral aspect; it can teach artistic discrimination as well as display it.[100] As *Silv.* 4. 6 suggests, collecting can be far more than a matter of establishing an owner's social credentials; it can help define the owner's character (for good or ill) – in this case, his intelligence, his good taste, and his moral and artistic sensibilities.

From the start of the poem the character of Vindex is established as open and generous, *benigni Vindicis* (3–4).[101] As Nisbet points out, this is an oxymoron that belies the meaning of the cognomen, punisher or avenger.[102] Vindex is not a private hoarder but someone who gladly shares his wealth and treasures. Civic-minded beneficence is now relocated within the private sphere. In *Sat.* 1. 9, Horace's limits of linguistic decorum are tested in his encounter with a bore. Statius' interaction with his host, on the other hand, is friendly and conducted on seemingly equal terms. In *Silv.* 4. 6 the location of the viewer is specified and his relationship to the statue and its owner is articulated within a private, domestic space that provides intimacy and mutual respect. Consequently, whereas *Silv.* 1. 1 emphasises the isolation of the statue and its remoteness from its viewers, *Silv.* 4. 6 emphasises its congeniality with its owner and visitors.

The statue is viewed as more than a precious collector's item, moreover. As in *Silv.* 1. 1, there is slippage between the statue and the god that it represents. The statue, for instance, is given an active role as 'the household genius and guardian of Vindex's chaste table' (*castae genius tutelaque mensae*, 32). The statue thus wears a genial expression, appropriate to the house's civilised festivities; it seems to encourage such social gatherings (55–6):

---

[99] Plin. *HN* 34. 19. 61–3; Barkan (1999) 70.   [100] Goldthwaite (1993) 247–9.
[101] On the meaning of *benignus* as both generous and kind see Coleman (1988) 177.
[102] Nisbet (1978) 8.

> sic mitis vultus, veluti de pectore gaudens,
> hortatur mensas.

Thus his gentle face, as if rejoicing from the heart, encourages the feasting.

We may remember that the equestrian rider of *Silv.* 1. 1 was likewise described as *mitis*, gentle (15), an epithet that Statius follows with the more ambiguous statement that Domitian's face is 'mixed in signs'. Here, however, he makes a point of interpreting *mitis* as proof of heartfelt joy. In personifying the statue, he claims that the god's innermost feelings are open. *Veluti* ('as if', 55) points to the role of the poet as the interpreter of the statue's silent text who, indeed, gives the statue life and feeling. Like *Silv.* 1. 1, *Silv.* 4. 6 explores the gap between the lifelessness of the material, bronze, and the life to which it gives such realistic form. But in keeping with the relaxed, private surroundings and with a genial, hospitable host, the task of interpretation is presented, at least, as not apparently intermingled with anxiety and ambiguity. Statius humorously consumes the wonders of his surroundings like the dinner guest he is; he cannot be satisfied (*nec satiavit*, 34), a concept that has literary as well as physical resonance.[103] Hyperbole here is directed to praise of the miniature rather than the colossal. As he plays upon the gap between the size of the statue and the importance of the god, Statius makes an important distinction between sight and perceptual response. The statue is small to look at but has a powerful emotional effect on the viewer.

As interpreter and animator of the statue, Statius subtly positions his own poetic art on a level with that of the sculptor. Indeed, when he dissociates the artistic origins of the miniature statue from the public art of the equestrian statue, the aesthetics of the *Silvae* and those of the statue of Hercules significantly intersect. The emperor's equestrian statue is associated with the art of the Cyclopes (*Silv.* 1. 1. 3–4). Not so the statue of Hercules (47–9):

> tale nec Idaeis quicquam Telchines in antris
> nec stolidus Brontes nec, qui polit arma deorum,
> Lemnius exigua potuisset ludere massa.

The Telchines in their Idaean caves and dull-witted Brontes could not have played with such a tiny mass, nor could the Lemnian, who polishes the gods' armour.

---

[103] See Gowers (1993) 126–35 who discusses 'satisfaction' in Horace's *Satires* as a sign of the observation of physical, moral and literary limits, and of Callimachean affiliation. Statius plays with Callimachean notions in this poem as he engages in the interplay with familiar literary categories of big and small, high and low.

The rejection of Brontes, one of the possible sculptors of the equestrian statue, suggests a different set of criteria at work here not only for
private sculpture, but also for poetry. The Telchines were skilled metal-
workers.[104] Yet they were better known in literature for their programmatic appearance in the prologue to Callimachus' *Aetia* (7–10), where they
are associated with the lengthy poem that is antithetical to Callimachus'
refined art. Significantly, they appear again in the *Thebaid*, as craftsmen
of Argia's ill-omened necklace (*Theb.* 2. 269–96).[105] By rejecting the art
of the Telchines, the statue of Hercules is brought strikingly within the
orbit of the Callimachean literary aesthetic.

Indeed, its refined sculptural art complements that of the present
poem, for both the poem about the tiny statue and the statue itself elevate
an art that is sophisticated, finely nuanced, learned, and exceptional.
Vulcan's art, which made the famous shields of Achilles and Aeneas
and generated two famous epic ecphraseis, is here despised. Vulcan is
mockingly reduced in role to polisher of the gods' arms; enormous size is
here given negative valuation, for Vulcan and his helpers could not 'play'
(*ludere*, 49) with such a tiny mass (*exigua*) of metal, the implication being
that they were too clumsy to do so. Again the sculptural and the literary-
critical fields intersect. *Ludere* is the term Statius uses to introduce and
characterise his own *Silvae* (*praeluserit, praef.* 1. 9). The quality signified
by *exiguus* is a term frequently applied to the refined short poem.[106]
Statius here adopts a Callimachean arrogance to disparage the epic
workers in metal; the small statue, the short poem, require a sophisticated
skill of which Vulcan or the Cyclopes, unflatteringly called *stolidus*, dull-
witted, are incapable. But more than sophisticated skill is at stake in
this reformulation of Callimachean categories. In Statius' own epic, the
Thebaid, the Telchines are responsible for making a small-scale work of
art – not a shield, but a necklace. On the other hand, this work of art
contributes significantly to the evil of the Theban conflict. The miniature
statue of Hercules, however, furthers social bonds among friends. The
art of the statue brings pleasure and gathers friends together in mutual
appreciation.

Here Statius, with a backward glance at the equestrian statue and his
own poetry, indicates the cultural and indeed moral divide between the
spheres of public and private art. And this division is pursued with further
reference to another key moment in Callimachus' poetry, the meeting of
the humble peasant Molorchus with Hercules (50–4):

---

[104] Coleman (1988) 185.   [105] McNelis (2000) chapter 2.
[106] On *exiguus* as a literary-critical term see *TLL* V. 1475 12–32.

> nec torva effigies epulisque aliena remissis
> sed qualem parci domus admirata Molorchi
> aut Aleae lucis vidit Tegeaea sacerdos,
> qualis et Oetaeis emissus in astra favillis
> nectar adhuc torva laetus Iunone bibebat

His appearance is neither fierce nor unsuited to informal banquets; rather he looks as he did when the household of frugal Molorchus gazed wonderingly at him or when the Tegeaean priestess of the Alean grove saw him or when, released from the ashes of the Oetaean pyre to the stars, he drank nectar, joyful, though Juno was still bitterly opposed.

Molorchus is a programmatic figure for the Callimachean aesthetic, a sign of the virtuous, humble host who nonetheless 'appropriates' the heroic. He figures in the first narrative of *Aetia* 3 where he humbly entertains Hercules on the eve of the slaying of the Nemean lion.[107] He then appears in *Georgics* 3 as a sign of the poetry that Virgil plans to reject in his move towards epic. In Statius' *Silvae*, Molorchus appears here and in *Silv.* 3. 1, another poem about Hercules.[108] In *Silv.* 4. 6 Molorchus, as virtuous host, is an appropriate figure to invoke in a poem about a supremely private occasion, the dinner party with friends.[109] 'Molorchus' furthermore acts as a textual cue that conflates the art of the statue – a work of art that is designed to adorn a table – and the art of the symposiastic poem.[110] Both poem and statue share a mutual value. Indeed, the statue is also eroticised through reference to the Tegeaean priestess, Auge, mother of Telephus by Hercules.[111] The god here is represented as relaxed, genial, and beyond political cares; Juno's hostility cannot affect his state of transcendent happiness in heaven's court. The statue therefore participates in a significant shift of categories: between public and private, heroic and erotic, transitory and enduring.

---

[107] See Parsons (1977).

[108] Verg. *G.* 3. 19 provides the first post-Callimachean reference to Molorchus, Statius, who mentions Molorchus three times, the first post-Virgilian references (*Silv.* 3. 1. 29, 4. 6. 51; *Theb.* 4. 159–64); Thomas (1983) 94–5, 103–5, and Newlands (1991) 445–6.

[109] In *Silv.* 3. 1, Hercules is specifically dissociated from 'the fields of Molorchus' (29). Hercules here is humorously presented in full divine strength and size as a genial but active superhero, a civiliser who makes the building of the temple a thirteenth labour. Here the magnificent temple and the elevated language in which it is described suggest a new poetics of grandeur that elevates the short, private poem through the witty exploitation of the gap between epic motifs and occasion. As we shall see in chapters 4 and 5, in his villa poems Statius particularly mediates between the public and the private spheres. The poetics of *Silv.* 3. 1 are geared to an occasion that mediates between the public and the private – the dedication of a temple and the celebratory games.

[110] On the probable function of the statue as a table ornament – Statius refers to the poem in the preface as *Herculem Epitrapezion* (*praef.* 4. 14) – see Coleman (1988) 174.

[111] See Coleman (1988) 186 on 52.

The dissociation of the sculpture from the public, political art embodied within the equestrian statue is thematised in the political genealogy with which it is endowed. For the statue, however, did once have a public context, and its expression was different from the genial one it displays, according to Statius, in the home of Vindex. The statue was formerly the property of Alexander, Hannibal, and Sulla, famous rulers who are placed in temporal succession as a tacit *memento mori* to holders of worldly power. As Alexander lay dying, the statue altered its expression and terrified the famous man (71–4), an implicit suggestion that for all his greatness, Alexander was not prepared for intimations of his own mortality. The statue, we are told, hated its next owner, Hannibal, who, despite the vast extent of his power, failed to placate the tiny statue of the god with offerings (75–84). We are not told what the statue thought of its third owner, Sulla (85–8), but a concluding reference to *saevi ... vox horrida Sullae* ('the grating voice of cruel Sulla', 107) suggests that the moral and literary sensibilities of the god would have been offended by this owner. As in *Silv.* 1. 1, the statue is inserted into a temporal context that, in this instance, clearly demonstrates the succession and transience of rulers. The ascription of feelings to the lifeless statue opens the text up to political and moral commentary.

Indeed, the statue, lacking power to alter its circumstances when in the possession of those who pursued *regius honos* ('regal glory', 91), articulates the relationships of domination and subordination on which royal or imperial power is founded. The inertness of its material metaphorically represents the lack of personal freedom or autonomy of the servant of the court, the person whose existence depends entirely on the will of others. At the same time, the statue's situation as the possession of great men creates a disjunction between their large, yet transient ambitions and the statue's tiny but perfect and enduring art. Removed now from an unstable political context, the statue exists in harmony with its present owner, the cultured and congenial Vindex, and enjoys *laeta quies* ('joyful quiet', 96).

The rupture in genealogical succession represents a break also with the valued beliefs and *mores* of the past, a past in particular dedicated to the pursuit of political power. The mention of Sulla complicates any backward look at the Republican past; the history of autocracy is seen to extend far back beyond the Augustan 'revolution'. The text endorses new values that accord with imperial realities. Thus Vindex's ownership of a statue that was once the possession of rulers draws attention to the new significance of his own private way of life. Indeed, in the home of

Vindex, Hercules can now be interpreted in accordance with the values of his new environment – not as a political figure but as a genial, virtuous god released from the labours and duties imposed on him by harsh deities and rulers. The statue's value is emphasised by its transference from the transitory, troubled public sphere to the safe, cultured environment of Vindex's home. Traditionally, Romans had felt that the ownership of precious works of art was morally acceptable only if they were publicly displayed; Horace's *Carm.* 2. 15 provides a ringing endorsement of public magnificence as opposed to private and self-indulgent pleasure. Statius however seems to suggest that the ownership and appreciation of proper works of art now more safely belongs to the private sphere. Vindex's home therefore provides a counterworld to the public realm where works of art owned for political ends have uncertain futures. This statue does not lose or change its head!

The statue's political genealogy problematises the issue of patronage. As the former possession of rulers, the statue marks the division between the political and the private world. That Vindex now owns a statue which was once the property of a divine king, a general, and a Roman dictator – a statue of a god who, moreover, has links with imperial cult – provocatively questions the notion of cultural authority and leadership within Flavian Rome. Statius opens Book 4 in a striking and unusual way, with three poems addressed to Domitian, two of which praise his artistic and engineering achievements (4. 2 and 4. 3). But now, with *Silv.* 4. 6 he writes an entirely different type of poetry that exalts the private world. Might not the statue of Hercules, once in the thrall of political leaders but now secure and cherished in the home of Vindex, provide a model for the workings of patronage that is applicable to Statius also? If so, the poem also provides a critique of the public world that cannot, it seems, properly protect or comprehend its precious works of art. For unlike Augustus, whose artistic patrons such as Maecenas and Messalla linked poets to the imperial court, Domitian in Statius' poetry is constructed as separate from the world of literary patronage that is revealed to us in the *Silvae*. Statius' patrons either live in the country well apart from Rome or, as in *Silv.* 4. 6, they have their own private enclave within the capital city.

Yet despite the apparent cultural divide between the public and private spheres, the terms public and private are not mutually exclusive. What is at stake in the poem celebrating this exquisite work of art is the fame of the poet and of the patron, whether emperor or private collector. Vindex seems to be a worthy, indeed better successor in possession of the statue than political leaders. His new ownership destabilises the workings of a hereditary system according to which shared values (and possessions) enjoy a stable transmission from past to present in a guarantee for the future. With the high priority it gives to moral and aesthetic values, the poem thus raises the question of where the true centre of cultural authority within Flavian Rome is located – in the ruler's palace or the private mansion.

This question is also treated as a moral as well as a social and political issue. Towards the poem's end, then, Statius draws a clear ethical contrast between the political world of the court and the private world of the poet and connoisseur (89–93):

> nunc quoque, si mores humanaque pectora curae
> nosse deis, non aula quidem, Tirynthie, nec te
> regius ambit honos, sed casta ignaraque culpae
> mens domini, cui prisca fides coeptaeque perenne
> foedus amicitiae.

Now too, if gods care to know the minds and hearts of humans, neither the court nor the desire for regal glory attracts you, Tiryuthian, but rather the mind of your master that is chaste and ignorant of guilt, committed to an ancient sense of loyalty and to a bond of friendship that once begun will endure.

The text does not elaborate directly on the meaning of *aula*, 'court', and *regius honos*, 'regal glory', but explains them through contrast with the values contained in Vindex's world.[112] As Wallace-Hadrill points out, the word *aula* is almost unknown in Republican literature 'both as an institution and as a word'. Derived from $\alpha\dot{\upsilon}\lambda\dot{\eta}$, the standard Greek term for Hellenistic courts, it is used in Roman imperial literature to refer 'to the physical location of imperial power and to the type of power, the personnel, and the perilous way of life that were associated with it'.[113] In *Silv.* 4. 6, it is suggested, the hearts and minds of human beings (*mores humanaque pectora*) cannot be properly known in a court society, for, as 'the font of power and favour', the court was also 'the scene of anxieties and humiliations' and hence of competition and mistrust.[114] It was, moreover, difficult to read the imperial mind. Hence the dangers, the uncertainty, and the ambiguity, as we have seen in *Silv.* 1. 1, of the public image.

The openness of the miniature statue's expression accords, however, with its present domestic environment, where there is no need for

---

[112] Martial is more blunt, referring to *variae tumidis terroribus aulae* ('the courts unpredictable with turbulent, arrogant terrors', 9. 43. 11).

[113] Wallace-Hadrill (1970) 283.   [114] Wallace-Hadrill (1970) 296.

occlusion. Purity and innocence of mind, loyalty, and enduring friendship are enshrined within the private sphere. The statue of Hercules articulates an alternative set of values to those embodied in a public work of art. Its value is ethical as well as economic and aesthetic; it endorses friendship and the companion attributes of hospitality and genial, sophisticated discourse. Friendship then, in contradistinction to the life of the court, is presented as the most enduring of values. It stands apart from the life of ambition with its rivalries, its uncertain feelings and motivations.

Indeed in this poem, as Konstan has observed, friendship is strikingly honoured in famous Catullan terms as *perenne| foedus amicitiae* ('a bond of friendship that will endure', 92–3), a direct allusion to Catullus' poem 109 where the poet presents an exalted definition of his relationship with Lesbia as *perenne foedus amicitiae* (6). Statius appropriates this term for a non-sexual relationship, his friendship with Vindex, and he stabilises it within an address to the god himself. The Catullan allusion demonstrates the extraordinary value that is being put on friendship here – understood as a bond founded on shared interests and tastes and mutual affection.[115] As Konstan observes, in this passage 'loyalty to friends is not inflected according to rank'.[116]

Yet friendship, it seems to be suggested here, does not entirely abolish the social hierarchy that matters in the world of public affairs. For at the same time, the Catullan allusion very subtly problematises the actual power relations between poet and patron. Statius may be hinting that his situation is that of the outsider to the world of the wealthy Vindex. Yet the inequality between poet and patron could work both ways. Habinek has argued that friends of lower social status often took on an advisory or admonitory role towards their more wealthy, influential patrons.[117] Even as he praises Vindex's excellent taste and character, Statius presents him with a hortatory model of the ideal patron. As Griffin and Myers remind us, moreover, a poet is no ordinary friend, for he can offer his benefactor immortal glory.[118] Literary and social power, therefore, may be oddly unequal. The relationship between the patron and poet is a delicate one that rests on the former's anxieties about his reputation and the latter's anxieties about his social acceptance and the reception and circulation of his poetry. By impersonating Catullus' voice here, Statius provides a

---

[115] See Konstan (1997) 148 on the development in the Empire of a concept of friendship based on a private bond of shared interests and values rather than on public services rendered to one another.
[116] Konstan (1997) 145.   [117] Habinek (1990).   [118] Griffin (1984) 217, n. 43; Myers (1996) 17.

discreet reminder of the memorialising power of the poet, a reminder
that is surely addressed not to Vindex alone but perhaps the emperor
himself who, after all, claims the first three poems of this book.

Towards the poem's end, then, Statius shifts attention from the statue
to poetry, for *Silv.* 4. 6 is as much about Statius' poetics as it is about sculptural art. In this poem, Statius uses the private work of art to present his
readers with a concept of the social function of poetry as therapeutic. A
poem such as he has written, celebrating a friend's precious work of art,
does not provoke anxiety but cements bonds between friends. Poetry of
this type elevates virtues to which the court is hostile. The allusion to
Catullus situates the poem within a poetic as well as a political genealogy in which friendship is the concomitant of the short but exquisitely
rendered poem. The new poetic traditions developed by Callimachus,
Catullus and Horace therefore legitimate Statius' own innovative poetic enterprise, which, by taking the short poem and its themes to a new
level of structural and thematic importance, attempts to grapple with the
changed conditions for poetry and patronage in the late first century AD.

The harmonious relationship between verbal and sculptural art in this
poem culminates in the conclusion where, as in *Silv.* 1. 1, Statius subtly
suggests the importance of the poet to the enduring fame of the statue.
Statius envisages the song that Vindex will sing about the statue and its
deeds, *memorabit* (99), even as he himself is in the process of commemorating the statue in verse – a dexterous sleight of hand that compliments
the patron while acknowledging the poet's importance and primacy.

Indeed, the poem concludes with a striking conflation of the political
and the poetic (106–9):

> nec te regnator Macetum nec barbarus umquam
> Hannibal aut saevi posset vox horrida Sullae
> his celebrare modis. certe tu, muneris auctor,
> non aliis malles oculis, Lysippe, probari.

The ruler of the Macedonians, barbarous Hannibal, or the grating voice of
cruel Sulla could never have celebrated you in verses such as these. Certainly
you, Lysippus, as the creator of this work, would prefer to be approved by no
other eyes.

Alexander, Hannibal, and Sulla, the statue's former owners, reappear
here at the poem's end as figures incapable of doing justice to the refined
work of art. The divine king, the famous general, and the Roman dictator
offer striking examples of political power, and yet they are here shown
to lack cultural authority. The most famous rulers of the ancient world

were not worthy of owning this statue for they were not capable of its proper commemoration. It rightly belongs only to a private citizen whose authority is located in his aesthetic and moral wisdom. This then is a final, striking demonstration of the way in which the poetic genealogy of this poem about the pleasure of friendship and the feast is intertwined with a political genealogy that moves the poem well beyond the occasion of the dinner party to social and moral commentary. With *his modis* ('in verses such as these', 108), Statius refers to the poem that he imagines that Vindex will compose about the statue, but again he is drawing attention to his own poetic achievement as alone capable of celebrating properly a ruler's work of art – whether rulership itself is to be understood in a political or more strictly ethical sense.

The poem ultimately stands apart from the statue in its final assertion of the poet's importance. Indeed, there emerges in these final lines of the poem an element of competition between the poet and the sculptor as well as the patron. In *Silv.* 1. 1, the sculptor of the equestrian statue remains a matter of mystification; here, in accordance with the open, disingenuous appearance of Hercules, the sculptor is named as the famous Lysippus, Alexander's court sculptor (37, 109). Statius' poem therefore represents an implied contest between the poet and one of the finest artists of Greece. By addressing Lysippus in the poem's last line he honours the artist, but he also appropriates him by memorialising him within the confines of his own new type of poem. Indeed, the visual artist seeking perpetual fame, as well as the ruler or collector, is dependent on the poet's text.

As Goldthwaite has argued, people collect art for a variety of reasons, among them respect for the artist, who in this case is Lysippus.[119] Vindex, then, has used his wealth wisely. His protection of the statue and respect for its sculptor provides, furthermore, a model for his relationship with the literary artist.

The mention of Alexander's sculptor Lysippus creates a final allusion to the question of patronage and the role of the court. In Horace's *Epistle to Augustus*, he tells us that Alexander had wonderful taste in the visual arts but was a dullard in his judgment of poetry (*Epist.* 2. 1. 232–4). His fame, then, was not well served by his poets. As a patron, indeed, he was inadequate. As Oliensis has shown, Augustus serves in Horace's poem instead as a model for the truly discerning political patron who knows how to reward his poets rightfully.[120] But for Augustus as the ideal patron

---

[119] Goldthwaite (1993) 244.   [120] Oliensis (1998) 194–5.

Statius provocatively substitutes Vindex, his private host. Statius can offer Vindex far better poetry than that received by Alexander, according to Horace, from the worthless Choerilus. He thus compliments Vindex as a patron at the same time as he reminds his readers of the superior role of the poet not just in commemorating the patron's deeds and virtues but in guiding and creating his taste. The substitution of Vindex here for political leader or emperor in the patronage stakes provocatively marks the separation of discriminating, effective patronage from the realm of politics and the imperial court.

A statue made by an artist who worked in the service of a great ruler is here, through Statius' poem, given a new set of meanings in a celebration of private life that challenges imperial authority. In his books on art in the ancient world (34–6), Pliny the Elder inveighed against private collectors; art, in his opinion, should be put on public display for everyone's delight.[121] Yet Pliny also laments that there are so many public works on display in Rome that they are easily erased from the memory of a public intent on business affairs.[122] As Barkan notes, the term Pliny uses to describes erasure from memory is *obliteratio*, a term whose physical meaning of erasure – literally the loss of letters that identify the work of art – is transferred to a metaphorical meaning of loss of fame.[123] Pliny thus openly acknowledges that the public work of art is particularly vulnerable to effacement and decay. Indeed, he claims that true appreciation of art can be cultivated only in conditions of silence and leisure – such as that provided by the house of Statius' friend.

Significantly, although the statue of Hercules is inserted into a temporal context through its possession by various political leaders, it is in this instance only the rulers that change, not the statue, which is neither defaced nor ravaged by time or human action. Kept safe within Vindex's house, it is unaffected by the political upheaval, social tumult, and forces of nature to which the publicly situated statue is vulnerable. The ethical and artistic values that the miniature statue of Hercules embodies are thus, so the poem implies, enduring ones that reflect upon the immortality of the poem itself. For enduring fame, it seems, can be found in a private home removed from the centre of political power. At the same time, however, through his meticulous description of the statue of Hercules, Statius brings Vindex's wonderful statue more safely, perhaps, into the public domain where it subtly yet eloquently can express the

---

[121] For references and discussion see Gordon (1979) 23–4.
[122] Plin. *HN* 36. 4. 27.   [123] Barkan (1999) 1–2.

importance of artistic and literary patronage to the cultural and moral vitality of the state.

The equestrian statue of Domitian and the miniature statue of Hercules are artistic forms that express different cultural attitudes. The one celebrates public power and magnificence, the other private friendship and refinement. The statue, a controversial object, provides an exaggerated figure of the two oppositional trends in Statius' *Silvae*, that between public and private poetry, and that between political aspirations and private friendship. Yet both poems are linked, in that ecphrasis of a statue, whether an impressive colossus or a precious miniature, proves a particularly dynamic, evocative way in which Statius can comment upon the social conditions of art and patronage within Flavian Rome while exploring the limits and possibilities of his experimental, poetic voice in the *Silvae*.

CHAPTER 3

Engendering the house: Silvae *1. 2 and 3. 4*

> Her snowy neck like to a marble tower,
> And all her body like a palace fair,
> Ascending up, with many a stately stair,
> To honor's seat and chastity's sweet bower.
>
> Edmund Spenser, Epithalamion

Silv. 1. 1 and 4. 6 stand at opposite ends of the poetic and political spectrum in Statius' poetry book. Statius' poetry of praise, however, contains a variety of negotiatory positions. This chapter will consider two poems that once again structurally and thematically complement one another, *Silv.* 1. 2 and *Silv.* 3. 4. They are admittedly addressed to people of very different social status – in *Silv.* 1. 2 the aristocratic Stella and his new wife Violentilla, in *Silv.* 3. 4 Domitian's court eunuch Earinus. Yet both poems explore social and sexual identity through the domestic space of a grand house and palace respectively. Gender and architecture are here integral to both the reinforcement and the questioning of traditional values in the Flavian age. Indeed, the literary construction of a woman and a eunuch through their houses implicitly raises the question of what constitutes 'Romanness' at the end of the first century AD.

Silv. 1. 2 celebrates the marriage of a couple who were fairly prominent figures within Roman society, Arruntius Stella and his wife Violentilla. Stella is the subject of several poems by Martial.[1] *Silv.* 1. 2 tells us that at the time of his marriage Stella was one of the *quindecimviri* (176–7), hoping, it seems, for further speedy advancement (174–81).[2] Both Stella and Violentilla boasted distinguished lineage (70–2, 107–9), but they are praised too for the quality of their minds (121–2, 172–3). Statius dedicates his first book of *Silvae* to Stella, representing him in the preface as a distinguished man of letters, *iuvenis optime et in studiis nostris eminentissime*

---

[1] Mart. 1. 7; 1. 44; 4. 6; 5. 11; 5. 59; 6. 47; 7. 36; 8. 78; 9. 89; 11. 52; 12. 3.
[2] On Stella see White (1975) 267–72; Hardie (1983) 68; *PIR* (1933) 227–8; Tanner (1986) 3044.

('most excellent young man, and highly distinguished in our field of literature', *praef.* 1. 1–2). Although Stella had a political career, Statius represents him primarily as a poet. Statius addresses him as *Latios inter placidissime vates* ('most peaceful among poets of Latium', 201). Stella has the same poetic tastes as Statius, *tecum similes iunctaeque Camenae* ('our Muses are alike and linked', 257); he is a fellow poet with whom Statius has drunk from the same poetic stream (258–9).[3] Statius represents himself as linked to Violentilla also, for she, like Statius, was from the Bay of Naples (260–5); 'my Parthenope', he says, raised her (260–1). Through both literature and birth Statius participates in the same cultural values as the newly wed couple.

In the preface to Book 1 (17–23), Statius draws attention to the fact that *Silv.* 1. 2 is longer by far than his opening poem to Domitian and indeed is the longest poem in the collection: one hundred hexameters for the equestrian statue, three hundred for the epithalamium. Although Statius claims that he begins his poetry book with 'Jupiter' (*praef.* 1. 17), the extraordinary size of his Jupiter's equestrian statue is not matched by extraordinary length of description – an imbalance between theme and structure found, as we have seen, in Callimachus' opening *Hymn to Zeus*.[4] As Zetzel has noted, works such as the *Hymn to Zeus* and the *Victoria Berenices* provided a precedent for the new idea in Hellenistic poetry that 'a great subject need not be dealt with in a grand style'.[5]

Here in *Silv.* 1. 2, on the other hand, Statius gives a topic that appeals to Callimachean sensibilities, the epithalamium, particular length, thereby attesting to the importance of the poem that stands second in the collection. Once again Statius engages creatively with notions of poetic decorum, elevating the personal occasion of a wedding through epicising play. Vessey regards *Silv.* 1. 2 as trivial in subject and in execution, the sad rhetorical exercise of a poet deprived of freedom of speech, the victim of both despotism and rhetoric.[6] But as with *Silv.* 1. 1, there had been nothing like *Silv.* 1. 2 before in Roman poetry. This second poem, like the first, is strikingly innovative, for it is a long, elaborate epithalamium that celebrates the marriage of a widow, not a virginal bride, that is

---

[3] On Stella as poet see *Silv.* 1. 2. 7–10, 94–102, 172–3, 195–9 and 247–55.

[4] See chapter 2 above, 54.

[5] Zetzel (1983) 100. He notes that one of the major breakthroughs of Hellenistic poets was their freedom from conventional strictures of genre and metre.

[6] Vessey (1972). But cf. Newmyer (1979) 29–31, 83–7, who acknowledges the complex originality of *Silv.* 1. 2 in its adroit play with structure and genre. Pavlovskis (1965) points to the innovative qualities of *Silv.* 1. 2 and to its important, foundational influence upon the later Latin epithalamium. See also in this regard Roberts (1989a).

'sung' _after_ the wedding, and that is interwoven with a central aetiological narrative in the manner of Catullus' _Carmen_ 64.[7] Furthermore, although the poem is written in hexameters, the personified Elegy is programmatically introduced at the poem's start as the 'tenth Muse' (7–10), thereby suggesting the generically innovative 'wedding' of epithalamium with elegy and endorsing the treatment of the marriage as the culmination of an elegiac love affair.

Silv. I. 2, I suggest, functions as a second programmatic introduction to the collection, honouring in second place to the emperor the friend to whom the first book of Statius' new poetry is dedicated. Stella is both politician and poet, celebrated here on an occasion that is both very public and very intimate, his marriage. _Silv._ I. 2 forms a bridge between _Silv._ I. I and _Silv._ I. 3, moving the reader from the public spaces of the emperor in _Silv._ I. I to the more domestic spaces of the senator and literary friend and his wife; it also forms a bridge with _Silv._ I. 3 where the patron and his home are physically and politically removed from Rome. As we shall see, moreover, _Silv._ I. 2 also corresponds, by position and theme, to the penultimate poem of the first collection, _Silv._ 3. 4, where marriage is given new, fantastical expression in the heart of Domitian's Palatine court.

Statius' treatment of Stella and his new wife suggests the subtle way in which patronage could work in Roman society. Garnsey and Saller define patronage as 'a reciprocal exchange relationship between men of unequal status and resources'.[8] But as Konstan points out, friendship and shared poetic tastes could, at least to a considerable extent, erase social and economic differences and form the basis of a genuine affection.[9] In _Silv._ I. 2 the subordination of Stella's role as politician to his role as poet manoeuvres Statius on to equal ground with his patron, for Statius' poetic resources are not inferior. Praise of a patron, then, can subtly become the means by which Statius can draw attention to his own poetic virtuosity. But Statius' relationship to Stella is rather unusual, for Stella himself seems to have been a poet of some distinction. Martial tells us that Stella was particularly famous for love poetry written in imitation of Catullus' short love poems to Lesbia.[10] Statius' reshaping of the epithalamic tradition in _Silv._ I. 2 thus delicately suggests the element of

---

[7] In his discussion of _Silv._ I. 2 Vessey (1972) draws attention to the importance of Catullus 64 and cites the allusions to it in _Silv._ I. 2 (178, n. 2). On the innovative nature of _Silv._ I. 2 see Roberts (1989a) 321–8. Roberts questions Vessey's notion that myth here provides a universal cultural language for Statius' audience. Rather, Roberts argues, Statius uses myth in this poem to play with traditional morality, as in the poem's treatment of chastity/virginity (327–8).

[8] Garnsey and Saller (1987) 152–3.   [9] Konstan (1997) 143–6.   [10] Mart. I. 7; 4. 6; 7. 14.

cultured competition between himself and Stella. Structurally modelled
upon Catullus' ambitious and complex *Carmen* 64, Statius' poem is both
a compliment to Stella and an affectionate act of poetic one-upmanship.
In *Silv.* 1. 2 poetry and friendship form the basis of an encomiastic tour
de force that celebrates both Stella's good taste and Statius' own considerable poetic powers.

In *Silv.* 1. 2 Statius brings together the public and the private sphere,
and he does so most strikingly here, I shall argue, through an architectural
figure of immense importance in Statius' *Silvae*, the house. The Roman
house was generally perceived as a sacred symbol of its owner's status and
virtus.[11] The word for house, *domus*, meant not only a physical dwelling
place but also the people within it, wives, children, slaves, and ancestors –
the household.[12] The *domus* was the site where the busts of the family's
ancestors were displayed and honoured, and thus was closely associated
with family renown and lineage. Indeed, the architectural form of the
house was inseparable from its social function.[13] The house mediated
between public and private space. It served both as a private shrine to
family tradition and vitality, and as a public shrine to its clients, a visible
sign of the owner's social standing.

In the period in which Statius wrote, however, social status and economic status were no longer necessarily equivalent. There was an influx
of new families into the senatorial order; families with a distinguished
lineage, moreover, could be poor.[14] Thus, as Garnsey and Saller have
argued, in a society offering a degree of social mobility, the private house
became the focal point for the transmission of wealth and status.[15] The
need to find new standards for social status other than ancestry devolved
then upon the *domus*, the house, where wealth could be displayed to the
crowds flocking to the morning *salutatio*.

The house was a highly visible sign of its owner's worth. Economic and
social status, aesthetic tastes or even moral values could all be expressed

---

[11] Bodel (1997) has pointed out that the Roman house in general was viewed as an extension of
its owner's character, in particular as a *documentum virtutis*, proof of virtue. See also Saller (1994)
88–95.

[12] Saller (1984) 343.

[13] See for instance Wiseman (1982b); Wallace-Hadrill (1988) and (1994); Saller (1994) 71–101. Bek
(1976) is seminal. Discussing Vitruvius, for instance, she argues that Vitruvius saw a building
'not in its appearance as an artistic particularity, but in the general aspect of its functionality
dependent on the human, social and natural factors' (159).

[14] A point made by Friedman (1989) 12 in her excellent study of the Elizabethan country house.
On changing conditions in the social hierarchy of the early Empire see Garnsey and Saller
(1987) 118–25.

[15] Garnsey and Saller (1987) 122.

through the style and location of the house. Indeed, since the emperor held a monopoly over public building, private houses became all the more important as centres for aristocratic patronage. Since much of an aristocrat's business took place in the house, where he needed to host many clients, it had to be impressive. Writing in the time of Augustus, Vitruvius insisted that, according to social and architectural decorum, the important man of affairs should own a large, spacious house.[16] Although the emperor was physically dominant within Rome through his construction of monuments, new imperial fora, and, in Domitian's case, the Palatine palace, he was not omnipotent; senatorial houses in particular remained an urban phenomenon of great importance.[17] Thus in the imperial city 'the substitutes for the public places and public buildings, the *opera et loca publica*, were the senatorial mansions and parks'.[18] The architectural style of a house formed an important indicator not only of the owner's wealth but also of his or her social rank and standing within the community.

As we shall see in the next three chapters, Statius' descriptions of houses interpret the social and indeed religious and moral value that the Romans put on their houses – that revered place where the honour of the family was preserved and displayed. Statius uses the house not only to document social change, but also to explore its implications for the poet and for the literary community for which he writes. For houses occupy a place that can be both oppositional and also contiguous to that of the court. Through houses, which employ their own architectural language of power, Statius articulates the ambiguous relationship of the aristocracy to the emperor, who limited the political authority of eminent citizens in constant awareness of their threat to his supremacy. Through houses too, Statius articulates his ambiguous situation as imperial poet, looking both to his aristocratic friends and to the emperor for public recognition. Finally, houses provide a complex meditation on the new poetics of Statius' *Silvae*. Through his descriptions of houses, Statius enters into a discursive competition with his patron in which, as he praises a work of art or building, he emphasises his own celebratory and analytical power. The house, then, forms a key feature of Statius' thinking about the role of praise poetry in Flavian society.

---

[16] Vitr. *De arch.* 6. 5; Saller (1984) 352–5.

[17] Eck (1997a) especially 162–3. Since Rome was the central point for the senatorial rank in the early and middle principate, almost every senator was compelled to acquire a house within the capital appropriate to his standing.

[18] Eck (1997b) 78.

THE HOUSE OF VIOLENTILLA

The novel form of *Silv.* 1. 2 – its union of epithalamic, elegiac, and aetiological narrative elements – is complemented by its unusual subject. Violentilla did not conform to generic expectations, for she had been married previously, and the conventional reluctance of the virginal bride is here transformed to her unwillingness to bear the yoke of a second wedding, *thalami secundi* (138). Her status as widow posed Statius with a particular challenge, for the traditional imagery of virginity was unavailable to him here. Violentilla was also a woman of substance, a fellow Neapolitan whom Statius honours with separate, special praise (106–36, 260–5). A sign of her high social position was her possession of her own magnificent house within Rome.[19]

In *Silv.* 1. 2 Statius explores two ways of praising Stella's bride and defining Violentilla's authority. First, he portrays her as an elegiac *domina* in a mythological narrative in which Venus arranges her marriage to Stella; second, as part of this narrative, he provides an elaborate ecphrasis of the house in Rome that she occupies before marriage. In an unconventional treatment of the nubile mistress, we are introduced to Violentilla not through her female body, but through her house. In *Silv.* 1. 2 a house, not the traditional epithalamic flower, becomes the site through which Violentilla's female identity is constructed and explored.

Newmyer has pointed out that Statius' descriptions of his friends' houses are characteristically fashioned to reflect their characters.[20] But such descriptions also suggest the social and political positioning of the owners. In his study of English country-house poetry, Molesworth has noted that a chief characteristic of this genre is metonymy, a strategy which connects the value of the property to the moral or spiritual value of the owner as well as to his economic and social standing.[21] Saller has pointed out that recent studies of the Roman house have overlooked the role of women in design and decoration.[22] We cannot tell from Statius' brief description whether the decoration of Violentilla's house reflected specific feminine sensibilities. Yet ecphrasis, offering a perceptual response to a monument or work of art, can open the way to ideological analysis. Statius' description of Violentilla's house is a gendered one in

---

[19] For a woman to possess her own house was not uncommon. Eck (1997a), from a study of *fistulae* (water pipes) in the city of Rome, attests to the presence of 32 out of 208 townhouses belonging to women of the senatorial order.

[20] Newmyer (1979) 40.   [21] Molesworth (1968) 7–9.   [22] Saller (1999) 196–7.

that it articulates conventional feminine virtues of beauty and chastity as well as, significantly, her considerable socio-economic status and her cultural origins which bring a new vitality to the concept of Roman tradition and family.

In both *Silv.* 1. 1 and 1. 2 human identity is constructed through architecture: through the sculpture of *Silv.* 1. 1, and through the house of a wealthy woman, Violentilla, in *Silv.* 1. 2. The fact that the house belongs to a woman indicates Statius' interest in reinterpreting cultural codes through bold, literary experimentation. Ecphrasis was tradition-ally concerned with objects of outstanding value – Achilles' shield, the emperor's statue, for instance. In Catullus 64, to which *Silv.* 1. 2 with its inset, aetiological narrative is indebted, the gorgeous palace of Peleus is briefly described (43–9). Martial tells us that Stella's house in Rome was a handsome building with expensive works of art.[23] In *Silv.* 1. 2 a woman's house, not the house of an élite male, becomes the non-traditional transmitter of a new sense of Roman identity that combines civic and national loyalties with friendship and love of the arts.

In *Silv.* 1. 2 the ecphrasis of Violentilla's house is particularly com-plex as it mediates between myth and reality. It is described as part of a mythological narrative, like the marvellous bedspread of Peleus and Thetis in Catullus 64, and yet the house nonetheless belongs to a historical person, Stella's bride, and it is situated in the heart of the city of Rome (144–5). Moreover, the description of Violentilla's house in *Silv.* 1. 2 is presented from Venus' point of view as she flies into Rome to arrange the marriage of Violentilla and Stella. Venus here, like the house, mediates between private and public space. She plays a dual role in this poem as both marriage-broker and imperial god-dess, founder of the Roman race. She is introduced to the poem in the traditional role of *pronuba*, leading the bride by the hand (11–15), but the description of her as *genetrix Aeneia* ('mother of Aeneas', 11) as-sociates her also with Rome's political origins. Thus the description of Violentilla's house should be understood as a function, in part, both of Venus' special hopes and of that goddess's complex role within the poem. It is thus intimately connected with changing ideas about Roman identity.

Violentilla's house, then, is a magnificent mansion that testifies to the economic power and high social standing of the bride. The ecphrasis of the house serves the complex function of mapping the moral as well as

---

[23] Mart. 6. 47. See also Almeida (1995) 37–8.

the social and physical attributes of Violentilla upon architectural space
(145–57):

> pandit nitidos domus alta penates
> claraque gaudentes plauserunt limina cycni.
> digna deae sedes, nitidis nec sordet ab astris.
> hic Libycus Phrygiusque silex, hic dura Laconum
> saxa virent, hic flexus onyx et concolor alto
> vena mari, rupesque nitent quis purpura saepe
> Oebalis et Tyrii moderator livet aeni.
> pendent innumeris fastigia nixa columnis,
> robora Dalmatico lucent satiata metallo.
> excludunt radios silvis demissa vetustis
> frigora, perspicui vivunt in marmore fontes,
> nec servat natura vices: hic Sirius alget,
> bruma tepet, versumque domus sibi temperat annum.

The lofty house opened wide its gleaming *penates* and the swans in delight
clapped their wings at the shining threshold. This is a house worthy of a
goddess; it stands comparison with the gleaming stars. Here there is Libyan
and Phrygian stone, here the hard Laconian rocks glow with green, here is the
spiralling onyx and the marble the colour of the deep sea, and here gleams the
marble that is often a source of envy to the Oebalian purple and the supervi-
sor of the Tyrian vat. Countless columns support the ceilings; the woodwork
shines with a lavish veneer of Dalmatian gold. The coolness streaming from
ancient woods excludes the sun's rays, clear fountains spring up in marble
basins, and nature does not observe the seasons: here the Dog Star is cold,
midwinter is warm, and the house turns and controls the seasons to its own
advantage.

An elegant chiasmus opens the description (145), linking poetic style with
the architectural display of the house. Each word carefully delineates the
essential characteristics of the house. *Pandit* suggests the house's openness
to visitors as well as its spaciousness. The verb identifies the house as a
domus frequentata, a crowded house open to many clients, an indicator
of the owner's high rank and social and political importance within the
community.[24] Venus and her swans thus approach Violentilla's house like
one of the many clients that thronged the open houses of the rich every
morning in Rome – a stylish image that combines beauty and humour.

The striking height of the house (*alta*, 145) suggests that the house
stands out and is noticed amidst the urban congestion of Rome. In
Roman moralistic discourse, architecture was frequently employed as

[24] Saller (1994) 92.

a paradigm of luxury and progressive moral decay.[25] In particular, a tall-standing house was viewed as the material expression of pride, of excessive and potentially ruinous ambition.[26] Statius' ecphrasis gives a new, positive valuation to height. Often deployed as a sign of masculine power, the physical height of the house here, however, is specifically correlated with the female body of its owner, who has been described by Venus as standing taller than any Roman matron (114–16).[27] Height is more than a physical marker, therefore. It is intertwined with rank, with the high social status of Violentilla. It is also a symbol of moral and economic superiority, of the power and influence of an exceptional matron.

Violentilla's house is luxurious in its size and the costly materials that adorn it – marble (148–51) and gold (153). Luxury here is given a positive valuation through a skilful mediation between moral and material values. For instance, the household gods, the *penates*, here connect the house with traditional Roman virtue and religiosity, with the ancestral conception of the house as a sacred place, centred upon its household gods.[28] Violentilla's *penates*, however, are 'gleaming' (*nitidos*, 145), like the precious stones and marbles that adorn the house (*nitent*, 150). The *penates*, Venus' first glimpse of the house's interior, point to the way in which Violentilla's house represents an adaptation of tradition to the changed economic and social value of the Roman house. Wallace-Hadrill's exploration of the social function of architectural decoration has stressed that the luxury of the Roman house, so firmly castigated in moral tradition, had a social function as a necessary marker of the owner's prestige and social standing; the underlying impulse of the Roman house 'is not to display wealth but to affirm status'.[29] Thus the brilliance of the *penates* can be understood not as a sign of luxurious decadence but rather as an affirmation of Violentilla's economic worth and also, one may infer, her

[25] There is a considerable literature on this topic, both ancient and modern. Since luxury is an important theme of this section of my book, I will direct the reader for now to Edwards (1993) 137–72, and my brief discussion in chapter 1 above, 4–6. Edwards provides an excellent, comprehensive discussion of the ancient sources and modern criticism. I will provide other, specific references as the occasion arises in the following chapters.

[26] For instance, at the end of the second book of the *Georgics* Virgil satirises the lofty townhouse with its proud doors – *foribus domus alta superbis* (461) – that spews forth its morning tide of clients. There was of course a practical element behind such moral strictures against height. Tall buildings in a crowded city were a hazard, subject to fire or collapse. They could cause severe bodily and financial harm. See for instance Sen. *Controv.* 2. 1. 11–12; Juv. *Sat.* 3. 190–222; 14. 303–16 and Mayor's (1878) commentary on these lines.

[27] See for instance Weisman (1992), especially chapter 1 where she discusses the sexual symbolism of architectural form.

[28] Saller (1984) 350: 'the Roman house had a sacred aura, embodied in the *dii penates*'.

[29] Wallace-Hadrill (1988) 56.

moral worth as a noble Roman lady upholding the glory of her family through her stylish and careful maintenance of the ancestral gods.

The social and economic importance of Violentilla is further marked by her house's prominent use of marble (148–51). The many columns that support the house (152) were a feature of public architecture applied to the private house to give it grandeur; the radiance of the marble, furthermore, was redolent of wealth.[30] Vollmer claims that Statius' listing of marbles is a standard topos of the rhetorical schools.[31] Marble here, however, participates in a rich semiotic system. Marble was an obvious sign of social status as well as material wealth.[32] It was also a prime target of moralistic discourse against luxury.[33] Marble used in private buildings was a fairly late phenomenon in Rome.[34] White Luna marble from north of Rome was the most common type of marble used for decoration until the end of the first century AD when coloured marbles from the East began to replace it.[35] Violentilla's house boasts all foreign marbles, and therefore represents the cutting edge of innovation in the decorative arts at this time.[36] As Fant observes, 'marble made a particularly appropriate symbol of wealth and power because it was expensive, imported, and unnecessary'.[37] Indeed, marble retained royal associations. In the first century AD, the major quarries fell under imperial control, for it was such a symbolically powerful material.[38] In *Silv.* 4. 2 Statius describes the wealth of marbles that adorn the *aula regia* of the Palatine (26–9). Violentilla's house, in its variety and abundance of marble, is as richly adorned as the imperial palace. Marble too, of course, is often used in an erotic context to describe beautiful human flesh.[39] Marble links sexual desirability to social and economic status, making Violentilla's house an

---

[30] Wallace-Hadrill (1988) 64–8 notes that the column was a feature of Greek public and sacred architecture. In a house, 'columns, whether in an atrium or a colonnade or within a room have the effect of marking out a space as prestigious' (68).

[31] Vollmer (1898) 251.

[32] Warde-Perkins (1992) 23 has pointed out that marble was 'the great prestige building material of its time'.

[33] Plin. *HN* 36. 1. 1–3. 8 attacks the quarrying of marble as a sign of Roman decadence.

[34] According to Pliny, the first man to veneer his house with marble was Mamurra, Julius Caesar's *praefectus fabrum*, chief engineer in Gaul. This, according to Pliny, merely confirmed Catullus' accusations of decadence against the man (*HN* 36. 7. 48).

[35] Warde-Perkins (1992) 15–16.

[36] See Vollmer (1898) 251–2 for identification of the various types of marbles used in Violentilla's house.

[37] Fant (1988) 149. The importation of foreign marbles was unnecessary since Italy had plentiful and good local stone.

[38] Fant (1988) argues that 'the imperial system is firmly at the center of the trade in marble and marble objects in the high Empire' (147).

[39] See *OLD* 2 on *marmoreus*.

appropriate site therefore for a woman described as a worthy object of
Jupiter's desire (133–6).

Marble, then, also makes Violentilla's house a gendered space, for it is
associated here with Violentilla's unique beauty and character. Indeed,
the shine of the marble and gold (153) with which the house is adorned –
nitidos (145), *nitent* (150), *lucent* (153) – contributes to a metaphorical identification of Violentilla as the perfect partner for Stella. Her house 'stands
comparison with the gleaming stars' (*nitidis nec sordet ab astris*, 147). The
starry radiance of the marbles makes Violentilla's house worthy of a man
whose name means 'star'. Here is one of several examples in the poem
where Statius plays with Stella's name.[40] Marble, an élite material, identifies Violentilla not only as one of the nobility but as an elegiac mistress
par excellence. Indeed, the house, we are told, is a worthy seat for a goddess
(*digna deae sedes*, 147). Violentilla's literary role within Stella's poetry as
the desirable yet distant elegiac *domina* is neatly fused with her superior
socio-economic standing.

Statius also perhaps plays off the aural association of Violentilla's name
with the violet flower.[41] The description emphasises the colour of the
marbles in her house; their predominant colour is purple mixed with
some green. Libyan marble (148) has a subtle colour modulating between
'golden yellow and red'.[42] Phrygian marble (148) has a white surface
mottled with purple circles.[43] Laconian marble, as the passage explains,
is green.[44] Carystian marble had greenish-blue veins.[45] The passage
ends by emphasising the brilliant purple of a stone that is probably
porphyry (150–1).[46] The onyx (149), a light-coloured stone marked with
spirals whose most desirable colour, according to Pliny the Elder, was
pale honey, is perhaps the only odd one out in this list.[47] Otherwise,
in his description of the marbles of Violentilla's house Statius seems to
play off the association of its mistress's name with the violet flower –
in literature best known as a purplish red flower with green leaves.[48]

---

[40] See also *Silv.* 1. 2. 73, 212–13, 228.
[41] Vollmer (1898) 237 suggests that the more likely derivation of the name Violentilla is from
     violentus, 'violent' or 'impetuous'. The notion of violence does not suit Violentilla's restrained
     character, however. Rather, the sound of the name, and the epithalamic context in which
     it appears, suggest a strong association with the *viola*. On the species of violet see Plin.
     HN 21. 14. 27.
[42] Vollmer (1898) 251.   [43] Cf. *Silv.* 2. 2. 87–9 and Van Dam (1984) 248.
[44] Cf. *Silv.* 2. 2. 91 and Van Dam (1984) 249–50.
[45] Cf. *Silv.* 2. 2. 95 and Van Dam (1984) 250–1.   [46] Vollmer (1898) 251.
[47] On onyx see Plin. *HN* 36. 12. 61. However, Pliny does catalogue three kinds of violet, the purple,
     the yellow, and the white. See *HN* 21. 10. 14.
[48] E.g. Verg. *Ecl.* 10. 39; see also *OLD* 2. I am grateful to Catherine Connors for making this
     connection between the marbles and Violentilla's name in her paper 'Statius and the Language

Violets were a symbol of beautiful but transient youth, an image of fragile virginity.[49] By transmuting the flower into solid stone, Statius thereby alters its associations to represent not the woman's fragility but her economic power and high social status. Thus one radical way in which Statius departs from the epithalamic tradition is in his treatment of virginity. Since Violentilla has been married before, he can depict her as chaste, but not as virginal. Instead of the traditional epithalamic imagery of flowers and fruit, therefore, he substitutes a house, a much more substantial and lasting image through which Violentilla's female identity is constructed.

The presence of woods (*silvis*, 154) as a feature of the townhouse is a little puzzling.[50] Moreover, these woods are specifically described as 'ancient' (*vetustis*, 154), an atypical feature of an urban landscape. In Statius' descriptions of houses, the symbolic importance of the design is often what matters, and it is fruitless to try to reproduce an architect's plan. The shady grove with its marble fountains reformulates within the villa the conventional imagery of virginity, applying it to the expression of Violentilla's chastity. The rays of the sun, an image that frequently is used as a metaphor for sexual passion, are excluded by the woods from Violentilla's house (154).[51] The clear fountains also suggest female purity, their liveliness (*vivunt*, 155), however, suggesting procreative power.

In these two lines we have the essential ingredients of the type of ideal landscape or *locus amoenus* we find prominently associated with virginity in Ovid's *Metamorphoses*: the ancient woods that shut out the sun's rays and preserve coolness, the clear living fountains.[52] Comparison with Ovid shows, however, that Statius has a very different approach to this topos. Ovidian landscapes, as Parry points out, do not protect but are the scene of violent acts of passion. They are particularly dangerous places

---

of Place', delivered at the Statius Workshop, Trinity College, Dublin, 21 March 1998. See also now Connors (2000) 512–13, who argues that the marbles reflect Violentilla's emotional shift in the poem.

49 Thus Proserpina picks both lilies and violets before her abduction by Pluto (Ov. *Met.* 5. 392). Violets were the first sign of spring (Plin. *HN* 21. 38. 64). They are associated with love (Hor. *Carm.* 3. 10 . 14) and with rites for the dead (Ov. *Fast.* 2. 539).

50 We might think that a garden is being described; Purcell (1987) mentions the Roman fashion of including landscaped woods within the villa complex (197). Perhaps, then, we are to imagine some woods around which a peristyle has been constructed. In *Silv.* 1. 3 Vopiscus' country villa boasts a tree within a central, inner courtyard (59–63).

51 Thus for instance, Ov. *Met.* 4. 192–5 plays with the conceit of the Sun, in love, burning with a new fire.

52 On the typology of the Ovidian ideal landscape see Parry (1964), and Segal (1969a). Segal discusses the sexual ambiguity of the Ovidian ideal landscape; Parry demonstrates its startling effectiveness as the scene of violent crime.

for women and for feminised males. Narcissus' pool in *Metamorphoses*
3. 407–12 provides perhaps the paradigm of the Ovidian landscape with
its water clear as glass, but entirely sheltered from the sun – a mirror image of Narcissus' own fatal virginity. In Violentilla's house, however, the
fountains spring from marble, a sign of a controlled, human-made environment rather than the natural landscape of Narcissus' pool. In Ovid's
Metamorphoses marble is the material to which the flesh of a beautiful and
virginal human body is compared. Thus for instance Narcissus, trans-
fixed by his mirror-image like a marble statue (3. 419), beats his breast
with 'marble palms' (*marmoreis . . . palmis*, 3. 481).[53] In Violentilla's house
the gleam of marble is implicitly transferred back from body to house
where it reflects not only the owner's beauty but also symbolically suggests her self-control and her power to construct and maintain her chaste
environment. Chastity, rather than virginity, is a concept involved with
independence and self-control. Beauty here is an ethical commodity, not
a vulnerable one.

The spondaic metre and central position of *silvis* in line 154 gives
that word special emphasis. As Statius perhaps plays upon Violentilla's
name, so here he perhaps puns on the title of his own *Silvae*, which are
architecture in verse. He thereby suggests that his poetry helps adorn the
house. Moreover, as Hinds has suggested, the mention of *silva* in Latin
literature frequently evokes a poet's relationship to earlier tradition, the
raw material or woods out of which the poet carves his own cultural
space.[54] The reference to ancient woods at a point where Statius evokes
an Ovidian landscape draws attention to Statius' heuristic engagement
here with the Ovidian typology of the *locus amoenus* as well as with earlier
epithalamic traditions. Indeed, in Statius' poetry, the house represents
the new type of *locus amoenus*, offering (in contrast to the *Metamorphoses*),
a safe space where nature is under human control and gods visit to aid
humans, not destroy them. In *Silv.* 1. 2 the ideal landscape, located within
Violentilla's house, reformulates the ideas of beauty and chastity within
the protective environment of a wealthy villa, where they become signs
not of transience and fragility but of feminine authority and power.

The description of Violentilla's house ends by making symbolic capital
out of the climatic orientation of Roman villas, which were specially
constructed so as to control both view and temperature.[55] Pliny's villas,

---

[53] See Ahl (1985) 238–9.   [54] Hinds (1998) 12–14.
[55] See Vitruvius' prescriptions for the proper orientation of a house in *De arch.* 6. 4. Rooms should
be designed to take advantage of the light and season of year in accordance with their function.

for instance, had rooms suitable for winter or for summer use; one private room in his Tuscan villa, decorated with a painted arbour, commanded a wonderful view of the sea that allowed Pliny to enjoy the pleasures of nature without its inconveniences.[56] Violentilla's house controls the climate and creates a moderate temperature all year round (157). In a series of final paradoxes we are told that the house shines brilliantly but excludes the sun's rays; the late summer heat of Sirius feels cool within the house, while midwinter cold feels warm (156–7). The house reflects the paradoxes out of which Violentilla's character is constructed in this poem: the nubile protégée of Venus and the independent, wealthy widow, the desirable elegiac *domina* and the chaste, modest young woman.

In *Silv.* 1. 2 control over nature's seasons is linked with Violentilla's ethical control of her own body. Unlike Stella, she has not impetuously demanded marriage but has been slow to accede to his pleas (162–93). She has 'grown warm' (*tepuisse*) towards her husband as her house is warm (*tepet*, 157) in winter; her husband by contrast is ardent, suffering on tides of passion (*aestus*, 91).[57] Violentilla embodies temperance. *Temperat* (157) then suggests more than climate control. Rather, it points to the good breeding and good sense of Violentilla herself, who agrees to remarry but does not rush to do so. Through her house she appears as a woman of high reputation in whom the influence and good sense of the matron is united with the beauty and desirability of the unwed.

The house, then, becomes the site through which the identity of the new Roman imperial woman is constructed. Economic wealth and power enter alongside the conventional female virtues of beauty and modesty; virginity, a sign of a woman's vulnerability, becomes transmuted to chastity, a sign of independence and self-control. Not surprisingly, Violentilla is described from Venus' point of view as *potentis*, powerful (158). The house, rather than the body, is represented here as the primary site of definition for the woman of high social and moral standing.

In *Silv.* 1. 2 the ecphrasis of Violentilla's house provides interesting evidence of the greater economic independence and social importance of the imperial Roman woman both within and outside marriage. Saller has noticed, for instance, a change in this period in concepts of the family, which came to include and value female ancestors as well as male ones.

Thus, for instance, winter dining rooms should have a sunny western exposure; libraries should face the east to keep the morning light.

[56] Plin. *Ep.* 5. 6. 11.

[57] See Cupid's speech to Venus (esp. 74–102) in which he describes Stella's passion for Violentilla as surpassing that of famous ancient lovers.

Since most senatorial families in this period could not boast a long agnatic lineage, the idea of the family shifted its emphasis from agnatic to cognatic kin.[58] A well-connected circle of kin traced through the female as well as the male line was indispensable to the new standards of social status that were being sought during the early Empire; so too was a fine house large enough to accommodate the morning _salutatio_.[59] Violentilla's separate wealth and fine lineage are praiseworthy features of her marriage with Stella, a means by which she can enhance the distinction of the family she joins (260–5). She herself distinguishes her own separate family line. Significantly, Venus mentions that Violentilla's beauty derives from her upholding of her ancestral _gloria_ (108, 261) and the honour of her race (109); through a woman, 'the glory of fathers' (_gloria patrum_, 108), is carried on. A woman's beauty here both incorporates and furthers traditional patriarchal values.

Statius ends _Silv._ 1. 2 with a wish for children who will perpetuate the family line and talents of both parents (266–77). Violentilla will pass on to her children the quality of _decus_ (272, 275) which she possesses, a concept hard to translate into English, for it suggests that beauty is a quality inseparable from nobility and good breeding. Both husband and wife possess this quality, but Violentilla does so to a greater degree (272–3). She will endow her children with _decus_ whichever of their sex (271–3). Violentilla here plays a key role in the creation and perpetuation of a strong family unit. More so than Stella, she is to be the transmitter of values traditionally thought of as male. Thus the children of both Stella and Violentilla will be leaders in the Roman community, lawyers, generals, and – in acknowledgment of the importance of literature to both Statius and Stella – poets (266–7).

But we must keep in mind that in _Silv._ 1. 2, the reader is invited to view the house from the point of view of Venus, who, in the poem's delightful fantasy, flies to her Rome and to Violentilla's house, anxious to find that her foster-child has lived up to her standards. This imperial Venus acts here in the role of _pronuba_, arranger of marriages. Venus' most famous literary role as _pronuba_ occurs in the _Aeneid_, where she engineers the relationship between Dido and Aeneas. Like Dido, Violentilla is Venus' protégée, and a wealthy widow. Indeed, a complimentary connection is made between Dido and Violentilla when, in the brief description of the latter's beauty (112–16), we are told that she is very tall; indeed, that she stands out among the Roman matrons as Diana stood out among her

---

[58] Saller (1984) 348–9; also (1994) 74–88.   [59] Saller (1984) 355.

nymphs (115–16) – an allusion to *Aeneid* 1. 501, where Dido is described as surpassing all her female companions in height, and is likewise compared to Diana. Violentilla's high standing in the community is thus indicated by her subtle and playful association with Virgil's queen. But the comparison also suggests the new positive valuation that has been put upon wealth. Unlike Dido, Violentilla will not be rejected by an Aeneas who spurned love, luxury and the material splendour of Carthage for sterner virtues. She is marrying Stella, a poet more than a politician, and the gods are on their side.

The house moreover as well as Violentilla herself is what first pleases Venus on her arrival in Rome, *exsultat visu tectisque potentis alumnae* ('she exults in the sight of her powerful foster-child and her house', 158). With a touch of social realism, then, Statius makes the house the significant marker of Violentilla's eligibility both as foster-child of Venus and as potential wife of Stella. Violentilla meets divine expectations because she owns a house 'worthy of a goddess' (147). Indeed, through Venus' gaze, we see that female identity in the imperial age is tied up with the importance of property even more than with irresistible beauty. Violentilla's marriage with Stella offers a different view of cultural identity from that expressed in the *Aeneid*; one in which luxury, wealth, and material splendour are assimilated to traditional Roman *mores* centred on the house. Violentilla will fulfil a traditional female role, but from a strong and separate social and economic base. Indeed, as a Neapolitan marrying a Roman, she realises a new concept of Romanness based on the union of both cultures to which Statius felt himself connected.

Violentilla's house represents a meeting-place of Greek and Roman culture within the imperial city. The house embodies traditional Roman ideas about the social and political function of the house – its open doors, for instance – as well as Greek ideas about art and design – all the marbles are Hellenic and in newly fashionable colours. The house thus incorporates both the new imperial glamour of Rome and traditional virtues centred on the family and linked closely with successful public life. Property, more than ancestral lineage, is a marker of social status; the wealth and power of Empire is openly displayed in the costly Hellenic materials that adorn the house; the new importance of women as propagators of family honour is marked by the attention that Venus, mother of the Roman race, *genetrix Aeneia* (11), focusses upon Violentilla's house. Indeed, as founder of the Roman race, Venus here, with her approval of Violentilla's splendid mansion, endorses a shift in cultural values whereby luxurious architecture and great wealth, conventionally features of the decadent Greek East, are assimilated to a traditional system of ethics.

Venus' role as mother of the Roman race as well as arranger of marriages introduces a political aspect to the ecphrasis. Read within the collection as a whole, the second poem offers through Violentilla's house important political as well as social and cultural ideas. Violentilla's house, like Domitian's statue and his palace, participates in a culture of display; it is worthy of a goddess, and Violentilla is the counterpart of Venus (the goddess's 'sweet image', 112), much as the emperor is the counterpart of Jupiter. Violentilla's house and Domitian's equestrian statue share a similar aesthetic based on extraordinary height, size, and shine.[60]

Yet the splendour of Violentilla's house is moderated by the notion of temperance and self-control. The house is both a public landmark, open and welcoming, and a private space that encloses and shelters Violentilla with its ancient woods. The equestrian statue, on the other hand, is an object of fear as well as wonder. The massive physical dominance of Domitian's statue, like his palace, corresponds to the political and social dominance of the emperor in Rome. Fashioned in colossal bronze, the head wreathed in the upper air of heaven, the statue offers an image of the emperor as superhuman and all-controlling. But Statius' description of the statue also brings out the isolation of an emperor who wields such enormous power. Violentilla's house, by contrast, is welcoming and 'open-doored'. The two forms of architecture, embedded within the two opening poems, discreetly suggest the tensions at play within imperial society between a remote emperor intent on expanding his authority well beyond traditional bounds and an aristocracy that laid claim to its own forms of cultural autonomy.

In *Silv.* 1. 1 the emperor's identity is fashioned through his equestrian statue, just as in *Silv.* 1. 2 Violentilla's identity is fashioned through her house. The equestrian statue enshrines the concept of the emperor's isolation and divine distance from human conduct and affairs. A woman's house, located within a mythological narrative, provides a safe site through which the ambiguous situation of an imperial nobility that was both subservient and ambitious could be explored.[61] As part of a mythological narrative, the house delicately and skilfully adumbrates a different kind of social order from the competitive environment found

---

[60] On the statue's size and brilliance see *Silv.* 1. 1. 1–2, 11, 56–60; on height, 32–3.

[61] On the constant tension between the emperor and the nobility see Hopkins (1965), especially 19–23.

on the Palatine where the court seems to have revolved around a remote
and childless ruler.

EARINUS' PALACE

In *Silv.* 3. 4, for instance, to which in concluding this chapter I will turn,
a new view of success within imperial society is articulated through the
eunuch Earinus, brought as a foreign slave to the Palatine where he
became the favourite of Domitian. At the time of the composition of
the *Silvae*, he was a freedman successful enough to request a poem on
the dedication of his first cuttings of hair.[62] He represents therefore a
different route to fame and wealth from that undertaken by Stella and
Violentilla.

Silv. 3. 4, though probably the most derided of all Statius' poems, is
a poetic tour de force that is not to be understood in isolation from the
rest of the *Silvae*.[63] There are, for instance, several significant points of
contact between *Silv.* 1. 2 and *Silv.* 3. 4. As the penultimate poem of
the collection, *Silv.* 3. 4 corresponds in position to the second poem
in the first collection of the *Silvae*, *Silv.* 1. 2. There are other, thematic
correspondences, despite the social differences between the addressees.
Violentilla and Earinus are both represented as protégés of Venus
(*Silv.* 1. 2. 107–13; *Silv.* 3. 4. 31–8). Violentilla resembles Venus herself
(*Silv.* 1. 2. 112–13), while Earinus resembles one of her children (*Silv.* 3. 4.
28–30). Both, then, possess a divine beauty, worthy of the gods. Both
poems are constructed around a fantastical narrative in which Venus
undertakes a journey to the imperial capital and is impressed by the
great buildings she sees, in particular Domitian's palace in *Silv.* 3. 4
(47–9) and Violentilla's house in *Silv.* 1. 2 (144–57). Both poems deal
in complex ways with a challenging and unconventional situation, in
Silv. 1. 2 the widowed status of Stella's bride, in *Silv.* 3. 4 the sensitive situation of the eunuch, whose castration took place before the passing of
Domitian's law forbidding this practice. Several of the important strategies of *Silv.* 1. 2 – inset mythological narrative, the prominent role of Venus
as the facilitator of divine and earthly union, the theme of marriage,

---

[62] *Praef.* 3. 16–20. This is the only occasion when Statius makes it clear that he acceded to a definite
request for a poem, unless perhaps we adopt M's reading *iussum* in the preface to Book 1. 19
instead of the emendation *ausus sum*. See the discussion of *praef.* 1. 17–20 in Geyssen (1996) 27–30.

[63] Vessey (1973) 28–36. Cf. however Garthwaite (1984) who reads the poem as an extended gibe
against Domitian, portrayed here as a sexual pervert; Hardie (1983) 121–4 and Laguna (1992)
308–10 who discuss the poem as an elaborate expression of a dedicatory epigram. Verstraete
(1989) counters Garthwaite's ironic and subversive argument in detail. See also Pederzani (1992).

ecphrasis – receive fantastical reprise in *Silv.* 3. 4. As we shall see, the later poem provides a kind of reverse image of *Silv.* 1. 2 in which a different vision of Roman identity is imagined and contested.

As Hopkins notes, imperial freedmen and court eunuchs, particularly in the later Empire, provide dramatic examples of upward mobility because they were not identified with aristocratic interests and therefore were more dependent upon the emperor for social advancement.[64] The trajectory of Earinus' career, from Eastern slave to imperial freedman, important enough to command a poem from one of the leading writers of the day, certainly provides an early example of this phenomenon. Nonetheless, the eunuch was a constant figure of physical and moral repugnance in Roman society.[65] How then does Statius deal with the derogatory, conventional stereotype of the decadent, feminised male, the 'puer delicatus'?

For one thing, this poem lies fully within a distinguished literary tradition of court poetry that uses fantasy to play upon the ruler's sexuality and divinity. In particular, with its metaphorical theme of haircutting, *Silv.* 3. 4 looks to Callimachus' *Coma Berenices* and to Catullus' *Carmen* 66, court poems which deal with highly sensitive topics with imagination, and also pathos.[66] Like *Silv.* 3. 4, Callimachus' *Coma* forms the penultimate episode in its poetry collection, the *Aetia.*[67] Callimachus' influence upon Statius' own 'hair' poem is revealed particularly in the way in which Statius deals with difficult topics such as castration and the eunuch's relationship with Domitian, as well as the notion of divine rulership; mythological fantasy and a certain urbane wit inform both poems.[68] More specific motifs, such as the cutting of a lock of hair, the journey of the lock accompanied by divinities, the prominent role of Venus, and the importance of perfumes for the hair, also connect the two poems.[69] Earinus is diplomatically honoured by being praised within a format formerly reserved for a queen even as Statius plays upon the ambiguous

---

[64] See Hopkins (1965) 20–3.   [65] See Roller (1998).

[66] On the pathos of Catullus 66 and its connection with the death of the poet's brother see Griffith (1995).

[67] Koenen (1993) 90–4.

[68] See Koenen (1993) especially 97, who argues that Callimachus in the *Coma Berenices* attempts playfully to acclimatise the Greeks to the alien notion of brother-sister marriage – an essential issue of the ideology of Ptolemaic kingship – while simultaneously making an urbane compliment to the queen. For further discussion and bibliography on the poem and its Roman influence see Barchiesi (1998) 212–17.

[69] Journey of the lock: Callim. *Aet.* 110. 51–6; Catull. 66. 51–6; *Silv.* 3. 4. 1–5, 81–98; Aphrodite/Venus: Callim. *Aet.* 110. 56–64; Catull. 66. 56–64, 90; *Silv.* 3. 4. 3–5, 21–59, 71–72, 91–2; perfumes: Callim. *Aet.* 110. 77–8; Catull. 66. 77–8, 91–2; *Silv.* 3. 4. 82, 92.

gender of Earinus, a feminised male.[70] In keeping with the tenor of the *Coma Berenices*, Statius' approach to Earinus is both complimentary and urbane.

But in particular here, the poem reveals some of the disturbing implications of Domitian's development of a divine ideology, in particular his close association with Jupiter himself. The poem rests upon the paradox that Earinus, as divinely beautiful, must rightfully be the possession of Rome's 'Jupiter', Domitian. Thus Statius represents Earinus as a divine child, a Cupid (26–30) or a Ganymede (12–20); found by Venus playing before the altar of Aesculapius at Pergamum (21–7), this seemingly parentless boy has the sacred status of a divine initiate, for the imperial transaction of slavery is mystified as 'sacred rapine' (*sacrae rapinae*, 13). The divinisation of the emperor and the boy provides a means by which Statius can elevate and distance his subject from reality; Earinus is set within an imaginative environment that endows him with legendary status – but it is the strictly subordinate status of Jupiter's cupbearer, Ganymede. Earinus' divinisation suggests his superlative value within the economic and social system of the imperial court. Yet the oxymoron 'sacred rapine' also hints at his ambiguous status as a highly precious object of exchange in the commercial transactions between East and West.

In this poem Statius pushes the limits of divine ideology on which the court rests to fantastic and, I believe, troubling lengths by insisting on the Jovian ideology of Domitian.[71] According to the poem's basic premise, if Domitian corresponds to Jupiter in imperial ideology, then he must of course have a 'cupbearer'. The relationship between Earinus and Domitian is suggestively represented as a sexual one; Earinus is described by Venus as 'a slave to Palatine love' (*Palatino famulus amori*, 38).[72] By treating Earinus in the poem as the emperor's 'Ganymede' (13–20), Statius reinforces the exotic nature of the court and suggests that the emperor operates by a different sexual and moral code from his Roman subjects. The different sexual *mores* of Berenice and her husband

[70] On play with gender/genre through allusion to the *Coma* in Catullus and Virgil and Statius' *Achilleid* see Barchiesi (1998) 212–17.

[71] On the close connection between Domitian and Jupiter in imperial ideology see Fears (1977) 135–6. Fears here surveys the literature which depicts Domitian as the earthly equivalent of Jupiter, and he discusses the issue of sesterces which show Domitian in military garb, holding the thunderbolt and being crowned by Victory. Such coins represent 'the first extant official proclamation of the emperor's status as the divinely invested vicegerent of Jupiter' (136). See also Alexandropoulos (1994) who notes that from AD 85 the theme of the liaison between Jovian and imperial cult emerges notably on the sestertius.

[72] Thus Cancik (1965) 61–4 notes the erotic vocabulary of *Silv.* 3. 4 and its seemingly uncomfortable linkage with religious vocabulary.

underlie Callimachus' poem uneasily, for brother-sister marriage was an alien concept to his Greek readers.[73] Similarly, the sexual relationship of Domitian and Earinus, though conducted on a divine plane, represents a major point of friction that provides a significant catalyst for the set of tensions that run throughout this poem: between East and West, past and present, traditional and contemporary *mores*, male and female, the simultaneous power and subjection of Earinus himself. For *Silv.* 3. 4 makes clear that Rome is not yet a Hellenistic city – although its 'monarch' may be moving in that direction. The poem uses encomiastic fantasy not only to praise and elevate the relationship between Earinus and Domitian but also to probe the dynamics of Flavian court society and its shifting categories of value. Indeed, the specific praise of Domitian and his favourite is part of a larger project within *Silv.* 3. 4 that invites analysis of courtly society rather than mere adulation. The potentially problematic theme of the emperor's divinity lies at the poem's core.

What I wish to look closely at here is the brief description of Domitian's palace, viewed by Venus as she flies from Pergamum into Rome with Earinus. As I have suggested, Violentilla's house rivals the emperor's palace on the Palatine in its luxurious marbles and radiance – as her house stands comparison with the gleaming stars (147), so too, we are told in *Silv.* 3. 4, Domitian rivals the stars with his lofty palace (47–9):

> nec mora, iam Latii montes veterisque penates
> Evandri, quos mole nova pater inclitus orbis
> excolit et summis aequat Germanicus astris.

There is no delay, and now here are the Latian hills and the *penates* of venerable Evander, which Germanicus, the renowned father of the world, reshapes with a new mass of buildings and has raised to the tops of the stars.

As in *Silv.* 1. 2, here again the ecphrasis is part of a narrative journey made by Venus, taking a new protégé, the slave boy Earinus, from Pergamum to Rome. But their journey here evokes that of Aeneas from Troy to Rome as well as the one undertaken for Violentilla, for Earinus' first sight of Rome is, like that of Aeneas in Book 8 of the *Aeneid*, Evander's Palatine.

In this brief ecphrasis, offering a bird's-eye view of the Palatine, the contrast between early and new Rome is compressed and sharp. Evander's piety – his reverence for the state, its gods, and his family – is evoked through his *penates*, the gods of his hearth. Violentilla's *penates* in

---

[73] See note 68 above.

Silv. 1. 2 gleam in modern style; Evander, however, is venerable (*veterisque*) and his *penates*, it is suggested, are likewise. We are reminded then of his humble dwelling on the Palatine, of the low doorway under which Aeneas had to stoop in his acceptance of humility as a regal virtue.[74] Domitian's buildings express a different concept of power and morality. The hill has now been transformed by a new mass of buildings that challenge the stars. The ruler's authority is expressed not through humble religiosity, but through his physical supremacy; the height of the new buildings asserts his divinity. The swift encompassing of ancient and contemporary Rome in this ecphrasis draws our attention to both difference and continuity. We are inevitably reminded too of Augustus, who first built up the Palatine hill as an imperial residence. Yet does the Palatine hill provide a narrative of progress, of cultural and religious development according to which Rome now has a ruler so powerful that he is not just descended from a god, as Augustus claimed, but equal to them? Or is this a narrative of aesthetic progress yet moral decline? This ecphrasis provokes such questions, but it does not provide answers. Nonetheless, it offers some insight into the dynamics of court society and the development of ruler-cult within Rome, a development that Statius' language here suggests far exceeded traditional Roman concepts of governance.

Earinus belongs to this new, shining palace through his exceptional beauty. The extraordinary height of the palace suggests not only the superiority of the ruler to his subjects but also his distance from them. Earinus is a sign too of that distance. By representing him as a precious object of exchange between Venus and Domitian, his special status within the court as well as Roman society at large is marked. He is not given any of the stereotypical negative attributes of the eunuch that the ancients found offensive, such as a weak, high voice.[75] Instead, he is described as outstandingly lovely. His star-like beauty (*egregiae praeclarum sidere formae*, 26) forms an appropriate adornment to the new palatial buildings of the imperial residence, which equal the stars (49). As Hariman has pointed out in his study of court society, the mastery of appearances is there of primary importance.[76] Earinus' beauty is all that counts. Unlike the other people whom Statius honours in the *Silvae*, he is not given any moral or intellectual attributes.[77]

---

[74] Verg. *Aen.* 8. 306–61.

[75] Sen. *Ep.* 47. 7 inveighs against effeminate slave boys, 'cupbearers adorned like a woman'. On the negative characteristics of the eunuch and the effeminate male in ancient society see Gleason (1995) especially chapters 3 and 4.

[76] Hariman (1995) 51–94, especially 76.   [77] See Verstraete (1989) 407.

Earinus therefore represents a new, untraditional way to gain success and power in Domitian's Rome. The gorgeous materials of gold and jewels that adorn the mirror encasing his votive lock of hair (94) suggest the high economic and social value placed upon Earinus' one important attribute, his beauty. Statius' poem too offers Earinus a pleasing reflection of himself.[78] But the mirror is also a symbol of entrapment. It metonymically represents the palace itself. It encloses in splendour Earinus' image (95–8) as well as the lock of hair, both preserved forever as perfect emblems of his unchanging and narcissistic condition. Like his own image encased in the gorgeous mirror, Earinus is a fixed, irremovable part of the palace's inner décor.

Earinus is an appropriate adornment then for this Palatine that raises its towers far above mortal experience and limits. He testifies to the rarified atmosphere of the court, its separation from ordinary society, its foundation in a new, divine ideology and in new ideas about social advancement that are founded on extravagant display.[79] But Earinus is a sign of difference as well as distance. Through the motif of Earinus' journey from Pergamum, the Palatine palace, like Violentilla's house, is represented as the meeting point of Eastern and Roman cultures – but it is an uneasy meeting point. Earinus represents what is foreign and new in Domitian's court and unassimilated to Roman ways, for his identity remains oriented towards the East, his place of origin. Although Rome had imported its own major cult of Aesculapius, he sends his dedication of hair to the temple of Aesculapius in Pergamum. When Aesculapius comes to perform the boy's castration, he comes not from the centre of his cult on Tiber island but from Pergamum (67–8) – castration is thus dissociated from Roman religious practices.[80] Arrested in eternal youth, Earinus seems destined to remain always different and unRoman. His identity, closely tied up with the East and femininity and yet firmly located within the imperial palace, is jarringly disruptive of Roman social and moral as well as physical norms.

Characteristically, in addition to the ecphrasis of the palace, mythological comparisons, even as they playfully honour Earinus, interrogate the values that Earinus embodies in Domitian's Rome. Only one lock of hair can travel to Pergamum (81–2), for Earinus as eunuch has little hair on offer (78–82).[81] But this lock is more famous than the lock of king

---

[78] Pederzani (1992) 93–4 has noted that the poem itself has a 'mirror' structure.
[79] See Wallace-Hadrill (1970) 293.
[80] On the cult of Aesculapius on Tiber island see Ov. *Met.* 15. 622–745; *Fast.* 1. 289–94.
[81] Morgan (1997) argues that Earinus substitutes for the bashfully bald Domitian. But Morgan

Nisus, or the hair that Achilles cut in mourning for Patroclus (84–5). In these two mythological examples the cutting of the lock of hair is associated with defiance of a father, daring action, and untimely death or metamorphosis. Scylla killed her father Nisus by treacherously cutting his special lock of hair; though female, she acted, at least according to Ovid, with daring and passion, thus defying the stereotype of weakness assigned to her sex.[82] When Achilles dedicated his hair to the memory of Patroclus, he did so in full knowledge that the cutting of his hair meant for him an early death; he was violating his father's vow to the river Spercheius that he would dedicate Achilles' hair as an offering of thanks for his homecoming. The cutting of these locks of hair recalls a society founded on meaningful moral codes; even as Scylla violated the sacred bond between father and child, Achilles honoured the sacred bond between friends. Both Scylla and Achilles provide reminders of a heroic world in which men and women through passion – even if misguided – defied their fathers and the warning of fate; in Achilles' case, he did so out of a higher sense of loyalty and love.

These two mythological comparisons encapsulate Earinus' divided sexuality, and they suggest, in a typically nuanced way, that Earinus is only half-man, half-woman. He is not only less than Achilles, he is also less, in a sense, than Scylla, who acts decisively if wrongly in defiance of authority. The identity of Earinus is constructed as both feminised and also, unlike Scylla, as passive; he is entirely in the possession of his 'father' and 'spouse' Domitian. Not for him an early heroic death; not for him metamorphosis. His lock of hair, cut by cupids and lovingly drenched in perfume by Venus and preserved (90–92), functions metonymically for Earinus himself, objectified through his only source of power, his physical, unchanging beauty.[83] He himself does not act but is acted upon. Only his lock makes a journey; he himself cannot leave the emperor's palace. Thus, when we are told at the poem's beginning that the lock, encased in

wrongly assumes that Earinus is long-haired (214, n. 35); although Statius addresses the hair in the plural in his opening propempticon (*ite, comae,* 1), at the poem's end we are told that Earinus can send to Pergamum only one lock, *solus crinis* (81). The inconsistency between plural and singular may be due to the inconsistency between Statius' two main models; in Callimachus the hair is singular and masculine, in Catullus the hair is plural and feminine. On the varied rules of votive haircutting in antiquity – sometimes only one lock was dedicated, often more – see Griffith (1995) 53.

[82] See Ov. *Met.* 8. 1–151; Hom. *Il.* 23. 140–51. On the influence of this Homeric passage on Catullus 66 see Griffith (1995) 54–5.

[83] The journey of Earinus' lock of hair from Rome to Pergamum elegantly frames the journey of Earinus from Pergamum to Rome, providing a kind of mirror structure for the poem. See Pederzani (1992) 92–3.

gold, travels *molliter* (2), softly, the adverb defines the physical condition of the eunuch, which is *mollis*; Venus herself is described as gentle, *mitis* (3) as she sends the lock on its way.[84] Spectacle here legitimates Earinus' only source of power. The ambiguity of his gender replaces moral and heroic values with the new valuable aesthetic qualities of sexuality and beauty.

The ecphrasis of the Palatine in *Silv.* 3. 4, then, encompasses the new social and moral as well as architectural codes of the court. It offers for scrutiny the new form of government to which Domitian gave monumental expression on the Palatine, a court society in which social status was expressed and won through the reliance on the power of the personal image – from the magnificent buildings of the palace to the beauty of Domitian's slave boy and his lock of hair. Yet, in the hierarchical structure of the court, there is little freedom, it seems, for autonomous expression.

Critics seeking from this poem a fuller understanding of the practices of ancient slavery will be disappointed. We need, after all, to take into account the requirements of the person to whom this poem is addressed, Earinus himself. The poem, beginning with its initial address to the hair as it sets out on its voyage to Pergamum, sustains a mythological fantasy in which the transactions of slavery are realised on a divine plane. Such mystification would doubtless have pleased Earinus, as the poem's recipient. The illusion is broken only once, when Statius indignantly inveighs against the former practice of castration (73–7). Critics have found this note of social realism jarring and intrusive. Yet it serves to emphasise Earinus' state of subjection and draws a metaphorical link between the cutting of the hair and the far less pretty cutting of the genitals.[85] The act of mutilation, moreover, locates Earinus within the conceptual field of autocracy. The artifice and ceremonial that sustain the hierarchical relations of the court are here briefly exposed.

---

[84] Thus the act of castration is described as *puerum mollire* (68), literally 'to soften a boy'.

[85] Statius deals openly both with Earinus' castration (65–82) and with the law passed against this practice (73–7). According to Vessey (1973) 35–6, Statius is here conforming to the demands of Domitian's regime. Cf. however Verstraete (1989) who argues that Statius' freedom to raise the topic of castration suggests that Domitian's court was more liberal than has been thought. Martial, not normally a squeamish writer, does not mention castration in the six epigrams on Earinus in Book 9 of his *Epigrams* (11, 12, 13, 16, 17, 36), although he does mention the law shortly before (9. 5 and 9. 7). See Hofmann (1990) who argues that Martial shows more tact than Statius, and Lorenz (1997) 82–91 who argues that Martial's two poems about the law forge indirectly a connection of thought with the following Earinus sequence. Dio Cass. 67. 2–3 puts a negative construction on the law against castration, claiming that Domitian passed it purely to spite Titus, who had been fond of eunuchs. For Ammianus Marcellinus, however, the reputation of Domitian is partly redeemed by his excellent law against castration (18. 4. 5).

Silv. 3. 4 demonstrates that, as Fitzgerald has argued, slavery provided the Romans with a language with which to think about other relationships and institutions.[86] Not surprisingly perhaps, slavery began to take on particular currency as a political metaphor in the early Principate.[87] Through Earinus, whose body is the property of others, Statius can explore the paradoxical situation of the courtier, powerful enough as the emperor's favourite to order one of the leading poets of the day to write a poem in his honour, and yet, as the fate of his body suggests, at the whim of his master's wishes. As a castrated slave and Domitian's prized possession, Earinus provides an extreme example of the condition of the courtier. The paradox of Earinus – emperor's favourite and slave, object of erotic desire and castrated male – suggests the courtier's uneasy position between 'power and powerlessness'.[88] Hariman well expresses the paradox of this condition when he comments that the task of the emperor or monarch is to keep his courtiers 'properly humble while holding the superior positions that they deserve'.[89]

It is not enough, then, to dismiss such poems as *Silv.* 3. 4 as flattery or to assume that Statius simply mirrors imperial ideology.[90] We may not like *Silv.* 3. 4 in this present age, but we should recognise that Statius' court poems are poems of anxiety as well as praise and that they are to be examined within the complex dialectic of the *Silvae* as a whole. *Silv.* 3. 4 forms an important part of the continuing dynamic in Statius' poems between public and private life, engagement and withdrawal. Indeed Statius' poems of imperial praise, including *Silv.* 3. 4, demonstrate the social and political constraints operating upon a poet with high personal aspirations and a strong desire for public significance. This poem clearly was a major diplomatic challenge for Statius. It was not dashed off in the heat of the moment. Rather, he tells us that he delayed a long time over fulfilling Earinus' request (*praef.* 3. 16–20). Even as he exalts and compliments Earinus with extensive play upon the myth of divinity, Statius establishes his distance from such representations of divine power by exploring the limits of their fictionality and by inviting reflection upon the political and social function of poetry in an autocratic society.

---

[86] Fitzgerald (2000) 10–12, 69–86.   [87] Fitzgerald (2000) 71.

[88] I borrow here a phrase of Henderson (1998) 39 used of the reader and suggesting that 'within the tasteful privacy of Statius' book-roll, the grandeurs of the Empire fold back into a reflection on the undecidable ironies of writing. There we may at leisure ponder powerfully/powerlessly how come it (and the rest of us) are so stuck between power and powerlessness'.

[89] Hariman (1995) 55.

[90] Pederzani (1992) argues that *Silv.* 3. 4 is court propaganda, devoid of irony or of any other signals in the text that suggest the poem is other than direct eulogy.

Thus although in *Silv.* 3. 4 Statius impersonates the voice of the Hellenistic courtier, he also marks his own separateness from court society by his exploitation of geographical and mythological distance. Whereas he represents himself as a joyful participant at the wedding of Stella and Violentilla, in *Silv.* 3. 4 he does not represent himself as physically present at the dedicatory ceremony of Earinus' locks. He visits Stella's house, not the Palatine. In *Silv.* 3. 4 Statius observes, fashions, and interprets divinity from afar, thereby marking not only his own separateness but also the separateness of the court from long-standing Roman traditions.

The position of the poem within the *Silvae* lends support to this interpretation. Both the poem that precedes *Silv.* 3. 4 and the poem that follows it reveal court society as uncertain, in part because the courtier was subject to the often arbitrary power of the emperor. *Silv.* 3. 3 laments the death of a courtier known to us only as the father of Claudius Etruscus, like Earinus a slave who had risen to be an important imperial freedman, although his route was through finance (he was put in charge of the imperial treasury). As an old man, he was dismissed by Domitian and exiled for an unspecified offence. Even an imperial servant who had enjoyed a long and successful career was not immune from the blows of fortune administered by the imperial master.[91] In *Silv.* 3. 5, the concluding poem of Book 3 and of the first collection, Statius expresses his disaffection with Rome and with Domitian, whom he describes as a 'cruel and ungrateful Jove' (*saevum ingratumque | Iovem*, 32–3), for he did not award Statius the prize at the Capitoline games. *Silv.* 3. 4 then is flanked by two poems that portray the life of those who seek the emperor's favour as profoundly uncertain. In *Silv.* 3. 4 Earinus is surrounded by the emperor's *former* (*priores*, 56) favourites; he too, it is implicitly suggested, will eventually be displaced from his preeminent position. *Silv.* 3. 4 emphasises the lack of freedom that makes even the highly favoured courtier totally subject to the whims and desires of the emperor.

Moreover, although Earinus is nominally the addressee of this poem, its other main recipient is Pollius Felix to whom Book 3 as a whole is dedicated. *Silv.* 3. 1 celebrates Pollius' refounding of the temple of Hercules on his Campanian estate, an act that in the public sphere was traditionally associated with the emperor; significantly, Pollius' home is founded on a prosperous family line of children and grandchildren (143, 175–79). Here on a private estate in the Greek part of Italy far removed from the court, traditional Roman civic virtues centred on worship of

---

[91] On Claudius Etruscus see chapter 6 below.

the gods and the honouring of the family seem, ironically, most vital.[92] According to the dynamics of the *Silvae*, the family, at the centre of a social order founded on friendship, perpetuates and reorients civic identity.

But the tension between Domitian's new Rome, shaped by Hellenistic ideas of monarchy, and the Rome of Statius' literary friends emerges most clearly from the interaction between the second poem in the collection and the penultimate one. *Silv.* 1. 2 begins and ends with a festal marriage celebration in which gods and humans mingle. Indeed, the gods, who appreciate Stella's poetic skills and treat him as a friend (*comitique canoro*, 225), bring Stella gifts (225–8) and sing for the wedding (1–10). The interaction between deities and humans in *Silv.* 1. 2 should not be seen simply as mythological embellishment. Rather, the gods here participate in the construction of a society where hierarchical distinctions are softened in a community based on generosity, friendship, and a shared love of the arts. As in Catullus 64, the harmonious interaction between humans and gods suggests a re-creation of Golden Age felicity – not in the mythic past but rather in the imperial present. In *Silv.* 3. 4, however, the relationship between Jupiter and his Ganymede is portrayed as an exclusive one. This 'god', it seems, does not participate in social relationships outside the glittering mass of the Palatine. Indeed, Earinus' isolation from external society, his lack of autonomy, is represented through the image of his enclosure within the space of the temple at Pergamum, within the space of the palace on the Palatine, and finally within the jewelled mirror.

As a eunuch, moreover, Earinus is a sign of the troubling sterility of Domitian's household. He is daringly represented in *Silv.* 3. 4 as both the perpetual child which Domitian and Domitia never had (21–30), and as the sterile marriage partner of Domitian (50–8), an Eastern eunuch who will never change or breed.[93] *Domus*, house, means not only a physical place of dwelling and a household; in a natural extension of the house's close connection with lineage, it also can refer to the imperial dynasty.[94] Earinus' protection by Venus, Rome's procreative goddess, has dynastic precedents in the situations of both Aeneas and Violentilla. When

---

[92] See chapter 5 below.

[93] Venus mistakes Earinus at first for one of her own sons (*Silv.* 3. 4. 28–9). Laguna (1992) 310 finds disturbing the marriage imagery used to describe the presentation of Earinus to Domitian although he exaggerates its extent. For instance there is no ceremonial joining of hands such as Laguna suggests; rather, at line 61, Earinus is granted permission to touch the emperor's right hand, the hand of power, many times. Such boldness about marriage and sexual matters is in a sense authorised by the precedent of the *Coma Berenices*, which treated brother–sister marriage as a routine part of royalty, however the poem's readers may have found it.

[94] Saller (1984) 343–51. Cf. Tac. *Hist.* 2. 101.

terms of peace are finally made between Aeneas' Trojans and the indigenous peoples of Italy, the best of both cultures is brought together in a productive union.[95] Violentilla's house, too, is the site of a procreative union between Greek and Roman, the place where future leaders – and poets – of the Roman world will be born, a new nobility who will form the mainstay of the state (266–7). In its cohesive fusion of Naples and Rome, her house embodies continuity and fertility as well as stability. The Palatine, by contrast, according to its representation in *Silv.* 3. 4, is filled not with children and heirs but with a changing succession of pretty slave boys, *priores deliciae famulumque greges* (55–6) who now give way to Earinus, surrogate son of Rome's Jupiter and Juno (18) and surrogate spouse. The supreme artifice of the court finds ultimate expression in its negation of the biological drive for reproduction. Yet such negation has troubling implications for an heirless ruler such as Domitian. Earinus is the new Trojan refugee, brought to Rome like Aeneas under the protection of Venus. Though Venus now acts as *pronuba*, bringing Earinus and Domitian together, she has abandoned, it seems, her traditional dynastic imperative.

In *Silv.* 3. 4, Earinus' journey with Venus to become an intimate part of Domitian's *domus* subtly hints at the faultlines underlying the ideology of the ruler-cult in Rome. Sexual and dynastic politics here collide. A major theme of Hellenistic court poetry was the fertility of the ruler.[96] Indeed, a ruler's divine authority was closely associated with the power to produce children and thus ensure continuity of family line and stability for the country. Thus Waters argues that 'the idea of divine kingship in itself almost necessitates a dynasty if there is to be a monarchy at all'.[97] Statius' poems of imperial praise draw upon a rich and complex tradition of Alexandrian and Roman court poetry, yet strikingly absent from Statius' court poetry is the prominent Hellenistic theme of the ruler's fertility, the crucial factor that stabilises a dynastic regime.[98] For Domitian had no biological heirs.[99] The designation of Earinus as Ganymede both honours the association of Domitian with Jupiter at the same time as it subtly points to the real limitations of a divine ideology that lacked a viable

---

[95] Verg. *Aen.* 12. 819–42.   [96] See for instance Theoc. *Id.* 17.   [97] Waters (1963) 200.

[98] Syme (1958) 208 remarks of the chaos following upon Nero's deposition that 'stability demanded a strong monarchy. In this period a strong monarchy meant the existence of heirs'. Thus according to Tacitus, *Hist.* 2. 77, Vespasian had the dominant claim to the throne because he had two sons to succeed him, and the prospect, therefore, of at least two future reigns.

[99] Suet. *Dom.* 3. 1. The date of the child's birth, who died in infancy, is disputed, but it fell between AD 74 and AD 80, before Domitian became emperor. See Southern (1997) 28. See chapter 2 above, 67–8.

future. The seemingly exalted distance of Earinus and his Palatine home from traditional Roman *mores* and normative sexual practices suggests, in this instance, a dangerous instability in the glamorous, new society being developed on the Palatine. Divinely unreal and artificial, the court exists in a never-never land that ignores human and dynastic needs at its peril.

Silv. 1. 2, by contrast with *Silv.* 1. 1 and *Silv.* 3. 4, celebrates marriage and its hopes for a fruitful union. It ends with an exhortation for children who will perpetuate the family line and talents of Stella and Violentilla (266–77). Both Stella and Violentilla boast distinguished lineage, a valued aspect of traditional Roman nobility (70–2, 107–9). They are also praised not only for their beauty but also for their minds and love of poetry that they will transmit to their children (121–2, 172–3).[100]

Although similar in many ways to *Silv.* 1. 2, *Silv.* 3. 4 charts the difference between the world of Statius' friends and the world of the court. The court in *Silv.* 3. 4 revolves around external appearances and hierarchical relationships, not on friendship and shared intellectual interests. It looks to the East in its refashioning of Roman traditions. Earinus represents a new way to acquire status within imperial Rome, not through birth or virtue but through beauty, sex, and the total subjection of personal needs to those of the emperor. He symbolises the powerful, contemporary challenge that the court represents to the hegemony of traditional Roman civic values. *Silv.* 1. 2, on the other hand, celebrates the regrounding and revitalisation of Roman traditions through a marriage that brings together in harmony the best of Greek and Roman culture.

In *Silv.* 1. 2 Statius offers a new definition of Roman nobility in which poetry is put on a par with legal and military ability. Predicting the character of the couple's children, Statius asks for offspring 'who preside over laws and military camps and who compose delightful poetry', *qui leges, qui castra regant, qui carmina ludant* (267). Through the marriage of Stella with Violentilla – a symbolic union between Rome and Naples – Statius constructs a new concept of political and civic service where breeding, brains and skill are properly rewarded, where strong marriages produce children who will assume with honour their parents' mantle, and where poetry plays an important role in the state. The marriage of Stella and Violentilla assumes programmatic importance at the start of the *Silvae*. Through this marriage Rome and Naples, imperial service

---

[100] On Stella as poet see lines 7–10, 94–102, 172–3, 195–9, and 247–55.

and poetry, are prospectively integrated in a creative, fertile union.[101] Violentilla's house, along with her marriage, encodes a protreptic vision of nobility, one that is created, sustained, and perpetuated by a social order built upon friendship and upon a harmonious union between Greece and Rome, the arts and politics, luxury and morality. Juxtaposed with *Silv.* I. I, *Silv.* I. 2 provides a subtle response to the threat of cultural eclipse.

Venus' approval of Violentilla validates this new and powerful construction of Roman nobility based on the arts as well as on virtue. In *Aeneid* 6. 847–53, Anchises exempted the Romans from practice of the arts and sciences, excluding in particular, as Edwards has pointed out, the kind of aetiological poetry in which Iopas, the poet at Dido's court, engages; the suggestion then is that 'imperial missions have no place for such a theme'.[102] Subtly encoded in Violentilla's house, and imagined in the children she will produce, is a redefinition of the imperial mission for the late first century AD as an enterprise founded on a union of traditional authority and enlightened cultural practices. In particular, Statius' protreptic vision makes poetry foundational to this new concept of Roman leadership. In this delightful, imaginative and playful poetic exchange with his friends, Statius fashions Roman identity in his own self-interest.

The house, then, is also the site in which the creative poetic power of Statius is fully displayed. Like Violentilla, Statius brings together Greek and Roman poetic traditions and creatively transforms them, making the house central to a new concept of the *locus amoenus*. Indeed, architectural display and poetic display are closely linked; luxury is the counterpart of bold and innovative literary style. In Statius' *Silvae*, the house becomes an important vehicle through which the poet can subtly express his own poetic virtues. Through the house, moreover, he can meditate on the social function of his poetry and can suggest political and cultural ideals that offer alternatives to those embodied within the court society of Domitian's Palatine.

---

[101] See Pederzani (1991) 22, who argues that Stella and Violentilla constitute ethical figures related to the world of the court; their virtue springs from their balancing of ancient and modern, tradition and contemporary reality, Roman dignity and Greek grace.
[102] M. J. Edwards (1994) 821.

CHAPTER 4

Imperial pastoral: Vopiscus' villa in Silvae *1. 3*

Magnae numina Romae
non ita cantari debent, ut ovile Menalcae.
Calpurnius Siculus, *Eclogue* 4. 10–11

If you possessed too delightful (*amoenior*) a villa in Domitian's reign, Pliny tells us in the *Panegyricus*, the emperor was likely to snatch it away for his own private use.[1] The *Silvae*, however, do not seem to suggest that owning a fine villa under the last of the Flavians was a risky investment. Rather, four of these poems (1. 3, 2. 2, 2. 3, and 3. 1) openly celebrate the villas of Statius' friends and enthuse over their superb location and landscape design, their opulent decoration, their contemporary amenities, and their privacy. If it seems prudent to discard here Pliny's image of the acquisitive, tyrannical emperor, nonetheless, as we shall see, in Statius' descriptive poems the emperor and the villa are not unrelated. Although these poems offer little in the way of systematic architectural detail, they provide yet another site for meditation upon the relationship between imperial and poetic authority.

Statius' villa poems testify to a new important notion in imperial culture, namely, as Bodel puts it, 'that the domestic environment in which a gentleman cultivated his leisure was itself worthy of poetic commemoration.'[2] Indeed, with these poems about the Roman villa, Statius became the founder of a new poetic genre, the villa or country-house poem. But this literary innovation has not been widely recognised. Indeed, these poems have been eclipsed by the fame of Pliny's letters on his villas (especially 2. 17 and 5. 6) and Martial's epigrams on rural life. Pavlovskis, for instance, regards Statius' villa poems as poetic counterparts to Pliny's prose epistles about his villas.[3] Thus she does not take account of a fundamental difference between them, namely that Pliny describes his villas from the point of view of a landlord, whereas Statius

---

[1] Plin. *Pan.* 50. 5   [2] Bodel (1997) 17.   [3] Pavlovskis (1973) 1.

always represents himself as a guest.[4] The basis of Statius' perceptual, interpretive responses to his friends' villas is thus entirely different from that of Pliny, who uses the descriptive epistle to conduct his readers on a self-promoting tour of his properties.[5] Martial's approach to the villa is also different from that of Statius. Not only are his several epigrams about villas short, of course; they also have a physicality alien to Statius' villa poems, for they focus on food, drink, hunting, and sex as rural occupations. In addition, slaves and rural labourers, absent from Statius' poems, intermingle with owner and guest.[6]

Critics have argued that the country-house poem of English literature, which first makes its appearance in the seventeenth century, drew its inspiration from Martial's epigrams on villas, in particular *Epigram* 3. 58.[7] But, as I have argued elsewhere, Statius' villa poems also influenced the genre of the English country-house poem, in particular its foundational poem, Ben Jonson's 'To Penshurst'.[8] Jonson derived from Statius the concept of a full-length poem that united the description of a country house with the encomium of its owner and that was founded upon common topoi such as the generosity of nature, its harmony with human needs, and the alignment of the house with the character of its owner.

Williams criticised the country-house poem of English literary tradition as an artificial genre, a celebration of exploitative opulence that mystifies the rural economy by removing the notion of labour – and indeed the labourers themselves.[9] Later critics however have argued that

---

[4] Bek (1976) 162 makes this important distinction at the start of her brief discussion of *Silv.* 1. 3.

[5] See Bodel (1997) 17 who suggests that Pliny's letters on his villas are meant to perpetuate his reputation as a cultured and highly talented gentleman.

[6] On food as a metaphor for the variegated style, theme and persona of Martial's poetry see Gowers (1993) 245–67

[7] Wayne (1984) 193 suggests that Horace, Martial, and Juvenal, along with myths of the Golden Age, provide the origins of the country-house poem. Cubeta (1963) 17 more specifically argues that Penshurst is conceived as a combination of Bassus' and Faustinus' farms in Mart. 3. 58. McClung (1977) 16–17 is unusual among critics in referring to Statius' villa poems at all, but he dismisses any idea of their influence upon Jonson's poem in a footnote (17, n. 10).

[8] Newlands (1988). Jonson's poetry owed a considerable debt to Statius' *Silvae*. 'To Penshurst' belongs to a collection called *The Forest*. The epigraph to another of Jonson's collections of poetry, *Underwood*, explains the meaning of *silva* with reference to the classical definition of a varied poetic collection. Fowler (1982) acknowledges Jonson's debt to Statius' use of the term *silva* but does not explore the relationship between the poetic texts beyond this theoretical basis. For specific verbal allusions to Statius' *Silvae* in Jonson's poetry see Herford, Simpson and Simpson (1952).

[9] Williams (1973) attacks pastoral poetry and the country-house poem on the grounds that they recreate an artificial world remote from the harsh realities of rural life (30–47). His work has been widely recognised as a necessary starting point for any investigation of the politics of place within the formation of cultural identity. See Maclean, Landry, and Ward (1999) for a re-evaluation of Williams's critical importance and the development of his work in new directions.

although the genre occludes the processes of labour and the circulation of capital, it is nonetheless a literary form that looks beyond the specific occasion of praise. Wayne for instance has argued that in 'To Penshurst' Jonson invents a form that investigates social and historical change.[10] The 'invention' in fact belongs to Statius. From Statius' *Silvae* Jonson learned the possibilities of employing the country-house poem as a vehicle for social and political analysis.

The focus of this chapter will be the villa poem placed first in Statius' collection, *Silv.* 1. 3. This poem honours a wealthy literary friend, Manilius Vopiscus, through the description of his estate. As in *Silv.* 1. 2, the concept of space and that of social and cultural identity are closely related. Here the estate – the house along with the garden with which the buildings were closely articulated – reflects the prosperity of Empire in its wealth, its order, its superb technology, and its control of nature. At the same time, the estate represents also a place of withdrawal for its owner, where poetry and philosophy can be practised in peaceful seclusion. Poetry in particular is central to Statius' concept of the villa and its landscape. Empire makes possible the pastoral dream of a landscape harmoniously attuned to poetic composition.

Through the villa then, Statius articulates a new form of social and cultural identity made possible by the benefits of Empire, that of the independent, wealthy man of letters who is entirely divorced in his pursuits from the world of imperial affairs. Yet the seclusion made possible by imperial prosperity also raises questions about the value and place of poetry that is dependent on comfortable material circumstances and that is composed and practised outside the parameters of Rome and its court.[11] But before we look in detail at *Silv.* 1. 3, let us first look briefly at the general concept of the villa in Roman thought.

THE VILLA

In Ackerman's comprehensive study of the villa and country house, the Roman villa is described as 'a building in the country designed for its owner's enjoyment and relaxation'.[12] 'Designed' is a significant word, for the villa rested upon the notion of a 'designer nature', fashioned to suit the urbanised tastes of its occupants for comfort and luxury. Nature existed to be dominated and exploited by humans. Ackerman

---

[10] Wayne (1984) 28.   [11] A point made also by Myers (2000) 125–38.   [12] Ackerman (1985) 9.

asserts that what distinguishes a villa from a farm (or the *villa rustica*) is the 'pleasure factor'.[13] The luxury villa of imperial times rested upon a paradox. Although country living was extolled over living in town, the villa was economically, socially and artistically dependent on urban culture. Imperial Romans did not value rusticity; their villas provided all the comforts of the city without the inconveniences of noise, dirt, and crowds. Paradoxically then, the country villa represented 'the desirable end of urban aspirations'.[14] Indeed, as Bodel has suggested, in the country there was even greater scope for innovative forms of architectural display than in the town, since social constraints upon self-expression could be somewhat relaxed.[15]

Three hundred years before Statius wrote his *Silvae*, Cato the Elder conceived of the villa as a working farm geared to maximum profit, not as a place for relaxation and pleasure. Even at that time, however, an ideological shift was taking place in the concept of the villa. In 184 BCE Scipio Africanus retired in political disgrace to his villa on the Campanian coast.[16] He was the first documented aristocratic Roman known to possess a country villa.[17] The villa thereafter became increasingly associated with *otium*, the life of leisure, and the agricultural economy that was necessary to support such a life was concealed behind elegant and grand buildings designed for personal enjoyment but also for impressive display of the owner's wealth and influence. For the facade of architectural magnificence made public the owner's high social status; in advertising leisure, the villa advertised the wealth, the tastes, and local influence of its owner.

A similar development is observable with the English country house, the Roman villa's descendant. Friedman has defined the country house as a place divorced from its agricultural context. Discussing the Elizabethan country house Wollaton Hall, she argues that 'emphasis on the niceties of architectural style and on increased spatial segregation of the family from the agricultural functions of the estate . . . make Wollaton Hall a country house rather than a house in the country'.[18] The same distinction can apply to the Roman villa. The agricultural underpinnings of the great Roman country houses were subordinated to the impulse for architectural display. The letters of Pliny, the poems of Statius, and the numerous wall-paintings of Roman villas emphasise innovative architecture and landscape design, not agricultural production. The spread

[13] Ackerman (1985) 9. For the identification of the three types of villa, *villa rustica, villa suburbana,* and *villa maritima,* see McKay (1975) 100–35.
[14] Maclean, Landry, and Ward (1999) 5.   [15] Bodel (1997) 7.   [16] Livy 38. 52. 1.
[17] D'Arms (1970) 1.   [18] Friedman (1989) 13.

of villas through the Italian countryside and in Campania in particular has been commonly interpreted as the aristocracy's response to their political disenfranchisement in the imperial age.[19] Yet it was the wealth of Empire that made these country villas possible. The economic prosperity of Rome as the dominant colonial power of the Mediterranean allowed the aristocracy to build their villas from expensive, gorgeous materials culled from all over the Empire and to fill them, moreover, with wonderful works of art from Greece. The abundant resources of Empire made possible then the cultivation of rural leisure in magnificent style. Aesthetically as well as economically the Roman villa and the Roman provinces were interdependent. Thus the villa was not a solitary retreat; it served as a site both for pleasure and for the bold articulation of personal power, interests, and worth.

Indeed, even if a villa did not include a working farm, it remained, it seems, an important centre of local patronage.[20] In the villa of the imperial period there was no clear division between public and private space.[21] The placement of the peristyle instead of the atrium at the front of the house, for instance, allowed the owner to present himself in a theatrical setting of both physical and social dominance.[22] The peristyle, then, functioned not as a garden of withdrawal but as a dramatic site where business, through the conduits of patronage and friendship, could be conducted.[23] As Wallace-Hadrill argues, 'the luxurious "private" life of the rich and powerful of the imperial period is precisely their public facade, and access to it is a privilege carefully guarded'.[24]

---

[19] Thus for instance Bek (1976) 164, who argues that Pliny the Younger enjoyed a 'splendid isolation' in his villas that for Cicero was an unobtainable privilege. Cicero complains that his villa at Cumae was a miniature Rome, such was the crowd of visitors (*Att.* 5. 2). Yet Pliny uses his villas as temporary retreats from Rome in which he can carry on his work for the capital, while also maintaining his interests in the local community. He goes hunting on horseback with his writing tablets, and he tries to do his duty as landowner – hearing complaints, checking accounts, managing property. See for instance *Ep.* 5. 14. 8 and *Ep.* 9. 36. 1–4.

[20] Indeed, as Wallace-Hadrill argues (1994) 51, this is the period when our literary sources give fullest attestation to the rituals of patronage.

[21] Thébert (1987) 321–34 makes the point that the Romans had a rather 'distended view of private life' that is reflected in the fluid design of their houses. 'It would be a mistake to suppose that a Roman house was an incoherent juxtaposition of two distinct areas, one essentially private, the other essentially public' (321). He sums up: 'Individuals could dwell in a house in many different ways, ranging from isolation to the receiving of large numbers of visitors with whom the owner was not on intimate terms' (353).

[22] Wallace-Hadrill (1994) 51–52. Vitruv. *De arch.* 6. 3 points out that in the *villa* the relative positions of the peristyle and the atrium are reversed from those of the townhouse.

[23] Plin. *Ep.* 9. 7, acknowledges the theatricality of the villa by calling his villas at Como 'Tragedy' and 'Comedy'.

[24] Wallace-Hadrill (1994) 52.

But since architectural display was often associated with new wealth, the villa became a target of a moral discourse against luxury that was fairly consistent in its images and vocabulary through the periods of the late Republic and early Empire.[25] In Augustan literature in particular the villa appears as a common figure of excessive consumption and immoderate pleasure, symptoms of moral decline.[26] Whitehorne has argued that the image of 'the ambitious builder' of private mansions became a stock type in Roman literary discourse, an 'extremely useful literary peg on which to hang a variety of ideas concerned with *luxuria*, moral decadence and the place of man in nature and society'.[27] The association of the villa and its builder with moral decadence, however, can be understood as deriving in part from a competitive social system in which architectural display represented new wealth and a possible threat, therefore, to the established social as well as moral order.[28] Moral anxiety was closely implicated with anxiety about social change.

True, as I mentioned in the introduction, at the same time there is evidence that social change also brought a more positive attitude towards leisure as well as towards luxury.[29] Republican Romans had nourished a long-standing suspicion of leisure; the proper occupation of a respected Roman male during the Republic was *negotium*, not *otium*.[30] The works of Seneca, however, reveal a shift in élite attitudes towards leisure. As Griffin has argued, Seneca reveals acute anxieties about the question of political participation, given the instability of a career in imperial service; in grappling with the question of '*res publica* vs. *otium*' he promotes the value of a 'leisured' life devoted to philosophy.[31] But

---

[25] See Edwards (1993) 144. See also her detailed discussion of the house and luxury in chapter 4, 137–72. A brief, useful discussion is also found in Beagon (1992) 75–9.

[26] There were also valid economic as well as ethical concerns influencing the discourse against the villa: houses could catch fire, or they could collapse in ruin, creating fear and constant worry for occupants and owner and, in the worst instance, bodily harm and financial ruin. See chapter 3, note 26 above.

[27] Whitehorne (1969) 37.

[28] Wallace-Hadrill (1990) especially 90–2. As he has argued, 'by offering new symbols to define social dominance, luxury threatens to redefine the social structure'.

[29] Cic. *Fam.* 9. 6. 5 chafes in his retirement from public affairs, despite his engagement in intellectual pursuits. On shifting cultural attitudes towards *otium* from the Republic through to the early Empire see André (1966), Griffin (1976) 315–66, and Connors (2000). D'Arms (1970) chapters 1 and 2 provides an excellent discussion of the social and cultural attitudes towards *otium* in the late Republic. On the cultural significance of the villa in the early Empire see now Myers (2000) 108–11.

[30] Varro *Rust.* 3. 2. 3–11, insisted that a villa, no matter how luxurious, should be self-sufficient.

[31] Griffin (1976) 315–66.

otium did not necessarily entail political and intellectual withdrawal. The imperial state itself sanctioned *otium* through frequent public entertainments.

The attractiveness of villa culture in the popular mentality can be seen from the many villa paintings that decorated modest Campanian homes, which seem to express aspirations for both an opulent leisure and high social status – 'large pictures for small dreams' as Zanker puts it.[32] Indeed, Zanker's study of the houses of Pompeii argues that their decoration, much of it dating from the Flavian period, was heavily influenced by the culture of the luxury villa: 'what had once been decried as corrupting *luxuria* was now obviously perceived, in the context of domestic space and its associated symbolic forms, as an important value, in some sense embodying abundance and enjoyment'.[33] Moreover, as Connors suggests, readers of the *Silvae*, particularly his villa poems, could at the very least imagine that they too shared in the extravagant wealth that made leisure possible.[34] The villa of the late first century AD, therefore, was broadly implicated in the diffusion of ideas about wealth, social status and artistic taste; it stood at the heart of social, moral and political change.

With his foundation of a new poetic genre, the villa poem, Statius boldly introduced to conservative literary tradition a social phenomenon fraught with contradiction.[35] The villa was the object of ethical criticism as a symbol of decadent luxury; it was also the object of popular aspirations for a life of leisure and wealth. Associated with political withdrawal from Rome, it was often at the same time the lively centre of local political life and a showcase of imperial wealth and power. The villa is the pre-eminent symbol of luxury in Statius' *Silvae*. Expensive decoration and bold architectural display are predominantly represented as positive and wonderful features of the villa. Statius thus found in the villa a powerful figure that embodied significant tensions within society of the late first century AD.

Running counter to the strong strain in Roman, and specifically Augustan, moral discourse, Statius' villa poems are provocative in their bold endorsement of luxury. Private architecture, a frequent sign in his Augustan predecessors of dubious morality, assumes a new role in Statius' poetry as an expression of high aspirations. As I suggested in the introduction, the villa poems in particular participate in, and even propel, a shift in attitudes towards luxury. Even more provocatively, however, they

---

[32] Zanker (1998) 184–6.   [33] Zanker (1998) 23.   [34] Connors (2000) 508.
[35] *Silv.* 1 .3, 2. 2, 2. 3, 3. 1.

redefine luxury as the enabler of virtue. In Statius' villa poetry luxury is celebrated as a sign not of moral decadence but as an essential component of moral virtue and philosophical value. The resources of wealth, technology, and nature create enjoyment and abundance that are not ends in themselves but means by which an owner can be free to practise poetry and philosophy; indeed, the villa landscape is assimilated to poetic ideals. The villa thus assumes in Statius' poetry a larger significance as a complex figure of the intellectual life. Moreover, the luxury of the villa is a counterpart to the 'luxury' of Statius' dazzling style in the *Silvae*. Architectural and literary brilliance complement one another and promote the villa poem as an important new genre within Flavian culture.

Statius' villa poems, then, do more than validate popular aspirations for comfort and wealth. They should be seen as imaginative, literary responses to the magnificent houses of his friends, not as guides to the architecture and social *mores* of the period. In their articulation of the special relationship between space and social and cultural identity, these poems invite us to look beyond the confines of privilege and the estate to broader cultural and ethical concerns. Through metonymy, for instance, the villa can act on one level as a model of the inner state; on another level it can act as a model for society as a whole.[36] Indeed, it can provide a special vantage point for the scrutiny of public ambition as well as for the condition of both poet and literature. Thus, as I shall argue later in this chapter, Statius makes the villa central to a new form of pastoral revitalised for the imperial age.

Silv. 1. 3 follows the brief yet richly evocative description of Violentilla's town house in *Silv.* 1. 2. It is the first full-length villa poem in Latin literature, and it can therefore be regarded as programmatic for a new type of poetry. Wonder and joy, rather than a zeal for systematic description, inform Statius' response to Vopiscus' home. Works of art abound (47–51); there is a wonderful mosaic floor (53–6); Statius feels he is treading on riches (53); and yet the reader has little idea in what parts of the house these marvels are to be found. Although the poet gives the impression of a response to the villa that is direct and immediate, he is in fact recollecting his day spent on Vopiscus' estate: *o longum memoranda dies* (13). Viewing here involves remembering and writing. Thus, when Statius says that his emotions make it difficult for him to know where to begin, what to put in the middle, or where to

---

[36] On metonymy as a fundamental mode of the country-house poem see Molesworth (1968) 7–9.

end (34), he is in fact drawing attention to the verbal processes of selection, amplification, and reordering endemic to the ecphrastic text. He thus invites simultaneously the reader's emotional engagement and critical detachment. Through expressions of wonder and joy Statius stresses the privileged nature of his viewing, and consequently of his writing about it. An observer and guest of Vopiscus' estate, not a user like Pliny, he presents himself to the reader not as an architectural guide but as an outsider who has temporary access to a very special privilege.[37] Description then includes the emotions and judgments of the describer as well as the visible appearance of the work being described.[38] And we as readers are consequently granted the critical privilege of reading the new type of poem developed in the *Silvae*, the villa poem.

Of course, with this type of response the poem moves beyond the immediate subject of the estate to honour the patron and host, Vopiscus. Statius' villa poems praise the owners through their properties; the properties in turn define their owners. Yet the poem goes well beyond praise of friend and host. Statius fashions Vopiscus' villa as the idealised site for poetic, not agricultural production, making it central to a new form of pastoral in which the boundaries between city and country are permeable rather than rigidly opposed.

My discussion of *Silv.* 1. 3 will focus upon two main areas of innovation: first, the poem's provocative challenge of the literary discourse against luxury. Private architecture is used in the villa poem both as a sign of ethical supremacy and of the writer's dynamic relationship to a literary tradition that he reveres, audaciously redefines, and develops in new directions. Second, I will focus on Statius' bold rewriting of pastoral in the villa poem. Like Statius' other villa poems, *Silv.* 1. 3 goes beyond the realm of social compliment to reflect more widely on the role of literature and philosophy within Flavian society and the obligations of the intellectual to the state.

LUXURY REDEEMED

The villa of Manilius Vopiscus was situated at Tibur. His precise identity remains uncertain. There is epigraphic evidence from AD 60 and 114 of two Vopisci, both of consular rank, and perhaps father and son.[39] We cannot tell however whether the elder Vopiscus was Statius' friend.

---

[37] Bek (1976) 161–2.   [38] Becker (1992) 11–12.
[39] On the epigraphic evidence for the Vopisci see Cancik (1978) 120–1.

Statius' poem provides no suggestion of a political career for Vopiscus or any insight into the origins of Vopiscus' wealth. It does not explain the circumstances that brought Statius to Vopiscus' villa one memorable day (13), nor does it define the relationship between Statius and Vopiscus. The pastoral atmosphere excludes such practical details. The preface to Book 1, however, describes Manilius Vopiscus as 'a very erudite man especially concerned with the rescue of a declining literature from decay': *vir eruditissimus et qui praecipue vindicat a situ litteras iam paene fugientes* (*praef.* 1. 24–5). This provides our only direct testimony for Statius' Vopiscus. He is introduced in Statius' poetry as a man of letters, not as an entrepreneur or tycoon. Poetry shapes his identity and that of his estate.

There is no epigraphic evidence for the situation of Vopiscus' villa at Tibur, although many villas were built there, since it was a popular resort, conveniently close to Rome and famed for its coolness.[40] *Silv.* 1. 3 however mentions no other villas, and makes no reference to the famous landmarks of Tibur such as the acropolis with its two temples.[41] The villa of Statius' first villa poem is introduced in exalted isolation. The description therefore is focussed on the poet's response to the landscape and its buildings. Yet Tibur, as the opening lines of the poem suggest, is important as a literary construct rather than as a geographical site (1–8):

> Cernere facundi Tibur glaciale Vopisci
> siquis et inserto geminos Aniene penates
> aut potuit sociae commercia noscere ripae
> certantesque sibi dominum defendere villas,
> illum nec calido latravit Sirius astro
> nec gravis aspexit Nemeae frondentis alumnus:
> talis hiems tectis, frangunt sic improba solem
> frigora, Pisaeumque domus non aestuat annum.

If anyone has had the opportunity to view the cool Tibur of eloquent Vopiscus or to become familiar with the twin *penates* threaded by the Anio or the interchange between each sociable bank and the villas competing to defend their master for themselves, then Sirius with his hot star has never barked at him nor has the oppressive offspring of leafy Nemea gazed at him: there is such a wintry coolness in the buildings, a persistent chill breaks the heat of the sun; the house does not swelter through the season of the Olympian games.

---

[40] Cancik (1978) 123; Troxler-Keller (1964) 133–4.   [41] Cancik (1978) 122.

The poem opens with an elegant, eight-line period in ornate style. Almost every noun is adorned with an adjective, and the importance of the occasion and the place is signalled by the elaborate mythological periphrases for time (5–6, 8). The ornamentation of these first lines suggests a luxury of style that complements the luxury of the villa, composed of two enormous, richly adorned mansions in which artifice triumphs over the natural hostility of climate. As in *Silv.* 1. 1, Statius' enthusiastic and elaborate response here to Vopiscus' villa marks the importance not only of the villa and Vopiscus but also of his new kind of poem. The juxtaposition of *facundi* (describing Vopiscus) with *Tibur* in the opening line locates the villa suggestively in a landscape that is shaped by literary tradition as much as by social and cultural circumstances. For Tibur had been made famous in Horace's fourth Book of *Odes* as the new Roman site of poetic inspiration, and Horace was an influential poet for Statius in his *Silvae*.[42]

Vollmer notes that Statius characteristically pays great attention to the openings of his poems.[43] The first word of the poem, *cernere*, alerts us to the importance of the viewer, here the poet, in the construction of the villa's meaning (1–8). Moreover, the opening verb *cernere* also serves as a warning that we should not regard this first villa poem as a guidebook, for ecphrastic texts are dubious sources of archaeological data. Although the rhetorical handbooks which deal with ecphrasis stress that its goal is to make the reader see vividly what is being described, they also suggest that the perceptual response of the viewer, and his interpretation of visual phenomena, is part of ecphrasis.[44] Indeed, the question of point of view, of focalisation, is crucial to this poem as it is to ecphrasis in general.[45] Two types of interaction are at work in the ecphrastic poem: that between the describer and the work described, and that between the describer and the audience.[46] Although in *Silv.* 1. 3 the viewer is Statius himself, the opening lines declare that a common perception and experience bind anyone (*siquis*, 2) who has seen Vopiscus' villa. The reader is thus invited in these opening lines to share in the viewer's experience and adopt his enthusiastic and learned perspective on the

---

[42] Hardie (1983) 170 suggests that the work which Statius held in highest esteem was the *Odes* of Horace. In Book 4 of the *Silvae* he modelled two of his poems, 4. 5 and 4. 7, upon the Horatian ode.

[43] Vollmer (1898) 265 on *Silv.* 1. 3. 1.

[44] Becker (1995) 24–31 quotes the initial definition of Aelius Theon, probably of the first century AD and basically repeated in the other handbooks: '[ecphrasis is] descriptive language bringing that which is being made manifest vividly before the sight' (25).

[45] Fowler (1991) 28–29.   [46] Becker (1992) 13.

wonders of Vopiscus' estate. As readers of this poem, we too become
viewers and critics.[47]

In these opening lines, Statius boldly throws down the gauntlet to
the critics of luxury, particularly Horace. The central position of Tibur
in the opening line as well as its juxtaposition with *facundi* (1) boldly
connects Vopiscus with the Augustan poet for, like Horace in *Carm.* 4. 2.
27–32 and 4. 3. 10–12, Vopiscus is presented as a poet living in Tibur.[48]
Yet Horace dissociates Tibur from its well-known villa culture. Tibur in
Horace's poetry is primarily described in terms of the idyllic features of
shade, water and song – a type of landscape often classified as a *locus
amoenus*.[49] This was generally conceived as a place of natural beauty
and the ideal environment for philosophy and poetry.[50] Moreover, this
minimalist landscape of only water and trees is assimilated in Horace's
poetry to the Epicurean landscape of Lucretius' *De Rerum Natura*, which,
through its simple elements of trees, water, and shade, symbolises the
correct way of living, untrammelled by desires for luxurious possessions
(2. 20–33).[51] The villa on the other hand appears frequently in Horace's
poetry as a perversion of nature, a symbol of physical and moral excess.[52]
For Horace, the amenities made possible by technology and riches are
unnecessary and the desire for them is irrational.[53] Although Horace
himself owned a villa, the so-called Sabine farm, its buildings, which
have been revealed by archaeologists to have been fairly substantial, are

---

[47] But, as Becker (1992) points out, this too involves us in a double movement of engagement
and withdrawal, for even as the writer encourages his readers to enter his world, we are made
'aware of our relationship to the describer and the language of the description' (14). Thus we
too engage in the act of interpretation at a further remove than the poet from the object of
description. These ideas are elaborated upon in Becker (1995).

[48] Tibur appears in Hor. *Carm.* 1. 7, 1. 18, 2. 6, 4. 2, and 4. 3.

[49] The Romans associated *amoenus* etymologically with either *amor* (Servius, on *Aen.* 6. 638) or
with *munus* (Servius on *Aen.* 5. 734). Although Servius defines the *locus amoenus* as 'places full
of pleasure from which no profit is derived' (*solius voluptatis . . . unde nullus fructus exsolvitur*), it is
frequently associated with fertility. See *TLL* i. 1962. 29–53; Ernout-Meillet 44.

[50] These are the minimum features of the *locus amoenus* as described by Curtius (1973) 195. Other
features that Curtius describes are a breeze, birdsong, and flowers. See also the discussion of
the *locus amoenus* in Rosenmeyer (1969) 179–205; also his critique of the unnecessary distinction
Curtius makes between 'grove' and 'pleasance' (189–90).

[51] In his later *Odes*, as Troxler-Keller (1964) 131–62 has argued, Horace removes from the landscape
of Tibur any of the details of daily living that colour his Sabine landscapes. Tibur was thus more
easily accommodated to an ideal of civic poetry that was rooted in the Italian countryside.

[52] See Nisbet and Hubbard (1978) on *Carm.* 2. 18, 288–92 and 2. 15, 241–4; Edwards (1993) 139–41.
The extravagant builder of these villas, moreover, lacks an understanding of the inevitability of
death that levels all social hierarchies. See Pearcy (1977).

[53] See the discussion of *Epist.* 1. 10 in Schmidt (1997) 146–54. Schmidt demonstrates that the
contrast between *rus* and *urbs* at the poem's start develops through the opposition of wealth and
poverty into a contrast between freedom and its lack.

never described.[54] Like Tibur, the Sabine farm is a *locus amoenus*.[55] It figures in Horace's poetry as a symbol of the moderate life devoted to poetry and virtue.[56] Thus for instance *Carm.* 2. 18 begins with Horace's proud assertion that his Sabine farm possesses no ivory or golden ceiling, no columns of foreign marble (1–5).

Statius on the other hand unashamedly conveys his enthusiasm for the luxury of Vopiscus' property. There are no houses in Horace's Tibur, just water, trees and shade.[57] But in Vopiscus' Tibur water and trees function as part of an opulent estate; the coolness created by shade in the *locus amoenus* is procured here by the architectural design of the house. The house itself is built of the most expensive materials and enjoys the amenities of the latest technology. Statius tells us, for instance, of golden roof beams, citron wood door posts, gleaming marble, piped water in every bedroom (35–7). Furthermore, Vopiscus is a collector of precious works of art – although it is typical of the magical, pastoral atmosphere of the villa that nothing is said about their origins. The house is adorned with ancient, lifelike sculptures of precious gold, silver and bronze; there is precious jewellery too (47–51).[58] Statius is so overwhelmed, he claims he was treading unaware on riches, *calcabam necopinus opes* (53). Indeed, Vopiscus' mansion is so vast that Statius can talk of it in the plural, *villas* (4). His home is made up of two symmetrical sets of buildings that match one another on either side of the river Anio. The man is so rich that he has doubles of everything!

Vopiscus' villa estate seems far then from the Epicurean or Horatian ideal of moderation, for it is vast, elaborately designed, and richly decorated and equipped. Yet Statius suggests Vopiscus' adherence to Epicureanism through the concluding comment that Epicurus would have preferred Vopiscus' estate to his own gardens in Athens (93–4). Is

---

54 On the archaeological remains of Horace's villa and their lack of correspondence with details in the poem, see Schmidt (1997) 13–52. Schmidt argues that we should not read Horace's poems for topographical and architectural veracity; rather, the poems that refer to the Sabine farm articulate a poetic landscape.

55 Hor. *Carm.* 1. 17. 1; *Epist.* 1. 10. 6, 1. 14. 20, and 1. 16. 15.

56 Schmidt (1997) especially 53–5 argues that the central principle of the Sabine farm is moderation, articulated in different ways in the three genres of satire, ode, and epistle.

57 Horace's first description of Tibur occurs in *Carm.* 1. 7. 13–14, 20–21. There the topographical details of the Anio and the groves of Tiburnus localise the *locus amoenus* in a famous Italian resort without, however, mention of people or houses; Tibur is a site distinguished by its rushing water, its trees, and thick shade.

58 Vollmer (1898) 273–4 on *Silv.* 1. 3. 50 assumes that Statius here is describing the decoration of the baths. But Statius' enthusiastic style does not allow for such certainty as to location. Note too *dum vagor* ('while I wander around', 52) which suggests Statius' unsystematic approach to description.

this not stretching a point too far? Yet such an exaggerated gesture is typical of Statius' boldness in the *Silvae*. As we shall see, Statius' first villa poem, *Silv.* 1. 3, directly evokes the hostile tradition against luxury in order to disarm it.

The extravagance of the house is fully matched by the extravagance of nature's own designs. Contrary to moralising strictures against architectural excess, Vopiscus' house is in harmony with its environment, not in violation of it. Roman gardens, in any event, were conceived as architectural elements, an extension of the house that was adapted to the building's disposition.[59] But Statius tells us little of how the garden was organised. Rather, the work of taming a landscape is effaced by the magical cooperation of nature with human needs. Like the house, nature is luxurious: *non largius usquam | indulsit natura sibi* ('nowhere else has nature indulged itself so abundantly', 16–17). On Vopiscus' estate, the pastoral ideal of nature unadulterated by human intervention is assimilated here to a georgic ideal of an improved landscape through the willingness of nature to cooperate with human needs; the georgic ideal in turn is assimilated to the pastoral ideal through a technology that celebrates art while occluding all notion of human labour.

Thus the villa landscape is fashioned in *Silv.* 1. 3 as the new *locus amoenus*, formed uniquely and seemingly effortlessly from the resources of technology as well as the cooperation of nature; the ideal site for poetry and the practice of virtue is now centred on a luxurious house and its carefully landscaped grounds.[60] The key features of the *locus amoenus*, water, trees, and shade, are boldly assimilated to those of the villa, which dominates the landscape. The river Anio, for instance, is 'threaded through' the twin mansions, as if the buildings had existed prior to the river, and its water is channelled and piped through rooms (37) and into baths (43–6); the trees are landscaped to provide views and shade (17–19, 40); shade itself is provided by the artful design of the house (1–8).

At the beginning of *Silv.* 1. 3, then, Statius suggests that his new poem poses a direct challenge to Horace. Tibur, the home of another eloquent poet, is now conceived as a villa landscape that links material values

---

[59] Grimal (1969) chapter 8 argues that the architecture forces the garden into a decorative frame for its constructions, while the garden in turn becomes a form of architecture (271).

[60] *Amoenitas* is a quality also attached to the Roman villa from late Republican times. See D'Arms (1970) 47–8; *TLL amoenitas* i. 1961. 4–14. Pliny quite freely attaches this quality to his own villas. Indeed, he applies the superlative form of the adjective *amoenus* to the villa, a form that seems only to occur at this period. See Plin. *Ep.* 1. 3. 1, 2. 17. 25, 5. 6. 3, 5. 6. 32, 9. 7. 3, 8. 18. 8; Tac. *Hist.* 3. 30.

to poetic and ethical ones. To illustrate my point further, let me look at Horace's *Epistles* 1. 10, which is a key work in the Augustan poet's programmatic opposition to the luxuries of the villa. Here, in an affectionate letter to his friend Aristius Fuscus, Horace praises the country with a string of questions that essentially beg the question of the inferiority of urban luxuries.[61] I shall briefly consider three of Horace's examples.

For instance, Horace provocatively asks his friend whether 'grass gleams or smells worse than a mosaic floor' (*deterius Libycis olet aut nitet herba lapillis*, 19)? Vopiscus' villa has a very special mosaic floor, of the type known as the 'unswept pavement' (55–6).[62] In *Silv.* 1. 3 this floor, however, represents an improvement upon nature, one that is 'justified' since the earth rejoices in its transformation, *varias ubi picta per artes | gaudet humus* ('where the decorated earth rejoices in its varied arts', 55–6). The grateful response of nature suggests that Vopiscus can be seen as a benefactor and civiliser whose luxuries benefit the land. Indeed, the light streaming from the ceiling and reflecting the vivid colour of the floor (53–6) forms another image of silent, harmonious reciprocity between art and nature, here located within the house itself.

Horace further provokes Aristius Fuscus by asking whether piped water is superior to an open stream (20–1):

> purior in vicis aqua tendit rumpere plumbum,
> quam quae per pronum trepidat cum murmure rivum?

Is water struggling to burst through the lead pipes in the streets purer than the water that purls with a murmur through the running brook?

Horace here denigrates, for the purpose of good-natured argument, the city dweller's reliance on the Roman system of water distribution through aqueducts and pipes, one of the enduring contributions of Roman technology to civilisation. The abundance of water and its diversion for plumbing are among the prominent marvels of Vopiscus' estate. Indeed, the perfect villa had to possess water in profusion.[63] One drawback of Pliny's Laurentine villa, for instance, was its lack of water.[64] On Vopiscus' estate, there is plumbing in all the bedrooms (37) and wonderful baths (43–6); one can dine at tables set on either bank and enjoy the sight of the clear pools of water, the deep fountains, and the Marcian aqueduct

---

[61] See Mayer (1994) 183 on *Epist.* 1. 10. 15–21.   [62] Plin. *HN* 36. 60. 184.
[63] Grimal (1969) 293.   [64] Plin. *Ep.* 2. 17. 25.

itself, which crosses under the river Anio on Vopiscus' territory, bearing
its piped water to Rome (64–9):[65]

> Quid referam alternas gemino super aggere mensas
> albentesque lacus altosque in gurgite fontes,
> teque, per obliquum penitus quae laberis amnem,
> Marcia, et audaci transcurris flumina plumbo,
> ne solum Ioniis sub fluctibus Elidis amnem
> dulcis ad Aetnaeos deducat semita portus?

What shall I say of the matching dining tables on the twin banks, the clear lakes,
the deep-pooled springs, and you, Marcia, who glide underground across the
depths of the stream, traversing the river with audacious lead, so that the channel
which draws the river of Elis under the Ionian waves to a Sicilian harbour is not
alone in its fresh, sweet water?

Natural and architectural pleasures are here breathlessly combined,
but the climax of this period is the aqueduct, the modern invention
humorously and outrageously compared to the traditional figure of the
underground river Alpheus (66–7). Horace's lines in *Epist.* 1. 10 suggest
the violent straining of the water to burst out of the pipes, an unnatural
confinement (*tendit, rumpere,* 20). On Vopiscus' estate the piped water
glides, *laberis* (66), a peaceful action; there is no struggle to break its bonds.
But *audaci*, which modifies *plumbo* (67), suggests the heroic, pioneering
spirit of Roman technology. The piped water represents material advance
rather than moral decadence. Indeed, the aqueduct points to the self-
sufficiency of the estate which has all the amenities to be found in the
capital city. Marcia, personified, represents a new mythical figure being
fashioned for Flavian society, worthy of comparison in its wonderful
structure and course with the legendary Alpheus celebrated by Virgil and
Ovid.[66] Thus, the aqueduct symbolically marks the close identification
of the estate with literary tradition as well as with urban values and
imperial prosperity.

Moreover, Statius takes away the negative valuation of technology as
the despoiler of nature by again showing that nature enjoys improvement.
The river deities of the Anio and its tributaries, the Tiburnus and Albula,
come at night to enjoy the beautiful, clear waters (70–5). Although baths
that use the Anio's water have been built on its banks (43–6), there is
no sense here that the river, though treated like a servant, is resistant or
hostile in any way to its confinement. The Anio is a most gentle stream,

---

[65] On the meaning of *alternas... mensas* as dining tables placed on each bank see Vollmer (1898)
276 and 269 on *Silv.* 1. 3. 64 and 25 (*alternas*). As I shall argue later, reciprocity and duality are
the principles on which this estate is founded.

[66] Verg. *Ecl.* 10. 4–5; Ov. *Met.* 5. 572ff. See Vollmer (1898) 255 on *Silv.* 1. 2. 203.

mitissimus amnis (24); though yoked (*iunctus*, 45) to the baths, the river
god laughs with pleasure, *ridet* (46). Szelest has commented on Statius'
innovative use of myth in the *Silvae*, in particular the way in which the
gods harmoniously mingle with humans in a contemporary landscape.[67]
We find a parallel development in art of this period.[68] In Statius' villa
landscapes, the gods consort amicably with humans without threat or
harm; indeed, rather than directing human needs, they cooperate fully
with them. This throwback to the Golden Age, an important part of
the poem's pastoral economy, is made possible by a technology that
painlessly removes the implicit violence from nature and god. Indeed,
the Marcian aqueduct represents a new process of myth-making in which
the new deities of technology emblematise the power of nature directed
productively to human use and the celebration of imperial grandeur.

Finally, in *Epist.* 1. 10 Horace criticises the villa for demanding a
panoramic view (23). A good view was an important feature of the
Roman villa, and one that Vopiscus' house typically enjoys (39–42):[69]

> te, quae vada fluminis infra
> cernis, an ad silvas quae respicis, aula, tacentes,
> qua tibi tuta quies offensaque turbine nullo
> nox silet et nigros imitantia murmura somnos?[70]

What of you, the hall that looks at the pools of the river below, or of you who
face the silent woods, where there is safe serenity and night is silent, undisturbed
by any wind, and there are only the murmurings that imitate dark sleep?

View here is connected not just with visual pleasure but with control
over nature, a control that Horace derides as a false form of pleasure.
Control of sight also involves control of sound. The sounds of nature
are suppressed so that Vopiscus can dream in peace as a man free from
mental and moral disturbance, his serenity safe (*tuta quies*, 41). Moreover,
Vopiscus' dreams, we are told elsewhere, inspire poetry, *habentes carmina
somnos* (23). Nature, made silent and acquiescent, creates the conditions
for literature. The control of view and sound metaphorically points to

---

[67] See Szelest (1972) 315–17.   [68] See chapter 1 above, 16.
[69] E.g. Plin. *Ep.* 2. 17. 5 and 15; *Ep.* 5. 6. 7–19.
[70] Courtney emends *nigros imitantia*, the reading of M, to *pigros mutantia*. See Courtney (1984). *Niger* in
Statius' *Thebaid* almost invariably has negative associations. See for instance *nigra Tartara* (*Theb.* 1.
307–8); *nigrae ... mortis* (*Theb.* 9. 851); and *niger ... lucus* (*Theb.* 5. 152–3), the grove where the
Lemnian women swear to murder their husbands. It is used five times in the *Silvae* outside the
present context, twice to suggest unpleasantness (*Silv.* 1. 3. 103, of satire; *Silv.* 4. 4. 62, of Thule)
and three times to describe death (*Silv.* 2. 1. 19, 3. 3. 21, and 5. 1. 19). Nonetheless, I believe that
the reading of M should be retained here. '*Niger*' refers to darkness and lack of colour; the text
is conveying the idea of stillness, which involves the absence of both visual and aural stimuli.

the inner control of the poet, who orders his material as he orders his landscape.

Vopiscus lives in the country in the luxurious style that Horace derided, yet in Statius' poem architectural and moral order are closely related. Vopiscus seems to have the best of both worlds. He possesses the peace and harmony with nature that Horace sought after in the country at the same time as he enjoys the comforts and luxuries of the city. The pleasure that the land takes in its improvement provides a strategy that seems implicitly to justify the urbanisation of nature. Moreover, the metonymical relationship that Statius constructs between the managed landscape and its owner defines Vopiscus' moral and social worth. The architectural aesthetic of the estate, with its union of order and abundance, provides a paradigm for social and moral relationships, including that between poet and patron.

At the start of the poem Statius describes the landscape of Vopiscus' estate as naturally gentle and cooperative with human endeavour, yet also lavish in its gifts (15–17):

> ingenium quam mite solo, quae forma beatis
> ante manus artemque locis! non largius usquam
> indulsit natura sibi.

How gentle the creative disposition of the land! What beauty in these fortunate places before the intervention of human beings and their art! Nature has nowhere indulged itself more lavishly.

Here the 'indulgences' of technology harmonise, then, with nature's own propensities. This combination of gentleness and lavishness is also reflected in Vopiscus' own character. At the end of the poem Statius singles out for praise Vopiscus' virtues; paradoxically, Vopiscus is outstanding in his quiet virtue and moderation (91–3):

> hic premitur fecunda quies virtusque serena
> fronte gravis sanusque nitor luxuque carentes
> deliciae.

Here is to be found productive peace and calm-browed, serious virtue along with a healthy brilliance and pleasures untainted by luxury.

Statius expresses the harmony within Vopiscus' character through a union of virtual opposites: quiet is productive, serious virtue is calm-browed, brilliance is *sanus* (that is, healthy and restrained), delights are untainted by luxury. With the words *quies* and *serena* Statius equates the philosophical serenity of Vopiscus with the peacefulness of his estate, which is described as possessing a *quies* ('peacefulness', 29) that is both *aeterna* ('eternal', 29) and *tuta* ('safe', 41). Vopiscus' *sanusque nitor*, 'healthy, transparent brilliance', corresponds to the radiance of the house's interior with its 'gleaming floor' *(nitidum . . . solum*, 54–5), as well as to the gleam of fleeting reflections on water (18–19). Although the 'fecundity' or creative potential of this *quies* is related to the generosity of nature, productivity here is not agricultural but ethical; it is related to a munificence of character that may extend to acts of patronage.

Thus, with the provocative, concluding statement that the pleasures of the estate lack luxury (92), Statius argues for a new valuation of wealth as the enabler of virtue. When Statius finally invokes a blessing upon Vopiscus' *bona animi* ('goods of the mind', 106), he uses a metaphor that brings out the link between material and moral well-being. The powerful fictions of a nature cooperative with aesthetic and moral order and of a stable, prosperous Empire are mutually reinforcing.

But Statius further challenges Horace by linking luxury explicitly with an Epicurean life-style. On one level, of course, Venus (9–12), along with Voluptas (9), signifies the urbane sophistication of Vopiscus' estate and its *amoenitas*.[71] In *Silv.* 1. 3. 10–12 Venus treats the house much as she treated Violentilla as a girl *(Silv.* 1. 2. 110–12), anointing both with special ointments. Venus' seductive treatment of the house as a human body suggests that the house is a metonym for Vopiscus himself. But here Vopiscus' status as a protégé of Venus also has a philosophical meaning. The close association of Venus and Voluptas is found also in the opening of Lucretius' *De Rerum Natura* where Venus is addressed as *Aeneadum genetrix, hominum divumque voluptas,| alma Venus* ('mother of Aeneas' race, pleasure of men and gods, / kindly Venus', 1–2). Venus and Voluptas are important Epicurean signs of pleasure rightly understood as moderation and freedom from excessive desire.[72] The linkage of these two figures at the opening of *Silv.* 1. 3 boldly introduces another novel and important theme of Statius' villa poems – the assimilation of Epicurean philosophy to a life of wealth and privilege.

On Vopiscus' estate technology and a cooperative nature are represented as providing protection from harmful human passions; they help create that 'safe serenity'. The villa buildings on either side of the river, for instance, struggle to 'defend' their master (4). With the notion of defence, Statius constructs Vopiscus' estate as a separate, safe world, far

---

[71] Cf. the definition of the *locus amoenus* offered by Servius as a place 'full of pleasure alone'. Cf. note 49 above.

[72] On *Voluptas* as the goal towards which the Epicurean strove see Bailey (1947) 60–6.

from the turbulence of public life. The vaunted coolness of the house, which does not swelter (*aestuat*, 7) with heat, assumes correspondingly metaphorical significance as a sign of the inner calm of both house and owner. The peace (*quies*, 41) that Vopiscus enjoys on his estate is safe (*tuta*, 41). The quiet and indeed silence of the estate, upset by no disturbance or whirlwind (41), both provide and reflect Vopiscus' philosophical calm, his freedom from passions. Boldly then, Statius represents technology, along with a cooperative nature, as playing an important role in the provision of Epicurean *ataraxia*.

Vopiscus' wise and generous use of wealth provides a model for patronage and is in accordance with what seems to have been a particularly Roman development of Epicureanism. A stimulating article by Asmis has shown that Philodemus' teachings on wealth, specifically the *Oeconomicus*, insert into an Epicurean framework a new aristocratic ideal that valued the life of the philosopher and gentleman farmer over that of the soldier and the politician.[73] Philodemus' Epicurean 'gentleman' lives in leisured, learned retreat, enjoying the *docta otia* (108–9) of a Vopiscus. Instead of participating in politics, he 'is relaxed about making money and uses it to enjoy philosophical leisure with friends'.[74] Philodemus is not changing Epicurean doctrine about wealth but he does give it a different emphasis. As Asmis points out, 'Epicurus is more comfortable with giving away wealth than preserving it. In a variation on Epicurus' recommendation, Philodemus has the rich man share with others while keeping his wealth.'[75] Philodemus' invitation to Roman aristocrats to open up their estates to philosophy is directly relevant to the social and political conditions of the first century BCE, a period of great private wealth and political anarchy when attitudes towards leisure were changing and the villa was developing in importance as a site for aristocratic leisure.[76] The accommodation of wealth to the life of the villa owner is also particularly appropriate to the circumstances of the late first century AD, when the chief means of public expression for the élite lay in private architecture.

THE POETIC LANDSCAPE

Although Statius 'answers' Horace on moral grounds, the two writers' primary field of engagement is poetry, for in *Silv.* 1. 3 philosophical quietude provides the proper conditions for poetic composition. The

---

[73] Asmis (forthcoming). I am grateful to the author for sharing the draft of her article with me.
[74] Asmis (forthcoming).   [75] Asmis (forthcoming).
[76] On the development of the villa in Campania in the late Republic see D'Arms (1970) 39–72.

coolness and the abundant waters of Vopiscus' villa are features for which Tibur was famous, and they are also its defining characteristics as the landscape of poetic inspiration in Horace's poetry, particularly in *Carm.* 4. 2 and 4. 3.[77] In *Carm.* 4. 3. 1–9, for instance, Horace sets Tibur against famous centres of power and worldly ambition in Greece and Rome.[78] Quiet, peaceful Tibur with its flowing waters and thick shady groves will fashion Horace as a noble Augustan poet in the Greek lyric tradition (10–12):

> sed quae Tibur aquae fertile praefluunt
> et spissae nemorum comae
> fingent Aeolio carmine nobilem.

The waters which flow through fertile Tibur and the thick foliage of its groves will fashion me as a poet renowned for Aeolian song.

Vopiscus' landscape, despite the technological dominance of the villa, is also a poetic landscape. The opening lines of *Silv.* 1. 3 emphasise the importance of water and shade, essential for the civilised amenities of the Roman villa but also endemic features of the ideal landscape and of Horace's Tibur. The landscape also has *ingenium* (15), creative power. The peace that the water and woods of Horace's Tibur provide for the poet is mediated directly on Vopiscus' estate through a powerful technology that creates and ensures the peace necessary for the intellectual life.

In *Carm.* 4. 2. 27–32 Horace compares himself to a bee collecting sweet honey from the dewy banks and grove of Tibur:

> ... ego apis Matinae
> more modoque
> grata carpentis thyma per laborem
> plurimum circa nemus uvidique
> Tiburis ripas operosa parvus
> carmina fingo.

Like a bee from Matinus busily plucking the pleasing thyme among the groves and banks of dewy Tibur, I, humble poet as I am, compose carefully crafted verse.

In this poem Horace contrasts his carefully crafted poetry with the vehement productions of Pindar, described through the metaphor of a river that has burst its banks and is racing down a mountain out of control (5–8).[79] Horace here redraws the Euphrates of Callimachus,

---

[77] On the watery coolness of Tibur see Hor. *Carm.* 1. 7. 12–14; Troxler-Keller (1964) 135–6.
[78] See the discussion of *Carm.* 4. 3 in Troxler-Keller (1964) 141–50.
[79] See the discussion of Troxler-Keller (1964) 151–7; Harrison (1995b) 108–15

literary-critical sign at the end of the *Hymn to Apollo* of a weighty poetics and well-worn tradition. The Horatian bee, gathering honey around the river banks of Tibur, localises in Italy the pure stream of Callimachean literary polemic, source of water for bees.[80] Correspondingly, at Tibur Horace's poems are *operosa* (31), elaborately crafted, and he shapes them like a sculptor, *fingo* (32) – the same verb that he uses in *Carm.* 4. 3. 12 to suggest the formative influence of Tibur on his poetry.[81]

The river Anio on Vopiscus' estate is the bearer of similar literary-critical ideals (20–3):

> ipse Anien (miranda fides), infraque superque
> spumeus, hic tumidam rabiem saxosaque ponit
> murmura, ceu placidi veritus turbare Vopisci
> Pieriosque dies et habentes carmina somnos.

The Anio itself, though a foaming torrent below and above the villa, here (miraculously) sets aside its swollen rage and rocky roar, as if fearful of disturbing the Pierian days of peaceful Vopiscus and his song-filled dreams.

In *Carm.* 4. 2 Horace used the image of two types of river to define his own refined poetics and their separation from Pindaric violence and passion. With the Anio, Statius combines Horace's two rivers into one. Outside Vopiscus' estate the river represents epic or Pindaric passion, *tumidam rabiem* ('swollen rage', 21). But on Vopiscus' estate the river is tamed and peaceful, obedient to Vopiscus' needs. A quiet environment for Vopiscus' poetic reveries is provided not by a big, rushing river but by a calm flow of water that is resonant of the familiar Callimachean image of the small, pure stream. This image of the quiet, narrow river connects Vopiscus' Tibur to Horace's Tibur as a similar poetic landscape which embodies stylistic ideals of careful craft and refinement. But the river Anio is subject to the demands of the house and its owners. Although turbulent above and below Vopiscus' estate, it modifies its sound and flow as it threads its way through his territory like an obedient and respectful servant, fearful (*veritus*, 22) of upsetting its master's poetic reveries, a river both moderate and temporarily un-epic (20–3). The quiet, narrow river, then, is shaped by the demands of technology as well as poetry. The servitude of nature in a sense substitutes for and occludes the system of slavery that underpinned the villa's economy. Here, in the subordination of the river to its master, we have a hint of an idea that Statius will

---

[80] Callim. *Hymn* 2. 105–13.
[81] Harrison (1995b) 114–15 notes that the image of the bee conceals a Pindaric allusion. Horace thus is also using a Pindaric image for poetic activity as well as a Callimachean one.

develop more fully in *Silv.* 4. 3, namely that the Callimachean image of the narrow pure stream is particularly apt for an unambitious poet-ics that safely accommodates itself to the dominant ideology.[82] Here in *Silv.* 1. 3, however, Statius offers an expansive view of Callimachean poetics specifically formulated as a challenge to Horace. Epicurean phi-losophy becomes an important aspect of Callimachean poetics, while these poetics themselves are reformulated to encompass the grand, luxurious villa as well as the narrow stream, the celebration of grandeur as well as peace.

Indeed, there is another source of water on Vopiscus' estate, the Marcian aqueduct, which even in the moment of praise for one of Rome's technological marvels is filtered through the poet's literary-critical ideals (66–9):

> teque, per obliquum penitus quae laberis amnem,
> Marcia, et audaci transcurris flumina plumbo,
> ne solum Ioniis sub fluctibus Elidis amnem
> dulcis ad Aetnaeos deducat semita portus?

you, Marcia, who glide underground across the depths of the stream, traversing the river with audacious lead, so that the channel which draws the river of Elis under the Ionian waves to a Sicilian harbour is not alone in its fresh, sweet water?

What matters is not the impressive technology of the aqueduct so much as the sweet water it provides, a fact made known through the mythological comparison with the river Alpheus which flowed underground to emerge in Sicily. Water, along with paths or roads, is an important poetic image. Here Statius plays with these familiar Callimachean metaphors. *Deducat*, a catchword of Callimachean poetic style, joined with *dulcis semita* ('a sweet path'), suggests refinement and exclusivity. Statius filters the image of the aqueduct's water through a poetic consciousness that trans-forms Vopiscus' estate into a bearer of literary-critical ideals.[83] The aque-duct itself is associated both with epic grandeur and sophisticated novelty. Although a guest on a rich man's estate, Statius thus appropriates the villa landscape to promote boldly his own unique poetics of Callimachean craft and exclusivity united with luxuriance.

In *Silv.* 1. 3 the innovative architecture of the owner is complemented by the innovative pastoral poetics of the writer, obliquely expressed through the ecphrastic, textual fashioning of the estate. Voluptas, we are told in the poem's opening lines, 'wrote' (*scripsisse*, 9) upon the house with 'tender

---

[82] See chapter 9 below.
[83] On *deducere* see Verg. *Ecl.* 6. 5; Ov. *Met.* 1. 4; Myers (1994) 4–5.

hand'. Voluptas, the Epicurean principle of pleasure and architect of the house, is conceived as a writer who composes in Callimachean style, for *tenera*, tender, is an epithet used to describe poetic refinement and is particularly associated with elegiac poetry.[84] With this clear reference to writing, Statius identifies the house as a verbal construct. Yet, as he makes clear in the preface, Statius' new poetry, the *Silvae*, is also characterised by boldness: both the composition of a poem to the emperor, and the speed at which the epithalamium for Stella and Violentilla was written, are signs of Statius' daring (*ausus, audacter, praef.* 1. 19, 22); equally audacious presumably is *Silv.* 1. 3, which Statius claims was written in one day (*praef.* 1. 26). This boldness, as his titling of his poetic collection as *Silvae* suggests, creates order out of varied, and sometimes resistant, material. In *Silv.* 1. 3 the technology of writing complements the technology of the landscape architect and engineer whose 'bold lead' (*audaci . . . plumbo*, 67) of the Marcian aqueduct channels, tames, and makes productive the exuberance of nature.

The ultimately unequal relationship between Vopiscus and Statius as host and guest, however, constructs a critical distance between them. Statius' ecphrastic text uses Vopiscus' villa as a complex figure within contemporary life through which social, political, and literary ideals could be safely articulated. Statius offers for critical scrutiny a vision of a social order removed from the court and founded largely on harmonious, co-operative relationships rather than on strictly hierarchical ones. What, however, is the place for the ambitious poet within this complacent pastoral order? In *Carm.* 4. 2 and 4. 3 Horace's fashioning of the Italian landscape of Tibur as the locus of poetic inspiration marked his closer integration within the Augustan state. Although in his villa landscape Statius foregrounds the importance of poetry, he nevertheless, through his new version of pastoral for the Flavian age, marks his distance from Horace by suggesting that the relationship between literature and the state is now more difficult and uncertain.

IMPERIAL PASTORAL

The term 'pastoral' has been much discussed in the past decades and has been subject to rather broad interpretation.[85] Alpers excludes landscape

---

[84] See Ov. *Am.* 3. 15. 1; *OLD* 4e and 6b.

[85] Empson (1935) expanded the concept of pastoral to include works that function as social analysis and therapy through their translation of the complex into the simple. Poggioli (1975) derived his definition of the genre from a wide-ranging survey of works of European literature. For Poggioli,

from his definition of pastoral, which depends on the central fiction that the shepherds' lives 'represent' human lives.[86] In my view, however, the ideal landscape of pastoral poetry is inextricably linked with the 'representative lives' of its poets, whether these poets are shepherds or villa owners and their friends. In villa landscape and pastoral pleasance alike, water, shade and trees provide the stereotypical setting for poetic composition and song; harmony with nature provides the complement to friendship among poets.

Virgil's *Eclogues* have generally been seen as providing pastoral with its canonical form.[87] This perhaps inhibits us from seeing pastoral as a mode that is highly flexible in form as well as content – there is the pastoral novel or the pastoral drama, for instance.[88] At the same time, however, Virgil's exhortation in *Eclogue* 4 to sing of woods (*silvas*, 3) worthy of a consul provided a directive for the later involvement of pastoral with politics and the court. The Neronian *Eclogues* of Calpurnius Siculus, which boldly invert the pastoral themes of Virgil, provide an important intermediary between Virgil's pastoral poems and Statius': the countryside is presented as boorish, the home of rustics unable to provide suitable patrons for aspiring poets.[89] At the start of *Eclogue* 4, for instance, the poet Corydon sits silent beside a noisy (*garrulus*, 2) stream. His location is described as hostile (*infesta*, 3) by a fellow poet. The incompatibility of the country with a refined, ambitious poetics is expressed through a landscape that is

---

pastoral is analytical and moral in purpose and makes social justice central. Alpers (1996) argues that pastoral is a 'mode' which is based on the Burkean concept of 'a representative anecdote', here the lives of shepherds and herdsmen. See chapter 1, especially 13–16. Alpers's definition is close to that of Gutzwiller (1991), to whom strangely he does not refer (see the review of Alpers's book by Hunter [1997]). Gutzwiller (1991) 5 defines pastoral as '*representations* of the speech acts of herdsmen, their conversations, and songs'. Gutzwiller's first chapter, 'Pastoral as Genre', provides an excellent discussion of ancient and modern theories about genre, pastoral in particular.

[86] Alpers (1996) 22–8.   [87] See for instance Hubbard (1996) 67–8.

[88] On the definition of 'mode' see Alpers (1996) chapter 2, especially 44–50. 'Mode' suggests that 'pastoral is a broad and flexible category that includes, but is not confined to, a number of identifiable genres' (44). For Gutzwiller (1991), pastoral can be referred to as either genre or mode: when content rather than form is dominant, 'pastoral finds a home in other formal types – drama, romance, novel, and so forth – where it is sometimes referred to as *mode*' (13).

[89] See for instance Newlands (1987); Hubbard (1996). On the dating of Calpurnius' *Eclogues* see the detailed survey of the evidence for either a Neronian or a third century date in Keene (1887; repr. 1996) 2–14. Keene argued strongly for a Neronian date. The debate was reopened by Champlin (1978), who argued for a Severan dating. In response, the case for a Neronian date was argued in the pages of *JRS* by Townend (1980), Mayer (1980) and Wiseman (1982a). The case remains open. Although I myself favour a Neronian date, what matters most for my purposes is that the poetry of Calpurnius Siculus, like that of Statius, is shaped by the imperial system of government and patronage.

filled with harsh, grating sounds, sounds that the aspiring poets attempt to suppress.[90]

Statius' villa poems represent a further reinvention of pastoral, for a country house, not pasture land, acts as the locus of friendship and poetry. Patronage is to be found in the country after all. The emperor and the urban élite are displaced by an owner whose house testifies to his wealth, his high social status, and his urban sophistication. It may be significant that at Tibur the emperor Nero had a villa whose design was similar to that of Vopiscus' villa: a set of twin mansions on either side of the Anio. The grandeur of Vopiscus' estate suggests imperial splendour – without the demands of politics.

In the villa poems of the *Silvae*, the villas which were on the periphery of Virgil's pastoral world in *Eclogue* 1 now occupy centre stage. Yet contrary to its social function as a lively centre of personal patronage, the villa in the *Silvae* is represented as detached from the public world, open only to the privileged poet and a few like-minded friends. In Vopiscus' garden, gods and humans mingle in harmonious proximity. The villa landscape participates in both a historical and a mythical world – explicit in ownership and location, symbolic in topography. It represents a new, updated version of the idealised landscape of pastoral poetry.

In *Silv.* 1. 3 the *otium* of villa life is assimilated to the *otium* that is a definitive feature of the pastoral landscape.[91] As Rosenmeyer has suggested, at the end of *Georgics* 2. 458ff., Virgil removes labour from his encomium of the life of the farmer and thus redescribes him as 'pastoral man'.[92] Statius pushes this development one stage further, assimilating the leisured life of the villa owner to that of pastoral good fellowship, poetry, and contemplation. But in this new version of pastoral, technology and wealth are active agents in creating a vision of poetic leisure. The economic prosperity of empire makes possible the pastoral dream. Again, Virgil set the direction in which pastoral would develop. In *Eclogue* 1, Tityrus' leisure to compose and sing poetry derives from economic as well as political security: he bought his freedom thanks to hard-won savings and to a 'god' in Rome, generally identified with Octavian (27–45). While he relaxes in the shade, a hedgecutter trims the boundaries of his farm, a simple form of estate management (56). Vopiscus' freedom, however, is made possible not by the gods nor by an authority in Rome but by

[90] See Newlands (1987).
[91] On *otium* as a definitive characteristic of the pastoral landscape see Rosenmeyer (1969) 65–97.
[92] Rosenmeyer (1969) 65–7.

an unspecified wealth that gives him the technological means to remain
independent of the emperor while enjoying to the full the economic
benefits of imperial prosperity. The villa poems of Statius accommodate
the pastoral dream to certain socio-historical realities. Wealth buys freedom and independence from labour, while the luxury of a mansion and
well managed estate removes the anxieties inimical to philosophical and
poetic meditation.

Since the villa rivals the city in its material attractions, the familiar
pastoral dialectic between city and country is reformulated in this poem
as a tension between private and public life, specifically between the life
of the intellect and the life of political engagement.[93] Through the villa
poem Statius can promote the attractions of a social order based on
friendship and learning rather than the seeking of political power.

The predominant structural principle on which Vopiscus' villa estate
rests is that of duality, a form of reciprocity. The villa thus rests in part
upon a different aesthetic from that of the imperial statue. Both are marvellous objects in the eyes of the viewer, but whereas the statue exceeds
all known bounds in its form and relation to time and space, the villa
provides a model of reciprocity and order. The poem opens by establishing the unique architectural composition of the villa: it is composed of
two main blocks, with the river Anio forming the dividing line that separates the villa complex into two complementary halves with 'twin *penates*'
(*geminos . . . penates*, 2); the two building blocks on either side of the river
contend in 'defending' their master (4). The competition engendered by
this duality is productive. The villas compete for themselves, not against
one another. The banking term *commercia* ('exchange', 3) is applied to
the companionable (*sociae*, 3) banks and thus incorporates duality within
Roman civic norms.[94] Commercial exchange here is redirected to the
profitable creation of architectural, and, as we have seen, social and
moral order. The harmony contained within this duality is indicated by
the stylistic threading of the river Anio between the *penates*. These twin
gods establish duality as a sacred principle of the reciprocity between
human beings and nature on the estate.

Like the buildings, the landscape is constructed on dualistic principles.

---

[93] See Gutzwiller (1991) 13. Marx (1964) chapter 1 talks of a 'counterforce' that threatens from
outside the pastoral world (25–6). His view is shaped by his study of the impact of industrialism
upon the American landscape and nineteenth-century literary forms. Oppositions need not
take such threatening or destructive forms but can provide alternative perspectives.

[94] *Commercium* can be used as a metaphor for sociable human interchange. See Sen. *Tranq.* 4. 4;
TLL iii. 1876. 28–46, cites specifically exchange of speech.

Through reflection, in particular, nature reproduces the duality of the architectural disposition of the house (16–19):

> non largius usquam
> indulsit natura sibi. nemora alta citatis
> incubuere vadis; fallax responsat imago
> frondibus, et longas eadem fugit umbra per undas.

Nature has nowhere indulged itself more lavishly. Lofty groves brood over swift-flowing pools; the deceptive image mirrors the leaves and the reflection flees unchanging across the surface of the water.

The generosity of nature here complements the lavish architecture of the villa estate and is realised specifically in the reflection of the trees in the water of the river, leaves matching leaves as mansions match mansions. Nature here mirrors the principle of duality on which the house is structured. Although the reflection is not static but flees over the water, the adjective *eadem* ('unchanging', 19) emphasises at the same time the constancy of the reflection. In *Silv.* 1. 3 Statius substitutes for nature's resonance nature's reflection; pastoral reciprocity here consists in visual, not aural exchange: *fallax responsat imago | frondibus* ('the deceptive image mirrors the leaves', 18–19). In this line *responsat* and *imago* teasingly lead the reader to expect a reference to sound, until the enjambment of *frondibus* in the following line. *Imago* in this landscape consists of reflection, not of echo. The absence of echo points yet again to human, technological control over the landscape; both sight and sound are carefully and harmoniously managed to create order and protect the interests of their owner.[95] The architecture of both landscape and house puts nature strictly into the service of Vopiscus.

Such duality simplifies Vopiscus' world into a pattern of symmetry that suggests human victory over errant nature. Symmetry restrains individual detail and subdues movement. Here for instance the river Anio does not cascade in the torrential waterfalls for which it was famed at Tibur, but suppresses its movement and its sound, creating an almost silent landscape (20–4, 39–42).

The silence of Vopiscus' landscape is consistent with post-Virgilian pastoral poetry which, as Rosenmeyer observes, removes the resonance of nature; shepherds and poets sing to a hushed landscape.[96] In Virgil's first *Eclogue*, the *locus amoenus* is founded on the notion of reciprocity, initially expressed through aural exchange. Tityrus for instance teaches the

---

[95] Cf. also the importance of reflection within the house. Light streaming down from the ceiling reflects back the gleaming mosaics of the floor (53–6).

[96] Rosenmeyer (1969) 149.

woods to sing his song, which they in turn echo back to him (4–5).[97] The echo is a sign of the mutual exchange between human and nature in the pastoral landscape.[98] It also has a symbolic function as a sign of Virgil's relationship with Theocritus, and thus establishes pastoral as an allusive mode, capable of reinvention.[99] Crucial to a definition of pastoral, then, is the myth of a cooperative nature which is itself a sign of the reciprocal relationships that inform the pastoral landscape between poet and nature, poet and predecessor, and poet and patron.[100] It is this myth of cooperation and reciprocity that Calpurnius Siculus boldly distorts in his focus upon the relationship between poetry and Rome. In Calpurnius Siculus' *Eclogues* the poets can compose and sing only in seclusion from the noises of nature; the lack of aural exchange, of reciprocity, symbolically suggests the sterility of their poetic environment. Nature is silent on Vopiscus' estate, yet, thanks both to technology and nature's propensities, cooperative with human needs. The principle of reciprocity which informs Vopiscus' landscape as well as his house suggests both the morally balanced temperament of the owner and the overall harmony of his environment, which is conducive to the production of sophisticated poetry and philosophical thought, untroubled by the potential errancy of nature.

   Indeed, Statius' villa poem rests also upon the literary dialectic between pastoral and epic, for *Silv.* 1. 3 in particular embodies the qualities that are strikingly absent from the world of the *Thebaid*: unity in doubleness, peace, freedom from passion, creativity. The theme of duality involves Statius in an agonistic self-positioning with regards to his own poetry as well as that of Horace and Virgil. For Statius is self-consciously aware of the distance between his new poetic project and his epic, the *Thebaid*. In *Silv.* 1. 3 Statius appropriates epic motifs, in particular the topos of duality, and gives them new meaning within the peaceful, pastoral landscape of Vopiscus' villa.[101]

   The *Thebaid* is a poem about doubleness. Two brothers, two cities, struggling over one sceptre: *nunc tendo chelyn satis arma referre|Aonia et*

---

[97] Thus also in Hor. *Carm.* 1. 17. 12 the rocks echo back the music of the panpipes.

[98] The echo is a recurrent motif of pastoral poetry, what Marx (1964) 23 calls a 'metaphor of reciprocity'.

[99] See Patterson (1987) 2.

[100] For a more negative view of the function of 'echo' in Virgil's *Eclogues* see Boyle (1986) 15–35, who regards the echoic Muse as a sign of the impotence of pastoral poetry trapped in its own sound.

[101] Gransden (1970) has argued that Virgilian pastoral provides a version of the 'anti-heroic' and is constructed in opposition to the great public world represented by epic. See however Van Sickle (1978) who argues that the *Eclogues* (like the *Silvae*) belong by metre to the genre of *epos* and deal in part with epic, national themes.

geminis sceptrum exitiale tyrannis ('now it is sufficient to extend my lyre to tell of Aonian warfare and the sceptre that was fatal to the two tyrants', *Theb.* 1. 33–4). In *Silv.* 1. 3 however, doubleness is not destructive but a source of united strength. The villa with its double penates (*geminos penates*, 2) assimilates the epic tasks of competition (*certantes*, 4), defence (*defendere*, 4), and destruction (*frangunt*, 7) to an overall project of harmony. The poem's second line (appropriately) points to the doubleness of the villa, constructed of two sets of buildings on either side of the Anio, which nonetheless work together to defend their master and whose separation is slight: sight, voice, and almost hands can be exchanged across the river's divide (30–1), a further sign of a harmonious duality and reciprocity. This narrow river passage between the two sets of villas is compared in grandiose fashion to the Hellespont, heroically swum so many times by Leander (27–8). Of course this is an over-inflated comparison, but it does the work of demonstrating both the distance and the connection between Statius' new subject and his former epic themes. The *Silvae* provide Statius with a space where he can transform epic themes from tragedy into play and yet draw attention to the importance of that play.

The villa moreover is removed from the harshness of nature that fashions the epic landscape of the *Thebaid*. It does not, for instance, suffer the burning heat of the constellation of Leo, described significantly as the 'oppressive offspring of leafy Nemea' (*gravis . . . Nemeae frondentis alumnus*, 6). Nemea plays an important part in the centre of the *Thebaid* as the site where the infant Opheltes is tragically killed, and where funeral games are instituted in his honour. By referring to the constellation of Leo in this way, Statius marks the distance of Vopiscus' estate, and hence of his poem, from the Nemean grove and its public and tragic associations. A significant episode in the epic poem is the violation of the Nemean grove as its ancient trees are cut down for the funeral pyre (*Theb.* 6. 84–117).[102] The pathos of the cutting down of the grove is marked by its description as an ideal landscape, *umbrosaque tempe* (87).[103] Shaded and venerable, a sacred wood that goes far back in time to the start of the world (93–6), this *silva* represents protection and the stability derived from successive generations. The cutting down of its timber exposes it to the sun (89), a sign of physical and moral violation. Animals, birds, woodland deities and nymphs flee in distress, uprooted from their homes (110–13). The cutting down of the grove presages the devastation of the

---

[102] As Taisne (1994) 343 notes, Statius' tree-cutting scene is the longest such episode in ancient poetry.

[103] Tempe, a valley in Thessaly, became a figure of an idealised landscape. See McKeown (1989) 21.

Theban war, which is about to begin in earnest.[104] But within the centre of Vopiscus' villa a tree flourishes which will not be cut down and in which the nymphs rejoice (59–63). Such a tree has epic roots: the palaces of Homer's Odysseus and Virgil's Latinus, for instance, were both characterised by the trees that flourished in their midst.[105] The appropriation and transformation of epic themes ennoble Statius' new poetry, which is characterised by its themes of safety, peace, and harmony with nature. The flourishing tree, growing up within the centre of his house, is an appropriate symbol of his new imperial pastoral, his *Silvae*.

Statius then constructs Vopiscus' estate as a counter-world to the troubled, destructive world of epic and the public world at large. Vopiscus' pastoral enclave is formed in response not just to Virgilian pastoral or to Horatian rural poetry, but to Statius' own epic. Comparison between the *Thebaid* and the *Silvae* draws attention, despite Statius' protestations otherwise, to the importance of his new kind of poetry – both finely crafted and exuberant, a celebration of a new form of aristocratic identity in which wealth and power are devoted to aesthetic, intellectual, and beneficent ends.

The *Thebaid* is a poem about the curse of genealogy. Strikingly, although the concept of ancestral lineage was central to the Roman house, there is no mention of ancestors in *Silv.* 1. 3. Vopiscus' estate is located in a space devoid of genealogical lineage. He is a man without a family, a past or a future; his nobility is located in the antiquity of his land. The groves are ancient (38–9); the tree in the centre of the house has never been cut. Appropriately for a collection of poetry called the *Silvae*, tradition and continuity are symbolically located in the land, specifically in the trees that flourish on Vopiscus' estate under his protection. Aristocratic virtue then is seen as located not in family inheritance but in the land itself, whose antiquity suggests enduring value. And as a poetic landscape, the villa estate locates virtue within poetry itself, not agriculture or politics.

Statius' version of pastoral is a complex form that permits the exploration of cultural values in a period of political change and stress.

---

[104] Indeed, this passage marks the end of a lengthy digression from the war, as Hypsipyle entertains and delays the Argive warriors with her lengthy tale of the Lemnian women which begins in *Thebaid* 4. The ending of her female narrative, one concerning love and loss, is associated with the ending of the Nemean *silva* and, correspondingly, with a type of poetry associated with epyllia and elegy rather than with heroic narrative. The cutting down of the *silva* in the *Thebaid* symbolically marks a turning point in the epic towards battle narrative. See Taisne (1994) 343–4 and chapter 9 below, 295–6.

[105] On the epic analogues see Taisne (1994) 347.

The system of mutual allegiances at work in the pastoral landscape of the villa provides, for instance, a matrix for societal order. The estate as an ordered physical structure functions as a metonym not only for the character of its owner but for other inherited structures such as society as a whole, a code of morality, a system of poetic practices. In particular, poetics, and the question of the social function of poetry, remain central to Statius' version of pastoral.

Thus the patron, who figures obliquely in Virgil's pastoral, assumes an important socio-political as well as metaphorical function. In *Silv.* 1. 3 the governing presence of the patron, and his construction as an erudite man with shared poetic interests, a philosopher who controls his passions as he controls his estate, provides the poet with a safe site in which he can engage in a witty, innovative competition with his patron and his house, with literary tradition, and with his own poetic past. Vopiscus is clearly far from the mean patrons castigated by Juvenal in *Satires* 7. 36–49, who, busy writing their own verses, fob off their poets with dilapidated quarters for recitation. Statius, 'desirous of woods', as Juvenal describes the aspiring poet (*cupidus silvarum*, 7. 58), has been given at least temporary access to them.

Statius here offers some solution to the rural discontent of the Neronian pastoral of Calpurnius Siculus – but, as we shall see, it is only partial.[106] Calpurnius' 'shepherds' found the country boorish, and they desired to escape to the city, which they perceived as the centre of the arts and learning and the only source of patronage. At the start of *Eclogue* 7, for instance, Corydon returns reluctantly from the city, *lentus ab urbe* (1), an ironic echoing of the opening of Virgil's first *Eclogue* where Tityrus is depicted as *lentus in umbra* ('relaxed in the shade', 4). He has seen the emperor, and nobody else will do. Yet he is back in the country; he has not secured the emperor's patronage. Vopiscus' estate offers many of the attractions of the capital city – its artistry, its wealth, its culture. Moreover, contrary to Calpurnius' rural world, Vopiscus' estate is founded on the importance of poetry, for Vopiscus himself composes verse. The opening line of this poem describes him as *facundi* (1). In the preface to *Silv.* 1. 24–5, we are told that he has taken an active role in rescuing literature from decay. He is represented as having taken on the role that Calpurnius' poets, at least, expected from their emperor. And yet, at the same time, that role is confined to the pastoral enclave of his estate.

[106] See Newlands (1987).

In describing Vopiscus in the preface to Book 1 as the man responsible for rescuing declining literature from decay, Statius here represents the state of contemporary literature as rather desperate, despite the opulence of Empire; it is dependent on independent patrons rather than the emperor. Yet how adequate ultimately is the independent patronage such as Vopiscus can offer? Poetry is the path by which Statius can both pursue peace and contentment and also advance his desire for fame. But as an outsider to the Tiburtine landscape, a guest who has come to praise, Statius is in a different situation from Horace and indeed from Vopiscus, for whom poetry is the privilege of carefully constructed leisure. Even as he praises Vopiscus, Statius subtly suggests that his patron is no Horace or indeed Maecenas. Indeed, he is a local poet beloved by the home deities, the Tiburtine Fauns, Alcides, and Catillus, founder of Tibur (99–100).[107] Statius praises Vopiscus for his poetic pursuits, among his many virtues, but he subtly indicates that Vopiscus' poetry has little impact beyond the garden. The confinement of Vopiscus' poetry to an audience of local deities fits, however, Vopiscus' quietism and self-containment. The silence of his estate paradoxically creates the conditions for poetic composition and yet suggests his lack of an important audience. Silence acts as a metaphor for isolation from the circulation of poetry.

Vopiscus' construction as a poet here provides a focus for Statius' own meditations upon the role of art within society. Vopiscus mimics the role of imperial patron; he provides the right conditions for poetic composition including the sophistication of the city – but he cannot provide the political influence or the necessary audience for poetic advancement. The poem therefore provides a subtle critique not of Vopiscus himself but of the condition of literature within the Flavian state. Should it not be the emperor himself, after all, who is concerned to rescue literature from decay?

The villa landscape then is transformed by Statius into a metaliterary sphere. It is in this imaginative territory that he can negotiate on relatively equal terms with his patrons, such as Vopiscus. Although poetry is an important occupation of this new *locus amoenus*, the question posed by Calpurnius' 'shepherds' concerning the value and function of poetry composed and sung in retirement away from Rome, quietly remains an open one. Vopiscus is like Virgil's Tityrus, snugly content in his pastoral retreat. Vopiscus' audience likewise are the local deities. *Silv.* 1. 3 is a

---

[107] On Catillus see Hor. *Carm.* 1. 18. 2; Nisbet and Hubbard (1970) 230.

graceful, innovative compliment to a wealthy friend who has shared literary interests. As in *Silv.* 1. 2 it promotes a new concept of aristocratic identity to which poetry, not ancestry, is central, both socially and intellectually. But the celebration of this new version of pastoral centred upon rural patronage points also to its possible limitations for the self-reflexive poet seeking to make a national mark with a new kind of poetry. The value of Vopiscus' kind of lifestyle can be made known only by a poet willing to go beyond the confines of the ideal landscape and to look to the emperor and to Rome. Indeed, it is through the acts of collection and publication that Vopiscus and Statius' new version of pastoral can be inserted into a more public, but more contentious world. In *Silv.* 1. 3 Statius ultimately questions his own fantasies of pastoral retreat.[108]

In his discussion of Elizabethan pastoral poetry Montrose has coined the term 'aristocratic pastoral'.[109] With the notion of aristocratic pastoral as poetry that looks towards the court for definition, Montrose makes a careful response to Williams's criticism of both pastoral poetry and the country-house poem as élitist and artificial.[110] Montrose argues that the forms of Elizabethan pastoral which Williams particularly targets are indeed artificial in that such pastoral 'cleanses the taint of agrarian labour from pastoral imagery'. Yet, he argues, aristocratic pastoral is nonetheless a form that is culturally vital precisely because it belongs to a courtly milieu. For instance, aristocratic pastoral can be used to further social and poetic ambitions, or to refuse them.[111] Particularly in times of immense social and political pressure from the court, pastoral can create 'an imaginary space' in which 'virtue and privilege coincide'.[112]

Statius' villa poems are a form of aristocratic pastoral, although I prefer the term 'imperial pastoral', for their ideal landscape is openly sustained and created by the marvels of imperial technology as well as by the cooperation of nature. More importantly, however, the term 'imperial pastoral' expresses the tension at the heart of Statius' villa poems between private and courtly patronage. In its relationship with the court, the villa occupies a space that is both oppositional and contiguous. Indeed, the villa poems rest on a paradox, for the poet Statius cultivates a form that ostensibly, at any rate, rejects ambition in order to try to advance his own poetic ambitions. These ecphrastic poems are as much about the

---

[108] Note then that the following poem, *Silv.* 1. 4, honours Rutilius Gallicus, Rome's urban prefect, and Statius' most distinguished addressee apart from Domitian. See Henderson (1998).

[109] Montrose (1983) 426–33.   [110] Williams (1973) 30–47.

[111] Montrose (1983) 426–33 argues that 'aristocratic pastoral' is capable of embodying some of the contradictory values and pressures of social life.

[112] Montrose (1983) 427.

poet as viewer and writer of the villa as they are about the owner and his property. Indeed, as Myers has argued, Statius' poetic immortality, as well as the fame of his patrons, is at stake in his villa poems.[113]

Horace, Pearcy has remarked, used architecture to define his relationship to society: 'the comparison of the Sabine farm and the grandiose villa defined the poet: secure in his talent, set apart from the materialism and secularity of his society, and untroubled by the fear of death'.[114] Architecture likewise defines Statius' relationship to his society and also to his audience, for in *Silv.* 1. 3 he promotes the value of a life sequestered from political ambition while simultaneously revealing himself to be an audacious, innovative poet who seeks out challenges both in architecture and in literary tradition. Statius has no snug Sabine farm as a secure metaphor for his way of life.[115] The silence that surrounds his patron's villa marks its seclusion from the outside world; its woods are silent, *silvas . . . tacentes* (40). The villa then defines Statius' relationship to society in ambiguous terms, as an outsider looking in two opposite directions for ordered security but also fame. Calpurnius' 'sheepfold' of *Eclogue* 4 may have been transformed into a luxurious villa, but the aqueduct that boldly crosses Vopiscus' estate symbolically suggests that the path of ambition still inevitably leads to Rome.

[113] Myers (2000) 106.   [114] Pearcy (1977) 779.
[115] See Myers (2000) 131. She points out that Statius' landscapes in his villa poems always belong to someone else.

CHAPTER 5

Dominating nature: Pollius' villa in Silvae 2. 2

animus hominis dives, non arca
Cicero, *Paradoxa Stoicorum* 44

With *Silv.* 2. 2, Statius takes the reader far from Rome to the Bay of Naples and the luxurious villa of Pollius Felix and his wife Polla. This is Statius' first poem set in his own homeland of Campania. Whereas the impetus for the description of the villa in *Silv.* 1. 3 is not revealed, the occasion for Statius' visit to the villa is here made known. In the poem's opening lines, Statius explains that after competing at the Augustalia, the great Neapolitan quinquennial festival established by Augustus, he gladly accepted the invitation to relax for a while on his native soil with his friends before making his way to Rome (6–12).[1] The poem therefore is set between two significant poles in Statius' career, Naples and Rome, the region of his birth and the centre of Empire. The luxurious villa thus acts here as the particular focus for a set of tensions between Greek and Roman culture, between regional and national identity, and between the safety of home and the dangerous adventures of Empire.

Pollius Felix is the friend to whom, along with his wife Polla, Book 3 is dedicated (*Polli dulcissime, praef.* 3. 1); his Campanian estate forms the subject of two poems, *Silv.* 3. 1 as well as *Silv.* 2. 2. Pollius Felix was not a Roman aristocrat; he belonged to Campanian, not Roman society.[2] D'Arms has suggested that Pollius may well have been the son of a freedman.[3] Like Manilius Vopiscus then, Pollius Felix was not a major figure in Roman society by any means, although in Pollius' case we know from Statius' poems something about his life. *Silv.* 2. 2 tells us that Pollius had been a local dignitary of Puteoli and Naples (131–7) who, after a

[1] On the Augustalia (also known by the Greek name Sebasta) see Van Dam (1984) 197.
[2] See Van Dam (1984) 192–3 for an overview of Pollius' life.
[3] See D'Arms (1974) 111. Nisbet (1978) is sceptical and argues that Pollius' learning and culture suggests that he was a member of the local aristocracy (3–4). Statius of course was learned but not an aristocrat.

successful career in local government, was living in retirement in a *villa maritima* overlooking the Bay of Naples.[4]

The economic success of Pollius, whether he was the descendant of a freedman or not, testifies to his extraordinary abilities. As D'Arms has pointed out, Puteoli, where Pollius had conducted his public career, was particularly marked by both 'fluidity and tension' in its social life during the Flavian period and formed a highly competitive environment.[5] Like Petronius' Trimalchio, a fellow Campanian, Pollius was a successful example of the wealthy and socially mobile entrepreneur. But with the satirical portrait of Trimalchio we see that social status acquired through wealth could come into conflict with that acquired through hereditary rank.[6] In *Silv.* 2. 2, as in *Silv.* 1. 3, on the other hand, Pollius' wealth is conjoined with virtue. Here too, however, as befits a man who had been immersed in public affairs and had assumed a role of leadership in his community, time-honoured traditions of Roman governance are fused with Greek philosophical ideals in a concept of nobility untrammelled by hereditary ideals.[7]

This justification of wealth is more startling in the later poem, for the Bay of Naples was a region long notorious for its luxury. Cicero, who wrote *De Officiis* at Puteoli, and set *Academica*, *De Finibus*, and *De Fato* in Campania, called the Bay of Naples *cratera illum delicatum*, 'the Bay of Luxury'.[8] The location of Pollius' villa in this prime real estate region gave the poet his most audacious opportunity to overturn traditional moral discourse and reinterpret luxury as moral decorum. Thus the poem's emphasis upon Pollius' villa as a stunning technological achievement and a wonderful example of luxurious architecture is boldly heightened rather than diminished by its Campanian context. Moreover, since the region of the Bay of Naples was also more positively famed for

---

[4] For the characteristics of the seaside villa, the *villa maritima*, see McKay (1975) 115–28; Pollius' villa is briefly described as a fine representative of the type (121–2).

[5] D'Arms (1974) 111–14. The ceding of a large portion of Capua's territory to the coastal city of Puteoli after the eruption of Vesuvius, followed by the bypassing of Capua after the completion of the Via Domitiana, caused significant growth in Puteoli's population. Puteoli was the most important commercial centre in the Bay of Naples at this time. This undoubtedly created a highly competitive environment both for freedmen aspiring to infiltrate the established ruling families and attain local office, and for the local élite trying to retain their traditional hegemony.

[6] Garnsey and Saller (1987) 112–25. They argue that in the Empire the acquisition and transmission of property provided an important way for the non-élite such as freedmen to acquire social status through wealth and thus infiltrate 'the Roman framework of social and economic inequality' (110).

[7] At lines 133–6 Statius mentions that Pollius was a highly acclaimed magistrate of both Puteoli and Naples.

[8] Cic. *Att.* 2. 8. 2; D'Arms (1970) 40. See also Connors (2000) 499–504.

its literary and artistic culture, Pollius' villa provides a much more significant site of artistic patronage than does Vopiscus' villa.

Whereas duality is the principle on which Vopiscus' villa is founded, Pollius' villa is characterised by its domination of nature. Pollius' villa is of a different type from Vopiscus' well-watered, shady mansion, located not in the lush surroundings of the Tiburtine dell but in harsh coastal country on top of a cliff. It is a *villa maritima* of the type known as a porticus villa, with a colonnade connecting the buildings on the beach with the main part of the villa on high.[9] The land, rather than being innately cooperative with architectural design, is represented as an entity that needs to be reshaped and tamed. Like Vopiscus' estate, Pollius' estate is represented as a *locus amoenus*, a privileged space in which Pollius and his friends practise both Epicurean philosophy and poetry. But whereas in *Silv.* 1. 3 nature was spontaneously cooperative with human needs, the landscape of Pollius' villa is strongly marked by the georgic impulse to tame and improve a harsh, uncultivated nature. The rugged coastal landscape in which Pollius' villa is located needs drastic alteration to suit the needs of its wealthy, sophisticated owner – for instance, the removal of a mountain for an open view, of wild brush for elegant buildings.

Thus in *Silv.* 2. 2, there is a far greater emphasis on the important role that technology plays in taming and reshaping the landscape to human needs. The domination of nature is represented in *Silv.* 2. 2 and also *Silv.* 3. 1 as a heroic activity that glorifies the villa owner; the owner's special abilities and his close relationship with the gods at the same time allow the task of dominating nature to be performed without grinding labour. Thus georgic tasks are accommodated to pastoral ease, and the Roman impulse to dominate nature is accommodated to a Greek style of leisure. In *Silv.* 2. 2 Pollius commands and refashions nature with the wonderful authority of Orpheus, Amphion, or Arion, so that the act of contesting nature is subsumed in elevated, poetic production.[10] In *Silv.* 3. 1 the restoration of a temple to Hercules on Pollius' estate is specifically represented as a triumph of technological endeavour that is, however, swiftly and almost magically accomplished through the aid of Hercules. And in both cases the land is grateful for its drastic alterations.

Bergmann has drawn attention to Statius' engagement in *Silv.* 2. 2 with the Roman impulse towards domination and control of nature. She

[9] On the two basic types of *villae maritimae*, 'peristyle' and 'porticus', see McKay (1975) 115–18.
[10] See *Silv.* 2. 2. 60–2.

argues that in *Silv.* 2. 2, Statius' ecphrastic art conventionally reflects the common cultural and aesthetic attitudes of the wall painters who decorated villas and houses with 'villascapes' – paintings of grand villas and their estates.[11] Statius' poem has a temporal and topographical structure that imaginatively recreates the poet's 'tour' of Pollius' estate, approaching it first from the sea and then ascending the cliff via a handsome porticus to the main buildings on the cliff top. Like villa paintings, Bergmann argues, Statius' poem 'typifies and exalts a domestic context in which architecture imposes order on the land and nature is shaped into perfect views'.[12] It is this 'ordered access to nature' which, she claims, determined the appearance of actual and painted landscape in the Roman *domus.*[13]

Statius, however, produces a perceptual, interpretive response to Pollius' estate. Despite the systematic, topographical structure of *Silv.* 2. 2, the emphasis falls not upon architectural detail and design but upon the emotions and ideas evoked in an admiring guest by the estate.[14] As in *Silv.* 1. 3, wonder forms the guiding principle of description. As Bishop has argued in his study of the role of wonder in drama, wonder can serve as a conduit of truth.[15] Wonder characteristically creates 'a dynamic space of flux and intermediacy – between stage and audience, between the real and the impossible, between reason and feeling'.[16] The particularly visual power of wonder, manifested in Statius' vivid if unsystematic description of Pollius' house, forges an emotional bond in *Silv.* 2. 2 between text and reader, pulling readers into Pollius' world and at the same time preparing them for an understanding of the villa's larger signification. Wonder then sharpens the reader's or audience's critical faculties and makes them critically aware of the complex relationship between the poet and the object of his description.[17]

Moreover, the topographical location of Pollius' villa in a rugged coastal area lends particularly vigorous expression to Statius' inversion

---

[11] Bergmann (1991).   [12] Bergmann (1991) 66.   [13] Bergmann (1991) 61.

[14] Bergmann supplies more architectural detail than in fact exists in Statius' poem. See for instance the elaborate waterway scene that Bergmann imagines for Pollius' harbour (54–5). Moreover, a common feature of villa paintings is human activity, which is notably absent from Statius' poem.

[15] Bishop (1996) 1–4.   [16] Bishop (1996) 3.

[17] See also Becker (1995), who argues that the emotional response of wonder keeps prominently in the text the poet/observer, through whose words the experience of seeing the villa is mediated. Through wonder, 'the ekphrasis encourages both acceptance of the illusion that we are viewers *and* awareness of the describer who creates that illusion' (35).

of the literary trope of luxury. For building and landscaping here necessi-
tate extravagance of effort and design in order to 'improve' and thereby
benefit nature. Building therefore functions as a metaphor of human,
ethical control over stubborn and resistant passions. Not that Pollius'
estate is fashioned with 'the curse of labour' as Raymond Williams puts
it.[18] Although in *Silv.* 2. 2 and *Silv.* 3. 1 attention is drawn to the heroic
task of improving the land, the myth of a grateful nature and helpful divinities yet again obscures the social and technological realities of estate
management. Williams views the country-house poem as simply 'social
compliment', a form of flattery in that it offers a pastoralism which defends landed property on a very specious basis.[19] But pastoralism in
Silv. 2. 2, even more than in *Silv.* 1. 3, serves ethical analysis as well as,
in part, social compliment. The accommodation to Greek philosophical ideas of the Roman impulse to dominate and improve nature draws
attention to the symbolic significance of the land as the bearer of moral
and literary values.

As in *Silv.* 1. 3 then, the historical 'reality' of the villa is mediated
through the literary and ideological uses to which it is put by Statius.
His point of view is that of poet, not architect; he uses the villa, among
other things, precisely to challenge conventional ideas about luxury and
architectural and poetic excess. The villa is a site of close engagement
both with the traditions of Augustan poetry and with contemporary
social and political realities. Here in *Silv.* 2. 2, however, dominating nature
is an important new theme in which three semiotic fields, the moral, the
political, and the poetic, intersect in a bold negotiation with both Roman
and Greek culture.

Finally, Pollius' wise governance of nature is given here a strong political dimension, for through his ordering of his land as well as his self, his
estate can function as a metaphor for the well-ordered state. Human control over nature is represented as more than a sign of the owner's wealth;
rather, the successful cultivation and landscaping of nature marks his social dominance, his moral authority, and his ability to rule. His benevolent
landscaping of nature associates his estate with traditional Roman ideas
about the importance of the garden within civic life. Indeed, as Kuttner
has argued, the Romans regarded the garden as playing an important
role in the cultivation of political and social virtue. The benevolent cultivation of nature fashioned the garden as a site of religious, civic and
literary resonance.[20] Through Pollius' carefully landscaped estate then,

---

[18] Williams (1973) 45.   [19] Williams (1973) 39–47.   [20] Kuttner (1999) 8–11.

Greek and Roman notions of virtue both come together and interrogate one another. The leisured pastoral landscape of poetry and philosophy is reformulated in *Silv.* 2. 2 to reflect and scrutinise the sensibilities and needs of the Flavian age.

It is misleading then to reduce *Silv.* 2. 2 to a decorative work of art, a cultural commodity like a wall-painting whose art is, perhaps, purely conventional. *Silv.* 2. 2 is not a villa painting in verse. While *Silv.* 2. 2 certainly participates in a culture that celebrates artistic control and display, it also transcends the limits of that culture. For art in *Silv.* 2. 2 forms a richly symbolic realm offering opportunities for the articulation of political and moral as well as poetic ideas.

In *Silv.* 2. 2 Statius offers a provocative, alternative model of the ideal state situated, however, apart from the centre of Empire in the Greek region of Italy. The geographical separation of the villa here from Rome – there is no aqueduct to provide a symbolic link with the capital – provides a critical perspective upon the culture of Empire on which the imperial villa was founded. And it consequently raises the question also of where the centre of true patronage is located. It is significant, I believe, that *Silv.* 2. 2 is Statius' first poem set in his own homeland of Campania. Pollius' villa in many ways rests upon a successful fusion of Greek and Roman culture. Yet viewed from the periphery in Pollius' villa, imperial culture and Statius' place within it as an ambitious poetic outsider generate conflict between regional and national identities. Pollius' villa provides a richly evocative site for a complicated nexus of ideas not only about patronage but also about civic governance, imperial ambition, and regional loyalty.

In *Silv.* 2. 2, even more than in *Silv.* 1. 3, Statius creates an ideology of the villa as well as reflects one. Here he boldly relocates the Augustan pastoral dream of the ideal landscape – the *locus amoenus* – on a grand estate in the most popular playground of Italy. Indeed, this poem on Pollius' villa provides perhaps Statius' most elaborate articulation of the significance of the villa in his poetry, for it promotes a philosophical and pastoral ideal that is implicitly transferable to the larger critical issues involving imperial politics. The villa stands at the centre of a nexus of relationships: between word and image, poet and patron, poet and audience, poet and literary tradition, and here also Naples and Rome. The complex interaction among these various strands in *Silv.* 2. 2 creates an intricate poem in which poetics and politics seamlessly combine in a meditation upon the social function of art in the age of Domitian.

REWRITING HORACE

The provocative nature of Statius' poems on Pollius' villa is immediately emphasised by the adoption of the strategy he employed in *Silv.* 1. 3 but that is here significantly expanded: allusion to Horace.[21] The audacity of Statius' challenge to the Augustan poets, particularly Horace, is demonstrated through the union in Pollius' villa of literary and architectural principles of boldness with principles of moral and political control. In this way, the life committed to poetry and philosophy that was so cherished by Horace is given striking new definition.

At the start of *Silv.* 2. 2, Statius acknowledges his debt to Horace in a periphrastic reference to the vine-clad hills and pleasant climate of the area in which Pollius' villa is set (4–5):

> qua Bromio dilectus ager collesque per altos
> uritur et prelis non invidet uua Falernis.

Here is the land beloved of Bromius, where over the lofty hills the grape ripens with warmth and does not envy the Falernian presses.

Here Statius specifically evokes *Carm.* 2. 6 of Horace (18–20):

> et amicus Aulon
> fertili Baccho minimum Falernis
> invidet uvis.

And the Aulon valley, hospitable to friendly Bacchus, does not envy at all the Falernian grapes.

In *Carm.* 2. 6 Horace chooses Tibur and Tarentum as ideal landscapes where he can spend his old age in humble, poetic retirement and set, as he says, a limit (*modus*, 7) to his desires.[22] He loves Tarentum in part because of its agreeable climate, suitable for the growing of grapes. In Horace's lines, a pointed contrast is made between two quite different wine-growing regions of Italy, Tarentum and Campania. Statius' contrast

---

[21] The other poem that deals with Pollius' estate, *Silv.* 3. 1, likewise opens with direct allusion to Horace. Its opening lines, *intermissa tibi renovat, Tirynthie, sacra | Pollius* ('Tirynthian, Pollius renews your interrupted rites', 1–2) directly echo the opening of Book 4 of Horace's *Odes*, *intermissa, Venus, diu | rursus bella moves?* ('Venus, are you starting up your interrupted wars again?' 1–2). The initial connection drawn between the two poems points, among other things, to the self-reflexive nature of *Silv.* 3. 1 despite its opening address to a patron, for both poems are programmatic and are centred on the description of a temple. On the programmatic nature of *Carm.* 4. 1 see Putnam (1986) 41; on the metaphorical importance of the temple and statue of Venus see Hardie (1993b) 129–31.

[22] On the textual problem of *modus* see Nisbet and Hubbard (1978) 98–99. On the moral as well as physical meaning of *modus* see *OLD* 6 and Segal's (1969b) interpretation of *Carm.* 2. 6.

between only the northern and southern regions of Campania is basically unnecessary but draws attention to the Horatian allusion. Pollius, like Horace, has retired from public life (133–41). Statius' opening allusion to this ode suggests that Pollius' estate is like Horace's Tibur or Tarentum, both beautiful, fertile landscapes, both Greek in origin, both ideal places of retirement for poets.[23]

But there is a problem of course with pursuing this comparison. In *Carm.* 2. 6 Horace describes his ideal resting place purely in terms of landscape, not in terms of a house or its luxuries. Horace's goal in *Carm.* 2. 6 is *modus* (7), a word that suggests moral as well as physical limits.[24] Tarentum was a substantial Greek city in the south of Italy, but Horace talks only of its delightful natural beauty, its fertility – excellent honey, olives, wine – and its moderate climate (13–20).[25] Described as *beatae ... arces* ('beneficent citadel', 21–2), in *Carm.* 2. 6 Tarentum is assimilated conceptually to the Sabine farm, which is likewise described in *Sat.* 2. 6. 16 as *arx*, the 'citadel' to which Horace retreats to write poetry; in neither case are buildings described. Horace's concept of the 'citadel' is metaphysical and conveys the notion of moral and spiritual defence.[26] The last words of *Carm.* 2. 6, *vatis amici*, clearly associate the ideal landscape of Tarentum with two other essential elements of the pastoral world, poetry and friendship.[27] In Tarentum, so Horace imagines, the Epicurean life-style can be actualised and made of central importance to his poetic existence.

Carm. 2. 6 endorses the southern, Greek part of Italy as a place of poetic inspiration and philosophical contentment. With its luxurious architecture, however, Pollius' villa seems at first sight far removed from the *locus amoenus* of Horace, where poetry and the simple, modest life were closely linked. The buildings that boldly dominate the landscape, not the natural beauty of the site, are what draw the eye; the first attraction of the estate are the baths (17–18). Pollius' villa moreover is full of wonderful treasures of art; Statius hardly knows where to begin (36–45). Evidence

---

[23] Horace refers to the founding of Tibur by 'an Argive colonist' (5) and of Tarentum by the Spartan Phalanthus (11). See Nisbet and Hubbard (1978) 98 and 101.

[24] See above note 22. *Modus* is also applied in the first line of *Sat.* 2. 6 to the austere Sabine farm.

[25] The idealisation of Tarentum in this poem is discussed in detail by Troxler-Keller (1964) 119–26.

[26] According to Segal (1969b) 243–4, *arx* always carries the connotation of defence as well as height. The association of the *locus amoenus* with the 'citadel' represents Tarentum or the Sabinum as a powerful refuge from worldly cares and concerns, a place where simple desires can easily be met and poetry can be composed. See also Nisbet and Hubbard (1978) 105.

[27] As Troxler-Keller (1964) 126 notes, Propertius conflates the pastoral and the agricultural world when he imagines Virgil composing pastoral poetry in the region of Tarentum (2. 34. 67–8). Virgil's Corycian gardener is located in Tarentum (*G.* 4. 125–48).

of luxurious wealth is more prominent here than in *Silv.* 1. 3. *Silv.* 1. 3 emphasises the harmony of the landscape with the mansions; the fabulous wealth on display inside Vopiscus' home is given only twelve lines (47–58). The centre of *Silv.* 2. 2, however, is devoted to the treasures of the house. Chief among them are Greek statues and Corinthian bronzes (63–72) as well as Greek marbles (85–94), luxury materials that Pliny the Elder criticises in Books 34 and 36 of the *Natural History* as signs of Roman decadence.[28] Between these catalogues of a collector's art is a catalogue of the wonderful views that the villa commands from its myriad rooms (72–85); the windows function as frames so that the collected views form a gallery of landscapes perfectly arranged like wall-paintings. Pollius has nature so much under control that he can organise the landscape outside the bounds of his estate into a tasteful work of art. Unlike Vopiscus' villa, Pollius' villa looks out and commands the wider world of Greek culture.

Archaeological evidence suggests that Pollius' villa may have been rather modest compared to the neighbouring villas.[29] This is not the impression we get from Statius' poem. When Statius says at lines 121–2 that Pollius is richer in gold than Midas or the kings of Troy or Persia, we might remember there Horace's programmatic statement at the end of Book 1 of the *Odes*, *Persicos odi adparatus* (*Carm.* 1. 38. 1). At the same time as he evokes Horatian simplicity, Statius plays up Pollius' luxury and asserts its affiliations with legendary royal wealth.

By directly evoking here the Horatian concept of the ideal landscape, Statius boldly draws attention to his confrontation with the long-standing tradition of Roman hostility to luxury. The allusion to Horace demonstrates the way in which Statius enjoys a provocative relationship with Augustan poetry in the *Silvae* as well as in the *Thebaid*. In bringing Horace's Tibur and Tarentum specifically to mind at the start of *Silv.* 2. 2, Statius implicitly draws a contrast between Pollius' villa and Horace's ideal landscape at the same time as he also forges a relationship between them. Pollius' villa is represented as the locus of poetry and virtue not only despite the luxury, but also *because* of it. Luxury and technology make possible the pastoral dream. But pastoral reciprocity is to a large extent seen as created through the harmonious conjunction

---

[28] Plin. *HN* 34. 3. 5 (the art of bronze is now practised for gain); *HN* 36. 1–13. 63 (marbles).

[29] There remains controversy over which of the villa ruins on the three capes south of Sorrento in fact represents Pollius' villa. See Van Dam (1984) 192, and Bergmann (1991) 66 n. 3 for bibliography.

of god and mortal working the land, not through the innate workings of a compliant nature as in *Silv.* 1. 3. Through a new emphasis on georgic activity, Statius boldly joins the luxurious status of Pollius and his estate to moral and political as well as literary values. Once again, but more boldly, Statius in *Silv.* 2. 2 evokes the hostile tradition against villa luxury in order to disarm it.

In *Silv.* 2. 2, as we shall see, Statius overturns the conventional architectural figures of decadence: height signifies moral superiority rather than pride; riches signify abundant virtue rather than vice; alteration of nature signifies ethical control rather than transgression. The distance he has travelled from the Augustan poets can be seen clearly by a brief look at the end of *Carm.* 3. 1, where Horace uses the architectural figure of the lofty, colonnaded atrium in negative comparison with his Sabine farm (45–8):

> cur invidendis postibus et novo
> sublime ritu moliar atrium?
> cur valle permutem Sabina
> divitias operosiores?

Why should I strive for eye-catching pillars at my door and a lofty hall in the new style? Why should I exchange my Sabine valley for more burdensome riches?

The lofty hall (*sublime ... atrium*), modelled in the latest style, is presented as a sign of extravagant, misguided desire for the greater burden of wealth. In *Silv.* 2. 2 the luxury that Horace condemned is incorporated and justified within a new *locus amoenus* centred on a lofty villa, whose very height and grandeur symbolise the moral superiority of its owner.

As Myers has pointed out, Statius' villa poems draw on a more positive conception of the Roman villa as the 'locus for the statement of intellectual and social ideals'.[30] The peacefulness of the estates of Statius' friends is closely related to their cultivated pursuit of philosophy and poetry, for 'Statius' patrons seem to be immune to the potentially damaging effects of their luxurious environment'.[31] For Myers, these landscapes represent a decisive withdrawal from politics. Yet, as I hope to show, Pollius' villa exists nonetheless within a political frame of reference. Through the theme of the domination of nature, Statius offers a vision not of escapism but of a new civic ideal founded on a shift of the cultural axis from Rome to Naples.

[30] Myers (2000) 109.   [31] Myers (2000) 121.

DOMINATING NATURE

Admittedly, whereas in *Silv.* 1. 3 nature is innately harmonious with the needs of Vopiscus, in *Silv.* 2. 2 the maritime landscape is naturally more barren and rough, and the theme of the domination of nature is correspondingly given greater prominence. In the ideal landscape of Pollius' estate, the features of the *locus amoenus* are cleverly adapted to a maritime environment. Water and shade, for instance, are provided by the sea and by reflection through technological as well as divine intervention. Thus while, as in *Silv.* 1. 3, reflection plays a role in suggesting the harmony between nature and human needs, here the voluntary cooperation of nature with the house that we found in the earlier poem is replaced by a willing obedience to orders and subordination to architectural design; indeed, at one point the sea itself is transformed into a work of art (45–9):

> haec domus ortus
> aspicit et Phoebi tenerum iubar, illa cadentem
> detinet exactamque negat dimittere lucem,
> cum iam fessa dies et in aequora montis opaci
> umbra cadit vitreoque natant praetoria ponto.

This part of the house looks towards the gentle rays of Phoebus' rising, that part detains the falling light and refuses to dismiss it, though its term of duty is done, when now the weary day and the shadow of the darkening mountain fall upon the surface of the sea and the mansion floats on the glass-like waters.

The supremacy of technology is emphasised by the authority the house exercises over daylight itself. Like a *dominus*, master of slaves, the *domus* controls the sun's rays and refuses to dismiss them even at the end of day. But although the relationship between man and the landscape is represented as one between master and slave, benefactor and client, rather than between equals, there is a certain reciprocity about this relationship. Domination mediates between nature and culture in a mutually beneficial way. Thus, the shadow of the mountain falling into the sea might suggest the final dominance of nature, except for the fact that the *praetoria* float on top of the water in reflection. Instead of art imitating nature, the ultimate effect is that of nature imitating art. The sea has become a mirror of the house, transformed as it were into the luxury item of glass, *vitreo* (49) – a perfect image of nature's willing response to art.[32] Relations of domination and subordination ultimately bring out the best in nature

---

[32] As Van Dam (1984) 225–6 points out, ancient glass was glittering and reflective.

and create a self-sufficient world. The relationship between human and nature is represented here as a benevolent one.

Significantly, the landscape of Pollius' villa is shaped by Virgilian as well as by Horatian allusion. This is not coincidental: the Bay of Naples was the site both of Statius' birth and of Virgil's tomb. As Hinds has argued, in *Silv.* 2. 2 Statius is negotiating the geography of Virgilian literary history.[33] At the same time, the allusions evoke a specifically Roman, nationalistic agenda that is at odds with Pollius' ideal of cultivated leisure. In particular, the sea represents a site of cultural contest between the two poets. A realm of human danger and risk that is hard for humans to control, the sea is intimately connected both with war and trade and with the imperialistic drive for territorial aggrandisement. But in *Silv.* 2. 2, the tranquillity of the sea by Pollius' shores reflects the moral and social order of his peaceful, well ordered estate. Indeed, from the vantage point of the windows of the villa, the entire Bay of Naples is artistically framed and ordered, creating a self-contained world (74–85). There is no need for Pollius, like Aeneas, to voyage out on uncertain seas; the world itself comes to him and is contained and controlled according to his tastes and needs. In *Silv.* 2. 2 Statius rewrites the Virgilian landscapes of the *Aeneid* and removes their associations with a nationalistic imperative. Instead, he recreates through Pollius' estate a new form of Virgilian pastoral in which the high value placed upon luxury and technology helps effect a close connection between the landscape and the ideal state.

Domination is of course an important aspect of the imperialistic mission, a means of acquiring works of art and expensive goods that form an important part of the cultural capital of Empire. But in *Silv.* 2. 2 domination of nature is represented as a benevolent activity that is largely detached from a national agenda of expansion and appropriation. Domination of nature shapes the *locus amoenus* and participates here in creating a pastoral realm of mutual benefit to nature and human being.

Statius describes the estate from the point of view of a traveller approaching from the sea; thus he describes the seashore first. Yet observation here is shaped by literary history rather than by topography. As Myers has pointed out, the description of the shore of the estate (13–16) as a curving bay flanked by ridges of rocks echoes Virgil's disquieting description of the Libyan harbour at *Aeneid* 1. 159ff. where Aeneas' battered ships seek refuge after the storm.[34] The Trojan ships of course

---

33 Hinds (forthcoming).
34 Myers (2000) 118. She suggests that Statius' description here also alludes to Lucan's description of Brundisium at *BC* 5. 442–4. See also Van Dam (1984) 201–2 on *Silv.* 2. 2. 13–29.

cannot stay; Aeneas' imperialistic mission requires him to reject the stability offered him in Carthage and to voyage out to his uncertain future. If Pollius' villa, so this opening allusion suggests, is a type of Carthage, then the regional peace and security that Pollius enjoys is in important ways antithetical to the ambitious aims of national policies. From the beginning of the poem then, the villa is given a political as well as a literary frame of reference.

Like the Libyan harbour (*Aen.* 1. 168), Pollius' estate is the home of nymphs. Here, notably, it is not the natural features such as the sheltered bay – charming to our modern sensibilities, perhaps – that attract the sea nymphs. Rather, Pollius' smart new baths on the shore lure them to his estate; indeed, the man-made structure is so appealing that the Naiads themselves would like to swim there rather than in the sea (17–20):

> gratia prima loci, gemina testudine fumant
> balnea et e terris occurrit dulcis amaro
> nympha mari. levis hic Phorci chorus udaque crines
> Cymodoce viridisque cupit Galatea lavari.

The first delight of the place is the baths, which smoke from double domes, and the sweet water runs from the land to meet the bitter salt sea. The nimble followers of Phorcus and damp-haired Cymodoce and sea-green Galatea long to bathe here.

Virgilian allusions remind us that the sea is an important area in which Roman national agendas are contested and displayed. At line 19 Statius alludes to the contest of the ships in Virgil's *Aeneid* Book 5 where 'Phorcus' band' (*Phorcique chorus, Aen.* 5. 240) propels the winning ship to victory in a competition that paradigmatically displays the qualities of good leadership.[35] Cymodoce (20) likewise appears in Book 10 of the *Aeneid* as a nymph of the metamorphosed ships who is particularly gifted in speech. She explains the miracle and urges Aeneas and his men to action (*Aen.* 10. 225–48). On Pollius' estate, however, the sea deities and nymphs are detached from a national context and assume a passive role; they are the recipients, not the agents, of human pleasure. Like the estate itself, the nymphs are removed from the political initiatives of imperial Rome.

Seneca condemned elaborate baths as a sign of modern extravagance.[36] In *Silv.* 2.2 luxury removes conflict and engineers pleasure and friendship. Moreover the preference of the sea nymphs for the artifice of Pollius' baths rather than their natural element introduces an important

---

[35] Nugent (1992) 262; Feldherr (1995) 255–7.   [36] Sen. *Ep.* 86.

theme of *Silv.* 2. 2; the removal of destructive *furor* from nature and its
consequent delight in its improvement (21–5):

> ante domum tumidae moderator caerulus undae
> excubat, innocui custos laris; huius amico
> spumant templa salo. felicia rura tuetur
> Alcides; gaudet gemino sub numine portus:
> hic servat terras, hic saevis fluctibus obstat.

Before the home the sea-blue ruler of the swelling wave keeps watch, guardian
of an innocent hearth; his temple foams with friendly spray. Alcides guards the
happy countryside; the harbour rejoices in its two presiding deities: one guards
the land, the other blocks the savage waves.

The acknowledged existence of a hostile nature, *saevis fluctibus* (25), founds
Pollius' estate, more overtly than in *Silv.* 1. 3, on a pastoral dialectic between forces of order and disorder. Nature here is subjugated to the superiority of man's works – but, watched over by Hercules and Neptune,
bailiffs of the estate, the fields are happy, *felicia* (23); even the sea spray is
friendly to human endeavour (*amico*, 22); the harbour rejoices (*gaudet*, 24)
to be guarded by Hercules and Neptune as they themselves are happy to
guard Pollius. Virgil's rather ominous harbour has been transformed here
to a benevolent one where nymphs, deities, and indeed poets, can securely
enjoy the benefits of friendship and civilisation. The landscape, then, is
marked as a sacred space. Here Statius negotiates between myth and reality, as in an actual Roman garden, which was populated by statues of gods
and mythological figures, for instance, pleasing the aesthetic eye and also
inviting veneration and contemplation of the virtues there represented.[37]
But Statius also fashions Pollius' estate as a magical, pastoral realm, where
the gods help further human ease rather than ambition.

Pastoral reciprocity here is engineered then through the dual management of the gods and technology, rather than through nature itself.
Pollius' villa is fashioned as a *locus amoenus* where Neptune and Hercules
uniquely work hand in hand with technology to provide safety and protection from the harsh external elements. Religion in *Silv.* 2. 2 sanctions
the luxury of Pollius' estate. For Horace, the protection of the gods alone
made secure his ideal landscape and granted it peace and prosperity.
As he says in *Carm.* 1. 17. 13, *di me tuentur* ('the gods look after me').[38]

---

[37] Farrar (1998) 104–5; Kuttner (1999) 10–11; Myers (2000) 111. On Hercules as a garden god see
Farrar (1998) 116–17 and on the nymphs see 120–21.
[38] On the frequency of this assertion in Horace see Nisbet and Hubbard (1970) 221–2. In *Carm.* 1.
17 the gods' protection makes possible the ideal landscape where Horace can practise poetry in
peace. As Schmidt (1997) 89 notes, Horace here at line 13 broadens and develops the statement

The gods too protect Pollius. Statius, however, also makes technological achievement crucial to the construction and defence of the villa, the new ideal site for the practice of poetry and virtue.

Further justification for the artistic and technological splendours of Pollius' estate is found in the close ethical connection forged between the personified landscape and the ideals of its master, a connection that is again more fully developed than in *Silv.* 1. 3. The prominent position of *amico* (22) implies the importance of friendship in Pollius' home; indeed, friendship draws Statius to the villa (9–10).[39] *Felicia* (23) introduces the first pun upon Pollius' name and suggests the close identification between Pollius and the landscape he has shaped.[40] Control over nature is closely linked to Pollius' moral control. Pollius, we are told at line 9, is peaceful, *placidus*, in character, the bay where his villa is set is correspondingly *placido* (13). The occasional resistance of nature to its improvement helps metaphorically fashion Pollius as a man who can master his land as he can master his passions.

Neptune, guardian of the shore who is described as the 'ruler of the swelling wave' (*tumidae moderator . . . undae*, 21), functions as a preliminary sign of ethical as well as physical moderation, for *tumidus* frequently refers to human passion, particularly anger.[41] Again, the *Aeneid* comes into play here. Neptune appears at the start of the *Aeneid* as the calmer of the storm that threatens to wreck Aeneas' ships off Carthage. He programmatically introduces the tension that runs throughout the epic between the forces of order and destruction. In *Silv.* 2. 2 the rejection of the Roman imperialistic drive for territorial expansion is symbolised by Neptune's circumscribed role. He guards a garden estate of poetry and philosophy, not a fleet that is single-mindedly bent on the building of a nation. Hercules too was closely associated in Roman thought with the founding of Rome's national identity, as the lengthy aition of the Ara Maxima in *Aen.* 8. 184–279 demonstrates. On Pollius' Campanian estate, Neptune and Hercules are represented as agents of containment rather than expansion. They promote a new concept of cultural identity based on the civilising effects of intellectual and artistic life.

of the *Ode*'s opening lines, namely that Faunus' frequent epiphanies bring protection to this farm. Now the gods in general protect not only the animals, but also the poet himself, ensuring the peace and prosperity that make music possible.

[39] In the preface to Book 2 Statius refers to Pollius as 'mine' (*Polli mei, praef.* 2. 12) and as a 'friend' (*amicus, praef.* 2. 14).

[40] Puns on Pollius' name occur also at lines 107, 122, and 150. On the frequency of such punning on names in Statius see Nisbet (1978) 8 followed by Van Dam (1984) 207–8.

[41] On *tumidus* as a descriptive epithet of anger see e.g. Ov. *Met.* 2. 602, 8. 437, and 13. 559. On the sea as a symbol of human passion see below 170–2.

The correspondence between Pollius' character and that of the sub-jugated but harmonious landscape is made explicit in the following lines describing the wonderful calm of the seashore (26–9):

> mira quies pelagi: ponunt hic lassa furorem
> aequora et insani spirant clementius austri;
> hic praeceps minus audet hiems, nulloque tumultu
> stagna modesta iacent dominique imitantia mores.

There is a marvellous quiet upon the sea: here the weary waves allay their fury and the mad winds breathe more mildly; here there is less risk of violent storms, and without tumult the gentle waters lie still, imitating the character of their master.

Ethical terms in chiastic order inform Pollius' marvellously quiescent landscape: *quies*, *furorem*, *insani*, *clementius*, link the calming of the sea's violence with the control of human passion.[42] The climactic line spells out the correspondence between physical and ethical moderation. Thanks to divine and human control the waters imitate the character of their master (29). *Modesta*, which I have translated as 'gentle', occurs here in a striking and unprecedented usage, for this adjective is always used to describe the moderation or temperance of human character.[43] The bold personification closely links Pollius with the topography of his estate; the waters imitate their master's art, and they imitate his temperate character. Luxurious the villa may be, but through the resources of human technology that reshape and tame nature, Horatian moderation can be created without the harm to the landscape or to the owner's character that Horace feared. Pollius' villa is shaped by the Roman impulse to dominate nature, but this is interpreted as a positive, benevolent impulse, not a transgressive one. Within Statius' reformulation of literary tradition the villa is represented as a moral space protected from the unsettling passions that involve Aeneas, for instance, in the adventures of Empire.

Thus Statius here reinterprets the cultural code that shaped the villa's ideology. The grandeur of Pollius' house, conventionally a sign of enormous social prestige, assumes an ethical value – Pollius is rich above all in moral wealth, in control of self as well as of his property. When towards the end of *Silv.* 2. 2 Statius then addresses Pollius as richer than the treasures of Midas and Lydian gold (121), *ditior* should be understood as referring to symbolic as well as material wealth, in particular to the riches of Pollius' mind that have enabled him to make wise use of his

---

[42] On the physical and ethical application of these terms see Van Dam (1984) 209–11.
[43] See *OLD* 1c.

wealth by cherishing both the arts and philosophy.[44] Indeed, this comparison introduces the extended passage toward the end of the poem (121–32) in which Statius, far more explicitly than in *Silv.* 1. 3, describes the villa owner as the Epicurean *sapiens* who is free from the temptations of power and ambition.[45] As Myers points out, such a characterisation is in keeping with Pollius' regional identity, for the area of the Bay of Naples was closely associated with Epicureanism.[46] Epicureanism here then provides an implicit alternative to the imperialistic drive of Roman nationalism.

Characteristically, Pollius is described as an Epicurean through his villa. Its situation on a cliff, looking out over the sea, is given explicit metaphorical application in its description as the 'lofty citadel of the mind' (129–32):

> nos, vilis turba, caducis
> deservire bonis semperque optare parati,
> spargimur in casus: celsa tu mentis ab arce
> despicis errantes humanaque gaudia rides.

We, wretched mob, who are prepared to enslave ourselves to transitory goods and perpetual desire, are scattered to fortune: you, from the lofty citadel of your mind, look down upon errant humans and laugh at mortal pleasures.

Statius here recalls Lucretius' description at the start of Book 2 of the *De Rerum Natura* (1–14) of the Epicurean wise man, looking down from the high temples of wisdom at others struggling in the sea of error (1–4, 7–14):

> Suave, mari magno turbantibus aequora ventis,
> e terra magnum alterius spectare laborem;
> non quia vexari quemquamst iucunda voluptas,
> sed quibus ipse malis careas quia cernere suave est . . .
> sed nil dulcius est, bene quam munita tenere
> edita doctrina sapientum templa serena,
> despicere unde queas alios passimque videre
> errare atque viam palantis quaerere vitae,   10
> certare ingenio, contendere nobilitate,
> noctes atque dies niti praestante labore

---

[44] Thus also Cancik (1968) 74–5. Cancik however argues that Statius has downplayed the luxury of Pollius' villa (74); he thus ignores the superb paradoxes on which this poem is based.

[45] On the extensive allusions to Lucretius and Horace in this passage see Vollmer (1898) 351–2 on *Silv.* 2. 2. 121. Vollmer points out that Statius' description of Pollius as *sapiens* here resembles that of Horace in *Sat.* 2. 7. 83–7.

[46] Myers (2000) 122–3. Wallace-Hadrill (1995) 4–5 notes that Roman gardens characteristically possessed Epicurean connotations.

ad summas emergere opes rerumque potiri.
o miseras hominum mentis, o pectora caeca!

When the winds are whipping up the waves to a mighty swell, it is sweet to look at the toil of another; not because there is particular pleasure in someone's harassment, but because it is sweet to see the evils which you yourself do not have. But nothing is more pleasant than to possess the lofty temples of the wise well fortified by serene learning, from where you can look down upon others and see them wandering in error everywhere, seeking the way of making a good life, rivals in ability, competing in nobility, struggling day and night with exceptional effort to reach the pinnacle of wealth and material possession. O wretched minds of men, oh blind hearts!

As Konstan has pointed out, the motif of seafaring in the ancient world is gain. Those storm-tossed on the sea therefore metaphorically represent people in the grip of misguided desires and greed. Indeed, the common metaphor of the ship as soul also comes into play here, suggesting 'a soul labouring under the unsettling blasts of passion'.[47] The image of the forti-fied citadel, on the other hand, represents the teaching of Epicureanism. 'From this vantage point alone may one look down in safety upon the restless and futile activity of mortals who stray and wander, strive and contend, and reduce talent, station and industry [*ingenio, nobilitate, labore*, 11–12] to the service of empty and limitless desire. Amid the frantic, com-pulsive motion at sea, on the battlefield, everywhere, only the Epicurean is stationary and secure.'[48]

Thus the cliff-top location of Pollius' *villa maritima* and its superior relationship to nature, in particular the savage sea (*saevis fluctibus*, 25), symbolically express the virtue of the Epicurean wise man who, like Pollius, has learned to be unmoved by the ambitions of the world, to be physically and morally aloof from the sea which serves as a symbol of human turmoil and error.[49] Statius develops the nautical metaphor with the description of Pollius' soul as a ship that has reached a safe harbour (139–41):

> illo alii rursus iactantur in alto,
> sed tua securos portus placidamque quietem
> intravit non quassa ratis.

Others are tossed about again on the deep, but your ship unshaken has entered a safe harbour and calm quiet.

---

[47] Konstan (1973) 8. See also 3–12 for a detailed discussion of Lucretius' passage.
[48] Konstan (1973) 9.
[49] On the Lucretian and Epicurean motifs of *Silv.* 2. 2 see Nisbet (1978) 1–2.

In the light of the metaphorical function of the sea, the features of the villa's harbour described at the poem's start – its calm waters, its blocking of the violent waves, and the clemency of its winds (25–9) – retrospectively assume specific symbolic importance as signs of their owner's Epicurean calm and beatitude. *Quies* ('quiet'), at first applied to the wonderful calm of the sea in Pollius' harbour (26) here assumes specific meaning as a word used to denote Epicurean calm and freedom from passion.[50] Thus in the preface to Book 3 Statius neatly conflates the physical calm of Pollius' estate with his philosophical peace of mind when he addresses Pollius as *quiete dignissime* ('most worthy of quiet', *praef.* 3. 2).

But the Epicurean metaphor also has a specifically Roman resonance. The sea is also the site of nationalistic enterprise, of the imperialistic quest for gain, as the nymphs at the start of Statius' poem remind us. The ship too is a common metaphor for the state.[51] Thus the lofty villa, Pollius' well-provided and well-protected resting-place in retirement, by contrast represents a powerful set of alternative values to those that drive the Roman state. Poetry, philosophy, and friendship, the qualities cherished on Vopiscus' estate and in the house of Vindex, for instance, are here given particularly dynamic expression in a region famed for its intellectual and artistic life.

Indeed, even the villa's commanding views over the Bay of Naples from its myriad windows, elaborated upon at lines 73–82, represent Pollius' successful accommodation of Roman ambitions to Epicurean virtue (73–5):

> sua cuique voluptas
> atque omni proprium thalamo mare, transque iacentem
> Nerea diversis servit sua terra fenestris.

Specific to each room is its own delightful view of the sea, and a territory all their own serves different windows across the expanse of the sea.

On the one hand, the villa's appropriation of the various views marks the wealth and social prestige of the owner and the Roman impulse for control of land. A fine view was an essential feature of the Roman villa, and houses were designed with rooms on individual axes to frame artfully the most attractive landscapes.[52] Characteristically then, the interaction between man and nature in Pollius' ideal landscape is not spontaneous

---

[50] On the specific philosophical meaning of *quies* as the Latin equivalent of Epicurean *ataraxia* see the discussion and bibliography in Van Dam (1984) 209–11. See also on *quies* OLD 6.

[51] See Nisbet and Hubbard (1970) 178–82 on Hor. *Carm.* 1. 14.

[52] See Vitr. *De arch.* 6. 4; Bergmann (1991) 59–62.

but is carefully controlled by architectural design. As Bergmann points out, the verbs *spectat, prospectat* and *prospicit*, make the villa 'a dynamic image that ... subjugates the land it sees in a succession of framed views'.[53] Distinction here between the outside world and the inner one is blurred. The sea, spread out before the windows of Pollius' villa, conveys with the word *iacentem* (74) both submission and the stillness of painting, while *servit* (75) portrays the land as a servant of the villa in its provision of various fine views.[54] Transformed into decorative pictures, the landscape appears calm and unthreatening. The villa's role as controller of nature is thus yet again represented as benevolent. Essentially the villa assumes the role of artist, selecting and ordering the raw material of nature into attractive form so that the distinction between actual and painted landscape is pleasingly blurred. Once again, domination mediates between nature and culture in a way that is mutually beneficent and pleasant.

On the other hand, this ordering of nature into pleasant views is metaphorically related to the ordering of the passions. The active role of the villa here as the controller of nature emphasises the strong metonymical connection between house and owner. Architecture creates the calm waters that are metaphors of inner calm. Here then the imposition of artistic order upon nature is linked with moral and spiritual authority and control. In particular, the pleasure (*voluptas*, 73) of the view is incontrovertibly linked with the Epicurean concept of pleasure as freedom from anxious desire; indeed *voluptas*, as we saw in the previous chapter, is, like *quies*, another catchword of Epicureanism.[55] The physical eminence of the villa and its corresponding subjugation of nature through architecture have then philosophical application. Pollius has achieved Epicurean *ataraxia* by conquering hope and fear, as he earlier conquered the sea and land (125): *spemque metumque domas voto sublimior omni* ('you conquer hope and fear, raised above all desire'). The highly controlled interactivity between man and nature is a sign of Pollius' ethical as well as social authority. The physical and architectural dominance of the villa provides another way of suggesting Pollius' moral as well as economic security; the outside world poses no threat to his inner being.

The view from Pollius' villa encompasses the entire Bay of Naples, reaching to Cape Misenum in the north and including many of its islands. Yet unlike many Roman wall-paintings, the landscape seen from

---

53 Bergmann (1991) 60.
54 See Van Dam (1984) 241 on the suggestion of submission that is present in both *iacentem* (74) and *servit* (75). See also on *iacere TLL* vii. 10. 49–63 for the meaning of object submission.
55 See chapter 4 above, 137.

Pollius' villa does not present a series of never-ending vistas; it is confined within the bounds of the bay. By framing and thus enclosing the
bay the house reproduces in its viewing its self-contained world.[56] The
house looks to the outside world only to fashion it as a further model of
the idealised private life. At the same time, that life is shaped by a firm
sense of regional identity. The encapsulation of the Bay of Naples through
the framed viewing of its windows suggests that the villa, though in one
sense physically separate from the outside world, in another important
sense embodies the distinctive philosophical and artistic culture of the
region. Although Pollius lives apart from the public power and authority
entrenched in the capital city of the nation, his villa forcefully articulates
the virtues that compose his region's cultural identity. Indeed, his villa
is a highly organised community whose successful accommodation of
Roman values to Greek ideals is founded, nonetheless, on a critique of
Roman nationalism. The moral landscape of Pollius' villa then has also
a political frame of reference.

Paradoxically perhaps, the philosophical ideal is also in some ways
here a civic ideal. Statius' second villa poem is a particularly ambitious
one that through the moral and philosophical elevation of wealth moves
beyond Pollius' villa to invite reflection on the larger social and political
order. In the political use it makes of the villa, so I wish now to suggest,
the poem looks specifically towards Rome as well as Naples, assimilating
the Greek philosophical ideal to a civic model where the intellectual life
is central.

PLAYING THE EMPEROR

The transvaluation of luxury is closely connected with alienation from
civic life. The perception of the state as an inadequate or indeed dangerous source of patronage is accompanied by a shift to the private
sphere for true appreciation of the arts. Pollius coopts the public role
of literary and artistic benefactor; hence his possession of luxury goods
becomes morally as well as aesthetically acceptable. Indeed, through
Statius' poem, Pollius' wealth is put on display for us all to enjoy. Significantly, then, Pollius is represented on his estate as Roman emperor or
colonial governor as well as Epicurean sage. These two roles are not in
fact incompatible. For Pollius' enlightened and benevolent governance
of his estate, though shaped by Roman values, is related to his pursuit of

---

[56] Myers (2000) 120 emphasises that the stress on the wealth of the villas of Statius' friends implies
that 'the owners have created their own private and self-sufficient worlds'.

wisdom. Fabulously wealthy, with a house filled with luxury goods, he is represented as knowing how to use this imperial style of wealth wisely. His villa thus provides a powerful model of the ideal state that, from the periphery of Rome, challenges its imperial centre.

Purcell has argued that the building of a luxurious villa was the domestic counterpart of the activity of the tyrant, the stereotypical transgressor of nature's bounds.[57] In traditional Roman thought, the luxurious villa was regarded as morally transgressive. The villa's innovative architecture and often physically daring location challenged Roman ideas of decorum and the sacredness of nature. Villas clung to dizzying cliff tops or were built out over waves in audacious defiance of nature; they incorporated artificial woods and even mountains within their precincts. Thus the challenging of the natural order embodied in ostentatious architecture was conventionally interpreted as a potent symbol of human pride and moral perversion as well as a threat to the social order. Pollius' villa has an audacious situation on a cliff top above a rugged shore. Yet this location, as we have seen, can be interpreted symbolically in the light of Epicurean beliefs. Furthermore, in Statius' poem Pollius is represented as playing the good emperor, not the tyrant. His ordered landscape provides a positive model for a social order based on enlightened governance.

Silv. 3. 1 for instance, to which we will briefly turn, celebrates Pollius' restoration of a temple, an act traditionally associated with the Roman emperor alone.[58] The temple, moreover, is dedicated to Hercules, a god long associated with the foundation of Rome. Here however the temple is located on a private estate, and the god, as in the house of Vindex, is described as off duty, relaxed, genial and depoliticised (29–45); he is accommodated therefore to private life. Still, Pollius is engaged in an essentially imperial act of rebuilding a sacred site and honouring a god who protects his estate. The dedication of the temple too is celebrated on a grand scale with games and sacrifice.

Pollius demonstrates too the particularly Roman virtue of piety to the gods, although it finds significant expression, in part, through his enthusiasm for Greek art. The temple, formerly unadorned, impoverished, and a temporary refuge for vagabond sailors (3–4), is rebuilt in a grander style, with gleaming Greek marbles (3–6). Architectural

[57] Purcell (1987) 190–3.
[58] See Eck (1997a) 163. Balbus' theatre, built to celebrate his victory in Africa between 19 and 13 BCE, was the last building of such scale in Rome to be raised by a man of rank unconnected to the imperial family. We have no knowledge after him of any senator who privately financed and dedicated a public building in Rome.

magnificence here testifies to Pollius' religious reverence. As head of his estate, he demonstrates a right relationship to the gods.

Indeed, towards the poem's end Pollius is specifically compared to Hercules, here now in his role as important Roman imperial god who through domination of nature brings the benefits of civilisation (166–70):

> macte animis opibusque meos imitate labores,
> qui rigidas rupes infecundaeque pudenda
> naturae deserta domas et vertis in usum
> lustra habitata feris foedeque latentia profers
> numina.

Blessings on your mind and your wealth, you who have imitated my labours, who conquer the rugged rocks and the shameful wastes of infertile nature and turn to use wilderness inhabited by wild beasts and put on view divinities hiding in shameful obscurity.

Hercules here specifically validates Pollius' wealth, for he has used it wisely in his taming of nature. The analogy between Hercules and Pollius suggests that technological improvement is a civilising activity and that wise use of wealth has become a new kind of heroism. In particular, the close connection drawn here between Pollius and Hercules (*meos imitate labores*, 166) assimilates Pollius further to the idea of the good emperor. As a former mortal who underwent apotheosis, Hercules was important to the emperors. He was particularly important to Domitian, who built a shrine to Hercules outside Rome in which, according to three epigrams of Martial, 9. 64, 65, and 101, the statue of the god bore Domitian's features.[59] The close assimilation of Hercules to Pollius in *Silv.* 3. 1 provocatively suggests that Statius is using Pollius and his villa to explore ideas of good governance. Note too that Minerva, Domitian's patron deity, is also closely associated with the estate (*Silv.* 2. 2. 2, 117). In keeping with the character of the estate, however, her warlike function, which is prominent in her connection with Domitian, is here abandoned as she is disarmed literally and metaphorically by Pollius' music (117).[60]

The rebuilding of the temple and the revival of the cult of Hercules on Pollius' estate are themselves actions modelled on those of an emperor. Laguna has noted that the choice of *aula* (10) to describe the temple is a usage found only in the poetry of Statius and Martial; otherwise it is

---

[59] Scott (1936) 141–6.

[60] On the close association between Minerva and Domitian's military prowess see *Silv.* 1. 1. 37–40. On Domitian's predilection for Minerva see Scott (1936) 166–88, especially 176–9 on her predominantly martial image on Domitian's coinage.

used to refer to the imperial court.[61] He also notes that in the preceding line Statius' address to Hercules as the former guardian of 'a small altar' (*parvae . . . arae*, 9) makes covert allusion to the most famous and ancient cult of Hercules in Rome, the Ara Maxima.[62] Like Augustus, and indeed Domitian, who modelled himself on the first emperor by active and prolific building and restoration, Pollius rebuilds a temple and restores a cult.[63] He plays emperor in a microcosmic world removed from the stresses and uncertainties of public life. Religion on Pollius' estate is not a matter of public duty but is coopted by a private individual. The temple thus represents the poet's continuing scrutiny of the concepts and rituals that shaped Roman reality and his provocative attempt to reformulate civic values within the private sphere.

Of particular interest too is the programmatic role of Hercules here. Statius begins Book 3 with a god who participates in literary tradition with both public and private poetry, with both beginnings and endings. Hercules is introduced at the start of the third book of Callimachus' *Aetia* and the third book of Virgil's *Georgics* as well as at the start of *Silv.* 3. 1.[64] He also appears at the end of the first edition of Ennius' *Annales*, where the founding of the temple of Hercules Musarum by Fulvius Nobilior forms a triumphal conclusion to his Aetolian triumph of 187 BCE; Hercules is here closely associated with Roman victory and cultural imperialism, for the temple featured statues of the Greek Muses brought from Ambracia.[65] The temple of Hercules Musarum also appears at the end of Ovid's *Fasti* as part of the project of Augustan restoration and the promotion of the imperial dynasty.[66] The *Aetia* and the *Georgics* share with the *Annales* and the *Fasti* a political frame of reference.[67] Hercules appears in the *Aetia* as part of an epinician honouring Queen Berenice; in the *Georgics* he acts as a foil to Virgil's announcement that he will soon write an epic honouring Augustus. Hercules at the start of Book 3 of the *Aetia* and the *Georgics*

---

[61] Laguna (1992) 132.   [62] Laguna (1992) 131.

[63] On Domitian's conscious rebuilding of Rome in imitation of Augustus see Sablayrolles (1994) 123–30.

[64] Thomas (1983) notes the similarity.   [65] See Skutsch (1985) 553.

[66] On the political and metapoetic significance of the temple of Hercules Musarum see Newlands (1995) 210–19.

[67] The opening section of *Aetia* 3, an epinician honouring Queen Berenice, seems to have contained an internal aetiological narrative of Hercules' founding of the Nemean games that emphasised the god's visit with a poor man named Molorchus before the fight with the Nemean lion. See Parsons (1977). Significantly, both Virgil and Statius mention Molorchus at the start of their third books as a kind of Callimachean signature. Virgil provides the first post-Callimachean reference to Molorchus (*G.* 3. 19), Statius the first post-Virgilian references (*Silv.* 3, 1, 29; also *Silv.* 4. 6. 51; *Theb.* 4. 159–64). See Thomas (1983) 94–5; Newlands (1991).

forms part of the poet's exploration of political poetry of public praise. In *Silv.* 3. 1 Statius uses the ecphrasis of the temple of Hercules to praise a private friend and patron. Yet the ecphrasis of the temple to Hercules situates Statius' *Silvae* within a poetic genealogy that explored different ways of honouring and defining a ruler. Indeed, Pollius' estate forms an important site for the articulation of ideas both about good patronage and good governance.

In *Silv.* 2. 2 Pollius plays the emperor through his domination of nature and the opulence of his villa. The connection between the language of domination used to fashion this private, luxurious estate and that of war has often been noted.[68] In Virgil's *Georgics* too we find the language of military domination used to describe the farmer's relationship to a nature which is often resistant to human endeavour. As Bradley notes, this is a sublimated form of warfare: the farmer 'is at war with it . . . tearing, cutting and stabbing, in the interests of productivity'.[69] But even when brought under human control, Virgil's nature constantly threatens dissolution.[70] In Statius' villa poems, on the other hand, nature is happy to be dominated; there is no simple Levi-Straussian division between nature and culture. A crucial aspect of Pollius' *locus amoenus*, then, is the central fiction that nature, described in human terms, is on the whole happy and grateful to be subjugated.

What has not been remarked upon in this poem, however, is the way in which the language of domination evokes the Roman public world of civic, as well as military, affairs, particularly colonisation.[71] The first terms used to describe Pollius' villa – *celsa Dicarchei speculatrix villa profundi* (3) – encapsulate the complex elements of the villa's significance. It is in a lofty position (*celsa*), a sign of its ethical superiority. It looks out over the deep sea (*profundi*), a gaze later to be ascribed Epicurean and political relevance. The sea, moreover, is described with reference to the Greek founder and coloniser of Puteoli, Dicarchus, a sign of the importance of Greek culture and history in the ideology of the villa and the poetics of the *Silvae*.[72] Festus plays on the Greek etymology of the coloniser's name

[68] The military imagery of the poem was noted by Cancik (1968) 69–70, but not developed beyond the notion of Pollius as 'military victor' over nature. See also Van Dam (1984) 227–8; Myers (2000) 113–15.

[69] Bradley (1969) 350–1.

[70] The classic formulation of nature's resistance to human improvement occurs in *G.* 1. 197–203 where Virgil describes the farmer as a rower battling upstream against a heady current.

[71] For Van Dam (1984) 227 Pollius is a civiliser, like the farmer, whose activity is often described in military terminology. Statius actualises the work of the civiliser in terms of Roman military and political activity.

[72] *Dicarchei* also makes a compliment to Pollius, since Pollius was a citizen of both Puteoli and Naples (*Silv.* 2. 2. 133–7).

by explaining it to mean that this ruler was very just.[73] At the start of the poem colonisation is implicitly established as a potentially benevolent, productive act. Finally, however, the villa is described as *speculatrix*, a military term used of a spy or watchman on the lookout for danger.[74] The villa, then, is conceived as a defensive unit, protective of its owners and their special lifestyle. Statius thus establishes the military character of the villa as a physical and metaphorical defence against the inroads of politics and ambition.[75] But this notion of defence incorporates more than the idea of Epicurean moral and spiritual security. The villa 'estate' exists in synecdochic relationship to the 'state', providing an example of a well-ordered, harmonious community founded on friendship, trust and justice. Pollius' house is represented metaphorically as the headquarters of his well-governed estate, or, as I wish to argue, state or colony. The villa buildings themselves are called *praetoria* (49), a word that is first applied to domestic architecture only around this time.[76] The association with the *praetoria*, the general's headquarters of a military camp, surely is still in play here, with aesthetic values linked closely to correct governance.

At lines 52–62, the military metaphor is given extended application in the description of Pollius as a military general, and of nature as a conquered provincial:

> his favit natura locis, hic victa colenti
> cessit et ignotos docilis mansuevit in usus.
> mons erat hic ubi plana vides, et lustra fuerunt
> quae nunc tecta subis; ubi nunc nemora ardua cernis
> hic nec terra fuit: domuit possessor, et illum
> formantem rupes expugnantemque secuta
> gaudet humus. nunc cerne iugum discentia saxa
> intrantemque domos iussumque recedere montem.
> iam Methymnaei vatis manus et chelys una
> Thebais et Getici cedat tibi gloria plectri;
> et tu saxa moves, et te nemora alta sequuntur.

Nature favoured this site, here conquered it yielded to the coloniser and compliant grew amenable to unknown uses. There was a mountain here where you see an open expanse of lawn, and the houses you now enter were wild brush; where now you see lofty groves there was no earth: the owner has conquered and

---

[73] See Vollmer (1898) 340 on *Silv.* 2. 2. 3.
[74] See *OLD* 1b and 1c.
[75] Van Dam (1984) 196 suggests that the adjective *speculatrix* characterises 'the victory of man over nature'. This blurs the special meaning of the word which stresses defence against the threats of the outside world rather than victory over them.
[76] *Praetoria* is used of the villa first in the late first century AD in the poetry of Statius, Juvenal, and Martial (*OLD* 3).

the land follows and rejoices as he fashions the rocks and takes them by storm. Look now at the boulders learning the yoke and the mountain that tries to enter the house now ordered to retreat.[77] Now let the skilled hand of the Methymnaean bard, the unique Theban lyre, and the glory of the Getic plectrum yield to you; you too move boulders, and the lofty groves follow you.

The land is treated here as a provincial that yields before the conquering, civilising hand of Pollius. *Domuit possessor* ('the owner has conquered', 56): the language of domination is emphatic here and blunt.[78] Note too the military language of *expugnantem* ('taking by storm', 57), *iugum discentia* ('learning the yoke', 58), the mountain 'ordered' (*iussum*, 59) to retreat. Yet such domination is presented as part of a colonial project rather than outright war and devastation. The first stage in creating a colony involved the military marking out of a tract of land and its reshaping for settlement. Pollius is civiliser as well as conqueror, as the juxtaposition of *victa* with *colenti* attests (52). Moreover, this colonial project is lacking in friction, for the land is represented as *docilis* (53), compliant with its transformation into civilised form. Domination is represented as a process not of destroying but of taming, of making gentle and amenable, *mansuevit* (53); the consequence is a land happy at its new civilised state: *gaudet humus* ('the land rejoices', 58).

The personification of the land here plays upon the civic notion of the conquered provincial, eager for the benefits of Roman civilisation. Moreover, the description of the conquering Pollius as *colenti* suggests a certain reverence towards the land he has conquered, a reciprocal relationship of worship and reward. The idea that humans who work the land have a worshipful relationship to it is elaborated upon by the elder Pliny, when he actualises in Rome's past the metaphor of the farmer as soldier (*HN* 18. 4. 19):

quaenam ergo tantae ubertatis causa erat? ipsorum tunc manibus imperatorum colebantur agri, ut fas est credere, gaudente terra vomere laureato et triumphali aratore, sive illi eadem cura semina tractabant qua bella eademque diligentia arva disponebant qua castra, sive honestis manibus omnia laetius proveniunt quoniam et curiosius fiunt.

What then was the cause of such great fertility? The fields were cultivated then by the hands of generals themselves, and, as it is right to believe, the earth rejoiced in its laureate plough and triumphal ploughman, either because they handled the seeds with the same attention as they handled war, or because

---

[77] See Van Dam (1984) 230–1 on the textual and interpretive problem of *intrantemque domos iussumque recedere montem* (59).

[78] On the military associations of *domare* see *TLL* V. 1946. 45–1947. 54.

they marked out the fields with the same care as they marked out their camps, or because all things grow more fruitfully from virtuous hands since they are granted greater care.

In the early days of Rome, there was no disjunction between sign and signifier, for farmers were indeed generals, and ploughs were triumphal trophies. Cultivation of the land was given religious sanctification by man's moral and worshipful relationship to the land that he carved out as he would a military camp, and which repaid him with abundance. Culture and cultivation were thus essentially synonymous. In Pliny's passage domination does not signify oppression or exploitation; rather, it metaphorically involves the dispensation of social justice. Thus, as in Pollius' estate, the land rejoices in its cultivation, *gaudente terra*, and responds with abundance.

Colenti in Statius' passage plays upon all three meanings of the word as coloniser, cultivator of the land, and religious worshipper. Although Pollius' villa is new, audacious and filled with Greek works of art, Pollius himself is thus associated with the time-honoured morality and practices of Rome's early leaders. Colonising nature is a religious as well as a militaristic act. Through Pollius' domination of the land, what Bourdieu has called 'a good-faith economy' operates in the villa landscape.[79] In a 'good-faith economy', as opposed to a 'self-interest economy' which relies on money, the relationship between work and its product is socially repressed by various mechanisms of mystification such as gift-giving and other forms of symbolic exchange: 'in obedience to the logic of gift exchange, nature bestows its bounty only on those who bring it their care as a tribute'.[80] The emphasis in the 'good-faith economy' lies then 'in the symbolic aspect of the activities and relations of production' which 'prevent the economy from being grasped *as* an economy, i.e. as a system governed by the laws of interested calculating competition, or exploitation'.[81] A 'good-faith economy' lies at the heart of imperial pastoral. In *Silv.* 2. 2 Statius constructs Pollius' villa as a colony whose social order is founded on friendship and generosity – a 'good-faith economy'

---

[79] Bourdieu (1977) 171–83 draws upon Mauss's (1967) seminal, comparative study of the forms and functions of gift-exchange, which argues that the exchange of goods in archaic societies was a moral transaction that established and maintained personal communities. Bourdieu in turn insists that the custom of gift-exchange is itself a form of mystification and is always connected with material advantage.

[80] Bourdieu (1977) 174.

[81] Bourdieu (1977) 172 insists on the abandonment of the distinction between 'economic' and 'uneconomic'. Societies that engage in gift-exchange are simply involved in a different form of economic practice, one that conceals self-interest and its origins in material forms of capital.

brought about through the enlightened domination of nature. Exchange between master and land, art and nature, is represented as beneficial to both; the effort which the owner puts into improving the land is repaid by a nature made compliant and abundant. And this in itself provides a model for intellectual exchange as well as for governance. By providing Statius with an idyllic retreat, Pollius is repaid by two poems and the dedication of a poetry book.

In *Silv.* 2. 2 the new art of landscape architecture is thus provocatively associated with the ancient art of agriculture and its attendant virtues. But only a brief passage touches upon the rural bounty of the estate, *ruris opes* (98), specifically its abundant vineyards (99–106), for in Statius' reformulation of the villa, the ornamental landscape and the grand house have replaced the fields of ancient Italy as the home of civic as well as philosophical virtue. As the military virtues of the farmer were foundational to the early city-state of Rome, so now these virtues are applied to the metaphorical fashioning of a new, modern state that is the product of Greek culture as much as Roman. Mastery and domination of nature, broadly conceived, provide the foundation of social and political order. Thus the technological prowess evident in Pollius' villa contributes to its metaphorical, synecdochic refashioning as a model realm or province.

Paradoxically, then, ancient virtues validate new arts, not only landscape architecture but also philosophy and poetry. Thus the poetic metaphor of domination shifts its reference from the idea of the governor/general to that of the powerful poet, as Pollius is compared to Arion, Amphion and Orpheus, two of whom charmed animate nature and one, Amphion, who controlled inanimate nature to build Thebes (60–2). Poetry again establishes Pollius' relationship with the land as a magical one of mutual benefit. The comparison with Amphion furthers the implied link between Pollius and the builder of a city-state. At the same time, all three comparisons link Pollius' power as ruler and landscape architect to his power as poet. *Thebais* (61) perhaps is reminiscent of the counter-world of Statius' epic, but here the Theban lyre becomes part of the colonial project, yielding (*cedat*, 61), like nature, to the creative forces of harmony.

Reference to the 'unique Theban lyre' is also an allusion to Pindar and his unique lyric genius.[82] For, as praise poet, Pindar was an important influence upon Statius' *Silvae* as well as his *Thebaid*. Pindar honours his patrons, as does Statius, through their wonderful houses and

---

[82] See *Silv.* 4. 7. 7–8.

enormous wealth. Ostentatious expenditure was regarded as the path
to tyranny. But, as Kurke has shown, Pindar could validate his patrons'
wealth through the virtuous use that they were shown to have made of
it. The individual wealth of the patron was absorbed into a notion of
the larger, communal good.[83] In *Silv.* 2. 2 Pollius, so Statius implies with
this reference, perhaps, surpasses the Pindaric initiative in the use that
he makes of his wealth. His estate is private, and yet, in its synedochic
fashioning, it provides a model for the ideal state in which civic and
philosophical virtue are conjoined and literature is made central. Statius
thus reinterprets through Pollius' private estate the nature of the public
good. Poetic composition and landscape architecture are seen as complementary activities; in their various types of ordering both are crucial
to the well-governed state.

Poet-philosopher and governor, Pollius conquers and controls his estate. His villa, described initially with the military term *speculatrix* (3),
guards the estate and its precious life style as if it were a separate
province, self-contained and harmonious. Pollius is master of himself
and of his land, a benevolent autocrat over a private, enclosed, self-
contained colony that rivals or even supplants the city: it has temples,
a grand porticus (30–5), and its own presiding deities. Pollius plays the
good emperor on his estate, revitalising traditional Roman virtues in
the private sphere. Praise here has a protreptic function and looks to the
state as well as the individual for the model of ideal patronage.

Yet Pollius has not only revitalised traditional civic virtues in his close
involvement with the land. Pollius plays the emperor in another regard,
by engaging in the imperialistic project of acquiring Greek works of art.
The most eminent room of the villa, the *diaeta*, for instance, is adorned
with precious Greek marbles of various colours (82–94).[84] Statius provides a catalogue of seven different varieties of marble that emphasise a
wide range of foreign resources from within the Greek world: Egyptian
(86), Phrygian (87–9), Spartan (90–1), Numidian and Thasian (92), Chian
and Carystian (93).[85] There is no Italian marble, no plain white. Pollius'

---

[83] Kurke (1991) 163–94.

[84] The *diaeta* was clearly a special room or suite of rooms. The word occurs twice in Pliny's
descriptions of his villas. The Laurentine villa has a *diaeta* that seems to be a sort of separate
garden pavilion (*Ep.* 2. 17. 20–4). The *diaeta* of the Tuscan villa however is attached to the
porticus; it is secluded but not separate from the main buildings of the house (*Ep.* 5. 6. 20–1).
Common to both forms of *diaeta* is the notion of retreat and exclusivity. They are shielded from
the noise of the outside world and enjoy perfect quiet (*Ep.* 2. 17. 22; *Ep.* 5. 6. 21).

[85] See Van Dam (1984) 247–51 for a discussion of these types of marbles. Their colours are red,
yellow, and green.

wealth and social status are reflected in his varied possession of coloured marbles at a time when such marbles were just beginning to infiltrate the adornment of private housing in Rome.[86] Coloured marbles distinguish Domitian's palace on the Palatine. In his poem describing a visit to the imperial palace, *Silv.* 4. 2, Statius cites in the grand hall only six marbles, including native white Luna (27–9), to the seven in Pollius' *diaeta*. Pollius is described as possessing wealth that rivals that of the emperor himself, although it is discreetly displayed in one elegant, private room.

In Rome, the acquisition of Greek luxuries went hand in hand with the imperialistic impulse to conquer and reshape the land. Indeed, control over the earth's treasures signified the right to rule other lands and people. As Barkan comments, 'art. . . is a valuable commodity in the exercise of Roman imperialism'.[87] At the same time, in assessing Pliny's books on the history of art, Barkan provocatively describes Roman culture as based on an *alienation* of the visual arts, 'first in the sense that they are produced in a variety of foreign places with cultures that differ from one another and from that of the imperial center, and second in the sense that many of the works have been appropriated by conquest'.[88] But although Pollius' possession of gorgeous, expensive marbles to beautify his *diaeta* assimilates him further to the civic concept of the Roman ruler as the collector of wonderful works of art, there is a crucial difference. Pollius himself comes from the Greek part of Italy. The works of art that he collects represent a significant part of his cultural identity.[89] They are not the product of 'estrangement and theft' but are culturally connected.[90] The relationship between the wealthy connoisseur and his environment is here one based on cultural cohesion and mutual respect. Thus at the conclusion of this catalogue, Pollius' Greek marbles, we are told, make a formal salutation of the 'Chalcidian towers' (94) – a reference to either Naples or Cumae, both centres of Greek culture.[91] The room with its Greek marbles then synecdochically represents Pollius' reciprocal relationship with Greek culture: *macte animo, quod Graia probas, quod Graia frequentas | arva* ('a blessing

---

[86] See chapter 3 above, 97.   [87] Barkan (1999) 129.   [88] Barkan (1999) 129.

[89] Hinds (forthcoming) argues that *Silv.* 2. 2 invites us to consider how the sources of cultural prestige could be mystified within the Roman imperial élite. Pollius amassed 'cultural capital' by building a villa ornamented with precious Greek materials and works of art that demonstrate his wealth and taste. And Statius, by writing a stylistically elaborate poem in praise of the villa and his friend's connoisseurship, acquired a corresponding source of cultural capital. Yet it is important to recognise that the identity of Pollius Felix, though modelled here to some extent on the Roman imperial élite, is firmly rooted in the Greek region of Italy.

[90] Barkan (1999) 129.

[91] In Statius' poetry *Chalcidicus* is used to refer to either Cumae or to Naples, which was founded by the inhabitants of Cumae. See Van Dam (1984) 251 on *Silv.* 2. 2. 94.

on your mind, because you approve of Greek things, because you inhabit Greek fields', 95–6).

Although art, plundered and collected, was important in the Roman exercise of power, collecting too, as we saw with Statius' friend Vindex, could have a moral and educational value.[92] Indeed, the poem represents Pollius' collecting of Greek art not just as a quest for cultural prestige but as part of his fashioning as a moral leader. Like conquering the land, collecting here represents moral authority as inseparable from material display. The art of Pollius' villa has then a didactic as well as an aesthetic purpose. His villa is not so much a commercial space as a moral and educational one. Bodel has argued that the country house was particularly associated with personal commemoration of the owner and his family.[93] Pollius lacks distinguished family lineage, but he finds in art his own forms of self-authorisation. Thus the bronze busts which Pollius collects (69–72) represent 'the faces of leaders, poets, and sages of former times' who have served as important moral influences upon Pollius, *ora ducum ac vatum sapientumque ora priorum* (69). Pliny complains of the Roman fashion of collecting likenesses of others only for their material value.[94] Lacking aristocratic lineage, Pollius however finds in the Greek heritage new models for civic virtue – significantly expanded to include the poet and the philosopher. Works of art thus take the place of ancestors in the fashioning of a new concept of nobility. Pollius after all was perhaps of freedman status. His villa however provides a powerful symbolic challenge to the high value the Romans put on the qualifications of birth for the stable transmission of aristocratic values. On Pollius' idealised estate nobility, achieved through virtue as well as wealth, is potentially accessible to all.

The bronze busts then confer not only prestige but also the guidance and wisdom that ancestors traditionally provided. They shape Pollius' social, moral and intellectual identity, giving him models to emulate in his management of his estate and person. Indeed, these three categories of general, poet, and sage represent a small variation on the three virtues of leadership Statius desired in Violentilla's children – general, poet, and lawyer.[95] Pollius harmoniously combines the virtues of the Epicurean wise man, the poet, and the imperial *dux*; these virtues work together through the pastoral exchange of Pollius' well-governed, exemplary estate/state. Thus the essentially hybrid culture of this region schools

---

[92] See chapter 2 above, 76.   [93] Bodel (1997) 6.   [94] Plin. *HN* 35. 2. 4–5.
[95] *Silv.* 1. 2. 266–7.

him in Roman as well as Hellenic ideas and values. But Roman values operate in a sphere separate from the public power and authority embodied in the monarch.

Through this representation of Pollius as an enlightened governor of his estate, Statius makes poetry and philosophy the essential foundation of a harmonious social order – a provocative ideal, perhaps, in a period in which Domitian was suspicious of intellectuals. In the year of the publication of this poem, AD 93, Domitian expelled all philosophers from Rome and Italy as part of a political purge.[96] Statius' two poems on Pollius' villas mark a shift on the cultural axis from Rome to Naples. In its fashioning as a model of a well-governed realm, Pollius' villa subtly invites reflection on the character of governance and patronage in Rome itself.

Significantly, Pollius is not the sole manager of his wealth. Polla his wife is also an important figure in Statius' poetry. If we are invited in some sense at the poem's opening to consider Pollius' estate as a refuge like Carthage, then clearly it is a morally and socially superior Carthage. Like the Libyan colony it has grand new buildings and a sophisticated culture, but it is ruled over not by a vulnerable woman but by a long-married, harmonious couple of outstanding virtue. Book 3 is dedicated to Polla as well as to Pollius, and praise of her virtues forms the climax to *Silv.* 2. 2. The figure of Polla helps cement the social relations of the villa into harmonious order, for Pollius enjoys not only a community of friends, but also a firm, equal partnership with his wife, and the prospect of long and fruitful continuity through many descendants. Vopiscus, it seemed, lacked wife and heirs. The figure of Pollius' wife, however, provides an image of continuing productivity and stability. *Silv.* 2. 2 concludes by relating the wise governance of the estate to the stable marital union of Pollius and Polla, whose equal partnership, together with their fecundity, subtly offers a model of ideal social relations for rulers, one that stands in noticeable contrast to the dynastic politics of the day.

The partnership of Pollius and his wife Polla emblematises in social terms the reciprocity on which this home is founded: *sanctusque pudicae | servat amicitiae leges amor* ('their sacred love observes the laws of chaste friendship', 144–5). Their marriage, described as long-standing and chaste, is founded on a term not usually applied to marriage, *amicitia* ('friendship'). To represent the enduring bond between Pollius

---

[96] Suet. *Dom.* 10. 3; Coleman (1998) 347.

and Polla, Statius here draws on the ideal expressed in Catullus 109 for the relationship between himself and his mistress, *aeternum hoc sanctae foedus amicitiae* ('this eternal bond of sacred friendship', 6). With *pudica* ('chaste') Statius removes the destructive sexual tension from the Catullan allusion. The allusion then provides more than a sublime compliment to Statius' hosts. As Konstan notes, an echo of this striking Catullan image also occurs in *Silv.* 4. 6, where *coeptaeque perenne | foedus amicitiae* ('the eternal bond of the friendship we have undertaken', 92–3) describes the virtues according to which Statius' host and friend Vindex conducts his life.[97] The obligations of *amici* towards one another were fundamental to Roman social relations; they are here in *Silv.* 2. 2 given heightened, permanent form in a subtle 'correction' of Catullus.[98] Thus in *Silv.* 2. 2 Statius describes the union of Pollius and Polla in terms of the social ethic of *amicitia*, of reciprocity and exchange here represented in its most enduring and affectionate form in a non-Catullan, chaste marriage. Despite the hierarchical topography of the villa and the language of domination that informs it, harmony is the principle on which all types of relations are here ultimately founded.

Polla is given her own brief eulogy (147–54). Unfortunately the text of *Silv.* 2. 2 is confused at this point – is this not typical, that the existence of women in classical texts was constantly threatened with erasure? Nonetheless, it is clear that Polla is praised as a worthy consort in her own right; she too has learned the secrets of happiness in her pursuit of Epicurean *voluptas* (150). In this gendered encomium of Polla, she is firmly associated with interior, domestic space as Pollius was associated with outdoor space. Her control is exerted over the house, as his is over the land. Statius implicitly counters here the charge that such great wealth as the couple possesses is incompatible with Epicurean belief by portraying Polla as not avaricious but wisely generous (151–4):

> non tibi sepositas infelix strangulat arca
> divitias avidique animum dispendia torquent
> fenoris: expositi census et docta fruendi
> temperies.

The miserly strongbox does not sequester and strangle your riches nor does the loss of greedy interest on loans torture your mind: your wealth is open and your moderation in its enjoyment shows your learning.

---

[97] Konstan (1997) 146. See chapter 2 above, 83.
[98] See Coleman (1988) 191–2 on *Silv.* 4. 6. 91–3.

The vivid image of the 'miserly strongbox' suggests Polla's wise control over the household finances.[99] Their wealth is open to all (*expositi census*) but she has the wisdom to use it with moderation (*docta fruendi temperies*). Wise rulers, Pollius and Polla balance the seclusion their wealth has bought with an openness and wisdom about their means.

Polla is presented as the ethical counterpart to her husband in the domestic sphere, sharing with him the key virtue of a moderation (*temperies*, 154) that is based on education and learning (*docta*, 153). As White has observed, the word *docta* ('learned') 'always implies, if not literary production, at least an enthusiastic preoccupation with literature and litterateurs'.[100] Habinek has argued however that the epithet *docta*, when applied to women, participates in 'a pre-emptive strike' to silence women, and is increasingly so used in imperial times. For, while *docta* acknowledges women's evaluative power, it undermines their creativity. Women's learning redounds solely to the male's credit. She gives him back an idealised self-image.[101] But Polla's 'learning' is here illustrated in a sphere that is separate from that of her husband, the interior space of the household and its financial organisation. Images of openness rather than constriction characterise Polla here. Nisbet has argued that the phrase *docta fruendi temperies* alludes to Horace's description of Sallustius Crispus in *Carm.* 2. 2. 3–4.[102] If so, it is significant that such a description is given here to a woman, not a man. True, Polla is not represented as a poet like Pollius, but she has her own important sphere of influence. Through Polla, Statius offers us a glimpse of the imperial woman, like Violentilla an economic power in her own right and an authority within her household. Saller has argued that it is wrong to think of Roman society by this period as strictly patriarchal. A wife would bring her own property and wealth to a marriage.[103] Private property in Statius' poem is associated not only with material wealth and status, but also with the notion of home and family as the legitimating nucleus of material possessions.

---

[99] Nisbet (1978) uses this passage as evidence for the identity of Polla as Lucan's widow, seeing the monetary references as a playful punning upon Polla Argentaria. See the reservations in Van Dam's discussion of Polla (1984) 454–5. Note however the pun with *infelix* upon Pollius' cognomen and the other examples of punning elsewhere in the *Silvae* that Nisbet cites (8).

[100] White (1975) 283.   [101] Habinek (1998) 122–36.

[102] In *Carm.* 2. 2. 3–4 Sallustius Crispus is described as opposed to luxury goods such as silver unless it gleams from restrained usage (*nisi temperato splendeat usu*). Nisbet (1978) 2–3 assumes that Horace is linking poetic patronage with Epicurean moderation, a point that is applicable here in *Silv.* 2. 2.

[103] Saller (1994) 128–30. Although the husband had authority over property in the *familia*, he did not have a monopoly in the household, *domus*.

Characteristically, in Statius the material shades into the moral. At the end of the poem Statius exhorts both husband and wife to outdo the 'titles' of former fame – *priscae titulos praecedite famae* (146). *Tituli*, the public inscriptions recording the achievements of civic-minded leaders, here suggest the metaphorical identification between Pollius and Polla and leaders of the state.[104] But leadership is defined in a new way. Pollius and Polla exemplify leadership in the community not through noble birth or wealth *per se* but through an ethical way of life that includes the wise use of riches and the patronage and practice of poetry. Pollius embodies what Habinek, with specific reference to Seneca, has called 'an aristocracy of virtue'. Seneca, he claims, invented and promulgated an 'aristocracy of virtue' whose virtue is founded in ethics, not in birth.[105] Seneca however, was an aristocrat by birth; as Habinek points out, he cannot escape the social and political challenges posed by his ancestry. But as in *Silv.* 1. 2, Statius here reaffirms yet again a new concept of civic identity in which power is equated with private property and nobility is based on virtue – domestic as well as philosophical – rather than on aristocratic descent. Indeed, Pollius, unlike Stella, seems to have no aristocratic background but may well have been a freedman who rose to become a local dignitary. Through his success in business alone, he had become a member of the regional élite.[106] The union of Violentilla and Stella, I have argued, represented a symbolic fusion of Naples and Rome, of regional and national identities. Through Pollius and Polla, however, Statius articulates a new social ideal of nobility and active virtue that, while it accommodates Roman values to Greek ideals, is nonetheless provocatively and exclusively located in his homeland itself. To be noble does not mean to be Roman or even male. Since poetry is crucial to this ideal, Statius provides a new model for the community in which he himself can be integrated – at the potential cost, however, of dislocation from Rome.

Marriage and childbearing, indeed, promise the successful future of this new concept of aristocracy. Significantly, the partnership of Pollius and Polla is founded on continuity. In *Silv.* 1. 2 fertility was prospective; in *Silv.* 2. 2 Statius celebrates a union that has proved fruitful. The complimentary reference to Polla's 'youthful grace' (*iuvenilis gratia*, 10) in the opening of *Silv.* 2. 2 suggests that Polla was perhaps elderly by this time; she stands, however, at the head of an idealised dynasty. *Silv.* 3. 1. 175–9 represents Polla as enjoying the kisses of her grandchildren;

---

[104] See especially *OLD* 2b.   [105] Habinek (1998) 137–50.
[106] On Pollius' social background, see notes 2 and 3 above.

Silv. 4. 8 celebrates the birth of a third grandchild to their son-in-law Julius Menecrates, and Statius there represents Pollius and Polla as surrounded by a crowd of grandchildren, *turba nepotum* (10). The other poems that refer to Pollius and Polla, then, portray the marriage as fruitful, the family as closely united and loving, the dynasty as strong. The imperial dynasty of Rome, however, rested on fractured family politics. Domitian had notoriously strained relations with his wife Domitia, for instance. Suetonius and Dio Cassius claim that she was complicit in his assassination.[107] Whether this story was true or not, her lack of fecundity was undoubtedly a problem for the state as well as for her marriage.[108] Unlike Domitian's court, Pollius' well-governed state has a stable foundation in the continuity of a close-knit family line and a balanced sharing of power between husband and wife. The concluding wish in *Silv.* 2. 2 (145–6) for the long life of Pollius and Polla is then more than a conventional trope; it is a final acknowledgment of the way in which Pollius' villa offers a vision of continuity and fruitfulness that has political and social as well as moral force. For the social and spatial continuity of the villa guarantees a future for the poet who enjoys the couple's patronage.

In *Silv.* 1. 2 Statius projected through the union of Stella and Violentilla a notion of Roman leadership as founded upon poetry as well as civic duties. In *Silv.* 2. 2 this notion finds full and stable expression in a region socially, politically, and geographically removed from the imperial court, yet nonetheless culturally vital: the Bay of Naples. The union of Pollius Felix and Polla therefore ensures through their descendants not only, perhaps, the continuation of the private province that they own and control, but the continuance of the new concept of civic virtue that is there practised and defined and that importantly includes the arts. Whereas in *Silv.* 1. 3 the poetic landscape was sheltered and limited, here Pollius' villa is constructed as a viable counterworld to Rome in its architecture, art, poetry, morality, and governance.

In his study of the North African villa, Thébert has argued that the villa was designed as an ambivalent rival to the imperial court.[109] The aristocracy built their homes 'not just in the Roman manner but as veritable local emperors', conceiving of its power as 'a mirror of the central power'.[110] Thébert is talking here of Late Antiquity, and of another place, North Africa. But as he notes, there is a remarkable homogeneity in the design

---

[107] Suet. *Dom.* 14. 1; Dio Cass. 67. 15. 3–4.   [108] See Vinson (1989), especially 447–9.
[109] Thébert (1987) 404–5.   [110] Thébert (1987) 405.

and conception of the villa over time throughout the Mediterranean.[111]
In *Silv.* 2. 2 and 3. 1 we find an early, subtle and nuanced expression of
the ideology of the villa as a regional counterpart of the court. Pollius'
villa is fashioned then as an alternative 'state' to Rome. Here traditional
civic virtues such as reverence for the land and the gods, along with the
will to conquer and to improve, are given new vitality and expression
in their fusion with new ideas about Greek wealth and culture. Pollius'
villa estate as described by Statius is both an ideal landscape and an
alternative realm whose harmonious ordering is founded on intellectual
enlightenment as well as wealth. The *locus amoenus*, here transformed
into a private villa, provides the model of the perfectly governed state in
which the intellectual life is central.

In particular, with his praise of Pollius' villa, Statius offers here a new
vision of cultural identity that is shaped by the uncertainty of political life
in the Flavian era. According to this vision, the imperialistic impulse to
conquer and control new lands becomes redirected to the private citizen,
who reformulates civic virtues within the confines of a private estate that
he owns, controls, and shapes perfectly to his needs. Pollius' villa, set in
the orbit of Naples, the centre of Greek culture in Italy, provides security
not found in the stormy, uncertain world of Roman public, urban life.
The calm waters of the bay, controlled by the villa, are metaphorically
opposed to the open seas of imperialistic enterprise in a symbolic clash
of regional and national identity.

CULTURAL FAULTLINE

Although Statius represents himself as a close friend of Pollius – he is
taken into the most intimate parts of his home, including the *diaeta* – his
authorial position maintains a critical distance from him that is expressed
through both geographical and philosophical separation. Rome, which
has no seeming attractions for Pollius, nonetheless exerts a powerful pull
upon the ambitious poet who tells us at the poem's start that he is eager
(*cupidum*, 11) to head for Rome. Unlike Pollius, Statius has *desires*; at the
start of the poem he wishes to voyage out of his home region to the
imperial capital of Empire. The tension between Naples and Rome that
runs throughout *Silv.* 2. 2 is thus specifically embodied in the person of
the poet as well as the site of the villa.

---

[111] Thébert (1987) 329: 'the remarkable unity of Mediterranean domestic architecture is a consequence of the social homogeneity and political cooperation of the region's élites. Everywhere
the ruling classes built in order to live in the Roman manner'.

Pollius' villa is represented as a site of enlightened patronage. Intellectual exchange, manifested in the delight in poetry that Statius shares with Pollius, is an important aspect of the reciprocal relationships that inform the villa landscape. The social distinction between Pollius and Statius, for instance, an issue of crucial importance in the world of the court, is effaced by the mutual interest and support of their friendship and devotion to poetry. In *Silv.* 3. 1 we are told that while the rest of Italy was celebrating the festival of Hecate, Statius and Pollius along with other friends joined together in the study of philosophy and poetry on Pollius' estate – a symbolic gesture of rejection of public national rite for private virtue that nonetheless remains a communal activity (*Silv.* 3. 1. 52–67). In this poem in particular, Statius emphasises the way in which Pollius' estate provides an idealised community for friends and fellow-poets.

Moreover, like Vopiscus, Pollius is a poet, but of a more elevated sort.[112] Indeed, poetic composition is represented as another heightened aspect of philosophical and georgic behaviour: when Pollius performs his poetry, he is represented as bringing nature under his control (116–20):

> hinc levis e scopulis meliora ad carmina Siren
> advolat, hinc motis audit Tritonia cristis.
> tunc rapidi ponunt flatus, maria ipsa vetantur
> obstrepere, emergunt pelago doctamque trahuntur
> ad chelyn et blandi scopulis delphines aderrant.

On one side of the bay the nimble Siren flies from her rocks to the better songs, and on the other side Tritonia listens, taking off her plumed helmet. Then the swift-blowing winds die down, the waves themselves are forbidden to roar, dolphins emerge from the sea, drawn to the sound of the learned lyre, and soothed, they stray towards the rocks.[113]

Poetry here calms the winds, the sea, and its animals; it thus accomplishes the same effect as Neptune, the guardian of the shore (25–7), and as architectural design. His poetry has a didactic function that is designed to improve nature: it draws the Siren, for instance, to 'better songs' (115), and it pleases the gods, here in the person of Minerva who possesses a temple nearby.[114] Pollius' power to control the wild elements

---

[112] Pollius practises a wide range of poetry: didactic, epic, elegiacs, and iambi. On Vopiscus' similar wide range of genres see *Silv.* 1. 3. 101–4.

[113] See Van Dam (1984) 264 on the translation of *blandus* (120), which I have translated as 'soothed'. Commentators have been divided over interpreting the adjective with the meaning of 'coaxing for more' or as 'gentle'.

[114] Statius tells us at the start of *Silv.* 2. 2 (1–2) that Pollius' villa is situated between Sorrento and the promontory of Minerva, where there was a temple to the goddess. See Van Dam (1984) 195.

of nature is mythologised and elevated in his implied comparison with Arion, who charmed a dolphin with his poetry; *aderrant*, Statius' own linguistic invention, neatly suggests the unusual effect that Pollius' poetry has on nature.[115] Poetry and landscape architecture are complementary activities, for earlier, Pollius' efforts in clearing and reshaping the wilderness are compared to those of Arion (61). Pollius is defined as a 'learned' poet (his lyre is *doctam*, 119) whose poetic composition, regardless of genre, is a metaphor for philosophical ordering and control.[116] Poetry on Pollius' estate then is seen as a powerful, therapeutic activity that complements the practice of architecture and of Epicurean philosophy.

Silv. 2. 2 thus offers far more than a description of Pollius' villa. It provides high praise for Pollius, and through him for a life devoted to the arts. But the relationship between the poet and the people his poetry honours is an ambiguous one, resting on a complex exchange of authority.[117] Indeed, Statius' separation from Pollius establishes the critical distance that allows him to act implicitly as a preceptor. Hence perhaps the social and political imperative behind the poem which is addressed to a wider audience than Pollius alone, namely to encourage the privileged few who possess wealth and power to use those assets wisely. The praise of this particular man and his villa can be read as a protreptic encouragement to any member of the privileged class to adopt a socially responsible role. Statius writes not just to celebrate power but to provide a corrective to its potential abuse. Since he represents Pollius as a poet like himself, clearly there is special interest here in the hope that Pollius will continue to prove to be a supportive patron. But more importantly, the synedochic relationship established in this poem between the estate and the state provides a model of proper governance and patronage for the ruling powers in Rome itself.

Nonetheless, despite the flourishing of poetry on Pollius' estate, at the start of *Silv.* 2. 2, Statius resembles Calpurnius Siculus' Corydon of *Eclogue* 7, for whom Rome functions as the magnet of his social and poetic ambitions. But he is also reminiscent of Meliboeus of Virgil's *Eclogue* 1, the outsider to the pastoral enclave. Thus, at the end of *Silv.* 2. 2, Statius

---

[115] On this *hapax* see Van Dam (1984) 264–5 on *Silv.* 2. 2. 120.

[116] For instance, he weaves together (*nectit*) the dissonant metre of elegy (114–15); as *minax*, a 'threatening' attitude that commands fear and respect, he 'binds' (*stringit*) the iambus (115).

[117] Thus Goldhill (1991) in his discussion of ancient Greek lyric, comments, 'the patron as audience is also implicated in demarcating the praise he is offered by the poet. The ambiguous language of *kleos* manipulates and veils the lines of power in the poetic exchange' (119).

makes clear that despite his privileged view of the estate, he falls outside
Pollius' charmed position, like his readers (129–32):

> nos, vilis turba, caducis
> deservire bonis semperque optare parati,
> spargimur in casus: celsa tu mentis ab arce
> despicis errantes humanaque gaudia rides.

We, wretched mob, who are prepared to enslave ourselves to transitory goods
and perpetual desire, are scattered to fortune: you, from the lofty citadel of your
mind, look down upon errant humans and laugh at mortal pleasures.

With the use of the pronouns *nos* (129) and *tu* (131) Statius marks the
separation of himself and his community of readers from Pollius' privileged state.[118] By including us among his *vilis turba* (129), Statius makes his
readers other than Pollius outsiders too, cultural consumers of the wealth
and leisure of more fortunate others. But he also invites our judgment
upon the social function of poetry in the new world of Flavian politics
and culture. For Statius here replays the pastoral situation of *Eclogue* 1
where Tityrus, snug in his purchased pleasance, temporarily hosts the
exiled Meliboeus. We find a similar contrastive use of *tu* and *nos* at the
opening of *Eclogue* 1 (1–5):

> Tityre, tu patulae recubans sub tegmine fagi
> silvestrem tenui musam meditaris avena:
> nos patriae finis et dulcia linquimus arva.
> nos patriam fugimus: tu, Tityre, lentus in umbra
> formosam resonare doces Amaryllida silvas.

Tityrus, you, reclining in the shade of a spreading beech, practise the woodland
muse with your woodland pipe; we are leaving the boundaries of our native
land and its sweet fields, we are fleeing our native land: you, Tityrus, relax in
the shade and teach the woods to sing of beautiful Amaryllis.

As Patterson has pointed out, we are offered in these opening lines a
choice of identifying either with Tityrus, secure in his pleasance, and a

---

[118] This is an uncomfortable separation, one that hints at the insular pleasure he takes in the errors
of others. *Despicis* commonly means 'despise' as well as the purely visual 'look down'. Indeed,
the Lucretian passage on which Statius draws here has been open to the same charge of cruelty
and self-interest, a charge Lucretius himself tries to defuse with the caveat in lines 3–4, *non quia
vexari quemquamst iucunda voluptas,* | *sed quibus ipse malis careas quia cernere suave est* ('not because there
is sweet pleasure in any person's harassment but because it is pleasing to witness the evils you
yourself lack'). Konstan (1973) has argued that here Lucretius is claiming that the wise man does
not take pleasure in looking at the suffering of others; rather *malis* (4) refers to the general evils of
avarice and ambition from which people suffer. In Statius' rendering of the Lucretian passage,
however, Pollius is described directly as scornful of unenlightened people (*errantes*). Statius thus
establishes a gap between Pollius and himself and his other readers, for we are included in the
nos, vilis turba.

model of disengagement, or with Meliboeus, the exile involved in the historical world making a temporary stop in Tityrus' land – the voice of conscience.[119] For Statius too, Pollius' estate is a temporary resting-place on home territory. In a sense then, Statius plays Meliboeus to Pollius' Tityrus. Unlike the pastoral landscape shunned by Calpurnius Siculus' Corydon, Pollius' villa landscape is a site of enlightened patronage and elevated poetry. Yet Pollius' poetry, Siren-like (116–17), charms and soothes, detached from the ordinary turmoil of mortal life. Statius, moving out into the public world, seeks a wider audience, a more dynamic, socially and politically engaged form of poetics that can have impact in Rome itself, the final 'arbiter of taste'.[120] But as the example of Meliboeus suggests, leaving the protection of the homeland involves the poet in uncertainty and danger.

Silv. 2. 2 presents a cultural dilemma. Where is the true place of exile? Where is the periphery, where the centre? For Calpurnius' Corydon, the country represented poetic and spiritual exile; for Virgil's Meliboeus, on the other hand, the country was home, the centre of poetic production and economic and moral worth. By playing both parts, Statius with his self-fashioning, divided voice questions the role of Rome as the dominant source of cultural authority.

Silv. 2. 2 represents Statius as only a temporary visitor to Pollius' estate, a poet whose self is divided between Rome and Naples. In *Silv.* 2. 2 and 3. 1 Statius thus locates himself on the cultural faultline between Naples and Rome where he explores the social function of poetry and patronage. The villa landscape is geographically distant from Rome – the national arbiter of taste, the centre of cultural and political power – although Naples clearly poses a powerful cultural challenge.[121] Naples and Rome are represented in Statius' *Silvae* as the two powerful poles between which the ambitious poet oscillates. Naples provides the safety and appreciation of home, Rome the excitement of Empire with the possibilities for intercultural contact without, perhaps, the patronage.

The cultural dilemma of the poet for whom patronage is located at home, but far-reaching fame and cultural authority can be found far away in Rome, is expressed yet again through the image of seafaring in the important preface to Book 3 of the *Silvae*. Here Statius makes further metaphorical play with the literary topography of Pollius' estate by claiming that his third book of poetry has found here a safe 'haven'

---

[119] Patterson (1987) 1–2.   [120] Hardie (1983) 43.
[121] On the importance of Naples as a centre of high culture in imperial times see Leiwo (1994) 41.

(*praef.* 3. 1–7). Detached from political life at Rome, the Epicurean couple are appreciative recipients of Statius' poetry; his poetry book will be safe (*securus*, 6) with them. Pollius and Polla therefore provide a secure foundation of enlightened patronage from which Statius himself can experiment with the 'boldness of style' (*audaciam stili nostri, praef.* 3. 4) that, we are told, Pollius 'fears'. The navigational metaphor of these opening lines of the preface imagines the book of poetry as a ship that has been bold and ambitious enough to venture out on dangerous seas, but is drawn back to the shelter of the Neapolitan couple.[122] Statius thus draws attention to the pioneering boldness of the *Silvae* – not in style and genre alone but in the difficult and sometimes dangerous challenge of writing praise poetry in the Flavian age.[123] His book of poetry, so it is implied, like the storm-tossed mortals Pollius watches from his heights, has thrown its lot in with the struggles and ambitions of seafarers who seek profit and fame – with uncertain results, particularly in a period in which Domitian had a dubious relationship with intellectuals, including, perhaps, Statius himself.

The twin concepts of 'boldness' and 'safety' are related not just to the protection offered by patronage but to the kind of poetry that Statius has chosen to compose. In the preface to Book 3 Statius describes his last poem, *Silv.* 3. 5 – which urges his wife to retire with him from Rome to Naples – as 'safe,' *securus* (*praef.* 3. 22), the same adjective used to describe the condition of his completed poetry book within Pollius' hands (*praef.* 3. 6). In *Silv.* 3. 5 Statius represents himself as disappointed in his poetic ambitions by the emperor, described as a cruel and ungrateful Jupiter, *saevum ingratumque Iovem* (*Silv.* 3. 5. 32–3); he thus turns to the safety and patronage offered by his home region. The conclusion of this final poem is a powerful eulogy of Naples as a 'better Rome' (81–112), a city with all the cultured amenities of the capital but happily free from the legalistic wrangling of the forum and the unequal exercise of power (87–8). Naples here is imagined as a city where 'peace is safe' (*pax secura locis*, 85), like Pollius' estate. Poetry written about Naples – far from the centres of power – it seems, counts as 'safe'. Statius thus in the final poem of his first collection of *Silvae* reverses the movement of *Silv.* 2. 2 by turning from Rome to Naples and to the regional protection of his friends. But in *Silv.* 2. 2, while he compliments his friends, Statius

---

[122] On the idea of the poetry book as a ship see Kenney (1958) 205–6.

[123] Coleman (1988) xxvi counters Vessey (1971) in seeing speed of composition as constituting Statius' 'boldness', not 'strained' Latin usage. Similarly, Laguna (1992) 113 argues that *audacia* refers to improvisational style.

looks specifically towards Rome and suggests that in the *Silvae* the social function of poetry goes beyond the parameters of safe praise. Boldness, too, characterises his poetry. In *Silv.* 2. 2 the opening Virgilian allusion to the Libyan harbour suggests that Statius approaches Pollius' estate like Aeneas, as a temporary visitor and bold adventurer who is torn between the competing claims of security and the quest for national fame.

Indeed, publication brings Pollius' private enclave, as it were, into the public domain and traverses the safe boundaries of his personal patronage. As readers of this published poem about Pollius' villa we are privileged and treated like intimate friends, for we are taken behind the facade of the villas we observe painted on walls and are guided within the most intimate parts of the house. Thus the immediate occasion of the poet's visit and his respectful response to his host are transcended by the wider significance of the villa in Statius' carefully crafted poem. Publication dissolves the barriers between public and private, and propels into prominence the secluded estate. Publication launches the poetry book back onto the uncertain seas of our reception.

CONCLUSION

It is not surprising, perhaps, that in a collection entitled *Silvae*, 'Woods', the domination of nature should be an important theme. Indeed in *Silv.* 2. 2, this theme is refigured to represent human control over the self and the state. The *Silvae* offer complex meditations on the nature and exercise of state authority and on the importance of an alternative set of values based on friendship and the cultivation of moral and intellectual harmony. Poems such as *Silv.* 2. 2 that stress the value of peace, friendship and Greek culture form a set of counter-generic reflections upon imperial and heroic values.

In *Silv.* 2. 2 and 3. 1 Statius expresses not only the power of Pollius to create his own *locus amoenus*, but also his own power as the poet. Crucial to the shaping of that poetic self is the creative deployment of literary tradition that the poet contests and rewrites. In the *Silvae* Statius recreates moral and literary tradition in a new type of poem that articulates a new concept of Roman identity – the villa poem.

It has been commonly suggested that the title *Silvae* alludes to Virgil's *Eclogues*, particularly the well-known line *si canimus silvas, silvae sint consule dignae* in *Eclogue 4*. Virgil here identified pastoral poetry as the poetry of aspiration – well suited then to court poetry. Statius' *Silvae* can be seen as a reformulation of that Virgilian mandate in the Flavian age. Indeed, the

Silvae are a new kind of pastoral poetry if we accept that pastoral poetry is a dialectical mode that constructs and contests different views of society and history. In the *Silvae* domination of nature is a trope that provides different perspectives upon the nature of power – the power of a friend to fashion his own territorial and spiritual boundaries, the power of an emperor to transgress human and natural boundaries, and the power of the poet to shape and contain both within the reflective limits of his own verse.

CHAPTER 6

Reading the Thebaid: Silvae *1. 5*

Laudas balnea versibus trecentis
cenantis bene Pontici, Sabelle.
Vis cenare, Sabelle, non lavari.

Martial, 9. 19

Silv. 2. 2 provides Statius' fullest meditation on the meaning of the villa
in his poetry and its fashioning as a *locus amoenus*. The metaphorical
topography of Pollius' estate vividly expresses the value of the intellectual
and virtuous life set apart from the capital city. Pollius' villa is imagined as
a separate refuge that is nonetheless culturally integrated with its larger
regional environment, the Bay of Naples; it suggests a new political model
for a state in which literature holds a central place. Written from Statius'
homeland of Naples, the poem thus implicitly challenges the cultural
authority of Rome.

The *Silvae* however provide other models for the intellectual life set
apart from the court and yet located within Rome itself. In *Silv.* 2. 3, for
instance, the garden of Atedius Melior, set on the Caelian Hill in the heart
of Rome, is constructed as a realm apart from the anxieties of public life.
Melior's artful garden provides a sort of horticultural counterpart to the
home of Novius Vindex in *Silv.* 4. 6. It is symbolically, not geographically,
separate from the court.[1] The most unusual form of the *locus amoenus*,
however, occurs in *Silv.* 1. 5, where the ideal site of friendship, safety and
physical beauty is playfully and luxuriously actualised not in the country
or a private home but in the enclosed space of Claudius Etruscus' private
Roman baths. This *locus amoenus*, moreover, owes its existence entirely to
Roman technological skill: aqueducts provide the water, a hypocaustic
system creates a perfect climate! Yet the values attached to this artificial
environment remain those of the villa landscapes: in the healthful indoor

---

[1] On *Silv.* 2. 3 see Vessey (1981) who argues that Melior has retired from public life because of
specific political trouble with Domitian.

setting of the baths beauty, exclusiveness, and virtue are conjoined. The baths too provide a refuge from the pressures of public, political life, yet with the added edge that they are set within Rome itself. The baths indeed provide a site for Statius' most self-reflexive discourse on his new poetic art. Here, from the heart of the capital itself, he articulates a poetics that is formulated in resistance to his own *Thebaid* and that is simultaneously ambitious and therapeutic.

Hardie points out that in *Silv.* 1. 5 Statius, as in his villa poems, is once again treading new ground.[2] Apart from some of Martial's epigrams, most notably 6. 42 on Etruscus' baths, descriptions of baths mostly occur later in epigrammatic tradition, for instance in Book 9 (606–40) of the *Greek Anthology*. Statius may well have been the first poet to devote a full-length poem to the topic.[3] Yet characteristically, Etruscus' baths cannot be reconstructed from the details provided by Statius' poem.[4] Nor does Statius tell us anything of the clientele of the baths, for despite their public function, the baths, like the villa, are represented as a separate world characterised by the interpenetration of myth and architecture. Besides, *Silv.* 1. 5 concerns poetry as much as, if not more than, the baths themselves. In a bold combination of literary motifs, Statius accommodates ecphrasis to the personal occasion of a symposium, the traditional setting for poetry and literary critique. As master of ceremonies, Statius takes on here a more authoritative role than in the villa poems, controlling both the symposium and the style of poetic production.

In *Epigram* 9. 19 Martial satirises the long poem on a patron's baths as ingratiating. But in *Silv.* 1. 5 praise of a friend's achievements is once again connected with the poet's self-reflexive fashioning as an innovative poet of praise. In particular, Statius uses the occasion of praise to provide a programmatic reflection on the distinctive poetics of his *Thebaid* and his *Silvae*. Statius explicitly announces that *Silv.* 1. 5 was composed as a respite from his work on the *Thebaid*. He thus offers his readers an interpretive guide to reading his epic poem that simultaneously elevates his current poetic project, the *Silvae*.

---

[2] Hardie (1983) 132.

[3] Martial's poem on Etruscus' baths (6. 42) has drawn far more critical attention than Statius.' See Fagan (1999) 12–39 who does not mention Statius' poem at all. Busch (1999) 35–59 compares the two poems, with the focus however on Martial's epigram, which he sees as a parody of poetry on baths. On Busch see the astute review of Lorenz (2000).

[4] Busch (1999) 38 notes that Etruscus' baths are known only from the literary representations of Martial and Statius. As Yegül (1979) has shown, Lucian's description of the Baths of Hippias does by contrast seem to provide a systematic guide to their layout.

Statius sets this poem at a symposium in Etruscus' honour and, drawing on the fiction of performance, he represents himself as the master of ceremonies, selecting the guests and orchestrating the song of praise. He thus inscribes himself into the performative tradition of archaic Greek lyric, lending authority to the pursuit of aesthetic and emotional pleasure within Roman culture. At the same time, in a self-reflexive gesture that encompasses the *Thebaid* as well as his present poetry, Statius wittily fashions the baths as a new fount of poetic inspiration for the *Silvae*. Viewed from the perspective of a symposiastic poem, the *Thebaid* is a poem of pain, suffering, excess and mutability. By contrast, like *Silv.* 4. 6, *Silv.* 1. 5 elevates the social function of arts that support and celebrate friendship.

We know of Claudius Etruscus only through the work of Statius and Martial. He was the equestrian son of an imperial freedman.[5] The baths, as a site of sensual pleasure, intersect with the erotic pursuits of youth. Since, unlike Atedius Melior and Pollius Felix, Claudius Etruscus was a young man at the time of the poem's composition, philosophy does not yet, it seems, count among his pursuits.[6] Nor however is he engaged in the typical career moves traditionally expected of an élite young male. In *Silv.* 3. 2, for instance, Statius addresses Maecius Celer, a young man in imperial military service. Claudius Etruscus, on the other hand, is represented as separated from public life and engaged, through the construction of his beautiful new baths, in private, not civic, benefactions. Indeed, as we shall see, the baths are constructed in conscious opposition to imperial service. The acculturation of the concept of virtuous leisure within Roman society here involves the redirection of traditional virtues to purely private ends in a particularly provocative way, since, unlike Pollius Felix, who was retired and elderly, Claudius Etruscus is just at the start of adulthood.

The strong opposition between public and private on which *Silv.* 1. 5 rests is extended specifically to the realm of poetics. Youth and leisure allow Etruscus to participate in a novel way in the strategy of 'recusatio' so frequently employed by Augustan love elegists in opposition to epic and here adapted by Statius to provide a negative commentary on his own epic poem. In contrast to the *Thebaid*, which immerses its poet and his audience in the pain and trouble of public life, *Silv.* 1. 5 is represented as 'safe' and joyful poetry that is also elevated.

---

[5] On Claudius Etruscus see White (1975) 275–9.
[6] Statius calls him *puer* at *Silv.* 1. 5. 64, *iuvenis* at *Silv.* 3. 3. 154.

Markus has shown that in several passages in the *Silvae* Statius provides his readers with an elevated public image of himself as epic poet-performer.[7] From the vantage point of *Silv.* 1. 5, however, the epic poet-performer is negatively portrayed. Instead, in *Silvae* 1. 5 Statius provides a full and different representation of himself as a poet of praise; in this he was influenced both by the performative tradition of Greek lyric and by the improvisational display poetry of the Greek games in which he and particularly his father had participated.[8] The poem's extraordinarily long prooemium (1–30), which exactly matches the description of the baths in length (30–59), creates the dramatic illusion of performance in order to banish the Theban deities and even the epic poem itself from the symposium. This poetics of 'exclusion' establishes the joyful, therapeutic function of Statius' art in *Silv.* 1. 5.

Silv. 1. 5 is an ingenious poem. The description of a building's interior, empty in this case of its human bathers, could have been a lifeless exercise. There is nothing static, however, about the art of Etruscus' baths or of Statius' poem. In *Silv.* 1. 5 we see the poet, in keeping with the symposiastic atmosphere he invokes, at his most playful. He does not eschew epic themes, motifs and elements of style but rather transforms them through their application to entirely new contexts. In particular, through the domestication of myth here, Statius animates the interior space. Baths were showcases for gorgeous works of art, particularly statuary. But instead of describing the still materials of the plastic arts, Statius represents the baths as full of animate life and feeling; Venus and the nymphs here bathe and play, while even the water, the marble, and the fire itself are given human emotions. Mythical figures here please rather than disturb. Fuelled by the energy of an inebriated, joyful poet, this ecphrasis celebrates the revivifying power of both art and friendship.

The lavish, dazzling architecture of Etruscus' baths called for a new, distinct poetics paradoxically uniting the tenets of Callimachean refinement with epicising grandeur. The interpenetration of architecture and poetics in this poem is encapsulated in the description of the baths of Claudius Etruscus as architectural jewels, *nitidis . . . gemmantia saxis | balnea* ('baths bejewelled with shining stones', 12–13). *Gemma*, 'jewel,' is a sign of both extravagance and rarity; it is also a literary term for stylistic adornment. Roberts points out that *gemma* is first used in this way in the poetry of Martial, where it describes the dazzling poetic style of Stella, to whom

---

[7] Markus (2000) 163–8.

[8] On the Greek professional praise poet and the tradition of encomiastic performance see Hardie (1983) 15–36.

the first book of the *Silvae* is dedicated. Statius' own *Silvae* are described as *gemmea prata silvularum* (the 'bejewelled meadows of his little *Silvae*') by the late Antique poet Sidonius Apollinaris.[9] Roberts notes that 'jewels' were viewed with suspicion by writers such as Tacitus and Quintilian; their powerful influence on literary criticism persists in the negative appraisal of apparent stylistic 'excess' among the imperial poets.[10] All the same, Statius' 'bejewelled' *Silvae* were to influence decisively the direction of future Latin poetry. In *Silv.* 1. 5 the baths glittering with shining stones point metaphorically to the brilliance of Statius' new poetry, where Callimachean tropes are transfigured by a new aesthetics of splendour.

Writing about the baths, in addition, is conceived as a therapeutic project that provides relief from Statius' epic project, the *Thebaid*. *Silv.* 1. 5 was composed, so we are told, in a break during a dinner party, *intra moram cenae* (*praef.* 1. 30). Indeed, the swiftness of composition of *Silv.* 1. 5 and the joyful energy of poet and addressee are elements that implicitly draw a contrast with the laboured circumstances in which Statius tells us he composed his epic poem – the *Thebaid* took twelve years to compose (*Theb.* 12. 811) and was, he claims, 'tortured with much filing' (*cruciata*, *Silv.* 4. 7. 26). In this play upon Horace's notion of the carefully 'filed' work, Statius suggests that his epic is carefully crafted.[11] But *cruciata* too is an appropriately painful word for a deeply painful poem. *Cruciata* refers not only to the labour involved in writing the epic poem, as opposed to the fluid facility of the *Silvae*. The word suggests too that the *Thebaid* was painful to write because of its horrendous theme, described in *Silv.* 1. 5. 8 as *arma nocentia*. Indeed the unusual word here invites a reading of the poem as painful and disturbing – mental torment for the reader as well as for the writer.[12]

The *Silvae* as a whole are poems that not only contest and rewrite literary tradition; they also constitute a set of counter-generic reflections on the *Thebaid* and the world of pain, suffering, excess and mutability there so tragically displayed. In *Silv.* 1. 5, Statius engages most fully, perhaps, in a dialectic not just with epic in general but with his own *Thebaid* in particular. In *Silv.* 1. 5, Statius draws a full and explicit contrast between the opposed poetics of his epic and of his *Silvae*, in particular

---

[9] Mart. 5. 11. 3–4; Sid. Apoll. *Carm.* 9. 229. See the references and discussion in Roberts (1989b) 52–5.

[10] Roberts (1989b) 53.   [11] Hor. *Ars P.* 291.

[12] Coleman (1988) 204 suggests that Statius approaches the metaphor of the file literally, in the sense that the *lima* would physically cause pain. I argue for an expanded meaning of *cruciare* here as a word denoting emotional as well as physical pain. (Can the two indeed be separated?)

those poems that promote the virtues of private life. Politics and poetics are here seamlessly combined. *Silv.* 1. 5 in particular provides a special vantage point from which we can read the *Thebaid* as a great work, to be sure, but one that is intimately involved in personal suffering and civic dissolution.

Murray has commented that the symposium was in many respects 'a place apart from the normal rules of society, with its own strict code of honour in the *pistis* there created, and its own willingness to establish conventions fundamentally opposed to those within the *polis* as a whole'.[13] *Silv.* 1. 5 uses the symposium to offer a provocative alternative to the politics of both the Theban and the imperial court. Martial, in the brief epigram that heads this chapter, associates long poems praising baths with servile flattery; Sabellus sings for his dinner. But in *Silv.* 1. 5 Etruscus' baths provide the symposiastic poet with a richly evocative site for the exploration of the politics as well as the poetics of the *Silvae* and the *Thebaid*. The *Silvae* and the *Thebaid* are united, it is true, in a boldness of literary conception. The *Thebaid* is performed with a bold lyre (*audaci fide*, 4. 7. 27); Pollius fears the boldness (*audaciam, praef.* 3. 4) of the *Silvae*. At the same time, however, Statius' subject in the *Silvae* is not the suffering caused by hate or civic dissolution, but, broadly speaking, the pursuit and promotion of intellectual and aesthetic pleasure – whether within the garden or among the monuments of imperial Rome. In *Silv.* 1. 5 the poet at play unites extravagance and refinement, enthusiasm and wit, to bring into new prominence the virtues of private life and of his own new poetic art.

THE BATHS

The Roman baths were on the cutting edge of architecture in the ancient world.[14] They permitted the architect to experiment with bold and innovative designs that were intended to please and to impress the general populace.[15] They were gorgeously and expensively decorated; the finest statuary and mosaics gave the Roman people a daily encounter with luxury. From her study of inscriptions found in baths, Dunbabin notes that 'among the virtues for which the baths were praised, their physical beauty is almost always included'.[16] Specifically, light, the quality of the

---

[13] Murray (1990) 7.
[14] According to Plin. *HN* 36. 24. 123, there was nothing more wonderful than the baths and the technology employed to service them.
[15] Yegül (1992) 2.   [16] Dunbabin (1989) 8.

water, and the wealth of multi-coloured marbles are the features most frequently cited, as they are in *Silv.* 1. 5.[17] The common designation of the *Silvae* as 'occasional verse' slights the subject of *Silv.* 1. 5 in its failure to recognise the central social and architectural importance of the baths in imperial Rome – as well as the opportunity they provide in Statius' poem for sophisticated literary engagement and play.

In part, perhaps, the problem lies with our terminology. The English word 'baths' has the connotation of the faintly seedy and disreputable, perhaps in part because baths in the UK were until recently the venue for the underprivileged. The American-style gym, while incorporating several of the facilities of the Roman baths – not only the swimming pool, sauna, and jacuzzi but also rooms for exercise, relaxation, and massage – typically lacks the architectural splendour of the baths of antiquity.

Roman baths, then, were a major cultural institution of the Empire, visible and exciting architectural signs of Rome's power, wealth and global success. As Toner comments, 'the baths were multifaceted – both private and public, and also commercial – and multifunctional as well – for meeting, cleansing, exercise, health, relaxation, education, talking, eating, ostentation, and awe, for actor and spectator alike'.[18] The mingling of Romans of different social status at the baths, to some extent at least, broke down the barriers between social ranks and even sexes. Yet such levelling tendencies, as Toner points out, were in themselves problematic, since baths were central to ideas about morality and social status and thus 'represented the point about which many social and cultural tensions were articulated'.[19] Thus too Fagan cautions that we should not overestimate the impulse for social equalisation, for the baths 'fit neatly into the pattern of élite provision of popular leisure'.[20] All the same, the baths permitted Romans of all classes the opportunity to participate in élite surroundings of exceptional grandeur and beauty and thus to enjoy directly the privileges of Empire. Going to the baths was a custom by which Romans recognised and celebrated their common identity.[21] Hence statues and pictorial representations of Venus are frequently found in Roman baths. She was, of course, associated with the erotic licence and titillation that the baths provided. But, in addition, her religious and political associations with the founding of the Roman race helped establish the baths as magnificent signs of the greatness

---

[17] Dunbabin (1989) 8.   [18] Toner (1995) 53.   [19] Toner (1995) 57.
[20] Fagan (1999) 222.   [21] Toner (1995) 62.

of the Roman people and their leader.[22] And they testify to the new importance that the concept of leisure claimed in the lives of the citizens of Empire.

Silv. I. 5, then, focusses on a social institution centrally embedded in the daily life of Romans of all classes. Romans could visit not only the colossal edifices built by the emperors, the imperial *thermae*, but also the privately owned, small baths of which there were many in Rome.[23] Agrippa's census of 33 BCE established that there were 176 small bathing establishments in Rome.[24] The baths of Claudius Etruscus, it seems, were a small, privately run, luxurious establishment.[25] They are the subject of Martial's praise (6. 42) as well as Statius' and seem to have represented the ultimate in elegant bathing experiences – if you haven't bathed in Claudius Etruscus' baths, Martial repeats to an acquaintance, you haven't bathed at all.[26] In their union of extravagance and refinement, Claudius Etruscus' baths form a particularly appropriate subject for Statius' new art in the *Silvae*. In particular, in *Silv.* I. 5 the symposium, which builds a community apart from the state, here intersects through the baths with broader notions of Roman cultural identity.

As luxurious, visually impressive buildings devoted to largely physical pleasures, baths were frequently regarded as morally problematic in the ancient world. A commonplace inscription on an epitaph acknowledged the paradox of the baths' possible pleasures and dangers:

[22] On the prevalence of Venus in the decorative schemes of Roman baths see Dunbabin (1989) 23–5. She argues however that the erotic, rather than the political significance of the baths, is dominant in the private baths as opposed to the imperial *thermae*.

[23] There is considerable confusion over the terms used for baths. See for instance Fagan (1999) 14–19 who attempts to distinguish between *thermae* and *balnea* on the grounds that the former were magnificent and more luxurious establishments than the latter. Fagan relies largely on the evidence of Martial, who refers to Etruscus' baths as *thermae*. Statius adds to the confusion, however. He refers to Etruscus' baths as *balneolum* in the preface to Book I (30) and as *balnea* in I. 5. 13. His use of the neuter seems to conform with the distinction that Varro makes between *balnea* and *balneae*, namely that *balneum* (and its plural form) refer to private baths, whereas *balneae* refer to public establishments: *publicae balneae non balnea, contra quod privati dicunt unum balneum* (*L.* 9. 68).

[24] See Yegül (1979) 108–9 and n. 2.

[25] Thus Yegül (1992) 31–2 in his discussion of *Silv.* I. 5. We can only conjecture about their location. See Vollmer (1898) 296.

[26] Yegül (1992) assumes (without providing evidence) that Etruscus' baths catered for a wealthy clientele. Yet he also emphasises that the entrance fee for baths was generally trifling. Mart. 6. 42, recommending these baths to a certain Oppianus, suggests that they were not at any rate restricted in their clientele to friends and relatives of Etruscus. Busch (1999) 53 argues that Martial's epigram was a parody of 'bath poetry' of the sort that he satirises in 9. 19 – a claim hard to support, since Statius provides us with our first known example of an extended poem on baths. And we do not know the chronological relationship between the two poems, although Busch (54–7) speculates that Statius knew Martial's poem.

balnea, vina, venus corrumpunt corpora nostra, sed vitam faciunt ('baths, wine and women corrupt our bodies, but these things make life itself').[27] Seneca, comparing the baths of Scipio's villa to those of modern times, provides the most outright condemnation of the easy pleasures of the baths (*Ep.* 86. 4–13). Scipio's baths were plain and dark; Seneca castigates modern baths for the very qualities that Statius praises – radiance, warmth of water, marble, mosaics, even silver taps – for, in Seneca's eyes, these are signs of corrupting, sensual indulgence.[28] And such indulgences were connected with the softening and corruption of not only the human body but the body politic as well.[29]

Typically, in *Silv.* 1. 5 Statius praises the luxury and magnificence of the architecture while defusing implicit associations with moral decadence. In a gesture characteristic of his villa poems in particular, but briefly deployed here, Statius makes the beauty of the baths a reflection of Claudius Etruscus' special character. As their marble and mosaics shine, so do his friend's character and effort: *macte, oro, nitenti | ingenio curaque puer* ('may a blessing, young man, fall upon your shining talent and effort', 63–4). Luxury and seductive pleasure are here justified in part because they are the product of traditional Roman virtues: ability and attention to duty; and these, as the juxtaposition of *cura* and *puer* suggests, are unusual qualities in a young man.

Moreover, Statius humorously acknowledges the sensuous appeal of the baths while safely displacing their eroticism onto the mythological figures of the nymphs and the materials themselves. Thus the nymphs are summoned to the baths unclothed, as temptresses of the infatuated Satyrs (17–18); water hovers in gleaming basins in narcissistic self-admiration (49–50); the Latin term for basins, *labra*, plays upon the word's other meaning of 'lips'. Precious stones not used in Etruscus' baths mourn from afar, like lovers excluded from the object of desire: *maeret onyx longe, queriturque exclusus ophites* ('the onyx mourns from a distance, the serpentine complains that it is excluded', 35). Etruscus' baths are presented as splendid and seductive, but not as corrupting or dangerous for humans. Indeed, the human body is nowhere on display here. Rather, myth conveys the notion that these baths represent a safe as well as a sophisticated

[27] See Fagan (1999) 32, 319; on the moral and medical connotations of the 'balnea vina venus' motif see Busch (1999) 517–29.
[28] Radiance: *Ep.* 86. 6, *Silv.* 1. 5. 12, 42, 45–6; clarity and warmth of water: *Ep.* 86. 10, *Silv.* 1. 5. 55; marble: *Ep.* 86. 6, *Silv.* 1. 5. 34–41; mosaics: *Ep.* 86. 6, *Silv.* 1. 5. 41–3; silver taps: *Ep.* 86. 6, *Silv.* 1. 5. 48–50. See also *Ep.* 56. 1–2 where Seneca, living above baths, complains of the noise from the exercisers.
[29] See Toner (1995) 55.

retreat. Dangerous nymphs – Salmacis, seducer of Hermaphroditus; Oenone, who refused Paris healing when he was wounded; and Dryope, seducer of Hylas – have been excluded (20–2). Moreover, the clarity of the water, allowing Narcissus an improved reflection of himself, would, it is implied, have protected him from his fatal delusion (55); here too Diana would not have exercised her curse on Actaeon but would have welcomed his gaze (56). Both these myths are well-known Ovidian tales from the *Metamorphoses*.[30] But Statius rewrites the Ovidian mythological landscape, making it safe through the dominance of art and technology.

Statius, then, views the baths through the sophisticated filter of myth. With the exclusion of potentially harmful nymphs from the baths, Statius acknowledges the apotropaic function of the baths. Dunbabin has made the point that as a cultural institution, the baths were constructed and perceived as a religious as well as a luxurious space: 'water had its own sanctity; the Nymphs were objects of cult ... bathing itself could have a ritual significance'.[31] Certainly the baths were a place of refreshment and relaxation from the burdens of everyday life. But they were also potentially dangerous places. According to Dunbabin's study of numerous inscriptions and ornamentation from bathing complexes from the second century AD onward, the need for sacred protection for the bather was a common concern, since exposure of the human body put the bather at risk.[32] Hence the decorative scheme of the baths was sometimes, at least, dictated by a concern for the religious and physical protection of the bather from disease as well as from the shafts of erotic desire. Aesculapius and Hygeia, for instance, are common statue types found in baths, serving the apotropaic function of shielding the bather from illness; they were probably not just beautiful sculptural forms to be admired.

Silv. 1. 5 incorporates into its literary programme the apotropaic function of the baths. Thus, in his dual role of poet and master of ceremonies at a symposium, Statius uses the lengthy prooemium (1–30) to banish three groups of poetic influences that he regards as hostile to his present work. First, he excludes the major, foundational divinities of poetic inspiration: the Muses (1–2), Apollo (3), Bacchus (3), and Mercury (4). Next, he excludes personifications: his epic poem of

---

[30] Narcissus: Ov. *Met.* 3. 339–510; Diana and Actaeon: Ov. *Met.* 3. 138–252.

[31] Dunbabin (1989) 32. She develops this argument with a discussion of the apotropaic function of decoration, 33–46.

[32] Dunbabin (1989) 11, n. 36. The inscriptions she studies are later than Statius' poem, but she argues that there is a remarkable uniformity in discourse about baths in the ancient world: 'literary and epigraphic testimony from the first century AD suggests that typical attitudes towards the bath had already taken shape'.

Thebes described as *arma nocentia* (8), then *Labor* (11) and *Cura* (12). Finally, he excludes the harmful water nymphs (20–2). Greek myths represent here dangerous, harmful territory. Only when transmuted into the beauty of marble, as the blood of Attis decorates Phrygian stone (37–8), can the danger they represent be neutralised.

Instead, Statius invents a new Roman mythology for his new Roman poem. In a witty burlesque of the summoning of divine aid, he invites as inspirers of his poem only divinities appropriate to his festive subject: water nymphs and Vulcan, god here of underfloor heating (6–7), and the Muse Clio in festive mood (13–14). The nymphs who will inspire his song are not the foreign, harmful nymphs of Greek mythology (20–2) but native, Roman nymphs who belong to the city's seven hills (23), to its river Tiber (24), and to its magnificent aqueducts that feed the baths, the Anio (25), the Virgo (25–6), and the Marcian (23–30) that crossed Vopiscus' estate.

For a new type of poem, then, Statius wittily creates a new Roman mythology that pays tribute to the technological triumphs of Rome. This new urban mythology, however, serves and glorifies private desires and ambitions, not civic ends. The wonders of Rome are concentrated in the confines of Etruscus' splendid new baths where the Roman nymphs inhabit incomparably rich and exclusive surroundings (30–1). Statius refashions mythical figures to reflect, create, and illuminate a private, separate space that is set within the heart of the city itself. The magnificence of the baths with the wonderful aqueducts that supply their water powerfully attests to the importance of the private life of virtuous pleasure and of the poetry written in its celebration.

Statius' tactics of exclusion extend too to the marbles with which the baths are adorned. Characteristically, as showcases of imperial wealth and power, Roman baths were adorned with the finest works of art and marbles from the Mediterranean world. Statius continues his authoritative, performative pose by curiously making a point of listing those marbles that are excluded from Etruscus' baths as well as those that are used (34–41). In his poem praising these baths Martial also provides a list of marbles (6. 42. 11–15). We cannot be sure, given the uncertain date of both poems, what their relationship is.[33] Yet apart from the difference in length (Martial's poem is only twenty-four lines long), there is a curious discrepancy over the marbles. Whereas Martial includes onyx and serpentine (14–15), Statius specifically excludes them along with Thasian

---

[33] See Busch (1999) 54–7.

and Carystian marble (34–5). Vollmer notes that the marbles which are included in *Silv.* 1. 5 reflect the skin tones of the bathers: tawny-coloured Numidian (36), purplish Phrygian (37–8), reddish Tyrian and Sidonian (39), and, as some contrast only, an incrustation of green Laconian (40–1).[34] They thus represent a 'highly refined' means of enhancing the bodies of the bathers. Again, the aesthetics of the materials and of the poetics coincide.

An explanation for Statius' particular selection of marbles lies in part also, perhaps, in the aesthetics of exclusion that are common to both the baths and their poetics in *Silv.* 1. 5. Pliny the Elder explains that Thasian was a white marble, popular before coloured marbles were introduced to Rome.[35] Perhaps then it was too plain and indeed common to be included in a sophisticated poem about Etruscus' baths. Carystian likewise did not have a unique lustre, for it came in many varieties.[36] Onyx was particularly used for small objects such as the legs of couches and would not have been appropriate, therefore, for a poem describing in an elevated style a work of monumental architecture.[37] Similarly, serpentine, Pliny relates, comes only in small columns and cannot therefore be used for large-scale works.[38] Statius' list of excluded marbles has symbolic value as inappropriate not just for the lofty vaulted spaces of the baths but for the elevated and sophisticated style of his poem.

Vollmer comments that the marbles of Etruscus' baths are to be compared in magnificence to those of Domitian's Palatine described in *Silv.* 4. 2.[39] The emperor's list however is less exclusive, for Luna, Italy's native white marble, is chosen for the columns (29).[40] Indeed, out of all the marble interiors praised in the *Silvae*, only the emperor's include Luna; the coloured marbles of the houses of Violentilla, Vopiscus, and Pollius, and of the baths of Etruscus, signify not only wealth and refinement but also separation from the world of the court. Such separation is further marked in *Silv.* 1. 5 by Statius' observation that Temesean copper is nowhere to be seen (47–8); the more precious metal – silver – complements the gleam of the marbles and the crystal-clear water (48–50). The emperor's equestrian statue made lavish use of Temesean

---

[34] See Vollmer (1898) 298 on *Silv.* 1. 5. 34 and Busch (1999) 45–7. Busch agrees with Vollmer that Statius' list of marbles reflects greater attention to their actual function within the baths.

[35] Plin. *HN* 36. 5. 44.

[36] Plin. *HN* 36. 7. 48. He seems to put Carystian on a par with Luna. See Vollmer (1898) 251 on 1. 2. 148.

[37] Plin. *HN* 36. 12. 59–61.   [38] Plin. *HN* 36. 11. 55–6.   [39] Vollmer (1898) 298 on *Silv.* 1. 5. 34.

[40] D'Ambra (1993) 23 notes that marble from Luni was, with a few exceptions, the material of choice for Domitian's building projects.

copper for the figure's breastplate; the mines, we are told, were drained of their ore in their fashioning of the gigantic armour (*Silv.* 1. 1. 42). Again, we are made aware of a subtly different aesthetic operating for emperor and for private friend. In the poem on Etruscus' baths extravagance is tempered with refinement; in the poem about the statue extravagance appears limitlessly expansive. Thus in *Silv.* 1. 5 Statius crafts from precious materials a *locus amoenus* where poetry and friendship flourish, values cemented by the gift of Statius' poem. The therapeutic environment of the baths is matched by the therapeutic art of *Silv.* 1. 5. And Statius' new poetics are directed to a new valuation of leisure as an honourable pursuit for Roman youth.

In *Silv.* 1. 5 Statius fashions the baths of Claudius Etruscus as an urban version of the *locus amoenus*, a world that offers peace and security apart from the stresses of a life of ambition. The gods and the nymphs have cooperated with Statius' masterminding of the festivities to create Etruscus' *locus amoenus*. There is no tension between nature and art because all possible tension has been removed. Nature here is fully cooperative and assimilated to its lavish surroundings; thus the water, described as *felix* (48), flows through and into silver (48–9); exterior and interior are united through the brilliance of light which reflects from the marbles (36, 42) and streams through the vaulted roofs (45). Myth imaginatively and wittily accommodated to the environment of the baths helps also to create 'safe' poetry that brings delight and banishes anxiety. There is no conflict in a poem that, the poet suggests, offers at least temporary relief from the trials of the *Thebaid*.

The lengthy prooemium to *Silv.* 1. 5 in particular allows Statius to assert and develop an active, performative role rivalling that of the architect. Through the poetics of exclusion, he simultaneously represents the baths as a safe space protected by benevolent divinities and his poem about the baths, correspondingly, as a grand and therapeutic art, a means of banishing toil and anxiety: *discede Laborque | Curaque* ('go far away, toil and anxiety,' 11–12). Statius announces at the start of *Silv.* 1. 5 that this poem was written as a pleasant break from his work on the *Thebaid*: *paulum arma nocentia, Thebae, | ponite; dilecto volo lascivire sodali* ('set aside your guilty weapons for a little while, Thebes, set them aside: I wish to play exuberantly for a beloved companion', 8–9). *Lascivire* defines the poet here at his most playful. But unlike Pollius' therapeutic art of *Silv.* 2. 2, Statius' art, performed here in a convivial setting, exists in a creative dialogue with Rome and his own Thebes. Whereas the *Thebaid* provides a grimly powerful Greek myth that invites reflection upon the contemporary world's

political realities – a protreptic on power – in *Silv.* 1. 5 the poet-performer
uses Roman myth in particular to create a delightful private world formulated in resistance to these political realities.[41] The social and cultural
tensions of the baths are played out, in Statius' poem, in the dialogue
between his two types of poetry. As we shall see, in *Silv.* 1. 5 the social
function both of the poem and of the baths neatly coincides. The poem
provocatively celebrates the private life of poetry and friendship within
a major imperial cultural institution in the heart of Rome itself.

READING THE THEBAID

In particular, the prooemium serves to define the special qualities of the
Silvae in contradistinction to the *Thebaid.* Whereas Statius' relationship
to his new subject is characterised through erotic play (*lascivire*, 9), his
relationship to his epic poem, on which he is still engaged, is represented
as antagonistic. This opposition thus suggests a method of reading the
Thebaid as well as the *Silvae.* Let us now consider more closely the first
lines of the prooemium. Here in particular Statius uses the fiction of
performance to articulate his ideas about the role of the poet in imperial
society (1–11):

> Non Helicona gravi pulsat chelys enthea plectro
> nec lassata voco totiens mihi numina Musas;
> et te, Phoebe, choris et te dimittimus, Euhan;
> tu quoque muta ferae, volucer Tegeaee, sonorae
> terga premas: alios poscunt mea carmina coetus.
> Naidas, undarum dominas, regemque corusci
> ignis adhuc fessum Siculaque incude rubentem
> elicuisse satis. paulum arma nocentia, Thebae,
> ponite; dilecto volo lascivire sodali.
> iunge, puer, cyathos, sed ne numerare labora
> cunctantemque incende chelyn;

My lyre, divinely inspired, does not beat upon Helicon with weighty plectrum,
nor do I summon the Muses whom I have so often wearied; we dismiss you,
Phoebus, from our celebrations as well as you, Bacchus; you also, fleet–footed
Tegean god, make the shell of your resonant lyre mute; my song demands
different gatherings. It is enough to have seduced here the Naiads, mistresses
over the waters, and the king of the flashing forge, still tired and flushed from
the Sicilian anvil. Set aside your guilty arms for a while, Thebes. I want to play

---

[41] Thus Hardie (1993a) 65 (speaking of Juvenal's sneers against mythological epic): 'He is deliberately
blind to the possibility that the exotic themes of mythological epic might be read as figuratively
relevant to the present day; after Vergil could any mythological epic escape such a reading?'

exuberantly for a beloved companion. Keep ladling out the wine, boy, without troubling to count, and ignite the lingering lyre.

In the prooemium of *Silv.* 1. 5. Statius brings together here symposium and 'recitatio', invoking an élite audience for appreciation and critique of his new poetry.[42] The youthfulness of the addressee (*puer*, 64) and the gaiety of the occasion are here matched by the energy of the poet, whose relationship to Etruscus is formal but not deferential. Rather, Statius assumes a position of authority as master of ceremonies and, turning aside from epic composition, infuses the ecphrasis of the baths with symposiastic life and wit.

Statius marks the distance between his epic and his new poetry through, as we have seen, the language of exclusion. In these opening lines then, a sharp distinction is drawn between the performative context of his epic and that of his *Silvae*. With *voco* (2), he evokes the persona of the grand epic poet, summoning the Muses with his voice. But this is a role he is gladly abandoning for now. Thus with *dimittimus* in the following line, he takes on the role of symposiastic host, stage-managing the participants and sending away unwelcome guests. The shift from the first person singular to the first person plural here marks the new direction of Statius' poetry, founded now on the shared, communal values that bind together the guests at a symposium.

The poem thus in its opening takes the form of a 'recusatio', a stratagem familiar to us from Augustan poetry. But in this unique case, Statius is rejecting his *own* epic poem. And as epic poet, he represents himself as a warrior, symbolically involved in the very violence that he now rejects. His lyre no longer beats upon Helicon, *pulsat* (1), a violent gesture that duplicates the martial subject of the *Thebaid*. Thus in the prooemium to the *Achilleid* Statius will reassert his commitment to epic poetry by beating once again upon the Aonian grove, *neque enim Aonium nemus advena pulso* (1. 10), language that, as Barchiesi comments, suggests a sort of military occupation on the part of the poet.[43] But the occurrence of the word in *Silv.* 1. 5 suggests too that in writing the *Thebaid* the poet has to arouse himself to the same sort of violent activity that infects the protagonists of the *Thebaid* – and this is completely inappropriate for his new symposiastic context. His epic Muses too are worn out, *lassata* (2), and he no longer badgers them. Like the grieving women of his epic, who articulate the suffering of war, the Muses too have become the objects of violence. At lines 3–5 he dismisses three gods who

---

[42] On 'recitatio' see chapter 1 above, 31–2 and Markus (2000).   [43] Barchiesi (1996) 54.

are intimately connected with the Theban conflict: Apollo and Bacchus, patron deities respectively of the rival cities of Argos and Thebes, and Mercury, Jupiter's unscrupulous go-between who arouses the demons of war.[44] The specific reference to the epic poem as *arma nocentia, Thebae* (8) – *nocentia* carrying the sense of criminality and guilt – sums up the subject of the poem directly in moral terms.[45] The *Thebaid*, it seems, is a poem that causes pain for both reader and writer. Its theme is described in *Silv.* 1. 5 not as glorious warfare but as ethically harmful warfare. From the perspective of the symposium, Statius offers a reading of the *Thebaid* as a highly disturbing work lacking institutional and moral authority. The process of composition torments him, torments his Muses, and, presumably, his readers.

Statius now boldly relocates in his symposiastic verse the moral authority that was traditionally associated with Roman epic. Through the language of exclusion, which has moral as well as aesthetic resonance, Statius makes a sharp ethical distinction between his public epic poetry and the private poetry of love, friendship and the arts with which he is now engaged. The theme of the *Thebaid*, a poem marked even more than the *Aeneid* by a pervasive, destructive dualism, is civil war, caused by the destructive hatred between two brothers.[46] By contrast, *Silv.* 1. 5 emphasises the value of peaceful affection between two friends. Instead of the dysfunctional families of Theban society, Statius here imaginatively creates a community of like-minded friends committed to the arts and to friendship. His poem, composed and performed on the spot, serves as a gift that forges and reinforces social bonds. The aesthetics of exclusion with which *Silv.* 1. 5 opens are thus constitutive of literary and social identity. Statius abandons his military pose as epic performer for that of the genial, but also inspired, symposiastic host who creates a convivial world of song, wine, and relaxation. The exclusivity of his baths is moral, not social. Through his stage-managed directions he creates a festive space from which pain, suffering and treachery are absent. Two different poetics then express two different social and political realities.

Statius' tactics in the prooemium map Callimachean tenets of exclusivity onto an ethical as well as a literary plane. All the same, unlike the Augustan poets, in this 'recusatio' Statius does not construct

[44] On Apollo's monstrous cruelty in the *Thebaid*, see Dominik (1994) 63–70. At the start of the epic, Jupiter commands Mercury to fetch Laius from the shades and take him to Eteocles, there to infect him with hatred for his brother (*Theb.* 1. 292–311, 2. 1–133); at the start of the poem's second half Mercury is dispatched to arouse Mars (*Theb.* 7. 1–89).

[45] On *nocentia* see *OLD* 2: 'stained with crime or guilty'.   [46] Thus Feeney (1993) 350.

a clear stylistic opposition between epic grandeur and Callimachean refinement. As we have seen, in *Silv.* 1. 5 he typically reworks acknowledged Callimachean categories, yoking grandeur to sophistication in a bid to honour appropriately Etruscus' achievements. Thus Statius' poem is in many ways as stylistically lavish as the baths he describes. As Hardie points out, sympotic epigrams commonly praise simplicity, a motif linked to Hellenistic poetic criteria.[47] Statius' call for heavy drinking of wine (10), as opposed to the pure, slender stream of water metaphorically associated with Callimachean poetics, boldly advertises his departure from epigrammatic containment. In addition, he links extravagant drinking with a lyre 'ignited' by inspiration and joyful enthusiasm (11); no longer 'lingering', it will produce a swift and dazzling composition. Statius plays here with familiar Callimachean metaphors; thus he will drink heavily, and his subject is not a pure stream but a magnificent body of water, the baths! The tension between the playful occasion and the elevated style of performance gives particular vitality to Statius' poem of praise. Callimachean stylistic tenets of exclusivity and refinement are asserted on a grand register that lays claim to the central importance of poetry and of leisure within Roman culture.

The prooemium culminates with a lofty invocation of new Roman nymphs that again boldly and wittily reworks Callimachean categories. The boundaries between the metapoetic and the descriptive, the fantastic and the real, here remain blurred, making the baths a symbolic space for poetic play and reflection (23–30):

> vos mihi quae Latium septenaque culmina, Nymphae,
> incolitis Thymbrimque novis attollitis undis,
> quas praeceps Anien atque exceptura natatus
> Virgo iuvat Marsasque nives et frigora ducens
> Marcia, praecelsis quarum vaga molibus unda
> crescit et innumero pendens transmittitur arcu:
> vestrum opus adgredimur, vestra est quam carmine molli
> pando domus.

But you nymphs who inhabit Latium and the seven hills and make the Tiber rise with your fresh waters, and you who are pleased by the aqueducts, the rushing Anio, the Virgo welcoming to swimmers and the Marcian, bringing the snows and icy waters from the Marsian region – all you whose waters travel and swell through the lofty structures and pass suspended over countless arches: we approach your work, yours is the dwelling I reveal in elegant verse.

---

[47] Hardie (1983) 133–4.

Statius here humorously invents a new Roman kind of nymph, who belongs to Rome's aqueducts. These nymphs of the aqueduct supply beautiful, pure water for Etruscus' baths, and correspondingly, fulsome, pure streams of inspiration for Statius' poem. The waters for instance are 'new' (24), appropriate therefore for a new type of poetry. They are also abundant and raised on high (27–8); *crescit* (28) in particular is a literary critical term referring to the grand sweep of the epic style.[48] Moreover, according to Frontinus, whose work on the Roman aqueducts was written close in time to the *Silvae* in AD 97, the Marcian aqueduct was particularly known for the purity of its water.[49] It was famous too for its length and height, which gave it an impressive appearance.[50]

With his grandiloquent invocation of the nymphs of the aqueduct, whose waters swell (*crescit*, 28) over countless arches, Statius provides a witty transfiguration of the Callimachean poetics of water to a new and grand Roman context which is to be treated, however, in elegant verse (*carmine molli*, 29); *mollis* is an adjective frequently associated with refined poetry.[51] Indeed, there is nothing vulgar about Etruscus' baths – *nil ibi plebeium* (47); the materials used in their construction are the most expensive, and the clientele is carefully chosen. Moreover, while the aqueducts themselves are enormous, soaring structures, the baths of Claudius Etruscus are themselves small (*parva*, 62) compared to the famous bathing complex at Baiae (60) or to the imperial *thermae* (62). The contrast in size brings into play here not only a contrast between public and private institutions but also familiar literary-critical criteria involving the carefully crafted shorter poem, as opposed to the long and verbose. The pure water of Callimachean inspiration springs here not from a secluded fountain but rushes along eye-catching, enormous structures. The aqueducts, then, dramatise the paradox on which Statius' new poetic style is founded. Together with the baths, they provide the new Roman fount of poetic inspiration – grandly elevated, and also sophisticated and refined. *Opus* (29) can commonly mean an architectural or a literary work.[52] The masterpiece of Roman technology metaphorically represents the virtuoso qualities of Statius' new monumental poetics.

[48] On *crescere* as a literary-critical term for the expansiveness of epic see *OLD* 4b; *Silv.* 3. 5. 36 (of the *Thebaid*).
[49] Frontinus 91. 3; Evans (1994) 83–93, especially 92–3.   [50] Evans (1994) 84.
[51] Hardie (1983) 135 notes the paradox between *lascivia* and the concept of *carmine molli*.
[52] For *opus* as a literary work see *OLD* 9c; as an architectural structure see *OLD* 10. The word may also have erotic connotations here, particularly in connection with the nymphs and bathing. See *OLD* 1d.

Although Statius does retain in his prooemium three deities from the *Thebaid* – Venus, Vulcan, and Clio – they too are transformed to suit their new poetic environment in the *Silvae*. For example, in *Silv.* 1. 5 Venus and Vulcan present a picture of marital accord. In the *Thebaid*, however, these two gods are associated with sexual jealousy and deceit.[53] Symbol of their epic discord is Harmonia's necklace, a gift designed by Vulcan to avenge himself on Mars and Venus through their daughter and her descendants (2. 269–305). Harmonia's necklace is an artefact intimately connected with sexual jealousy, deceit, violence, and the treacherous politics of the divine. The marital division of Venus and Vulcan plays out on the divine level the fraternal division of Eteocles and Polynices. Feeney has suggested that, unlike the broad visions of human life and empire provided by the shields of Achilles and Aeneas, Harmonia's necklace provides a summation of Statius' epic as 'an internally bound miniature of pettiness and vice, a catalogue of lust and madness'.[54] The dreadful history of the necklace, described as *longa series* (2. 267), is self-consciously linked to the subject of the poem, *longa series* (1. 7).[55]

This deadly gift is specifically evoked in *Silv.* 1. 5 by the reference to Vulcan's anvil as *Sicula incude* (7), a direct allusion to the forging of the necklace in *Thebaid* 2. 278. But by contrast, in *Silv.* 1. 5 Venus is shown working with her husband to create Etruscus' beautiful, life-preserving baths (31–3). Indeed, the construction of the baths is quite a family venture. In addition to holding her husband's hand and directing his arts, Venus lights the torches of her cupids (33). Venus is not, as in the *Thebaid*, the fomenter and victim of sexual jealousy. It seems hardly coincidental that the allusion in *Silv.* 1. 5 to the epic ecphrasis of Harmonia's necklace should precede another ecphrasis involving very different values: love, friendship, peace, the harmony of a beautiful work of art, and the positive role of gifts in social relations.

Clio, the Muse invoked in the prooemium to the *Thebaid*, also reappears in *Silv.* 1. 5 in symbolically altered dress: *procax vittis hederisque, soluta | fronde verecunda, Clio mea ludit Etrusco* ('flirtatious with garlands and ivy, freed from the chaste laurel, my Clio plays for Etruscus', 13–14).[56]

---

[53] Venus also plays a major role in the Lemnian episode as goddess of destruction (*Theb.* 5. 49–498). See Dominik (1994) 54–63.

[54] Feeney (1993) 364.   [55] A point made by McNelis (2000) chapter 2.

[56] The textual problems of line 14 have been well discussed by Harrison (1985) 337–40. M has *fronde verecundo*, a reading that is objected to on the grounds that it leaves *fronde* isolated, and that the epithet *verecundo* does not suit the symposiastic, erotic nature of the poem. The first argument is more persuasive than the second, for modesty is frequently a characteristic of Statius' friends. Harrison accepts Baehrens's emendation *fronde verecunda*, arguing that Statius here makes

In the *Thebaid*, Statius' invocation of Clio, *quem prius heroum, Clio, dabis?*
('which of the heroes will you give us first, Clio?' 1. 41) echoes the opening
lines of Horace's *Carm.* 1. 12, *quem virum aut heroa lyra vel acri | tibia sumis
celebrare, Clio? | quem deum?* ('which man or hero do you plan to celebrate
with lyre or resonant flute, Clio, which god?', 1–3). The *Thebaid's* invocation lacks Horace's celebratory tone; significantly, in Horace's *Ode*,
celebrare is juxtaposed with Clio, a name etymologically associated with
the Greek word for celebrating heroic glory, κλείω.[57] In the *Thebaid* Clio
is asked to 'give' rather than to 'celebrate', and the projected heroes she
provides problematise the heroic ethos: Tydeus, immoderate in wrath
(41–2), Amphiaraus, the seer swallowed by Hell (42), Hippomedon as
turbid as the river he chokes with corpses (43). The last two heroes
of the list, Parthenopaeus and Capaneus, encapsulate the dominant
emotions aroused by Statius' representation of the Theban war: lament
and horror (44–5).[58] In *Silv.* 1. 5 Clio is restored to her celebratory role,
but, since she sings not of gods or heroes but of a beloved friend, she is
removed from her august Horatian pedestal to play (*ludit*, 14) for Etruscus.
Clio is here accommodated to the poetics of the *Silvae* as programmatically announced in the preface; there, Statius comments, the greatest
epic poets indulged in 'foreplay' (*praeluserit, praef.* 1. 9) before completing
(or embarking upon) their great epics. Since baths were associated with
sexual pleasures, Clio is transformed into a flirtatious Muse (*procax*), her
solemn prophetic laurel discarded (13–14).

By coopting Clio, the Muse of his *Thebaid*, for service in his *Silvae*,
Statius underlines the difference between the two poems in social and
moral ethos as well as aesthetics. The Clio of the *Silvae* bestows pleasure in the service of friendship. She invites a reading of *Silv.* 1. 5 as a
humorous and witty poem that tests the bounds of poetic decorum; in
her transformed state, she is an appropriate Muse for a poem in which a
new set of nymphs, the Naiads of the aqueducts, is introduced to Roman
poetry! Yet, through her former association with Statius' epic, she is
well suited to a new type of hexameter poetry. Wit here combines with

reference to the laurel. This seems more reasonable to me than Courtney's further emendations
fronte verecundis, where the epithet refers to the *vittis* of line 13. I do not accept, however, Harrison's
argument that Statius evokes specifically here the myth of Daphne. According to his reading, Clio,
the representative of Apollonian epic, discards the emblem of chaste Daphne for the Dionysian
ivy. But the terms 'Apollonian' and 'Dionysian' are themselves problematic in the context of the
Thebaid, where such clear-cut distinctions dissolve in the physical and moral chaos of the epic
world.

57 Nisbet and Hubbard (1970) 146.
58 On Parthenopaeus as synonymous with lament see Hardie (1993a) 48.

epic hexameters to celebrate in elevated style both the magnificence of
Etruscus' baths and his youthful devotion to pleasure and festivity. After
the prooemium, the description of the baths themselves (30–59) unfolds
in the third person, unpunctuated by individual expressions of wonder
such as we find in *Silv.* 1. 3 and 2. 2; amazement belongs instead to
the fire, in awe of the riches it heats (43). Personification, an important
feature of the *Thebaid*, is here humorously deployed.

Clio's appearance in 'flirtatious' mood (*procax*, 13) accords fully with
Statius' desire, as he says at line 9, 'to play exuberantly (*lascivire*) for a
beloved friend'. *Lascivire* is an erotic term, appropriate to the flirtatious
context of both symposium and baths. It is also, however, a provocative
literary-critical term. It is used frequently by Quintilian to denote excess
in modern language and style.[59] Quintilian of course is mainly talking
about orators, who promote crowd-pleasing language over clear argu-
mentation. Yet he does accuse Ovid of lack of restraint in his bold transi-
tions in the *Metamorphoses*.[60] Statius' choice of *lascivire*, then, encompasses
the lavish expansiveness of his hexameter poem, directed here to joyful
celebration. Clio in undress, therefore, is Clio nonetheless, and marks
the importance of Statius' bold new poetic endeavour in the *Silvae*.

Statius' 'recusatio' is unique not just in its rejection of his own epic
poem but also in its turning not to love poetry but towards ecphrasis of
a building. The baths, not the bedroom, become the site of alternative
values to those associated with war and politics. Although Etruscus plays
a minor role in this poem, there is nonetheless particular significance in
his function as the addressee for a poem that offers a meditation upon the
poetics of the *Thebaid* and the *Silvae*. Statius seems to fashion this poem
in part as therapy for himself, wearied by the draining preoccupation
with a brutal and violent epic. But at the end of the poem he suggests
that the poem has therapeutic value for his friend Etruscus also, who was
a victim of imperial politics. Etruscus' choice of a private, secluded life,
expressed through his baths, seems to have had political motivation, for
his father was in exile at the time of this poem's composition. The poem
responds then not only to the *Thebaid*, but also to the particular political
circumstances of Etruscus' family. The two, however, are not unrelated,
as we shall see.

The concluding couplet of *Silv.* 1. 5 delicately touches upon Etruscus'
sad and difficult family circumstances. The conventional wish for long
life for Etruscus and his baths is capped by a final couplet expressing

---

[59] See for instance Quint. *Inst.* 4. 2. 39.   [60] Quint. *Inst.* 4. 1. 77.

hope for the rebirth of the family's fortunes: *tecum ista senescant | et tua iam melius discat fortuna renasci* ('may those baths grow old with you, and may a better fortune now for you learn to be reborn', 64–5). The verb *renasci* metaphorically links the healthful waters of Etruscus' baths with the desired regeneration of his family, an oblique wish for the return from exile of Etruscus' elderly father – described in *Silv.* 3. 3. 154 as 'reborn' (*renato*) on his return. The exaltation of friendship and private life in *Silv.* 1. 5 can therefore be seen as a political gesture, an assertion of enduring values in the face of an unpredictable world. But in order to assess fully the impact of this concluding couplet on the poem we need to consider what we know about Claudius Etruscus and his father.

Most of our knowledge of Etruscus' family comes from *Silv.* 3. 3, a poem of consolation on the death of Claudius Etruscus' father. We do not know the father's name, only the son's, although it was the father who became famous in a long political career as one of the most successful and enduring of imperial freedmen. *Silv.* 3. 3 documents that career – and the final loss of his name.[61]

The career of the elderly Etruscus illustrates the unpredictability of fortune for a servant of the court. According to *Silv.* 3. 3, he was a slave from Smyrna (43–6, 60) who was freed while in service to Tiberius (66–9) and rose in the administrative hierarchy to become secretary *a rationibus* under the Flavians, a position which put him in charge of the imperial treasury (85–105). He was elevated to equestrian status by Domitian, and thus came to equal in status his two sons (143–5), whose mother, dead in their infancy, had been of high birth (111–12). In 82 or 83, however, shortly after Domitian's accession, he was disgraced and sent into exile. He was then an old man of over eighty, an age when a man expects honourable retirement, not shameful banishment. Exile was in Campania, so his offence could not have been too heinous, particularly since we are told that his colleague was banished from Italy (160–4).[62] However, Claudius Etruscus' father was away from Rome for around seven years, a long time for an old man, and he died shortly after his recall when he was close to the age of ninety – a sad end to a promising career.[63]

We can only conjecture the circumstances that led to his downfall. Carradice has suggested that Etruscus' offence may have been the mere

---

[61] The value of *Silv.* 3. 3 as a source for the father's career is discussed in detail by Weaver (1965) 145–54. Because of its allusion to Domitian's return from the Sarmatian campaign, *Silv.* 3. 3 cannot have been written before January 93. See Weaver (1965) 145.

[62] Weaver (1965) 150 notes that in lines 164–5 Statius blurs the period of exile.

[63] Mart. 7. 40. 6 provides the age.

making of a mistake or, more seriously perhaps, opposition to Domitian's new policies with the coinage.[64] Statius, however, refers only vaguely to an error incurred either through advanced age or the tricks of Fortune (156–60). Essentially, *Silv.* 3. 3 represents Etruscus as a victim of court society. It suggests, in particular, that Etruscus may have incurred the emperor's displeasure because he was an old man, worn out with the duties of his work (*tarda situ rebusque exhausta senectus*, 156). The position of treasurer, we are told, was onerous, affording little time for relaxation; Etruscus led a hard-working, traditional life, eschewing any form of self-indulgence and supported chiefly by a loving family and loyal clients (106–10), yet such conventional virtues did not ultimately protect him. As Wallace-Hadrill has pointed out, the court was a site of anxiety and fear. Here the emperor demonstrated his power to bestow or withdraw favours; here the courtiers themselves lived in an atmosphere of hypocrisy, competition, and distrust. The court provided a context of instability and psychological strain to which Etruscus fell victim.[65]

Silv. 3. 3 raises the question of the value of service in the imperial system. Its rewards could be great, but they were unpredictable, for just when one might have expected Etruscus to enjoy the fruits of a long and distinguished service in the imperial treasury, he fell precipitately out of favour. Loyalty, trust, faithful service, such qualities, it seems, were not rated highly enough within the imperial system.[66]

Silv. 1. 5 suggests that the economic fortunes of his house did not suffer because of the father's exile.[67] Yet, it seems that the two sons shunned politics as a way of life.[68] Claudius Etruscus' eschewal of a public career, then, finds specific justification in the fate of his father. His wealth, however, came from the unstinting generosity of the father (*Silv.* 3. 3.147–50); Claudius Etruscus' customary *nitor* is a sign of the father's indulgence (149–50). The magnificence of the baths too then is a tribute to the father's love for his son and to hard work in a life of imperial

[64] Carradice (1979) 101–3 argues for AD 82 as the year of banishment on the hypothesis that the father of Claudius Etruscus opposed Domitian's reform of the coinage in that year.
[65] Wallace-Hadrill (1970) 305.
[66] *Silv.* 3. 3. 158–9. Compare the career of Rutilius Gallicus, Domitian's 'workhorse'. By the time the poem honouring his recovery from a serious illness was published, he was dead. The reader is left to conclude that the lines claiming that Gallicus became ill not because of age, but because of faithful and overworked imperial service (1. 4. 52–7), proved only too true. See Henderson (1998) who states that Gallicus' illness 'describes the syndrome of *power*' (64).
[67] J. Evans (1978) suggests that the important connections Etruscus' father made through his marriage to a woman of high birth were instrumental in cushioning the old man's exile and in securing his eventual return.
[68] See Weaver (1965) 153 on lines 147ff.

service. At the start of *Silv.* 3. 3 Statius encapsulates both these sides of the father's life by summoning as his Muse *Pietas*, the highest of the gods and the rarest of virtues (1–7). The invocation is in part ironic, for *pietas* has two meanings in the poem: familial love and devotion, and dedication to imperial service. Whereas Claudius Etruscus' grief and devotion for his father is described as exceedingly rare (*praef.* 3. 15–16), *pietas* in the sense of dedication to an emperor whose powers of governance are unpredictable is severely scrutinised in this poem.[69]

In his epigram on the father's death, 7. 40, Martial commemorates the father of Claudius Etruscus as a long-standing fixture of Domitian's court, *ille senex Augusta notus in aula* ('that elderly man who was well known in the imperial court', 1). *Silv.* 3. 3 suggests that his survival to old age in court service, through many changes of emperor, was extraordinary (83–4):

> tu totiens mutata ducum iuga rite tulisti
> integer inque omni felix tua cumba profundo.

You dutifully bore the yoke through many changes of leader, preserving your integrity, and you kept your small boat afloat no matter what the sea.

Survival in the unpredictable, mutable life of court is described as tricky navigation in precarious, unfathomable seas, an image reminiscent of the seafaring metaphors through which Statius advocated the Epicurean calm of Pollius Felix (*Silv.* 2. 2. 131–2, 138–42). The fall of the father of Claudius Etruscus is all the more shocking because it comes so late in life, and not surprisingly the disaster is described in terms of a storm (158–60). The common imagery here puts the father's career under ethical pressure as we, his readers, are invited to question the meaning and value of imperial service in contrast to the retired or philosophical life.

Indeed, Book 3 as a whole interrogates the value of a life devoted to imperial politics as opposed to a life lived far from the centre of imperial power in Naples. It begins and ends with two poems, *Silv.* 3. 1 and 3. 5, that assert the value of life in the Bay of Naples. *Silv.* 3. 3 is the central poem of the book, and the centrepiece of a series of three poems addressed to public figures engaged in imperial service. *Silv.* 3. 2 is addressed to Maecius Celer, a young man who is engaged in military service to Domitian, whereas *Silv.* 3. 4, as we have seen, is addressed to Earinus, a successful freedman and favourite of Domitian. As on a wheel of fortune,

---

[69] Thus Claudius Etruscus is made to complain against the inequities of a fate that deprived him of his father shortly after his restoration (182–7), a complaint that could as well (but with less tact) be made against an emperor who exiled an old man and recalled him too late.

the fates of Celer and Earinus are still rising. But, according to Statius' poem, the father of Claudius Etruscus, once a successful freedman like Earinus, suddenly and inexplicably fell from favour. The positioning of *Silv.* 3. 3 functions as an implied protreptic on the unpredictable dangers attendant on the life that strives for public success and imperial benefits. As Millar comments, paraphrasing Epictetus, slave of a freedman executed by Domitian in AD 95, 'Caesar's friend knows neither security nor freedom'.[70]

The concept of the baths as a safe, enclosed space, a site of resistance to the pressured vagaries of urban and court life, is similarly contextualised in Statius' poetry book not only through the later lament for Claudius Etruscus' father but through its juxtaposition with its surrounding poems, *Silv.* 1. 4 and *Silv.* 1. 6. *Silv.* 1. 4 likewise invites interrogation of the life devoted to public service, for the themes of public service and health link it with *Silv.* 1. 5. Rutilius Gallicus, Domitian's urban prefect, was perhaps Statius' most eminent dedicatee.[71] *Silv.* 1. 4 celebrates his recovery from a serious illness, brought on by overwork in imperial service (52–6). Yet by the time the poem was published, Rutilius Gallicus had in fact died. The fate of Rutilius Gallicus is similar to the fate of the father of Claudius Etruscus – both prominent public officials dashed unexpectedly from the heights of success. The curious inclusion of this poem in Book 1 of the *Silvae* after Gallicus' failure to recover draws particular attention to the stress and unpredictability of an imperial career. Reading this poem after Gallicus' death provides a different perspective upon public life from reading it while there seemed hope of his recovery.

In *Silv.* 1. 4 Statius employs a strategy of praise characteristic of his other imperial poems. In concern for Gallicus' health, Apollo speaks the encomiastic account of Gallicus' career to Aesculapius (58–105). This can of course be seen as a deferential gesture; the poet speaks not in his own voice but in words borrowed from a god. But Apollo's speech also brings into prominence the inequity of fate and 'Jupiter'. He is determined to rescue Gallicus from *iniquo . . . Iove* (94–5), a daring statement that the translator of the Loeb circumvents by rendering *Iovi* as 'Pluto'. But Domitian is consistently represented in the *Silvae* as Jupiter. Apollo's voice conveys an implied protreptic: Domitian makes excessive demands upon his servants. He is not figured, however, as a tyrant. Statius says that Gallicus was devoted to the emperor and overwork was, to him, 'sweet work' (*dulce opus*, 56). In this poem Statius explores the consequences of

---

[70] Millar (1965) 144.   [71] On Rutilius Gallicus see Henderson (1998).

the ideology of imperial divinity: how can imperial servants fulfil the expectations of a ruler who is semi-divine? Such ideology creates a gap between master and man, pushing Gallicus beyond his mortal limits. Thus in *Silv.* 1. 4 as in *Silv.* 3. 3 life in imperial service is represented as unpredictable and enormously demanding, while its rewards remain uncertain.

Unlike the father of Claudius Etruscus, however, Gallicus occupied a high position next to 'Jupiter' – nonetheless that did not protect him from a sudden, unexpected demise. In *Silv.* 1. 4 Statius effusively compliments Gallicus on his high position as a 'wandering moon surrounded by stars' (*uaga cingitur astris | luna*, 36–7), an allusion to the Augustan climax of Horace's *Carm.* 1. 12. 46–8:

> micat inter omnes
> Iulium sidus velut inter ignes
> luna minores.

The Julian star shines among the others, like the moon among lesser fires.

As Henderson puts it, Gallicus here is being conceived as 'an Apollo and Augustus rolled-into-one'.[72] Gallicus is essentially second in command to Domitian himself. And yet, Statius' subtle deployment of the Horatian allusion demands more attention. This final image of Gallicus as a 'wandering moon encircled by stars' shifts between deference and self-assertion on the part of the poet. As moon, Gallicus' relationship to Domitian, the sun, is aptly figured, for as imperial servant, he is a figure of borrowed light. With the addition of *uaga* to Horace's unadorned moon, Statius adds a special Flavian twist to imperial stellar ideology.[73] *Uaga* connotes errancy, wandering on an unpredictable course and contained only by the stars, themselves figures of imperial divinity.[74] The wandering moon, then, is an accurate image for life in imperial service as adumbrated in the *Silvae*; an uncertain life circumscribed and contained by the demands of the imperial hierarchy, yet exposed too to the whims of fate.

The juxtaposition of *Silv.* 1. 5 with *Silv.* 1. 4, therefore, lends particular force to Statius' exaltation of the son's devotion to the pleasures of private life. Instead, then, of the rough waters of the court, the son, Claudius Etruscus, has wisely chosen the still, protected waters of a quiet life,

---

[72] Henderson (1998) 56.

[73] On the apparently erratic course of the moon and its constant mutability see Plin. *HN* 2. 46–8.

[74] Cf. *Silv.* 1. 1. 97–8 where Domitian's Flavian ancestors are depicted as encircling the neck of the equestrian statue of the emperor.

metaphorically displayed in his magnificent private baths. The baths become a particularly potent image of the *locus amoenus* because they function as a refuge not from politics in the abstract but from politics in the bitter experience of Claudius Etruscus' family.

Poet and friend are here closely linked, for in writing this celebratory poem Statius seeks relief from his own source of grief and stress, the *Thebaid*. Its noxious subject and Muses must be banished from a poem honouring Statius' friend. While the exclusion of the *Thebaid* brings to the fore the importance of friendship and festive celebration, we are also offered here a way of reading this epic from the standpoint of the *Silvae* as a tale not of military glory but of psychological distress and civic evil that must be excluded from Statius' present work. The Theban myth is an examination of the uses and abuses of autocratic power; it provides a powerful civic paradigm for imperial Rome in its first-century struggles to negotiate and stabilise the position of emperor.[75] In particular, viewed from the perspective of *Silv.* 1. 5, the Theban myth provides an extreme, frightening version of the instability of the political world – the *labor* and *cura* (11–12) and the unpredictable rewards and failures – from which Claudius Etruscus himself has had good reason, it seems, to withdraw. Here in the centre of Rome itself, unlike in his more public poems such as *Silv.* 1. 4, Statius' art can be truly therapeutic and also exalted.

As Markus has shown, Statius counteracts Juvenal's savage portrayal of Statius as pimp, who prostitutes his *Thebaid* at a public performance before a vulgar mob.[76] Rather, Statius consistently represents his literary recitals of his epic as élite occasions where his audience consisted of senators or even the emperor himself.[77] Statius 'represents his poetic mission as continuation of the work of the early (*prisci*) composers of poetry, whose mode of composition was oral'.[78] Through his symposium in *Silv.* 1. 5 Statius likewise elevates his 'occasional' poetry, making its performance an élite and joyful occasion where he himself, through dramatic stage directions, selects the audience. Here he draws upon the performative tradition of Greek lyric in order to lend authority to a new Roman mythology and to a new concept of Roman identity that is dedicated to poetry and friendship rather than politics, traditionally the young Roman male's route to fame. At the same time, however, the poet's performance of an archaic lyric situation, though effective in its

---

[75] See Dominik (1994) 130–80.   [76] Juv. *Sat.* 7. 82–7. See Markus (2000) 171–5.
[77] Markus (2000) 163–8.   [78] Markus (2000) 163.

immediate context, reminds the audience and reader of liberties and status now lost. The poet's voice is now raised in support of the arts rather than the state, and in support of private virtues rather than civic ones. He plays the inspired poet at a very private occasion. Indeed, as the following poem *Silv.* 1. 6 suggests, the commanding position the imperial poet enjoys in the symposium is not matched in the outside Roman world, much as the poet may wish to integrate alternative cultural values into the fabric of public life and into a particularly Roman style of poetics.

CHAPTER 7

The emperor's Saturnalia: Silvae *1. 6*

Iubes esse liberos, erimus

Pliny, *Panegyricus* 66. 4

Duceris ut nervis alienis mobile lignum

Horace, *Satirae* 2. 7. 82

Silv. 1. 6 concerns a public, imperial peformance – the gifts, banquet, and spectacular shows – provided by the emperor for the people on the occasion of the Saturnalia. We move then as readers from the private enclosed space of the baths to the public enclosed space of the amphitheatre, from an atmosphere of exclusivity to one of inclusivity, as people of all ranks and races join together in the carnivalesque celebration of the winter feast. Unlike Horace, who in *Sat.* 2. 3 withdraws from Rome at the Saturnalia to write poetry, Statius takes on the challenge of describing the winter festival at which he himself takes part. But he abandons the authoritative, performative role of *Silv.* 1. 5 and, on the whole, presents himself as simply one of the spectators at the amphitheatre, viewing the performance of others through the collective pronoun 'we' (*nos*). Domitian, not Statius, is master of ceremonies here; the new culturally coercive power of the amphitheatre absorbs the poet's voice into the crowd. The poem thus mediates here between two types of consciousness that are not necessarily compatible. The poet represents himself as a spectator, not a performer; he is both part of the crowd and yet he is also separate from it in his attempt to commit to published form the day's events.

An important theme explored in the poem is the imperial appropriation of the discourse of popular liberty, for Domitian's spectacle takes place at the Saturnalia, the Roman feast of popular licence and social inversion.[1] The poem is therefore constructed out of two competing, contradictory occasions: the emperor's entertainment in the amphitheatre,

---

[1] Scullard (1981) 205–7.

site of imperial control, and the Saturnalia, festival of popular liberty. The literary paradigm for a poem set at the Saturnalia is provided by Horace's *Sat.* 2. 3 and 2. 7. In the latter poem Horace's slave assumes the liberty of speech associated with the Saturnalia to harangue his master.[2] As a literary setting, then, the Saturnalia provides an obvious occasion for rebellious, or at least questioning speech. How then does the temporal framing of *Silv.* 1. 6 and the spatial confinement of the events it describes affect its account of the people's traditional freedom on the Saturnalia to speak and act as they wished? To what extent does the poet, speaking as one of the enthusiastic crowd, interrogate or resist the emperor's power? As we shall see, the poet's necessary abandonment of the performative role of *Silv.* 1. 5 dramatises the constraints operating upon the imperial poet in his engagement with public, civic rituals. At the same time, however, the Saturnalia itself offers the occasion for a poetics that obliquely explores the paradoxical nature of the emperor's power and of *his* Saturnalia.

The poem is written in hendecasyllables, a metre not normally used for elevated occasions but rather for invective and displays of acerbic, irreverent wit.[3] By using this metre for the final poem of Book 1, Statius engineers a witty form of Saturnalian inversion, the rapidity of the short hendecasyllabic lines corresponding to the swiftly changing scenes of entertainment that flash past the spectators' gaze.[4] The metre exists in tension with the lavish nature of the imperial spectacle, and the dominating presence of the emperor. Here, for the first time in the *Silvae*, Statius brings the emperor himself into the public arena, where his power is displayed not in a colossal statue, as in *Silv.* 1. 1, but in his social interactions with his people. The amphitheatre itself, which may well have been the Colosseum, is not described.[5] Instead, the poem describes the

---

[2] On the Saturnalia as a framing device for Hor. *Sat.* 2. 3 and 2. 7 see Bernstein (1992) 34–55.

[3] See Morgan (2000) 115–16. Morgan emphasises that the metre, light and fast, is associated through Catullus with jocularity and is appropriate therefore for a festival notably lacking in constraints. If so, there is then a tension between the traditional associations of the metre as developed by Catullus and the Flavian form of the Saturnalia as described here by Statius.

[4] See Damon (1992) 304. She argues that Statius' use of the hendecasyllabic metre for varied occasions in the *Silvae* (such as *Silv.* 2. 7, the 'birthday poem' for the deceased poet Lucan) suggests that it should not necessarily create expectations of Catullan or Saturnalian irreverence. Van Dam (1984) 453 points out that Statius uses this metre for closure, with Books 1, 2, and 4 of the *Silvae* ending with a hendecasyllabic poem. H. B. Evans (1978) argues that Horace's second poem on the Saturnalia, *Sat.* 2. 7, functions as a closural poem to the *Satires*.

[5] Martial's *Liber Spectaculorum*, written to celebrate the inaugural games in the Colosseum, focusses to a far greater extent on the entertainment than on the amazing new building. The seventh *Eclogue* of Calpurnius Siculus, on the other hand, describes Nero's amphitheatre in detail (23–72) and overtly uses the architecture of the amphitheatre as a metaphor for imperial power.

entertainment the emperor provides in the amphitheatre.[6] The idea of the emperor is examined anew here through spectacle, rather than through architecture. All the same, the lavishness and unprecedented luxury of the spectacle recounted in *Silv.* 1. 6 correspond on the social register to the massive size of the statue in *Silv.* 1. 1. Both poems explore excess as a metaphor for imperial power.[7] While such a metaphor evokes the divine majesty of the emperor and the wonder and awe he engenders in his audience, it also points to the ambiguity inherent in a power that so ostentatiously exceeds human norms.

In *Silv.* 1. 6, this ambiguity is part of a larger response to imperial autocracy and Domitian's expansion of the imperial office into a divine monarchy.[8] In particular, *Silv.* 1. 6 explores the association that Domitian cultivated with Jupiter.[9] In the proem to the *Thebaid*, as Feeney has pointed out, Domitian's systematic cultivation of analogies with Jupiter produces anxiety in the poet, whose epic poem consistently stresses the dangers of human attempts to compete with the gods and appropriate the heavens.[10] As in *Silv.* 3. 4, *Silv.* 1. 6 takes a playful, yet also troubling look at the political, social, and indeed literary implications of Domitian's Jovian theology. In this poem, where Domitian is on public display, not secluded in his palace, the comparison between the emperor and Jupiter specifically brings out the dual aspect of this god, both provider and punisher. The threat of the unpredictable exercise of power is never absent from his representation here. The humour and playful inversions sanctioned by the Saturnalia provide an alternative channel for the expression of anxieties about Domitian's aspirations for divine rights and powers.

The Saturnalia itself, as Bernstein has argued, is a festival that 'can be interpreted as a specific kind of language through which the tensions in a society are articulated and made visible'.[11] Through the use of two politically highly charged occasions – the games and the Saturnalia – *Silv.* 1. 6 scrutinises the ideology of divine kingship on which Domitian based his rule, in particular the right the emperor assumes at the

---

[6] The classical definition of ecphrasis encompassed events as well as places. See chapter 1 above, 40.

[7] See Cancik (1965) 100, who argues that *Silv.* 1. 1 and *Silv.* 1. 6 correspond closely in structure and development of theme.

[8] As Millar (1977) 3 observes, the transformation of the emperor from *princeps* to Hellenistic king was not interrupted by 'good' emperors such as Trajan or Marcus Aurelius.

[9] On Domitian's association with Jupiter see Scott (1936) 133–40; Sauter (1934) 54–78; Fears (1981).

[10] Feeney (1993) 358–9.   [11] Bernstein (1992) 36.

Saturnalian feast to control his people's traditional liberties. *Silv.* 1. 6 thus explores the paradox at the heart of imperial culture, namely that the price the Romans had to pay for the immense extension of their power was lack of their former freedom. The poem investigates the limits of popular and poetic freedom under Rome's 'Jupiter'.[12]

THE POLITICS OF SPECTACLE

Any approach to *Silv.* 1. 6 and Domitian's Saturnalian games is undoubt-edly complicated by the hostile view of important imperial writers that public entertainment served as a sop to a servile nation. According to Tacitus, for instance, those upset by Nero's death were the *plebs* and the worst slaves, because they were addicted to the circus and theatres.[13] From this type of élite perspective, writing and reading about games, correspondingly, is a demeaning activity, particularly when done with enthusiasm. The subject of ceremonial, however, has come to be seen by modern critics as fundamental to an understanding of the political process and the structure of power.[14] As Cannadine observes, ceremo-nial and spectacle centred around a monarch or an emperor 'seem to confirm consensus, to disguise conflict, and to support both hierarchy and community'.[15] Spectacle was integral to the monarchical or impe-rial process, for by impressing and captivating the people, it persuaded them to acquiesce in a political system where power was unevenly dis-tributed. The political cannot then be separated from the spectacular. As Cannadine well puts it, 'politics and ceremonial are not separate sub-jects, the one serious, the other superficial. Ritual is not the mask of force, but is itself a type of power'.[16]

The political authority of the Roman emperors was committed to impressive display, and the theatre or amphitheatre provided the pre-ferred stage for the dazzling display of statecraft. Suetonius tells us that Domitian had a marked sense of stage presence. As he presided over the Capitoline games, for instance, he presented himself wearing a Greek-style purple toga and a gold crown elaborately decorated with the images of Jupiter, Juno, and Minerva. The two priests who stood beside him on

---

[12] By freedom I mean personal, not political liberty, in particular the freedom of speech associated with the Saturnalia since, as Wirszubski (1950) 171 has argued, 'autocracy and constitutional freedom are incompatible'.

[13] Tac. *Hist.* 1. 4. 14–16.

[14] For a fine discussion of the importance of the study of ceremonial to historians and anthropolo-gists, see Cannadine (1987).

[15] Cannadine (1987) 15.   [16] Cannadine (1987) 19.

either side were similarly arrayed apart from the crowns, which lacked the divine images.[17] But visual display of majesty alone was not enough to please the populace; rather, at the games the emperor had to earn the acclamation of the crowd through lavish gifts. The putting on of shows, like the raising of public monuments, was an important means then by which the emperor could display what Veyne calls 'euergetism', his largesse to the Roman people.[18] This largesse was an essential component of the good king, who in popular political philosophy displayed a natural liberality in the luxury of his buildings and the bounty of his gifts.[19] The shows provided a stage where the emperor could cultivate the convenient fiction that though he was raised far above his people, they were his primary care.[20]

At the same time, as Wiedemann observes, attendance at the games subjected the emperor to pressure from the people who expected the emperor to share his power, at least symbolically, by providing them with spectacular entertainment. In the amphitheatre the emperor was in an ambiguous position 'as both autocrat and servant of the Roman people'.[21] The murder of Caligula at the games provides an extreme example of the emperor's potential vulnerability in this enclosed and crowded public place.[22] The games therefore were managed through a system of organised licence and surveillance effectively designed to broaden and confirm the emperor's safety and authority in his social transactions with his people. Of necessity, the appearance of an emperor at the games was a carefully orchestrated act of statecraft and theatrical display. Hopkins has argued that the amphitheatre served as the people's 'parliament', the place where, in an age of diminished political rights,

[17] Suet. *Dom.* 4. 4. The mock-funereal dinner that Domitian staged for the senators (Dio Cass. 67. 9.1–6) arguably shows a sense of theatrical humour, if a perverse one, in the emperor. See Vismara (1994) 415–16.

[18] Veyne (1990) 320–419.   [19] Veyne (1990) 321.

[20] Veyne (1990) 398: 'Given by the Emperor or in his presence, the shows were a material satisfaction, but they also allowed the sovereign to prove to his capital that he shared popular feelings (*popularis esse*). They were also a ceremony at which the Emperor was acclaimed ... The material and symbolic satisfactions of the Circus subjected the *plebs* to their master. One could also say that there was something democratic in this *largesse* and this homage that the Emperor paid to the most representative city of his Empire'. I part company with Veyne here in the emphasis he lays on the emperor's demonstration of populist feelings, for this does not correspond to literary representations of Domitian's relations with his people.

[21] Wiedemann (1992) 171.

[22] Suet. *Cal.* 58. The games also provided the emperor with an opportunity for the abuse of power. According to Suet. *Vesp.* 4. 4 Vespasian fell from political favour because he fell asleep during Nero's performances or even left them. Worse of course are the examples of spectators supposedly dragged from their seats at the order of the emperor and forced to perform in the arena. E.g. Suet. *Cal.* 35. 2; *Dom.* 10. 1.

the people could directly confront the ruler with their needs.[23] In the case of Domitian, however, his cultivation of a close association with the gods endowed him with enormous symbolic power as a majestic, divine monarch. The amphitheatre of *Silv.* 1. 6 is represented not so much as a 'parliament' as a temple to Rome's new god, the vicegerent of Jupiter on earth.

Characteristically, the writings of Pliny and Tacitus provide a completely negative interpretation of Domitian's management of the games. For Bartsch, the Nero who oppressed his audience, forcing them to watch the spectacle of imperial decline, finds a worthy successor in the Domitian of Pliny's *Panegyricus*. At Domitian's games, according to the *Panegyricus* (33. 3–4), the audience is riveted by fear, unable to express its true feelings under the sinister eye of an emperor who used his public appearances to scrutinise his audience for any sign of disloyalty or disrespect. Bartsch interprets Pliny's Domitian as a paranoid tyrant, a master of dissimulation who in turn compels his audience to disguise its true feelings: 'Seated in the imperial box and not, like Nero, actually on the stage, Domitian nonetheless watches the audience not for signs of political disaffection but for the wrong responses to the show in the arena. These spectators simulate enthusiasms they do not feel – or literally become the spectacle themselves'.[24] For imperial writers, the theatre is not only an important staging-ground for the dramatic confrontation of emperor and people; as Bartsch has argued, it provides literally and metaphorically a highly charged paradigm for the workings of imperial power.[25] Thus in the *Agricola* Tacitus extends the theatrical paradigm to the political arena in his haunting portrait of Domitian 'as an observer who forces his audience to act against their will and who watches for their inadvertent betrayal of their true feelings'.[26]

Yet in *Silv.* 1. 6 Domitian, far from brooding over his people, is presented neither as an observer nor as the direct object of his people's gaze. An instructive contrast exists in the seventh *Eclogue* of Calpurnius Siculus, where the detailed description of the amphitheatre climaxes with the viewer's gaze drawn towards the majestic figure of the emperor.[27]

---

[23] Hopkins (1983) 15–16.   [24] Bartsch (1994) 2–33.
[25] As Bartsch (1994) 31 argues, the theatre provides 'literally and figuratively a microcosm for the workings of power'.
[26] Bartsch (1994) 33.
[27] Calp. *Ecl.* 7. 79–84. Cancik (1965) 106–8 discusses the differences between Calpurnius' seventh *Eclogue* and Statius' poem that he claims arise from different sets of generic expectations. Yet it is hard to see what the generic expectations of a reader of *Silv.* 1. 6 might be, given the unusual use of hendecasyllables and the novel topic of the poem.

Domitian, on the other hand, is never described in *Silv.* 1. 6. His
relationship to his people is thus presented as different from Nero's.
Goddard has suggested that Nero lost the support of the élite by court-
ing the favour of the general populace through his personal participation
in the games.[28] Nero's mistake lay in his failure to keep his people at a
respectful distance; in abandoning the performance of imperial majesty
for the roles of murderers and women, he confused appearance and
reality and subverted the notion of imperial hierarchy.[29]

Domitian, however, did not make Nero's mistake of descending to
the stage. Suetonius' anecdotal description of Domitian's divinely regal
attire suggests that at the games Domitian, on the contrary, preserved
a godlike distance from the crowd.[30] In addition, Suetonius tells us that
Domitian was particularly generous in his production of games for the
people and controlled his subjects through his munificence. He constantly gave magnificent and lavish spectacles, *spectacula assidue magnifica
et sumptuosa edidit* (*Dom.* 4. 1).[31] He was generous too at these shows, providing banquets and gifts of many kinds such as food and money.[32] In
Silv. 1. 6 Statius and the audience are represented as the enthusiastic
recipients of one of these shows. The day begins with a huge shower of
sweetmeats upon the crowd, moves on to a free and lavish banquet, and
continues with a seemingly endless succession of lavish and novel shows,
described by Statius as *novosque luxus* ('new luxuries', 51); the continuance
of the spectacle through the night, thanks to artificial illumination, is part
of the unprecedented novelty of delights, *noctem enim | illam felicissimam et
voluptatibus publicis inexpertam* (*praef.* 1. 31–2). The free food and gifts, the
novelty, the splendour, the rapid succession of entertainers, the extension
of the shows into the night by seemingly magical means, all form visible
proof of the emperor's munificence and superhuman capabilities.

In *Silv.* 1. 6 Domitian is presented as an emperor who fully understands
the dynamics of the amphitheatre, a magnificent controller and pleaser
of the crowd. The games that take place on his Saturnalia provide a
paradigm of empire that reinforces both community and hierarchy and,
through the controlling presence of the emperor, asserts the stability of
the regime. *Silv.* 1. 6 does not glorify the Empire through a magnificent

---

[28] Goddard (1994) 79. Nero's gravest mistake then, Goddard concludes, was his failure to please
those who would write his history. Goddard's analysis of Nero depends upon the thesis of Veyne
that the games created a division between the senate and the emperor, as the élite and the *plebs*
struggled for first place in the ruler's attention. See Goddard (1994) 76; Veyne (1990) 406–7.

[29] See C. Edwards (1994) 83–97.   [30] See note 17 above.

[31] He was not as lavish as Trajan however. See Jones (1992) 105.

[32] Suet. *Dom.* 4. 5.

building like the Colosseum. The poem looks at imperial power from the ground up, where it is realised in material terms appropriate to the Saturnalian celebration. Food and sex are what please the crowd; the freedom of speech traditionally associated with the Saturnalia is replaced by the passive reception of free gifts.

Silv. i. 6, then, suggests that Domitian perhaps had learned from Nero's mistake. This poem displays Domitian engaged in the cultivation of 'privileged visibility', a notion which Nero had apparently abandoned by his literal descent among the people to perform.[33] 'Privileged visibility' is a term I borrow from Greenblatt, who argues that the success of the Elizabethan monarchy depended upon histrionic display which, as in a theatre, both engaged the audience with the queen's visible presence of monarchy and held them at a respectful distance.[34] A related, important strategy of Elizabethan statecraft was the arousal of 'salutary anxiety' through the theatrical staging of public events such as executions and maimings, which displayed the monarch's power both to punish and to pardon.[35] The arousal of salutary anxiety likewise kept the general public at a respectful distance. As a hegemonic practice it was essential to the concept of 'privileged visibility', and it was deeply implicated in the fashioning of texts as well as the management of spectacle.[36]

In imperial Roman society artistic traditions and social institutions were similarly enmeshed in the mutual reinforcement of 'salutary anxiety', nowhere more explicitly perhaps than in the amphitheatre, where the punishment of criminals could be given spectacular form as elaborate mythological drama.[37] *Silv.* i. 6 presents Domitian as both a popular benefactor of his people and a figure of wonderful, even fearsome majesty who maintains a crucial distance between himself and his subjects. Through its exploration of the imperial fiction of divinity, *Silv.* i. 6 plays with the notion that although Domitian pleases the crowd with theatrical extravagance, the fundamental arbitrariness of such divinely conceived power underlies the comedy of the day's events. *Silv.* i. 6 reveals the ways in which the technique of 'salutary anxiety' in the amphitheatre

---

[33] Nero did not perform publicly in Rome until near the end of his reign, in AD 65. See C. Edwards (1994) 89.

[34] Greenblatt (1988) 64.

[35] For the term 'salutary anxiety' see Greenblatt (1988) 135, and for a discussion of its implications, 129–63.

[36] Greenblatt (1988) 133–8. Greenblatt argues that one of the defining characteristics of Shakespearean dramaturgy is its appropriation of an anxiety that was accepted by the audience because it was compounded with pleasure.

[37] Coleman (1990).

unifies the people in support of their emperor and thus brings about the resignification of the Saturnalia and the very notion of *libertas* itself.

CONTROLLING CARNIVAL

Complicating our approach to Statius' representation of the imperial games is their specific occasion, the Saturnalia. This festival was presumably an occasion when the emperor's authority could be tested to its limits.[38] Bakhtin viewed the Saturnalia as a paradigm of carnival, which he defined as an occasion of popular freedom that defied élite culture. Bakhtin idealised carnival as a place where the voice of the people could be heard without restraint and where bodily impulses and material pleasures could be frankly indulged: 'carnival celebrated temporary liberation from the prevailing truth and from the established order; it marked the suspension of all hierarchical rank, privileges, norms, and prohibitions'.[39] For the period of the Saturnalia social and ethical rankings were abolished, and masters and slaves ate together at the communal feast. For Bakhtin, carnival was liberating in a broad sense in that it made possible the scrutiny, mockery, and even subversion of social norms and institutions. The Saturnalia then was a potentially dangerous festival for an authoritarian élite.

Bakhtin's exuberant, utopian definition of carnival as a site of communal celebration has been criticised, however, as an oversimplification of its function. Bernstein for instance has located what he calls 'a bitter strand' within the Saturnalia, which can dramatise the tensions within society and even contains the potential for anarchic violence.[40] Bakhtin's theory too ignores the spatial, temporal and legal constraints upon the Saturnalia and other carnivalesque celebrations.[41] Carnival is generally a time of *licensed* festivity.[42] Thus in *Silv.* 1. 6, the emperor organises the entertainment for the Saturnalia, and he controls its time and place. Carnival, it is now generally agreed, is a powerful ideological tool and analytical concept whose functions are various. Myerhoff points out that

---

[38] On the Roman festival see Vollmer (1898) 304 on *Silv.* 1. 6. 4; Scullard (1981) 205–7.

[39] Bakhtin (1968) 10.   [40] Bernstein (1992) 17.

[41] For a discussion of critical attitudes to Bakhtin's formulation of carnival, see Stallybrass and White (1986) 1–31; Bernstein (1992) 17–18.

[42] In his study of the festive in Greek and Roman religion, Kerenyi (1962) 49–70, especially 64, has argued that the feast belongs to a stable pattern of religious events in which the festive is defined by the predictable alternation of complementary elements, the serious and the playful, the constrained and the free. According to Turner (1969) chapter 5, this licensed alternation of constraint and freedom can be seen as a sign of social well-being; carnival is not destructive of social rules but offers a fresh perspective upon them.

it can be used by writers to make a variety of statements about the social and political order: 'to affirm it, attack it, suspend it, redefine it, oppose it, buttress it, emphasize one part of it at the cost of another'.[43]

The association of the Saturnalia with social inversion and popular *libertas* undoubtedly endowed this Roman festival with the potential to challenge imperial authority. Britannicus' assumption of freedom of speech on the Saturnalia, for instance, led to his murder, for he misjudged his audience and, in front of Nero, he sang bitterly of his exclusion from the throne.[44] *Silv.* 1. 6 demonstrates the ways in which Domitian took control of this festival, using it to affirm his own supremacy before his people. Thus the Saturnalia is strikingly called the emperor's Saturnalia (*Saturnalia principis*, 82), a paradoxical resignification of the festival that buttresses the emperor's power over his people and calls into question the very notion of popular liberty. Control of the Saturnalia gave the Flavian dynasty the ultimate form of cultural legitimacy.

Statius invokes Saturn on the Kalends, and in the preface refers to his poem as *Kalendae Decembres* (*praef.* 1. 31). But all our surviving calendars that preserve the month of December mark 17 December as the date for the Saturnalia.[45] In his discussion of the origins of the Saturnalia, Macrobius explains that the Saturnalia was often celebrated over three days from 14 to 17 December, since the former was the date given by the Numan calendar, the latter the date given by the Julian calendar after Caesar added two days to the month.[46] Domitian, it seems, appropriated the Saturnalia for his own political use, placing its celebration in the most prominent position of the month, the Kalends. The first day of the last month of the year could be seen then to open with Domitian, as the first day of the new year opened with the emperor involved in the inaugural ceremonies of office, often indeed in the role of consul.[47] This manipulation of the calendar was a skill Domitian had undoubtedly learned from Augustus, and it had the major ideological advantage of allowing the emperor to dominate the two major end points of time, as he dominates the two end points of Statius' first book of *Silvae*.[48]

---

[43] Myerhoff (1978) 235.   [44] Tac. *Ann.* 13. 15. 2–3.
[45] See Degrassi (1963) 25, 83, 106, 199, 261.   [46] Macrob. *Sat.* 1. 10. 2–18, 23.
[47] See for instance *Silv.* 4. 1, which celebrates Domitian's seventeenth consulship in AD 95. Suet. *Dom.* 13. 3 tells us that during his rule as emperor Domitian was consul in seven consecutive years, AD 82–8, and then again in AD 90, 92, and 95, though he never held the office for a long period of time.
[48] On Augustus' manipulation of the Roman calendar to honour himself and his family see Wallace-Hadrill (1987).

Silv. 1. 6 provides our only evidence that Domitian perhaps changed the date of the Saturnalia to his own advantage.[49] We do know however of another change that Domitian made to the Roman calendar, a change that was cancelled after his assassination. Clearly signalling that he conceived of himself as Augustus' successor, Domitian named the months of September and October after himself, as *Germanicus* and *Domitianus* respectively.[50] The emperor's control over time firmly suggested his divine authority over both the human world of socially constructed points of celebration and the natural world of change and alteration. Moreover, the appropriation of the Saturnalia put Domitian fully in charge of the subversive tendencies of the winter feast. *Silv.* 1. 6 rests upon the paradoxical notion that the emperor decides when and how the people's freedom is to be celebrated. The conjunction then within *Silv.* 1. 6 of Saturnalia and imperial show strikingly reveals the temporal and spatial constraints upon this traditional festival – the emperor decides both when and where it will be celebrated. This traditionally subversive festival is thus reshaped within the poem as an instrument of official authority. Moreover, in openly acclaiming their feast day as *Saturnalia principis* (82), the people themselves in Statius' poem acknowledge the licensed and circumscribed nature of their festival.

As Wilson points out in his discussion of Shakespeare's *Julius Caesar,* Foucault defines discourse as 'not simply that which translates struggles or systems of domination, but is the thing for which struggle takes place'.[51] *Silv.* 1. 6 explores the implications of Domitian's absolutism, his control of discourse, for the poet himself as well as for the people. As we shall see, Statius' presentation of imperial majesty in this poem goes beyond surface impressions of wonder and pleasure to reveal the mechanisms that control and fashion both the imperial image and the people. Thus the poem itself exists as a discursive site of both celebration of imperial authority and resistance to it.

Silv. 1. 6 is not a swan song to lost Republican liberty. It focusses on the present, not on the past. One of its major concerns is to redefine, through the emperor's Saturnalia, the new social and political order under Domitian and the poet's place within it. Absolutism was the prerequisite of the Pax Romana, but the Romans were always aware that absolutism could descend into despotism. Stability of the imperial

---

[49] Vollmer (1898) 303–4, 310, assumes that the emperor's feast was separate from the 'real' Saturnalia. But the changing of the date is consistent with Domitian's attempt to rival Augustus – in the calendar, perhaps, as well as in building.

[50] Suet. *Dom.* 13. 3.   [51] Wilson (1987) 31–44.

system depended in part on the emperor's benevolence to his people. As
Wirszubski observes moreover, 'freedom is of necessity precarious under
absolutism because an unlimited power can cause just as much harm as
good'.[52] In *Silv.* 1. 6 the amphitheatre on the Saturnalia thus becomes
the site where the tension between the emperor's roles as servant of the
people and as autocrat is displayed in his specific enactment of the part
of Jupiter. Thus, while the poem celebrates the bounty and majesty of
the emperor and his Empire, it simultaneously reveals anxiety about the
retaining of cultural autonomy, or some degree of control over discourse,
in the face of a hierarchical and authoritarian power. As we shall see,
Statius examines the emperor's control over the Saturnalia from two
points of view, that of the adoring audience and, at the poem's end, that
of the master-poet who resists absorption by the crowd and anxiously
seeks personal *libertas* through his own fashioning of the emperor's feast.

THE EMPEROR'S FEAST

Like *Silv.* 1. 5, *Silv.* 1. 6 begins with formulae of exclusion that seem
initially to assert the poet's authority over the stage-management of the
proceedings (1–8):

> Et Phoebus pater et severa Pallas
> et Musae procul ite feriatae:
> Iani vos revocabimus kalendis.
> Saturnus mihi compede exsoluta
> et multo gravidus mero December
> et ridens Iocus et Sales protervi
> adsint, dum refero diem beatum
> laeti Caesaris.

Father Phoebus and stern Pallas and Muses, go far away and take a holiday: we
will call you back on the first of January. Let Saturn released from his bonds be
here, and December torpid with a lot of wine, and laughing Jest and wanton
Wits, while I tell of the blissful day of Caesar in mood for play.

Phoebus, Minerva and the Muses are banished in the opening two lines,
as they were from *Silv.* 1. 4, and they are joined by Janus, who will preside
over the following month with Domitian.[53] Statius here invokes deities
more congenial to his festive poem – Saturn and December, the namer
of the festival along with his month – and the personifications, *Iocus* and
Sales, who characterise the jovial nature of a holiday whose dominant

---

[52] Wirszubski (1950) 170.   [53] See *Silv.* 4. 1.

feature Bakhtin describes as laughter.[54] The brisk hendecasyllables and
the plural *Sales* announce a different atmosphere from the refined wit
(*salino*, 131) of *Silv.* 1. 4 – and also subtly introduce the notion of food
that is so important at the games.[55] The Saturnalia was a carnivalesque
occasion when the social hierarchy was overturned; the freeing of Saturn
from his chains (4) was an emblem of temporary popular freedom.[56] Thus
Statius abandons the high style associated with Apollo, the Muses, and
the state deity Minerva, Domitian's particular patroness (1–2). Nonetheless, the opening lines make clear that this is an occasion of *licensed* revelry;
the day is Caesar's (8). Thus, an immediate tension is introduced into the
poem between Saturnalian and imperial expectations. To write a poem
on the Saturnalia that praises the emperor is virtually a contradiction in
terms.

The dominant feature of the Saturnalia, and of the Saturnalian poem,
was freedom of speech. In *Sat.* 2. 7 Horace's slave freely criticises his
master; in *Silv.* 4. 9 Statius speaks freely and abusively of the present
he has received from a friend on the Saturnalia. Statius in the opening
lines to *Silv.* 1. 6 promises freedom of speech, in particular jests and
irreverent, racy wit (6). Yet this poem is in fact marked by the absence
of speech on the part of the audience. Its reactions to the spectacle are
interpreted in visual and somatic, not verbal terms. Statius too presents
himself for the most part as simply one of the observing crowd. Indeed,
despite the poet's opening gesture of control over his subject in his exclusion of unwanted deities, his person remains in the background until
the poem's end. His viewing of the entertainment is not personalised by
individual expressions of delight or indeed, as in *Silv.* 1. 5, by stage directions. The emperor instead dominates the poem. His presence is everywhere directly felt, but his actual person is nowhere described. He is the
silent and invisible orchestrator of the show, the puppet-master pulling
his people's strings. The strategy of 'privileged visibility' operates here
largely through invisible presence. The notion of popular freedom with
which the poem opens is thus offset by the persistent awareness throughout the poem of the emperor's unseen control over this highly public
occasion. Although the emperor is referred to as *laetus* (8), there is no apparent personal relationship between him and the poet or indeed verbal

---

[54] Bakhtin (1968) 74–82.
[55] On the literary metaphor of 'salt' see for instance Gowers (1993) 261.
[56] Macrob. *Sat.* 1. 10 provides less provocative, physical reasons for the binding of Saturn's feet: it
  represents the ten-month binding of the child in the mother's womb; and it represents natural
  law and the fluctuating productivity of the earth.

interaction – the emperor is too remote. Hence in the amphitheatre, the description of the feast and the permitted inversions concentrate on material, not verbal pleasures.

Critics have drawn a sharp distinction between *Silv.* 1. 6 and *Silv.* 4. 2, the poem in which Statius is invited to dine with the emperor at his palace. In *Silv.* 4. 2, so the argument goes, Domitian appears in the poem as a remote, lofty figure in the intimidating Palatine, whereas in the earlier poem Domitian, true to the Saturnalian occasion, at least mingles with the people.[57] On the contrary, Domitian is consistently represented in *Silv.* 1. 6 as a divine being of superhuman capabilities. Moreover, in *Silv.* 1. 6 the poet does not meet the emperor face to face as he does in *Silv.* 4. 2; his presence is implied rather than visible. Thus although in *Silv.* 1. 6 Statius removes the emperor from the pedestal of the equestrian statue and brings him into the public arena, the emperor continues to dominate his city as a remote, divine being.

Domitian, it is true, does we are told join in the banquet held in the amphitheatre (43–50):

> una vescitur omnis ordo mensa,
> parvi, femina, plebs, eques, senatus:
> libertas reverentiam remisit.
> et tu quin etiam (quis hoc vocari,
> quis promittere possit hoc deorum?)
> nobiscum socias dapes inisti.
> iam se, quisquis is est, inops beatus,
> convivam ducis esse gloriatur.

Every social rank dines at the same table, children, women, common folk, knights and senators. Freedom has relaxed respect for social rank. And you too (which of the gods could be summoned to this feast, which of them could promise this?) you entered upon our companionable feast with us. Now someone, whether he be rich or poor, is boasting that he was the guest of his leader.

Yet the emperor joins in the banquet as a god, not as one of the people. Indeed, the very mention of 'guest' (50) belies the notion of true conviviality and commensality here. Statius' language is reverent, almost incredulous that such a favour could be granted. The emperor's gracious bestowing of his presence upon the banquet outdoes the actions of the gods – it is a blessing none of the gods could promise (45–7). His

---

[57] Thus Goddard (1994) 69–70. Goddard argues that 'by graciously deigning to be present and to eat and drink alongside his subjects, Domitian displayed his *comitas*, his affability, the positive virtue of condescending to associate so closely with the mass of his people' (70). See also Damon (1992).

presence then does not create communal values, as at the symposium, but rather reinforces hierarchical divisions.

From the start of the festivities in the amphitheatre, Domitian plays the role of Jupiter. Statius' account of the day's events, for instance, opens with the people literally being showered with sweetmeats scattered from a rope extended high above the amphitheatre (9–27), as the emperor imitates Jupiter in his role of weather god by sending gifts from the sky. Geographical names stress the emperor's ability to draw on the resources of empire: nuts from the Black Sea region (12), dates from Palestine (13), plums from Damascus (14), figs from Asia Minor (15), fall down along with local fruits such as apples and pears and the old-fashioned rural must-cake (18–19).[58] These are described as *rapinis* (16), rapine, offering a view of Empire as a free plundering of its material resources in which the people symbolically share. The gifts illustrate the emperor's power to transcend the limits of space and time by magically bringing the world's bounty into the confines of the amphitheatre in December. Indeed, some of the fruits are out of season, for the apples are not quite ripe (*non perustis*, 18).

The descent of these gifts among the people is compared in mock-epic language to a mighty, devastating storm that explicitly associates Domitian with Jupiter in his control over nature (21–7):

> non tantis Hyas inserena nimbis
> terras obruit aut soluta Plias,
> qualis per cuneos hiems Latinos
> plebem grandine contudit serena.
> ducat nubila Iuppiter per orbem
> et latis pluvias minetur agris
> dum nostri Iovis hi ferantur imbres.

The tempestuous Hyades or the rain-bearing Pleiades do not overwhelm the earth with such rainclouds as the storm that battered with peaceful hail the spectators seated in the Roman amphitheatre. For all we care, Jupiter can shroud the world in clouds and threaten the broad fields with winter storms, provided rains like these are brought by our Jupiter.

The shower of fruits and cakes is so lavish and so intense that the people are battered (*contudit*, 24) by them – all the more so, since some of the fruit – apples or pears – is unripe (*non perustis*, 18) and therefore presumably hard![59] The paradoxical nature of this expression of divinely

---

[58] See Vollmer (1898) 305–7 for an explanation of the different foods and their varied provenance.

[59] Vollmer (1898) 306 on *Silv.* 1. 6. 18 notes that these Etruscan apples or pears are slow to ripen and must remain on the branch up to winter time.

exercised power is summed up perhaps in the phrase *grandine serena* (24), 'peaceful hail'. The emperor's generosity to his people is here humorously displayed, yet it is not without a hint of menace. The display of imperial beneficence with which the day begins provides a forceful reminder to the people of who is in control.

As Gowers notes, descriptions of food tend to steal language from other spheres of action remote from the feast such as war, for instance; in so doing, the literary representation of food provides an alternative perspective from which to scrutinise the larger world.[60] In *Silv.* 1. 6 the intensity of the storm of fruits and cakes hints through metaphor at the violence implicit in such excessive demonstrations of power. Indeed, as Sauter has argued, the association of Jupiter with the weather gives this god a double existence: 'einerseits drohend (Blitz und Donner), anderseits sanft, heiter (caelum serenum)'.[61] This duality, translated into anthropomorphic terms, represents the emperor as a figure to be both feared and admired.[62] As Millar observes, the imperial system rested on the 'arbitrary exercise of power and favour on the one side, and that ever-present fear and uncertainty on the other'.[63] In the amphitheatre, Domitian's power is comically and generously deployed in crowd-pleasing ways that nonetheless remind his people that, like Jupiter, he can also on other occasions wield the thunderbolt.[64] Thus Statius' text hints at the emperor's capacity to inflict harm as well as good on the days when he is not *laetus*. There is, then, a 'bitter strand' within such delights.

Although the poem pushes the implications of the divine analogy to a point that disturbs the faultlines underlying the discourse of imperial majesty and praise, Statius demonstrates the people's willing complicity in this particular imperial fiction, and he presents himself, for the most part, as one of the crowd. Using the communal first person pronoun to identify his views with that of the audience, Statius calls Domitian *nostri Iovis* (27), 'our Jupiter'. Here, Domitian's two roles of benefactor and god are combined. Playing Jupiter in the amphitheatre involves the emperor in a delicate balancing act between pandering to the crowd and also keeping them at a distance through marvellous effects that suggest the emperor's superhuman authority over nature itself; his lavish and even miraculous style of giving ultimately identifies him as divine. Here then

---

[60] Gowers (1993) 37–8.　　[61] Sauter (1934) 63.

[62] There were other aspects of Jupiter more closely tied to statecraft and the wise guidance and protection of one's people. See Dio Chrys. *Or.* 1. 37–47. On the specific identification of Domitian with the weather-god see Sauter (1934) 62–4; also 54–78 for an overall discussion of the identification of Domitian with Jupiter.

[63] Millar (1977) 10.　　[64] Cf. *Silv.* 3. 3. 158.

we have a demonstration of the mutuality involved in the fashioning of the emperor's divine image. For the Jovian ideology developed by Domitian is confirmed by the popular interpretation of the shower of fruit and nuts as the gifts of 'our Jupiter'.

True to the occasion of the Saturnalia then, this 'Jupiter' is also represented as a god who shares his boundless pleasures in sex as well as in food. And like the food, the sexual pleasures too come from heaven, since Domitian returns his 'Ganymedes' to earth for the people. For if Domitian is the equivalent of Jupiter, then he must also of course have a Ganymede and distribute on this special day comparable pleasures to his people.[65] The Jovian ideology of Domitian, then, is pursued in the description of handsome serving boys as so many Ganymedes (*Idaeos totidem . . . ministros*, 34), a striking plural that introduces new social values to Rome, a city where manly virtues were traditionally praised and effeminacy and homosexuality were derided.[66] The presence of these serving boys, however, suggests, as in *Silv.* 3. 4, the emperor's divinely sanctioned disregard for social and moral convention; yet here that disregard penetrates the heart of Roman society itself, challenging traditional Roman values with implications, moreover, for the people's liberties. No bluff, blunt Davus here interrogates the master, as in Horace's *Sat.* 2. 7. The presence of 'Ganymedes' suggests the high premium put on appearance and pleasure in Domitian's Rome rather than on discomforting speech. Later, prostitutes appear in the amphitheatre, 'girls easily bought' (*faciles emi puellae*, 67). Jupiter's traditionally voracious sexuality is here displayed in the comic inversion of the emperor's pimping for his people. But if Domitian loses some dignity by playing, in part, a jovial Jupiter, it is only for one day. Yet again, moreover, we see only the emperor's gifts, not the emperor himself. He himself acts always at a distance. The concept of 'privileged visibility' conceals the emperor's person behind the physical evidence of his munificence.

The somatic pleasures of food, drink, and sex, therefore, bind the people to the emperor. As Statius tells us in the preface to Book 1, Domitian's shows provide a vicarious new sexuality, for they thrill the people with a night of untried delights, *noctem enim | illam felicissimam et voluptatibus publicis inexpertam* ('that happiest night of experiment with public pleasures', *praef.* 1. 31–2). A rapid succession of 'new luxuries' (*novos luxus*, 51) that follow the banquet again flouts social and moral convention: women fight women (53–6), dwarves fight dwarves (57–64), and exotic

---

[65] On Earinus, the emperor's 'Ganymede', see *Silv.* 3. 4 and chapter 3 above, 105–17.
[66] Edwards (1993) 63–97.

entertainers from the margins of Empire dance and play loud music (70–4).[67] The fighting dwarves and women may well have been criminals, enacting their punishment for the Roman people.[68] As Stallybrass and White observe, 'carnival often violently abuses and demonizes *weaker*, not stronger social groups – women, ethnic and religious minorities, those who "don't belong" – in a process of *displaced abjection*'.[69] The Roman people's pleasure in the somatic abnormalities of fighting women and foreshortened men is an instance of 'licensed complicity' with the emperor. Essentially the people have substituted observation for participation, subjecting the exotic to their superior gaze.[70] The mixing of ranks at the banquet (43–5) only temporarily occludes the real hierarchical structuring of the amphitheatre, where the marginalisation of weaker social groups acts as a covert form of social control, uniting the Roman people with their leader in a reaffirmation of the dominant ideology of Empire. Dwarves, fighting women, criminals – these represent the aberrant elements of society and are chaotic forces whose subjugation metaphorically upholds Roman supremacy. Authorised by Saturnalian licence then, Domitian can transgress social as well as physical limits and categories outside the more private spaces of his court and impress the people at large with the sensuousness and novelty of his entertainment.

The amphitheatre itself provides a paradigm of Empire – all classes, many races, packed into the enclosed circular space of a magnificent monument to popular entertainment and mass consumption. The superiority of the Romans to the conquered races is visually confirmed by the ranks of seats, enabling the spectators to observe the fruits of empire from on high and to act as rightful consumers. The exotic provenance of many of the performers puts Empire on display, assuring the spectators of their right to enjoy and exploit its novel offerings. The performers come from the far reaches of the Roman world – girls from Lydia, musicians from southern Spain, jugglers from Syria (70–2) – and the servants are Middle Eastern in appearance (34). Birds too come from all over the world. Imitating the lavish shower of sweetmeats, they suddenly swoop down upon the crowd, flamingos from Egypt, pheasants from Phasis, and guinea-fowl from North Africa (75–8).[71] The spectators seize the

---

[67] On women as gladiators see Wiedemann (1992) 26–7.

[68] On the theatrical enactment of criminal punishment see Coleman (1990).

[69] Stallybrass and White (1986) 19.

[70] On the superior, respectable gaze at the fair, see Stallybrass and White (1986) 42–3. The gaze of the Roman people at Domitian's shows can hardly be characterised as respectable, however.

[71] There is some doubt as to the precise identity of these exotic birds. See Vollmer (1898) 309 on *Silv.* 1. 6. 75.

birds as another form of novelty, and there are too many for people to take them all (79–80):

> desunt qui rapiant, sinusque pleni
> gaudent dum nova lucra comparantur.

There are not enough people to seize them, and they rejoice, laps full, while their new booty is collected.

These birds reappear in *Silv.* 4. 6 (8–9) as the type of exotic food that does *not* appear on the table of the refined Vindex, for it was associated with overabundance and, by metaphorical extension, with lack of refinement in the arts. Vindex and his guests refuse the food of Empire, a gesture of definitive separation from the public world. *Silv.* 1. 6, however, takes place in a highly public, not a private space. The seizing of the birds in the amphitheatre visibly articulates an idea of Empire based upon limitless consumption. The world is the people's for the taking – especially if the emperor arranges it. Competition is purely material, not social or political, as people struggle to seize the prizes that chance, not labour, provides them. Because the emperor makes available for his people the fruits of Empire, Domitian and his people are bound together in licensed complicity. The emperor's Saturnalia lavishly provides the material pleasures associated with the popular festival, compensating for loss of individual liberties through overabundance.

The free food, the birds that fall with ease into the people's laps, constitute a comic version of the Golden Age. Indeed, Statius claims that the lavish bounty of Empire that Domitian provides for his people is superior to that of the first Golden Age under Saturn (39–42):

> i nunc saecula compara, Vetustas,
> antiqui Iovis aureumque tempus:
> non sic libera vina tunc fluebant
> nec tardum seges occupabat annum.

Come now Antiquity, compare the ages of ancient Jupiter and the time of Gold. Wines did not flow so freely then, nor did the harvest continue late into the year.

Saturn ('the ancient Jupiter') brought the arts of agriculture to Italy.[72] The depiction of Domitian as the new Jupiter asserts his superiority over the ancient Italian god in purely material, not moral terms. Domitian's Golden Age embraces the foreign and the exotic; it involves not so much the control of nature as its alteration, for Domitian can change its laws by

---

[72] Macrob. *Sat.* 1. 7. 18–21.

extending the time of harvest into winter (42). Saturn, we are told, is now
allowed to appear unbound only on the day appointed by Domitian for
his feast (4). Far from being a figure of unlimited freedom, the Saturn of
Silv. 1. 6, it turns out, has been resignified as an emblem of state-sponsored
licence. Indeed, the figure of Saturn points to another, less complimentary aspect of Jupiter: his association with dynastic strife. Thus the
literary topos of the Golden Age of Saturn removes the poem from
the restricted perspective of the pandered audience and opens it up to
some of the faultlines underlying imperial ideology. Playing Jupiter in the
amphitheatre involves the emperor in the slippery terrain of divine comparison with a god; a god, moreover, of particularly ambiguous power.[73]

The start of night as well as day is marked by special effects that
suggest the emperor's superhuman and even terrifying authority over
nature itself. Suetonius tells us that Domitian introduced the novelty of
staging gladiatorial shows at night by the special illumination of torches.[74]
Statius describes the wonders of artificial light not in practical terms but
in a striking image that attempts to recapture the marvellous visual effect
of this spectacle upon the observers (85–90):

> vixdum caerula nox subibat orbem,
> descendit media nitens harena
> densas flammeus orbis inter umbras
> vincens Cnosiacae facem coronae.
> conlucet polus ignibus nihilque
> obscurae patitur licere nocti.

Dark-blue night was hardly beginning to cover the world when there descends
amidst the thick shadows in the middle of the arena a flaming orb, outdoing the
brilliant stars of the Cretan Crown. The whole sky gleams with fires and allows
dark night no entry.

Statius describes the sudden arrival of artificial light from the point of
view of a spectator for whom, in the clamour and confusion of the ever-
changing shows, a burning orb of light miraculously descends out of the
darkness, burning more brightly than a constellation. The amphitheatre, presented at the poem's start as a microcosm of the earth ruled by
Jupiter, is yet again subject to divine, mysterious power as a constellation is apparently brought to earth in a striking inversion of the natural
hierarchy.[75] The poem and the entertainment climax at this point with

---

[73] Feeney (1993) 220.   [74] Suet. *Dom.* 4. 1. See also Wiedemann (1992) 14.
[75] For the myth of Ariadne's Crown, see Ov. *Fast.* 3. 359–516; *Met.* 8. 174–82; Bömer (1958) 174–75
on *Fast* 3. 459–516.

an incontrovertible demonstration of imperial power. The emperor, it seems, can transgress the laws of nature itself. Saturnalian inversion has become a function of the emperor's authority.

Like the grand 'rainstorm' of sweetmeats with which the shows and *Silv.* 1. 6 begin, the descent of the 'flaming orb' into the arena seems to me a strategy fully implicated in the theatrical production of 'salutary anxiety'. The sudden descent to earth of a flaming orb that to the poet's eyes resembles a constellation is an event productive of both fear and wonder.[76] This final demonstration of the emperor's power dramatises an important strategy through which he controls his people. In Statius' representation, the theatre of imperial majesty depends not simply on the emperor's physical presence but on dramatic, symbolic acts. The hyperbolic comparison of the wonderful light to the constellation of Ariadne's Crown is of course, on the one hand, a clever compliment to Domitian's technological mastery of nature, for the constellation was the gift of Bacchus to his wife, and Bacchus is a god fully implicated in the emperor's Saturnalia. At the same time, the myth suggests the emperor's aspirations to transcend human and even natural law. Thus in *Silv.* 1. 6 the emperor's deeds are presented as inseparable from the notion of force. That force is contained on the particular day on which the emperor is *laetus* (8), but its full potential is expressed here through the dramatic symbolism of the constellation. As Greenblatt remarks, a ruler's authority depends on both fear and beneficence: 'if there were only fear, the prince, it was said, would be deemed a tyrant; if there were only mercy, it was said that the people would altogether cease to be obedient'.[77] The flaming heavenly orb serves in the poem as a striking icon of the essential ambiguity of imperial power.

Up until this point in the poem, Statius has presented himself through the use of the first person plural pronoun *nos* as one of the crowd, a typical spectator.[78] His emotional responses are not separated from those of the people. It is their common responses and perceptions that he presents. Whether he towers over Rome in the symbolic form of an equestrian statue or orchestrates the people's games, in the *Silvae* the emperor is constructed as a remote figure whose control of his people seems paramount. The climax of Calpurnius Siculus' *Eclogue* 7 is the rustic Corydon's vision

---

[76] Luc. 1. 75–6 describes the descent of stars to earth as part of the Stoic cataclysm. Sen. *Q Nat.* 7. 20. 2 says that everyone is amazed (*stupent*) at the phenomenon of sudden fire streaking down from the heavens, and, despite the simple physical cause, regards it as a miracle.

[77] Greenblatt (1988), 137. Cf. Millar (1977) n. 63 above.

[78] Domitian is *nostri Iovis* ('our Jove', 27); he joins *nobiscum* ('with us') in the feast (48).

of the emperor Nero, viewed from a respectful distance (79–84). The climax of *Silv.* 1. 6 is formed not by the emperor himself but by a supernatural symbol of his power. The poem suggests that the precise workings of imperial authority are invisible to the people; only its marvellous and terrifying effects are to be seen. As a god, Domitian is an absent presence.

Calpurnius' seventh *Eclogue* presents Corydon's experience at the games in terms of a dialogue with his country friend Lycotas; there is an interior dialogue too when an elderly spectator is introduced (39) to explain the new sights of the amphitheatre. But the crowd in *Silv.* 1. 6 is virtually silent. Indeed, on this day traditionally associated with freedom of speech, the people are represented as speaking out only once, not in rebellion, but in acclamation of Domitian as their 'master', *dominus*. When they do speak, they metaphorically translate the overabundance of the day into their overly enthusiastic speech (81–4):

> tollunt innumeras ad astra voces
> Saturnalia principis sonantes
> et dulci dominum favore clamant:
> hoc solum vetuit licere Caesar.

They raise countless voices to the stars, echoing the emperor's Saturnalia, and they acclaim him 'master' with affectionate enthusiasm: this title alone Caesar refused to allow.

The title *dominus* when applied to the emperor was certainly controversial. Suetonius tells us that Domitian liked being acclaimed *dominus* on his feast days, and he sees Domitian's supposed introduction of the title *dominus et deus* as a sign of arrogance.[79] Yet Statius' poem tells us that the emperor forbade the people to use this title, but that their enthusiasm overcame his strictures. Does Statius here hint at a feigned modesty on the part of the emperor? The incident, I suggest, is provocative rather than subversive and tells us more about the status of Domitian's subjects than about Domitian himself. Statius represents the popular acclamation as voluntary, a sign of the people's affectionate enthusiasm (*dulci favore*, 83).[80] This phrase suggests that the term *dominus* can be interpreted in the light of the exchange between ruler and ruled that is enacted in the

---

[79] Suet. *Dom.* 13. 1–2. See Jones (1992), 108–9, who discusses the evidence and dismisses the idea that Domitian favoured the title *dominus et deus*.

[80] Hopkins (1983) 15, n. 23, has acknowledged that we do not know enough about the history of imperial 'acclamation' to determine normal practice. Many of the incidents reported concern 'acclamation' that was on command. The 'acclamation' of *Silv.* 1. 6, however, is represented as spontaneous and indeed against the emperor's orders.

amphitheatre, indicating the people's power to endow their favour on the emperor in grateful exchange for his benefactions.[81]

Yet the people's acclamation also reveals the paradox implicit in the occasion, the Saturnalia, festival of popular freedom. For the voluntary acclamation of *dominus* strikingly demonstrates the people's willing acceptance of the emperor's control over their festival and his success in bringing about communal support. Significantly they raise their voices to the stars, for that after all is where the divine authority of their 'Jupiter' seems to be located. The people's use of the term *dominus* on the Saturnalia, the one occasion of the year when such a title should surely have been avoided, dramatises the startling resignification of a festival of popular liberty that has been commandeered by the emperor with the complicity of his people. It is they, after all, who shout out that the Saturnalia is the emperor's.

At the same time as it celebrates and explores imperial majesty and theatrical display, *Silv.* 1. 6 plays upon the paradoxical nature of Roman *libertas* under Domitian. The somatic and material pleasures specific to carnival – the hectic bombardment of novelties, the abundance of food and drink, the availability of sex and the feasting of the eyes – here are shown as binding the Roman people closely in approbation and complicity to their emperor. In the amphitheatre he is seen as catering to 'safe' desires whose fulfilment does not challenge his supremacy. Indeed, far from challenging the emperor, the people use speech to endorse him enthusiastically. The concept of *libertas* thus appears as weakened and no longer functions as a powerful political ideal; indeed, the word appears in *Silv.* 1. 6 only to express the relaxed social relations among the different ranks at the feast (45). And even this social differentiation is spatially and temporally contained – by the elliptical walls of the amphitheatre, and by the imperial appropriation of the calendar. The celebration of the shows in *Silv.* 1. 6 is underpinned by a redefinition of *libertas* as a concept that is controlled by Domitian, who decides on what day the people can be 'free' and happy and what form that freedom should take. A cultural practice based upon freedom is shown in *Silv.* 1. 6 to have been resignified as willing compliance with the persuasive fictions of power.

Yet, as I have suggested, the development of the comparison between the emperor and Jupiter in this poem quietly raises the unsettling question of what happens when the emperor exercises such enormous power

---

[81] Thus *favor OLD* 1c: 'goodwill, favour ... shown in recognition of merit'.

on the days when he is *not* 'happy', *laeti* (8)? Indeed, the poem's strong
emphasis on the emperor's divine authority and control may in fact be
related to an underlying uncertainty about the stability of his rule. Let us
look briefly at the poem's closing lines which, in typical Statian fashion,
express the wish for limitless repetition of the day's events, *quos ibit procul
hic dies per annos!* ('this day will continue through many years!' 98), and
give the assurance that the day will never be forgotten as long as Rome's
hills, father Tiber, Rome and the Capitol endure (99–102). *Silv.* 1. 6 is
the last poem in the first book of the *Silvae*. Thus the acknowledgment of
Horace's famous closural reference to the Capitol in *Odes* 3. 30 (8–9) is
not unexpected. What is new, however, is the description of the Capitol
in the last line of *Silv.* 1. 6 as 'the Capitol which you restore' (*quod reddis
Capitolium*, 102), a reminder that twice within the Flavian years the temple
of Jupiter Capitolinus had been destroyed, first in AD 69 during the civil
war and then by fire in AD 80; civil war also caused its first destruction
in 83 BCE. In a key passage of Tacitus' *Histories*, the Capitol tracks the
development of Rome.[82] Tacitus interprets the temple's destruction by
fire in the civil war of AD 68–9 as a heinous crime intimately connected to
the evil of civic dissolution; a monument which had stood while Romans
fought on behalf of their country was burned by 'the madness of princes'
(*furore principum*).[83] In a specifically Flavian context, the temple of Jupiter
Optimus Capitolinus was an emblem of temporality and change, a constant reminder of the conflict through which the Flavians had come to
power. Since Domitian has been portrayed as Jupiter in this poem, he too
is intimately associated with the Temple of Capitoline Jupiter. Although
he brings renewal, the temple itself is set within a cycle of change. The
poem therefore ends with a subtle reminder of the human and physical
forces that can threaten the stability of a regime and its ruler.

Significantly then, while the shows seem designed to assert the stability
of the regime, they offer the people the spectacle of rapid change. The
amphitheatre is a restless place that creates anxiety mixed with pleasure.
Here, where sights and sounds constantly change, the Ovidian world of
change and flux is represented in microcosm (51–2):

> hos inter fremitus novosque luxus
> spectandi levis effugit voluptas

amidst the roar and novel luxuries the swift pleasure of viewing flies past.

---

[82] Tac. *Hist.* 3. 72. See Wiseman (1978) especially 171–2. On Domitian's restoration of the Capitol
see Suet. *Dom.* 5. 1.
[83] Tac. *Hist.* 3. 72. 1.

Unlike the stable, quiet world of the villa landscape, the amphitheatre offers fleeting impressions and lots of noise. The final dramatic expression of the emperor's metamorphic power is the huge and brilliant globe of fire that descends at night to illuminate the amphitheatre and that is described as resembling the constellation of Ariadne's Crown (85–8), that stellar symbol of metamorphosis. The metamorphic world of the amphitheatre with its fleeting pleasures and sounds produces a disjunction between the fluidity of pleasure and the purported stability of imperial rule associated with Golden Age bounty.

Studies of monarchical ceremonial have noted that theatrical display of a regime's prosperity tends to be particularly elaborate and ostentatious at times of crisis. Kuhrt, for instance, has noted that the Babylonian New Year Festival, which encapsulated notions of traditional order and prosperity, became prominent in a period 'of extreme and lengthy instability in the kingship'.[84] MacCormack points out that the great ceremonies of Late Antiquity generally occurred at times of political upheaval; the ceremonies then provided an urgent attempt to explain change and to reassert stability.[85] Thus Cannadine notes that 'the need for tradition and for order, as met by ceremonials such as these, actually increased as the stability of the state became ever more uncertain'.[86] Unfortunately we do not know in which year Domitian's Saturnalian games were performed. But the *Silvae* as a whole were composed in the late, difficult period of Domitian's reign, a time of increasing dynastic instability. Moreover, the Secular Games, the biggest festive event of Domitian's reign, were associated with a period of crisis. They were celebrated in AD 88, five years before their appointed time. Augustus had celebrated his Secular Games in 17 BCE. The games were supposed to be held every 110 years. By strict calculation, then, Domitian's Secular Games should have been held in AD 93, but Domitian recalculated the date, perhaps because this was a period of severe setbacks for him.[87] He had recently lost two commanders in the Dacian war, and unrest had been fomented by the appearance of a 'false Nero'; probably too there were warnings of the rebellion headed by Saturninus that broke out at the very beginning of AD 89.[88] In a time of military and political instability the Secular Games may well have fulfilled an urgent need for a great showcase ceremonial to validate and buttress Domitian's right to rule not just as a Flavian but

---

[84] Kuhrt (1987) 40.　　[85] MacCormack (1981) 12–13.　　[86] Cannadine (1987) 8.
[87] Jones (1992) 102–3 argues that Domitian calculated the date from Augustus' intended date of 22 or 23 BCE for the games.
[88] See Jones (1992) 141–9.

as the true successor of Augustus. It is tempting to speculate then that the extravagant entertainment described by Statius was part of a massive effort to control time and people's liberties in a regime and dynasty struggling to survive. For time was not in fact on Domitian's side.

The principle of change embodied in the shows is related to the concept of imperial power that is expressed in this poem. As Jupiter, Domitian is capable of change from beneficent to punitive ruler. Domitian's majestic presence at the games is shown to rest upon a powerful union of extraordinary control and the unpredictable exercise of authority. The prospect of rapid change, along with the duality of the emperor himself, provides a paradigm of the workings of imperial power consistent with its representation elsewhere in the *Silvae*: those who serve the emperor, whether by managing his city or treasury or by applauding his games, earn great rewards but remain subject to the unpredictability of a power that constitutes itself as divine and thus outside human or natural law.

Stallybrass and White have argued that carnival is 'ideologically powerful in the study of ideological repertoires and cultural practices'.[89] In the swift-moving hendecasyllables of *Silv.* 1. 6, a metre associated with social and political irreverence, Statius explores from within the public arena the hegemonic practices that attempted to confirm the social and political order under Domitian. Indeed, the particular occasion of the Saturnalia permits attention to be drawn to a sore point in imperial ideology, the myth that Jupiter came to power by violent and irreverent means through the brutal deposition of his father Saturn. Jupiter embodies a violent force that exists beyond human law. Feeney has suggested that in the *Silvae* Statius attempts to allay the anxiety that the association between Jupiter and Domitian arouses in the *Thebaid*.[90] Yet the paradoxical nature of Domitian's Saturnalia, combined with the troubling associations of the Jovian paradigm, unsettle the discourse of praise, revealing the paradoxes on which such imperial fictions could be based.

THE POET'S SATURNALIA

Although he includes himself among the admiring crowd at the amphitheatre, Statius expands the poem beyond a popular perspective through his manipulation of literary topoi that appeal to the competence of an élite audience. He matches the novelty of the emperor's shows with the novelty of his own verse and wittily accomplishes his own

[89] Stallybrass and White (1986) 26.   [90] Feeney (1993) 359, n. 151.

literary inversions. Although his poem follows the chronological order of the festival, beginning at dawn and ending at night, his swift-moving hendecasyllables playfully combine with epic language to create a novel and humorous tension between metrical form and style.[91] Thus, for instance, he describes popular entertainment in the élite terms of epic and myth. The day opens in epic manner with the stately introduction of Aurora – *vix aurora movebat ortus* ('scarcely was dawn beginning its risings', 9) – followed by the storm which involves obvious play with epic imagery.[92] Epic matter is played with in the carnivalesque inversions of the spectacle. Thus the grotesque character of the fighting between the women is magnified by the epic simile comparing them to Amazons (55–6); the fight of the dwarves plays with scale in its epic personification of *Cruenta Virtus* ('Bloody Courage') who, along with Mars, laughs at the flying of tiny fists (62); and this fight is followed by a Homeric allusion to the hostility between pygmies and cranes.[93]

The presence of *Virtus* as the inciter of dwarves and women in Statius' textualised amphitheatre provides a comic inversion of her traditional meaning as the manly virtue of courage. But Statius is also appealing here to a critically trained readership, people like Stella to whom Book 1 is dedicated and who know his *Thebaid*. The fights, comically reminiscent of the larger epic world, specifically replay the dualism of the *Thebaid* as entertainment. The presence of the personification of *Cruenta Virtus* ('Bloody Courage') undoubtedly refers to the gladiatorial nature of the grotesque combats and, presumably, to the killing that results. Yet this personification, along with Mars, keeps unusual company amongst the human performers. Indeed, she is a personification drawn from Statius' *Thebaid*. Feeney aptly describes her as highly indecorous whenever she appears in the epic.[94] She is part of Bacchus' drunken, staggering train in Book 4. 661–3, and later in Book 10. 639–49 she appears as a figure that is comically and ineptly transformed into a failed advertisement for peace. She thus invites a re-evaluation of the conventional Roman conception of *Virtus* as glorious courage in battle.[95]

In the *Thebaid Virtus* is also closely akin with Death. Her epithet *cruenta* in the *Silvae* harks back to that association. There is a certain overlap then between the *Virtus* of the *Thebaid* and the *Silvae*. Although

---

[91] Damon (1992) 304 has argued that the use of hendecasyllables for poems of imperial praise does not necessarily imply irreverence. This metre however does draw attention to the independence, if not irreverence, of the poet.

[92] The *Thebaid* of course, like the *Aeneid*, opens with a storm (*Theb.* 1. 336–89; *Aen.* 1. 34–156).

[93] Hom. *Il.* 3. 3–7.   [94] On *Virtus* in the *Thebaid* see Feeney (1993) 382–5.

[95] Feeney (1993) 383.

Virtus participates in a comic version of the epic's deadly duels, there is an uneasy disjunction between her laughter (*ridet*, 62) and her epithet *cruenta*, a term that makes her here, as in the *Thebaid*, a problematic figure, incompletely resignified as jovial. Her presence, along with that of Mars, provides a reminder of the possibility of uncontrolled violence that the games artfully occlude and contain. Although such literary inversion then reflects in part the jovial nature of the Saturnalia, it also allows the poet a degree of freedom in his representation of a day of *libertas* that seems so firmly in the emperor's control. Thebes, despite its comic dress here, provides an alternative story of a different social order, one based on conflict and dynastic instability. That story provides a salutary reminder that violence cannot always be contained, that there is a 'bitter strand' in every carnivalesque feast.

The presence of *Virtus* here points to Statius' management of spectacle in his own familiar epic terms. Thus on the literary level élite categories are challenged and overturned, as the themes of epic – storms, war, courage – are re-evaluated on the Saturnalia through the material, the marginal, and the grotesque. In form and style then, the poet in a sense appropriates the emperor's entertainment and rewrites his own Theban subject as comic and incisive entertainment.

But so overwhelming are the emperor's benefactions that, after the description of the pyrotechnics, the poem ends in an extraordinary way with a delayed *recusatio*. The poet becomes so sleepy with wine, he tells us, that he breaks off the poem abruptly at the nocturnal climax of the shows (93–7):

> quis spectacula, quis iocos licentes,
> quis convivia, quis dapes inemptas,
> largi flumina quis canat Lyaei?
> iamiam deficio tuaque Baccho
> *   *   *   *   *
> in serum trahor ebrius soporem.

Who could sing of the spectacles and the licentious jokes, who of the banquets and the free feasting, who of the rivers of abundant Lyaeus? But now I am faltering in song and with Bacchus ... drunken I am dragged to a late sleep.

The poet has said very little about himself in this poem. He has acted as an observer of the proceedings, not as a participant, and he has expressed the feelings of the spectators as a group rather than as an individual. But now at the poem's end he draws attention to himself and to his own state of mind. As in *Silv.* 1. 4, but at the conclusion here, the poet refers to his insufficiency to write a poem of imperial praise: *deficio*.[96] The solution here is not, as in *Silv.* 1. 4, to summon his imperial addressee, Rutilius Gallicus, as Muse but rather to end the poem.[97]

Here, instead of forging social bonds as in *Silv.* 1. 5, the emperor's wine ultimately alienates the poet from the spectacle and the crowd of which he has been part. For his response to the emperor's performance is to absent himself from it. Wine here does not inspire but leads to sleep and silence. As Henderson suggests of the beginning and the ending of the *Thebaid*, the 'humility' of a poem's apologies constitutes 'a rhetoric of deflection and meiosis, the characteristic décor of urbane discourse under the empire'.[98] Statius' failure to continue the poem through to the end of the festivities is a gesture that on the one hand acknowledges ultimately the inexpressibility of the emperor's munificence, but, on the other hand, allows the poet, under the guise of alcohol-induced drowsiness, to elude the emperor's control over the Saturnalia. Paradoxically, he recovers his own voice through silence. As Pagán comments of Tacitus' deployment of silence in the *Annales*, 'silence can be as powerful an expression of disaffection as speech'.[99]

The closing motif of drunkenness, moreover, suggests satiety as well as insufficiency. Eating and drinking, as Gowers has argued, provide aesthetic figures for literary composition and consumption.[100] Before the emperor's show is over, the poet draws the line and ends the show for us, his readers. He decides what and when is enough. Thus Statius reasserts control, if in a limited way, over the representation of performance. The poet's premature departure from the proceedings forms, then, a silent acknowledgment of the poet's own *libertas* on the emperor's day, his freedom both to leave and to end the poem as he himself wishes. Unlike the emperor too, whose shows are continuing with increasing lavishness into the night, Statius as a poet sets a limit to his extravagance in verse. He thus at the end tacitly marks his separation from the imperial culture of seemingly limitless consumption. Even as he acknowledges his failure to describe fully the wonders and delights of the emperor's feast, he asserts his right to carve out his own poetic space.

---

[96] Cf. *Silv.* 1. 4. 19–23.   [97] *Silv.* 1. 4. 19–37.   [98] Henderson (1993) 164.

[99] Pagán (2000) 364. Pagán shows that in the *Annales* only those about to die speak freely. Similarly, in Statius' *Thebaid*, the most open attacks on the tyrant Eteocles come in Book 3 from Maeon, just before he commits suicide (*Theb.* 3. 59–91) and from the elderly Aletes who, we are told, had nothing to lose as he was at the end of his life (*Theb.* 3. 176–217). Death alone liberates speech. On this motif in imperial epic see McGuire (1997) 200–5.

[100] Gowers (1993) 40–6.

As Wilson observes, carnival functioned in the Renaissance as 'a symbolic system over which continuous struggle to wrest its meaning was waged by competing ideologies'.[101] *Silv.* 1. 6 demonstrates the triumph of imperial ideology over the ideology of popular *libertas*. Yet the amphitheatre was not entirely under the control of the dominant ideology. Statius' representation of imperial spectacle reminds us that he is the master-poet of imperial epic – and also too of a new, refined and splendid aesthetic that resists absorption by the crowd. Greenblatt has argued that 'salutary anxiety' when transferred to the stage (or as here to a text) gives the author a measure of control, of analytical power, over this technique and can subject it to ironic scrutiny while containing it within the confines of his work.[102] Although Statius largely represents himself in *Silv.* 1. 6 as one of the complicatious public, applauding the benefits of Empire, the emperor's encompassing power inevitably poses a problem for the poet of imperial praise who attempts to portray the emperor's extravagances without eclipse of his literary worth. Thus he dramatically solves his aesthetic dilemma through his own final disengagement from the feast.

The juxtaposition of *Silv.* 1. 6 with *Silv.* 1. 5 provides an analytical perspective upon the splendours and extravagances of Empire that challenge a poet's power of speech to the point of silence. Indeed, freedom in *Silv.* 1. 6 consists not in openness of speech but in its withdrawal from a public occasion. Through the representation of performance in these two poems, Statius dramatises the difficult situation of the imperial poet struggling to assume a meaningful role within society.

In *Silv.* 1. 6, the amphitheatre and its games provide a strong, dramatic conclusion to the first book of the *Silvae*. December and nightfall are both powerful markers of closure; so too is the poet's withdrawal from the emperor's public performance – and indeed his own. In *Silv.* 1. 6 Statius' exploration of the new divine ideology of the emperor concludes with a final act of personal, poetic disengagement that prepares the way for the devotion of Book 2 to poems that celebrate the enduring, stable values of learning, friendship and poetry.

MacCormack has commented that ceremonial provided an occasion for 'tacit stock-taking'.[103] At the end of the first book of the *Silvae*, the poem on the Saturnalia participates in its own kind of 'tacit stock-taking'. *Silv.* 1. 6, after all, is simply one part of a mosaic of different poetic

---

[101] Wilson (1987) 42.   [102] Greenblatt (1988) 138–42.   [103] MacCormack (1981) 13.

situations. In other poems of the *Silvae*, Statius offers a different concept of pleasure, one in which freedom can indeed be found in the cultivation of philosophy and there is time and occasion for reflection, music, and poetry in a social environment detached from the ambiguity and ultimate uncertainty of imperial power. Indeed, at the end of Book 3, in the poem which closes the first collection, *Silv.* 3. 5, Statius represents himself as in flight from Rome itself, heading as a willing 'exile' for the alternative culture of Naples.

A Saturnalian poem, *Silv.* 4. 9, likewise closes Book 4 of the *Silvae*. This too is a hendecasyllabic poem, but the Saturnalia here involves a private occasion, the poet's exchange of gifts with his friend Plotius Grypus. The poem takes the form of a cascade of comic abuse against Grypus' gift, the works of the Republican Brutus, derogatively described by Statius as *Bruti senis oscitationes* ('the mumblings of old man Brutus', 20). In the world of Flavian Rome, so Statius suggests in this final poem, the political freedom of speech that Brutus represents has become irrelevant. His words are mere mumblings, *oscitationes*.[104] Even leftover foods such as onion skins (29–30) or haggis (35) would have made a preferable gift.[105] But in turn he gives Plotius Grypus this poem, a gesture that reinforces their friendship. In the preface to Book 4 (22–4), Statius says that he and Grypus laughed over these hendecasyllables together. In a humorous and provocative way Statius suggests the social importance of literary composition in an era that provided the leisure and the wealth to develop a sophisticated intellectual culture outside the public spaces of Rome.

Yet there is a bitter strand too in this Saturnalia. *Silv.* 4. 9 plays off Horace's *Ep.* 2. 1 addressed to Augustus. Habinek has called this a 'revolutionary' poem.[106] For in this poem Horace, like Statius in *Silv.* 4. 9, denies the usefulness of past writings to the present. At the end of the poem he imagines the fate that he hopes his own work will avoid, redundancy and consignment to the spice market as useless wrapping paper (*Ep.* 2. 1. 264–70). In *Silv.* 4. 9 Statius complains that Grypus has given him a worm-eaten book, the stuff of wrapping paper (10–13), which Statius tellingly associates with past literary works, old Brutus' rubbish. The material value of the book and its political value are here made

---

[104] The word *oscitatio* is associated with boring, deadening writing and speech. See Mart. 2. 6. 4; Quint. *Inst.* 11. 3. 3.

[105] See Gowers (1993) 37 on the comic phrasing of the paltry foodstuffs that 'contains all the fun of the festival'.

[106] Habinek (1998) 114.

equivalent: liberty is dead in Rome. Statius' book on the other hand is represented as a valuable economic commodity within the new culture of imperial consumerism. It cost ten asses, it is expensively decorated, and it is written on new papyrus (7–9).[107] With *novus* (7) he hints at the innovative nature of his poetry. Nonetheless, abandoning his customary rhetoric of self-depreciation, he promotes here the material value of his poetry book over its literary value.

Statius evokes here a different social context from that of Horace, one in which the production and circulation of poetry flourishes freely only within the parameters of private rather than imperial patronage. Horace speaks in an advisory fashion to Augustus, whereas Statius admonishes a private friend. As Oliensis has suggested, at the end of *Ep.* 2. 1 Horace detaches himself from the necessity of imperial patronage.[108] He can afford to do so, for he has his own sources of poetic autonomy and worth. Statius' new poetry, however, is here confined within a system of exchange between friends, an exchange, moreover, that is represented as unequal, for Grypus has not repaid him in kind. Indeed, at the end of his last published collection of *Silvae*, Statius suggests his wish to put a stop to this exchange when he asks Grypus not to send hendecasyllables in return.

Thus, at a convivial moment, Statius nonetheless concludes his poetry book with a rather bleak look at the conditions of patronage in Rome. What matters, as the appearance of his book suggests, is the outer wrapping, not the inner content. Poetry has lapsed into commodity.[109] The first three poems of Book 4 grandly celebrate the emperor. Statius' flagrant abandonment of the elevated, grand style in the final poem of Book 4 is accompanied by a new assertion of the expensive, outer appearance of the poetry book. As Coleman notes, the twin bosses on this book (8) suggest that it is the equivalent of our 'coffee table book'; that is, it is valued for its very expensive physical appearance, not its literary content.[110] Indeed, the poem that Statius now sends Grypus is almost a grocery list; if this is representative of their type of poetic exchange, then appearance and content are in fact strikingly mismatched. Statius' poetry now participates in the superficial culture of display, where appearance alone seems to matter, and from which, so he seems to suggest at the end of the *Silvae*, he wishes to withdraw.

---

[107] On the adornment of this book roll see Coleman (1988) 225–6 on 7–8.

[108] Oliensis (1998) 191–7.

[109] As Oliensis (1998) points out, the distinction between poetic value and market price is sometimes difficult to see, but it is a distinction that Horace is compelled to make in his own case (194).

[110] Coleman (1988) 225–6 on 8.

Part of the project of the *Silvae* is the critical examination of shifts in cultural attitudes and ideas, and the accompanying search for a new discourse that can authorise and analyse them. In *Silv.* 4. 9 Statius accomplishes through literary means yet another form of Saturnalian inversion. The political liberty of a Brutus may be obsolete, but the poet can explore other means of literary autonomy, even if that in the end means withdrawal from engagement with a poetics of Empire. *Libertas* now resides, if at all, in the realms of domesticity and aesthetics, not politics. Unlike Book 1, which is framed by poems that honour the emperor, Book 4 does not climax with praise of Domitian. Though now decked out in a suit fit for the emperor, including a purple stripe (7), Statius' poetry is represented as completely detached from a political or courtly context.[111] Instead, this last short poem of Book 4 of the *Silvae* decisively marks the poet's provocative withdrawal from the public project of imperial praise. The transvaluation of *libertas* in *Silv.* 4. 9 is perhaps Statius' most Saturnalian moment.

[111] On the meaning of *purpureus* see Coleman (1988) 225 on 7.

CHAPTER 8

Dining with the emperor: Silvae *4. 2*

'A poet cannot know his theme until the emperor orders it. Until then he should think of nothing but the sublime classics of the past. But I knew I would be commanded to celebrate a great act and the greatest act of our age is the building of the new palace ... How many captives died miserably quarrying its stone? ... Yet this building which barbarians think a long act of intricately planned cruelty has given the empire this calm and solemn heart where honoured guests and servants can command peace and prosperity till the end of time.'

Alasdair Gray, *Five Letters from an Eastern Empire*

Book 4, published as a separate collection of *Silvae* in AD 95, marks a new departure for Statius in that it begins with a sequence of three poems addressed to Domitian.[1] The emperor's assumption of his seventeenth consulship on 1 January AD 95, provides the occasion for *Silv.* 4. 1. As is characteristic of Statius' poems of imperial praise, the poet's voice is occluded by that of Janus who speaks the encomium of the emperor from his new temple in Domitian's Forum Transitorium, the Temple of Janus Quadrifrons.[2] Flanked on one side by Vespasian's Temple of Peace, and on the other by the Forum of Augustus and the Temple of Mars Ultor, the new forum of Domitian was symbolically linked with both peace and war.[3] As god of both war and peace, Janus appropriately emblematises the architectural programme of the new imperial complex. Fashioned by and for Domitian, the Flavian Janus of *Silv.* 4. 1 is an appropriate spokesperson for imperial encomium.

But in a surprising move of direction, *Silv.* 4. 2 presents Statius himself at the very seat of power, the imperial palace on the Palatine, which

---

[1] On the date of publication of Book 4 see Coleman (1988) xx–xxii.
[2] On the Temple of Janus Quadrifrons see Coleman (1988) 69–71; Anderson (1984) 136–7; D'Ambra (1993) 26–30; Darwall-Smith (1996) 120–4.
[3] For a full discussion of the Forum Transitorium see Anderson (1984) 119–39; D'Ambra (1993), especially 19–33. On the symbolic nature of the new forum's location see Turcan (1981) 387.

he describes as a sublime architectural expression of imperial majesty (18–31). The occasion is an imperial banquet to which Statius has been invited.[4] Here Statius encounters Domitian not as a statue and not as a remote Jupiter pulling the strings at the amphitheatre, but face to face. Unlike Calpurnius Siculus' Corydon, he has penetrated the inner sanctuary of power. Moreover, although Statius represents himself as a grateful, admiring beneficiary of imperial privilege, his voice is not absorbed by the crowd, as in *Silv.* 1. 6. *Silv.* 4. 2 therefore provides Statius' most direct exploration of the relationship between the poet and the emperor. Indeed, *Silv.* 4. 2 suggests on what terms poetry can and should be written for the emperor.

Characteristically, Statius' poem takes a new approach to two topics that had traditionally attracted hostile criticism in Latin literature: the banquet and the opulent house or, in this case, palace. The ideal associated with the dinner party, whether public or private, was 'commensality', of eating with one's guests and sharing the same food, wine, and conversation.[5] *Silv.* 4. 6 articulates this ideal through Statius' description of his dinner with his host Novius Vindex.[6] The meal is anything but staged. For a start, the invitation is impromptu. Vindex catches Statius wandering around the Saepta Iulia and rushes him off to his house for dinner. The food is unpretentious, and everything is shared: friendship, poetry, humour and art (12–13). There is no sense of distance between Statius and his host. Vindex of course is a private friend, yet in the topos of feasting, it seems, patrons and emperors were measured by virtually the same criteria.[7] The dinner party served as a marker of a host's character, for in his treatment of his guests the host produced his public image for the community. When the emperor himself was host, feasting, as Braund has argued, was treated as an important index of the character of his regime.[8]

Writers hostile to Domitian's reign used the banquet to illustrate Domitian's tyrannical nature. Juvenal's fourth *Satire* portrays Domitian as avaricious and self-absorbed, his senators as obsequious and craven. The catching of a gigantic fish in a specifically imperial tract of sea merits a more urgent council of state than matters of war. In Pliny's *Panegyricus*, the banquet dramatises the contrast between the 'good' emperor Trajan

---

[4] Domitian also had several palaces outside Rome. At his Alban villa, which like the Palatine was vast in scale, he performed many important imperial duties. Thus, as Jones (1994) remarks, 'real power resided wherever the emperor was, wherever he chose to establish his court, and nowhere else; that was not necessarily on the Palatine' (329).

[5] See Braund (1996) 37–52.   [6] See chapter 2 above, 73–87.   [7] Braund (1996) 49.

[8] Braund (1996) especially 51–2.

and the 'bad' emperor Domitian. The virtues of kind hospitality, good-natured wit, and love of culture are ascribed to Trajan's table (*benigna invitatio et liberales ioci et studiorum honor*).[9] At Domitian's banquets, by contrast, the emperor displays his greed, his boorishness, and his self-obsession. According to Pliny, Domitian ate nothing at his imperial banquets, having already gorged himself in private. Instead, he used the occasion to brood in sinister fashion over his guests, watching their every move as they coped with food that he himself did not deign to touch.[10] Here Domitian is presented as the bad ruler because he both eats alone and remains aloof from his guests. As Braund remarks, 'even though Domitian joins his guests at the *convivium*, psychologically he remains the sole eater in his failure to join with them on equal terms'. That is, through his portrayal of Domitian's attitude to feasting, 'Pliny has presented Domitian as a "bad" ruler. Whether he chooses to eat alone or to lord it over his guests, he is a paradigm of the tyrant.'[11]

The theme of the imperial banquet is handled quite differently in Statius' *Silvae*, for Domitian is presented as a generous host. In *Silv.* 1. 6, the emperor is pointedly included in the people's feast: *tu . . . nobiscum socias dapes inisti* ('you came to share in the feast with us', *Silv.* 1. 6. 46, 48). Not that Domitian in this poem is on any true terms of equality with his subjects, as we have seen. He remains on a divine, separate plane, as the reverent language here suggests. Yet he at least makes the appropriate gesture of commensality at the Saturnalia, a time when masters were expected to share with the common people. And his feast is lavish to the extreme. Likewise in *Silv.* 4. 2 there are a thousand tables set for the guests (33), the best food and drink provided by Ceres and Bacchus themselves (34–7), and squadrons of slaves in service (39).

In the *Silvae* Domitian is represented as a considerate, munificent host. But at the same time, in both *Silv.* 1. 6 and 4. 2, he is presented as a host who remains apart from his guests on a separate, divine plane. Even in the more élite setting of a dinner party at the palace, he cultivates the notion of privileged visibility. For Pliny, aloofness was one of the negative characteristics of Domitian, a sign of his fear and suspicion of his subjects.[12] But in *Silv.* 4. 2 Domitian is presented as a divine being. The soaring and opulent architecture of his palace expresses an idea

---

[9] Plin. *Pan.* 49. 8.   [10] Plin. *Pan.* 49. 6.   [11] Braund (1996) 46.

[12] Plin. *Pan.* 48. 3–49. 3. Domitian is represented as a brooding, blood-thirsty monster who only appears from solitude in order to create solitude (48. 5)!

of god-like majesty that symbolically separates the emperor from his guests. Aloofness can be understood in terms of the Flavian ideology of ruler-cult, which stressed the proximity of the emperor to the gods rather than to his people. Thus the Cancellaria reliefs, particularly relief A, depict Domitian in the close company of gods who both guide and honour him.[13] In *Silv.* 4. 2 Statius interprets Domitian's separateness from his people as a sign not of a tyrannical monster but of a majestic god.

In the *Panegyricus* Pliny describes Domitian's palace as a labyrinthine retreat, a barred and virtually inaccessible imperial wasteland where Domitian hid from his people to nurse his secret wrath.[14] There is none of the darkness and secrecy of Pliny's Palatine in Statius' description of the palace, however. Statius' encomiastic description of the palace lavishly expresses the concept of the emperor's sacred majesty through brilliant light and vast, soaring spaces. Playing the role of naïve outsider, Statius feels as if he is in heaven, reclining among the stars with Jupiter, *mediis videor discumbere in astris | cum Iove* (10–11). This then is no ordinary banquet. Indeed, Statius suggests the religious nature of the occasion by calling the feast *sacrae* ('sacred', 5), and in the preface to Book 4 he designates the banquet as *sacratissimis* ('most sacred', *praef.* 4. 6). The description of the emperor and his palace in *Silv.* 4. 2 articulates a new concept of imperial majesty that is concentrated on the sacredness of the emperor's figure and on the monumentality of the setting in which he is placed. Aloofness and distance evoke wonder and are an essential component of Domitian's self-fashioning as a god and absolute monarch.

Yet despite the divine stature of Domitian in this poem, Statius views and writes not from a position of subservience. The opening of the poem, as we shall see, is elevated, richly allusive, Pindaric in its self-reflexive statements on the social function of court poetry. 'With what lyre can I best celebrate the emperor's benefactions?' the poet asks (7–8).[15] As Goldhill reminds us in his discussion of Pindar's *Olympian* 6, 'the poet's glory – his self-glorification – is a constant grounding for the glorification of the victor'.[16] So here, despite the different social and cultural circumstances of the Flavian poet, the emperor's elevation in the poem as godlike victor over the world remains, to a certain extent at least, contingent upon the poet's powers and willingness to praise.

---

[13] See chapter 1 above, 15–17.   [14] Plin. *Pan.* 48. 3–49. 3.
[15] See Harrison (1995b) 120–1 on Statius' use of the 'lyre' as the symbol of either lyric or epic.
[16] Goldhill (1991) 165.

It has been assumed that the occasion of the banquet marks a turning point for the better in Statius' relationship with Domitian. *Silv.* 3. 5, the concluding poem of the first collection of the *Silvae*, had represented the poet, in an appropriate gesture of closure, taking his leave of Rome and of the opportunity, it seemed, to court favour with the emperor. Book 4, with its opening triad of poems addressed to the emperor, has been taken as a sign of renewed imperial favour.[17] Statius is not only back in Rome, he has also had an invitation from the emperor to attend a banquet at the Palatine. In *Silv.* 4. 2 Statius says that up until this day, he has spent sterile years (*steriles..annos*, 12). He presents himself at the start of the poem, Janus-like, on the threshold of a new life (*limina vitae*, 13), as he has crossed, for the first time, the threshold of the Palatine. The invitation to the court is strongly linked with the prospect of social advancement for the poet.

All the same, the poet's relationship to the emperor is clearly represented as uncertain. From the start of *Silv.* 4. 2, the poet reminds the emperor and his readers that he speaks here as the premier poet of imperial Rome, a poet surely worthy of standing beside Homer, Virgil and Pindar in the rankings of fame – worthy indeed of honour by the emperor. The epic and lyric resonance of the poem's opening lines echoes throughout the poem as an allusive plea for recognition of the poet's crucial importance to society and its ruler. The poem thus is both a celebration of imperial power and an *invitation* to Domitian to recognise and honour appropriately the poet's true worth. Praise and admonition are here intermingled.

In this poem Statius reveals the central importance of the palace as the new arena for social and political advancement. Seen from the perspective of an admiring poet, the palace lavishly reflects an elevated concept of imperial majesty that lacks the emphasis upon the foreign and the exotic found in *Silv.* 3. 4. Nonetheless, the architectural language of the Palatine also suggests the vast gulf between the emperor and his subjects, including the poet who craves public and imperial recognition. The poem thus conveys a certain ambivalence about the hierarchical relations between ruler and ruled within court society; it hints at the difficulties that stand in the way of the aspiring poet. Distance, moreover, creates awe in the viewer of imperial majesty but makes the emperor a text hard to read – and write about.

---

[17] Hardie (1983) 65.

In the opening lines of the poem, Statius boldly draws attention to a key element of Flavian ideology, the autocratic nature and style of the emperor's power. Significantly, the first word of the poem is *regia*, 'regal', used here in the opening comparison between the banquet of Dido and of Domitian. *Regia* connects this poem with the preceding one on Domitian's seventeenth consulship, which had ended with the bold appellation of Domitian as *rex* (46).[18] Roman writers, averse to the word 'king' and its associations with tyranny, did not normally apply the term *rex* directly to an emperor.[19] Yet treatises on kingship stemming from a rich Hellenistic tradition had become popular in Rome because of their clear application to the imperial system.[20] With the striking title of *rex*, Statius programmatically activates this tradition, inserting Domitian into a discourse of kingship by which he would be judged. *Rex* moreover was a term used also of Jupiter, king of the gods, with whom Domitian was openly associated. With the one word *rex* in *Silv.* 4. 1, Statius gives bold voice to what Domitian himself, it seems, had authorised to be said only in hieroglyphic code on his Pharaonic obelisk, that Domitian was monarch of Rome in all but name.[21] By introducing to imperial panegyric such a dangerous word as *rex*, Statius throws out an implied challenge to the reader to reconsider the word's meaning and to accept, perhaps, a new valuation of *rex* appropriate to the new court society through which power was mediated. Significantly, in the poem immediately following, *Silv.* 4. 2, monarchs provide an important point of comparison for Domitian himself; they invite the reader to consider the responsibilities and implications of Domitian's 'kingship', with particular reference to the situation of the aspiring poet. For Statius does not passively reflect imperial ideology. In *Silv.* 4. 2 he fashions a complex view of imperial divinity and court etiquette that is interwoven with allusions to the traditional importance of the poet as the commemorative and admonitory voice of the state.[22]

---

[18] On the problem of punctuation in the text of *Silv.* 4. 1 here – some editors have suggested taking *rex* in apposition to Jupiter, which would leave the vocative adjective *magne* hanging without a noun – see Coleman (1988) 81–2.

[19] On Roman dislike of the word *rex* see Dunkle (1967) 156–9.

[20] Such Hellenistic treatises became popular at the end of the Roman Republic. See Fears (1977) 94–5.

[21] On the obelisk see chapter 1 above, 11–13.

[22] Vessey's (1983) analysis of this poem as an expression of Domitianic ideology does not allow for the mediating influence of the poet. For Vessey, the *Silvae* as a whole contain 'an accurate and authentic statement of attitudes purposefully disseminated and encouraged by Domitian himself' (211).

THE PALACE

Next to Augustus, Domitian was probably the most ambitious of Rome's imperial builders.[23] There was not an area of the city that he did not transform in some way. Probably the most imposing monument Domitian built was his palace, which took over the Palatine hill. Symbolically as well as physically, the palace expressed the emperor's dominance over Rome; it provided an overt symbol of the transference of power from the Roman Forum to the emperor's residence.[24] Despite the destruction or defacement of most of Domitian's monuments after his assassination, the palace endured and became the permanent residence of future emperors, including Trajan. As Macdonald has argued, the Palatine complex was 'a panegyric in architecture of the emperor's claim to omniscience'.[25] It provided the Western world with 'a new concept of the palace', setting the pattern therefore for imperial displays of power.[26]

The palace was composed of two main parts: the official palace, known as the Domus Flaviana, and the private palace at a slightly lower elevation known as the Domus Augustana.[27] It was this bipartite division that perhaps contributed to Pliny's description of the palace as a secret and labyrinthine hideout for an imperial tyrant.

The banquet to which Statius was invited was held in a grand hall in the Domus Flaviana that was specially designed for formal receptions and was characterised by its spaciousness. There were, Statius says, a thousand tables set (33). This grand hall is perhaps to be identified with the *aula regia*, a vast, richly decorated public room that provided a highly formal setting for state occasions.[28] From archaeological remains and Statius' description it has been deduced that the walls and floors of the *aula* were sheathed in decorative marble, of several different colours according to Statius (27–9). Its size was broken up by columns and recesses

---

[23] See Gsell (1894) 90–119. He concludes his discussion of Domitian's building programme with the remark that 'Domitien fut, après Auguste, le prince qui modifia le plus l'aspect de Rome' (119). See also Sabayrolles (1994) 125–30; D'Ambra (1993), especially 5, 34, 43–4.

[24] Detailed discussion of the Palatine complex is to be found in Macdonald (1965) 47–74; cf. Darwall-Smith (1996) 179–215, who offers a cautious critique of some of Macdonald's assumptions. See also the discussion of Sablayrolles (1994) 117–23, for whom the Palatine complex is an expression of power come to maturity. Mart. 7. 56. 1 gives the name of the architect as Rabirius.

[25] Macdonald (1965) 71.   [26] Macdonald (1965) 129.

[27] See Darwall-Smith (1996) 185–99 (Domus Flaviana) and 199–203 (Domus Augustana).

[28] The *aula regia* was aligned along a central axis that ran from the great entry hall through a peristyle to the *triclinium*, the dining room. Thus Statius refers to a hall (*aula*, 23) and emphasises numerous pillars (18–20), details which suggest that the banquet was held in the *aula regia*. See Macdonald (1965) 53–4, 61–2. Darwall-Smith (1996) 196, however, says that Statius' description is too vague for us to determine in which of the staterooms the banquet was held.

in the walls. The emperor himself, it seems, occupied a commanding position by an apse at the head of the hall. Significantly, whether the banquet was held in the *aula regia* or in the adjacent *triclinium* or *basilica*, an apse was a striking feature shared by all three state rooms.[29] Like a monumental statue of a god within his temple, the emperor must have drawn all eyes towards him. Macdonald revealingly comments that 'the general appearance would have been that of stage-building architecture, for the *aula* is both theatre and temple, the place where Domitian puts himself on display in front of his guests to be worshipped'.[30] Indeed, the apse was a highly unusual architectural form in a secular context.[31] A new form of architecture, therefore, was linked to a new idea of the imperial banquet as sacred performance and hence to a new idea of the emperor, not as *princeps* but as Hellenistic-style monarch.[32] At a banquet, the emperor was on show, playing to full advantage his chosen role as divinely elected ruler of the Roman people. The theatricality of this representation forcefully emphasises the gap between the emperor's position, on the high stage of power, as it were, and his courtiers, there to watch the emperor and be in turn observed.[33] Yet in *Silv.* 4. 2 the poet clearly too is the manipulator of imperial representation.

Although in the preface to Book 4 Statius calls the poem an expression of thanks for the banquet (*praef.* 4. 6–7), he adopts the fiction that he is composing the poem on the spot at the feast.[34] He thus gives the poem the immediacy and grandeur of a public performance. The ecphrasis of the state hall in which the banquet is held powerfully expresses the poet's excitement and amazement at his surroundings (18–31):

> tectum augustum, ingens, non centum insigne columnis,
> sed quantae superos caelumque Atlante remisso
> sustentare queant. stupet hoc vicina Tonantis
> regia, teque pari laetantur sede locatum
> numina (nec magnum properes escendere caelum):
> tanta patet moles effusaeque impetus aulae
> liberior campi multumque amplexus operti
> aetheros, et tantum domino minor; ille penates
> implet et ingenti genio iuvat. aemulus illic

---

[29] Darwall-Smith (1996) 213.
[30] Macdonald (1965) 201; on the theatricality of the *triclinium*, see Bek (1983).
[31] Darwall-Smith (1996) 186.   [32] Bek (1983) 81–107.
[33] Bartsch (1994) 31–5. But we need not conclude that the emperor's gaze was necessarily 'oppressive' as Tacitus and Pliny, intent on describing the abuse of power, characterise it.
[34] See Coleman (1988) 83–8 on the conjecture that the poem was in fact written in advance and delivered immediately after the banquet or towards its end.

mons Libys Iliacusque nitet, <tum> multa Syene
et Chios et glaucae certantia Doridi saxa,
Lunaque portandis tantum suffecta columnis.
longa supra species: fessis vix culmina prendas
visibus auratique putes laquearia caeli.

An august building, huge and catching attention with more than one hundred
columns, indeed as many as could support the gods and the sky, if Atlas had a
holiday. The neighbouring palace of Jupiter Tonans is amazed, and the gods
are glad that you are situated in a comparable position (yet please do not hurry
to ascend to heaven). Such an enormous building opens before my eyes, the vast
expanse of an enormous hall more spacious than a plain and enclosing much
sky in its embrace, only lesser than its master. He himself fills the household and
brings pleasure to it with his mighty genius. The mountains of Libya and Troy
glitter there in rivalry, with much marble from Syene and Chios, the stone that
competes with the greenish Doric, and Luna marble used for the supporting
columns. The view extends upwards to a great height: you could scarcely take
the roof in with your weary vision, and you would think it was the ceiling of a
gilded heaven.

Statius' language is appropriately effulgent, not just because he is
attempting to convey to the reader the effect upon him of the enormous
size and height as well as the rich decoration of the palace. Rather, he
is presenting himself as a first-time viewer of the palace, who will therefore
be particularly overawed at what he sees. And, if there are any 'faultlines'
that run through his discourse of praise, such as the suggestion at line
21 that the price of parity with the gods is the possible invitation to join
them soon (!), then these can be cleverly ascribed to the poet's struggle to
describe adequately the direct impact of the palatial architecture upon
a first-time viewer.

Statius' description emphasises the enormous size of the banqueting
hall, the expensiveness and gorgeous colours of its materials, its drawing
of the eye up into the remote heights of the ceiling where reality dissolves
into divine fiction. The emperor himself is presented as a god, occupying
the centre of the description as he commands the attention of the diners
in the hall. Statius' emphasis upon the hall's vast scale situates the emperor at a far remove from his courtiers, vastly superior to mortal men.
The ecphrasis of the banqueting hall then serves to reveal the unspoken
assumptions upon which the architectural design of the hall was based:
it is an expression of absolute power and of the divine right to rule. Yet
awe is not the only emotion expressed, there is also humour, appropriate
to the festive occasion and an important feature of the *Silvae*. There are
so many columns that they could hold up the heavens on their own if

Atlas had a holiday (18–20). Statius describes the hall as *moles* (23), an enormous mass whose vast extent covers even the sky itself (23–5), yet these buildings are lesser than Domitian, who, in a variation upon the notion of divine weight, 'fills' this space with his majesty (26).

By wittily pushing the limits of imperial praise, Statius suggests the ways in which the emperor's monumental palace pushes the limits of architecture in its expression of imperial power. As the palace transcends the natural order in its breathtaking height and extent, so the emperor crosses mortal limits in his association with the gods. The unprecedented size and massiveness of the building correspond to the unprecedented grandeur and power of the emperor, while the vast distances within the *aula* also suggest his separateness. The ceiling, gilded like the starry heavens, is almost too much for Statius looking upwards to take in (29–30). Statius draws attention here to the deceptive nature of viewing and the subjective basis of perception. For the viewer in the emperor's palace, the boundaries between fiction and reality become blurred. The claims to divinity that the vast height and extent of the hall express become confused with actual divinity, as Olympus and the Palatine become interchangeable in Statius' playful trope.

The architectural elements of the palace also reproduce the dynamics of court society. Within the palace the rivalry among the marbles – the emulous (*aemulus*) Libyan (26), the competitive (*certantia*) Dorian stone (28) – replicates the social relations among the courtiers, who strive among one another for the attention of the emperor.[35] Jupiter Tonans – whose temple is significantly called a *regia* (21), for the homes of two monarchs are being compared here – is also constructed as a rival, who is struck with amazement at Domitian's palace (20). Domitian's palace matches or surpasses, it is implied, the home of the high god Jupiter himself, and thus any other building in Rome.

Significantly, the temple of Jupiter Tonans was associated in its origins with competition. It was built by Augustus on the Capitoline in fulfilment of a vow made after he escaped death by lightning bolt on his campaign against the Cantabrians.[36] But the temple, lavishly decorated and filled with fine works of art, was popularly perceived to challenge the honour due Jupiter Optimus Maximus Capitolinus.[37] The temple of Jupiter

---

[35] Cf. Coleman (1988) 191.   [36] Suet. *Aug.* 29. 3.

[37] Dio Cass. 54. 3–4 states that Augustus reported a dream in which he consoled Jupiter Optimus Maximus Capitolinus by designating Jupiter Tonans as his porter. A bell was added to the cult statue of Jupiter Tonans to signify this function. On the Temple of Jupiter Tonans see Gros (1996) 159–60. On its rich decoration see Plin. *HN* 34. 5. 10 and 36. 8. 50.

Tonans, then, was associated with competition between old and new, between imperial and Republican building projects. Its introduction in *Silv.* 4. 2 as a point of comparison for the Palatine places the palace within a teleological framework; Domitian's palace now surpasses even the clearly 'upmarket' temple of Jupiter Tonans, as Domitian himself as imperial builder surpasses Augustus. As Elias points out in his analysis of court society, when a monarch's power far exceeds that of the aristocracy, it finds symbolic expression in a house that surpasses any other in size, expense, or ornamentation.[38] With the Palatine palace, Domitian claims supremacy not only over the aristocratic élite and the temples they built for gods, but over the founder of Rome's first dynasty, Augustus himself. The politics of court society are expressed through an architecture of competition and intimidation through awe.

But writing poetry of praise is itself also a competitive endeavour. While Statius' expressions of awe and wonder, therefore, convey both the solemnity and the delight of the occasion as he crosses the threshold into a nobler world, at the same time, however, that awe is modified by the attention that Statius draws to the novelty and importance of his own poetic enterprise. The hall that he describes is far bigger than one supported by one hundred columns (18). With *centum . . . columnis* Statius gives architectural expression to the literary topos of 'many voices', which begins with ten voices in the *Iliad*, is increased to one hundred by Virgil, and expanded to a thousand by Ovid and then Statius in the *Thebaid*.[39] With his appropriation of this literary topos Statius suggests that panegyric, despite strictures on its length, is akin to epic in demanding a rhetoric of grandeur and expansiveness. Indeed, in his use of an architectural metaphor here he plays off the concept of the poem as a grand building, a metaphor that derives from the start of Pindar's sixth *Olympian Ode* (1–4), where Pindar compares the panegyrical poem to a golden hall, noble in design and splendidly wrought. Subtly then Statius puts high value on his own poetry of praise as an art deriving from both archaic lyric and epic and demanding elevation and expansiveness in form and conception.

There is a further metapoetic aspect to this line. It evokes the opening line of Virgil's description of Latinus' palace in *Aeneid* 7. 170, *tectum augustum, ingens, centum sublime columnis*. Here, Virgil tells us, Latinus held 'sacred feasts' (*Aen.* 7. 175); indeed, his palace is called a temple (*templo*, 192). As Wiseman points out, Latinus' palace is both home and

---

[38] Elias (1983) 62.
[39] Cf. Hom. *Il.* 2. 488–9; Enn. *Ann.* 469 (Sk.); Verg. *G.* 2. 43 and *Aen.* 6. 625; Ov. *Fast.* 2. 119; Stat. *Theb.* 12. 797–9.

shrine, 'above all a monument to his ancestral glory'.[40] Latinus' palace
provides a precedent of revered antiquity for Domitian's own palace and
sacred banquet, *sacrae . . . cenae* (5). Yet one room in Domitian's palace is
much larger than Latinus' entire palace of a hundred columns. Statius
places his ecphrasis within Virgilian epic tradition; indeed, he implicitly
sets himself above Virgil here, for Domitian's palace, being far grander
than Latinus' and indeed Augustus', provides the later poet with the
greater challenge.

The Virgilian comparison embodies protreptic, another aspect of
Statian panegyric. Vessey argues that the comparison to Latinus' palace,
with its evocative use of *augustum* (18), has special import in its suggestion
that 'the reign of Domitian – of which the completion of the *Domus* is a
crowning point – is nothing other than a refounding of Rome, the incep-
tion of a *novum saeculum* in a mystical sense, just as much as were Aeneas'
arrival in Latium and Augustus' establishment of the principate'.[41] Such
remarks might better apply to Aeneas' visit to Evander. Aeneas' arrival at Latinus' palace is disastrous for that monarch. It destroys him
and his family and ends his rule. The example of Latinus suggests the
fragility of monarchical power vested in a sole ruler. Although Latinus'
palace is filled with his long line of divine and noble ancestors (*Aen.* 7.
177–82), the sacredness of the monarch does not protect him, it seems,
from institutional collapse.

There are no divine ancestors in Domitian's hall to act as advisory,
stabilising models, however. The palace is new and wonderful, yet lacking a historical or dynastic foundation. Domitian's role as head of state,
it is clear, has reached an unprecedented degree of absolutism, but this
does not necessarily make him more secure, only more isolated. Does
the ecphrasis of Domitian's banqueting hall then chart a story of aesthetic and political progress? Or aesthetic progress only, with political
power dangerously embodied in a remote and isolated ruler? The social
function of praise poetry includes the examination of the cultural values
on which the ruler's ideology depends.

EMPEROR AND MONARCHS

The relationship between the poet and the emperor, then, is by no
means straightforward, but involves a delicate negotiation of positions
of dominance and subordination. Coleman claims that *Silv.* 4. 2 conveys

---

[40] Wiseman (1987) 397.   [41] Vessey (1983) 216–17.

'an impression of a relaxed and accessible emperor'.[42] On the contrary, distance again marks Statius' dealings with Domitian. In a court society relationships between courtier and emperor were fluid and imprecise and marked by varying degrees of proximity.[43] Statius is one of an enormous crowd at the imperial banquet. His access to the emperor consists purely in observation, not conversation. The emperor is not cracking jokes with Statius, or indeed with any of the more élite guests. He is represented in this poem as an aloof, divine being (14–17):

> tene ego, regnator terrarum orbisque subacti
> magne parens, te, spes hominum, te, cura deorum,
> cerno iacens? datur haec iuxta, datur ora tueri
> vina inter mensasque, et non adsurgere fas est?

You, ruler of the earth and great parent of the subjugated world, you, hope of mankind, you, care of the gods, is it you I see while reclining? Is it really granted me to look at your face close by amidst the drinking and feasting, and is it right not to rise in deference?

Certainly the juxtaposition of *tene* with *ego* suggests a certain equality between Statius and the emperor that is supported by the imperial protocol of allowing the guests to remain seated (17). Yet the gesture towards equality is modified by the ambiguity of *iacens*, which can express a position of extreme subjection, particularly towards the gods.[44] Furthermore, the hymnic form of Statius' address to the emperor – the repetition of *te* (14–15) and the apostrophes – presents Domitian as a god and separates him from the poet as an aloof, superior figure who maintains a sacred remoteness. Through viewing, Statius constructs the emperor as a god to whom he can in the special circumstances of divine beneficence come physically close (*iuxta*, 16). But physical proximity does not imply intimacy. Significantly, Statius observes the emperor but he does not talk with him – another sign of the social distance between them. The written text of the subsequent poem becomes the means by which the poet talks about, if not with, the emperor.

Bartsch observes that in the *Agricola* Tacitus presents Domitian as an observer, watching his audience for any slippage of their courtly masks that might betray their true feelings.[45] In this poem, however, only Statius is doing the viewing. At the banquet, the privilege Statius is granted is not conversation, but observation of the emperor's face from close at hand. The importance of observation is marked by the framing of line 16

---

[42] Coleman (1988) 82.   [43] Wallace-Hadrill (1970) 285–94.   [44] See *TLL* vii. 10. 64–11.
[45] Bartsch (1994) 39.

by two words of vision, *cerno* and *tueri*. As Elias remarks in his analysis of court society, observation there is brought to a high art.[46] Since freedom of speech is restricted within a court, appearance becomes crucial, and every gesture and expression is weighed carefully by courtier and ruler alike.[47] By presenting himself as an observer of the emperor rather than the observed, Statius thus tacitly asserts the poet's authority over the representation of the imperial image. Sinfield has noted that the lines of perspective that draw the eye towards the monarch's throne and that replicate the hierarchical structure of the court 'not only privilege the king's position, they also hold him trapped'. For the self-display of the monarch rests upon the hidden struggle between ruler and courtiers for a share in monarchical authority.[48] Statius does not describe Domitian's person or his accoutrements. Only his face, and the characteristics expressed there, command attention. How then does Statius interpret the face of Domitian? What is the character of the emperor as Statius perceives him?

Statius perceives Domitian here as a god, not as a human being. Immobile, inscrutable, the emperor is, in a sense, the culminating point of the palace's architecture. The grandeur, radiance, and remoteness of the palace are particularly replicated in the emperor's face (40–5):

> ipsum, ipsum cupido tantum spectare vacavit
> tranquillum vultu sed maiestate serena
> mulcentem radios submittentemque modeste
> fortunae vexilla suae; tamen ore nitebat
> dissimulatus honos. talem quoque barbarus hostis
> posset et ignotae conspectum agnoscere gentes.

I had leisure to look at him, eagerly at only him, tranquil in expression but softening his rays with serene majesty and lowering gently the standards of his pre-eminence; nevertheless the honour he sought to hide shone in his face. Seeing such a splendid sight a barbarian enemy and unknown tribes could have recognised him.

Spectare (40) marks the limits of the poet's interaction with this divine being at the banquet. The poet has the leisure (*vacavit*, 40) to survey the emperor's face. Yet the opening repetition of *ipsum* in line 40 negates any sense of relaxation or possible intimacy, as the poet views this god-like emperor with the desire fed by the novelty and possible uniqueness of the occasion.

---

[46] Elias (1983) 104. See also Wallace-Hadrill (1970) 295.
[47] Wallace-Hadrill (1970) 305.   [48] Sinfield (1992) 84.

Domitian is represented here refulgently, as if he were the Sun god shining from behind the clouds (41–4). Statius is not alone in commenting on Domitian's shining face. Others gave it a negative construction. Suetonius tells us that Domitian's face was notorious for its frequent flush and changing of colour, an index of powerful emotions that people found hard to interpret.[49] For Tacitus in the *Agricola* the glow of the emperor's face was a sign of his suppressed hatred.[50] Indeed, physiognomical explanations for character connected a reddish face with anger.[51] Presumably here however Statius is suggesting that the emperor's honour is so great that, godlike, it cannot be displayed to the full without harming mortals. Besides, Domitian's 'rays' are gentle and therefore suggestive of his care for his people. Indeed, his face metonymically expresses the brilliance of his palace. Its shine may also literally refer to the light that, reflected from the marbles (*nitet*, 27), gives Domitian's face a divine glow (*nitebat*, 43).

All the same, *dissimulatus* in line 44 is troubling.[52] Why does Domitian try to hide his honour? From modesty? Or is this a sign that there are other thoughts and feelings he is trying to hide? Yet we need not jump to a purely negative interpretation here and assume that the reference to dissimulation suggests that the emperor may be attempting to hide his darkest thoughts and feelings. It is clear, however, from Statius' description that Domitian presents to his subjects a carefully crafted image. *Dissimulatus*, then, suggests both the conscious artifice involved in the emperor's self-fashioning and also the sheer difficulty involved in interpreting the face of power – for who can interpret a god? Ultimately the word refers to the inscrutability of the imperial image. In *Silv.* 4. 2 Statius does not perceive the emperor as a human being; Domitian neither moves nor speaks. Rather he views the emperor essentially as a godlike statue, an object not of conversation but of the poet's gaze, and a figure whose face in its refulgent and ambiguous divinity ultimately eludes secure interpretation. But this in itself is unsettling.

---

[49] See Suet. *Dom.* 18. 1; also Plin. *Pan.* 48. 4. Pliny interprets the emperor's *rubor*, flush, as a sign of his shamelessness.

[50] Tac. *Agr.* 45. 2. See Coleman (1988) 97 on negative constructions of Domitian's face; Ash (1999) 141.

[51] Heat creates the reddishness of face in the angry person. On the ancient practice of inferring character from physical signs see Evans (1969) especially 22–4.

[52] On dissimulation in Domitian's face see Tac. *Hist.* 4. 40. 3–4: *et ignotis adhuc moribus crebra oris confusio pro modestia accipiebatur* ('and the frequently shifting expressions on his face were taken as modesty since his true character was unknown').

In *Silv.* 1. 1 Statius describes the face of Domitian's equestrian statue as 'mixed in signs' (*ora mixta notis*, 15–16), for it suggests both peace and war. Here in *Silv.* 4. 2 the martial aspect of Domitian adds to the ambivalence of his appearance. The military imagery of lines 40–5 is striking, particularly if we remember that Statius is viewing Domitian at a convivial social ritual. The emperor lowers the 'standards' (*vexilla*, 43) of his preeminence. Although he does not appear in his full public magnificence but tries to keep a low profile relative, of course, to his vastly superior position, he does not discard his lowered standards. He retains a military presence even at the banquet. Indeed, although Statius describes Domitian's expression as initially 'tranquil' (41), his appearance is such that barbarians would recognise him (44–5) – hardly a relaxed demeanour for a banquet. Indeed, the military imagery here marks the ambivalence of the palace itself as a highly ambiguous architectural space. As Wallace-Hadrill explains, the palace was 'a private household with a central role in public life, the *domus* of a citizen and simultaneously the *praetorium*, the headquarters of a commander protected by the praetorian guard'.[53] It was also, as Statius describes it, a temple to Rome's new god.[54]

As in *Silv.* 1. 1, Statius portrays Domitian as a leader in both peace and war, who never neglects his responsibilities to guard the boundaries of the Empire. Domitian's military image of course was very important to him. The Flavian dynasty had emerged from civil war thanks to the military success of Domitian's father Vespasian. By representing the emperor as lowering his standards, not discarding them, Statius conveys the idea that the emperor is always vigilant, never entirely off duty, although by AD 95, the time of this poem's composition, the major Danubian expeditions were over.[55] He thus plays here upon the imperial fiction that the empire was still expanding into uncharted territory, and that glorious military conquests were still to be made under a godlike emperor.[56] A subsequent series of comparisons between Domitian and Mars, Pollux, Bacchus, and Jupiter, all at rest after heroic struggles (46–56), further conveys the impression of the emperor as a martial figure of godlike stature whose responsibilities permit the enjoyment of only a temporary leisure.

[53] Wallace-Hadrill (1970) 287.

[54] Martial likewise describes the Palatine as the earthly equivalent of Olympus. See Mart. 7. 56, 8. 36, 8. 39, 9. 91.

[55] See Syme (1988); Jones (1992) 152–9.

[56] On global expansion as an important feature of imperial ideology from the time of Augustus see White (1993) 161–8.

With his description of the palace, Statius interprets for his readers the imperial ideology on which it was based. With his description of the emperor, he attempts to analyse the face of power itself. The result of this second effort is perhaps more worrying, for his face remains an unstable sign that resists a coherent interpretation. The threat of the exercise of power is never absent from it. In exploring the implications of Domitian's omnipotence, Statius suggests the worrisome, uncertain relations that exist between a people and a ruler set so high on a pinnacle of divinely conceived authority that no genuine communication, perhaps, can exist between them. In Statius' descriptions, both palace and emperor are linked in their crafting of an image that compounds fear with awe, distance with divinity. How then can a poet negotiate with such a being?

Myth characteristically provides a means for suggesting the ideal relationship between poet and ruler. At lines 53–6 Jupiter is described, like Domitian, at a banquet; unlike Domitian, however, he is listening to poetry, for he has ordered the Muses to sing private songs while he rests, *dux superum secreta iubet dare carmina Musas | et Pallenaeos Phoebum laudare triumphos* ('the leader of the gods orders the Muses and Apollo to produce private songs and to praise the triumphs of the Gigantomachy', 55–6). Jupiter provides a model for a desirable relationship of reciprocity between the 'monarch' and the poet. Jupiter patronises the Muses and Apollo, and they cooperate by honouring him with poetry that celebrates his exploits. Although he orders (*iubet*, 55) these songs, the commemoration of Jupiter's triumphs is nonetheless dependent upon the powers of his poets.

Yet why are these songs described as *secreta* (55), private? Coleman explains that the Muses and Apollo are performing at a banquet for Jupiter and his hosts, the Ethiopians; it is a private occasion to the extent that they are not singing to all humankind.[57] *Secreta*, I suggest, also looks back to the polemical preface to Book 4 in which Statius defends his *Silvae* from the charge that his poetry should not be published but rather circulate *secreto*, in private (*praef.* 4. 29–30). *Secreta carmina* connects the songs that Jupiter hears with the *Silvae*. His poetry too then, Statius implies, is worthy of the ears of *his* Jupiter, despite what his hostile critics say.

With his vignette of Jupiter's banquet, Statius transfers to the mythical realm the social conditions of literary composition and production of the first century AD. Apollo and the Muses are essentially trying

---

[57] Coleman (1988) 99.

out their new poetry at a *recitatio*, which, as Markus has shown, was a social institution central to the production of imperial literature.[58] The recital served as an intermediate stage between composition and publication where new poetry could be both advertised and tested in front of friends and critics. Jupiter's banquet in *Silv.* 4. 2 provides a model then for the production of poetry such as the *Silvae*, which claim to have been performed initially at private, relatively informal occasions, such as the dinner party of *Silv.* 1. 5.[59] Here patronage and evaluation at the highest level by Jupiter provides the ideal environment for aspiring poets of praise – and correspondingly draws attention to the absence of poetry at the earthly Jupiter's banquet. For Statius says in the preface that *Silv.* 4. 2 represents a *post eventum* offering of thanks (*praef.* 4. 6).[60] But there may be a further meaning to *secreta* here. The Muses sing for Jupiter a song of the gigantomachy, a highly delicate subject as it concerns a serious challenge to Jupiter's power. Prudently the ruler hears the song of his heroic struggle in private first before it reaches wider circulation. Now gigantomachy was often used in Roman poetry as a metaphor for civil war; it is used thus by Statius in *Silv.* 1. 1 for instance, where he refers to the civil wars that brought the Flavians to power as *bella Iovis* (79).[61] This phrase indeed refers specifically to the fighting on the Capitol that involved Domitian in a melodramatic nocturnal escape. In *Silv.* 4. 2 the evocation of the theme of gigantomachy suggests how crucial it was that any account of the founding events of the Flavian dynasty be gloriously represented and civil war itself be reinterpreted as an impious challenge to rightful rule.

With his portrait of Jupiter here, Statius subtly suggests then an ideal model for the relationship between the ruler and the poet. *Secreta* links Statius with the Muses and Apollo as singers of praise. If the emperor is truly worthy of comparison with Jupiter, then he should honour his poets. Moreover, poets make history, and thus it is prudent, as well as just, for a ruler who cares about the representation of controversial events to reward his poets. Whether enacted in public or in private,

---

[58] Markus (2000).

[59] See White (1974) 40, who argues that the *Silvae* and Martial's *Epigrams* were presented to a small group of connoisseurs through recitation and drafts, *libelli*. Fowler (1995b) accepts that such 'occasional poetry' was evaluated first in private recitations, but draws attention to the afterlife of such poetry within a published collection. For Fowler, the study of the reception of literature through books and reading is of prime importance. Patronage, Statius seems to be suggesting here however, is important at all stages of the production of poetry.

[60] See however note 34 above.

[61] On the events involving the Capitol see Jones (1992) 14; Tac. *Hist.* 3. 59–74; Mart. 9. 101. 13–16. Domitian escaped disguised as a priest of Isis.

the poet's role is crucial to the ruler's representation and place in history.

Indeed, from the start of *Silv.* 4. 2, Statius plays upon the idea that the poet has his own source of authority that resides in his ability to sanction and memorialise the temporal activities of gods and monarchs. In an allusive way, *Silv.* 4. 2 advances the idea that poets alone can provide rulers with a mainstay against mortality and transience. The poem begins, for instance, with the reminder of famous regal banquets that were immortalised by poets: Dido's banquet for Aeneas, and Alcinous' for Ulysses (1–8):[62]

> Regia Sidoniae convivia laudat Elissae
> qui magnum Aenean Laurentibus intulit arvis;
> Alcinoique dapes mansuro carmine monstrat
> aequore qui multo reducem consumpsit Vlixem:
> ast ego, cui sacrae Caesar nova gaudia cenae
> nunc primum dominaque dedit non surgere mensa,
> qua celebrem mea vota lyra, quas solvere grates
> sufficiam?

The regal banquet of Sidonian Elissa is praised by the poet who brought great Aeneas to the Laurentian fields, and the feast of Alcinous is displayed in immortal song by the poet who wore out Ulysses in his return over the vast tracts of sea. But I, to whom Caesar has granted for the first time the novel joys of his banquet and has given me the privilege of not rising at my master's table, with what lyre should I celebrate my devotion, what thanks can I find sufficient to express?

As I have mentioned, the opening word of the poem, *regia*, connects the banquets of Dido and Alcinous with that of Domitian, identified as a monarch when he is called *rex* at the end of *Silv.* 4. 1. 46. Furthermore, both the palaces of Alcinous and Dido were known, like Domitian's palace, for their magnificent opulence. In particular, the fabulous wealth of the Homeric king makes a highly complimentary point of comparison for Domitian. Yet through these examples of other famous feasts and palaces made known through literature, Statius honours himself as well as Domitian. The magnificence of Domitian's palace and the capaciousness of his power requires a second Homer or Virgil or even Pindar, for with *ast ego* (5) Statius suggests that the epic medium is not adequate for a new (*nova gaudia*, 5) and challenging occasion of praise. Although Statius expresses the conventional doubt that he has the ability to rise to the occasion (7–8), with *nova* (5) and *primum* (6) he stresses the innovative nature of

---

[62] Verg. *Aen.* 1. 695 ff.; Hom. *Od.* 8. 59 ff.

the challenge the emperor's banquet has given him. Statius thus here subtly acknowledges himself as a prime member of a distinguished tradition of poets whose immortality, unlike that of earthly monarchs, is assured through their verse. He thus places epideictic here on a level with epic; the immortal lyre (7), the instrument of inspired Pindaric verse, likewise asserts the importance of his new panegyrical poetry addressed to the emperor.

Moreover, the poet alone clearly controls the representation of the regal banquets. This, I believe, is wittily indicated by the unusual use of the word *consumpsit* ('consumed', 4) which makes possible a variety of metaphorical play. Coleman for instance has pointed out that Statius here suggests that Homer wore out ('consumed') his hero in his long voyage. Then again, *consumpsit* is a highly appropriate word to use in the context of a banquet, since it is also associated with 'eating'.[63] Saying that Homer 'consumed' Ulysses like a piece of food wittily implies the poet's ultimate control over his 'material'. The subject of his poem is dependent not just upon the desires of the host for commemoration but upon the poet's unique manipulation of the subject.

More sombrely, however, *consumpsit* evokes the transience of life and the mortality of even heroes and monarchs. A poem, on the other hand, performed on the lyre (7), is the only true, lasting monument of human achievement. In *Silv.* 4. 2, poetry is represented as an important instrument of immortality. Homer's poem was a work that would endure, *mansuro carmine* (3), unlike the mortal span of his hero Ulysses and unlike, too, the regimes of either Alcinous or Dido. These two monarchs were immortalised not through their kingdoms but through poetry. Domitian's palace expresses an idea of imperial authority destined to endure in peace and prosperity. Yet the examples of Alcinous, Dido, and later Latinus provide a warning that earthly power, no matter how magnificent, inevitably crumbles away or is suddenly and violently ended.

Through these examples of temporal power, Statius protreptically represents himself as a mediator between the godlike isolation of the emperor and the imperial desire for public fame and immortality. The feasts of Dido and of Alcinous, like that of Jupiter, suggest the sort of relationship that is to be desired between poet and monarch. At Dido's feast Aeneas told the story of Troy, thereby gaining her love and assistance. Similarly, at Alcinous' feast, Ulysses' song of his adventures helped secure the poet's

---

[63] On *consumere* in the sense of 'to eat' (often voraciously) see *TLL* iv. 612. 40–82. On the use of this alimentary word as a literary metaphor for fulsome literary composition see Gowers (1993) 192–3.

return home with the king's help and gifts of treasure. Both these feasts embody the ideal of commensality; the rulers mingle with and help their guests. The relationship between poet and ruler implied within these paradigms is one of mutual help and self-respect. By indirectly suggesting the obligations of a ruler to his poets, they contain an implied appeal for Domitian to recognise and honour Statius himself and give him scope and material for his poetry. For these examples also indirectly draw attention to the gap between the poet's potential and his actual situation. Despite the fiction of immediacy, he is not standing, lyre in hand, holding the court and emperor spellbound with his verse. Rather, he is one of the guests at a thousand tables (33), viewing a statuesque figure that is essentially detached from the social context of feasting and drinking; the emperor does not move or talk or reveal his feelings.

The uncertainty of the poet's relationship with his emperor is captured in the poem's opening, where the poet presents himself as caught on the cusp between public and private life (12–13):

> steriles transmisimus annos;
> haec aevi mihi prima dies, hic limina vitae.

> We have spent sterile years.
> This is the first day of my life, this is its threshold.

With another alimentary metaphor, Statius suggests that his past years have been 'sterile', that is, lived apart from the emperor's table and lacking, therefore, both in his food and in his patronage.[64] The emperor's interest in him now, and the consequent provision of material for poetry, it is implied here, can change his career.

Yet this state of liminality is never resolved, for the poem ends with uncertainty. Statius correlates his present day of good fortune with the time when the emperor awarded him the victory for his poem on the German wars at the Alban contest of 90 AD.[65] Yet the memory of this honour includes an implied critique of Domitian for having thereafter neglected the poet (57–67):

> di tibi (namque animas saepe exaudire minores
> dicuntur) patriae bis terque exire senectae
> adnuerint fines. rata numina miseris astris
> templaque des habitesque domos. saepe annua pandas
> limina, saepe novo Ianum lictore salutes,
> saepe coronatis iteres quinquennia lustris.

---

[64] See *OLD* 2.   [65] On the date of the Alban contest see Coleman (1988) 101.

> qua mihi felices epulas mensaeque dedisti
> sacra tuae, talis longo post tempore venit
> lux mihi, Troianae qualis sub collibus Albae,
> cum modo Germanas acies, modo Daca sonantem
> proelia Palladio tua me manus induit auro.

May the gods grant that you exceed twice, three times the life span of your father (for the gods are said to listen often to lesser souls). May you send your relatives deified to the stars, and grant temples and inhabit your palace! May you often open the threshold of the year, may you often greet Janus with a new lictor, may you often repeat the quinquennial games in prizewinning years. The day on which you granted me access to the blessings of your feast and the sacred rites of your table came to me after a long time, a day as bright as that one when beneath the hills of Trojan Alba your hand encircled me with Minerva's gold as I trumpeted in turn about the German wars and the Dacian battles.

Statius' wish for long life for the emperor climaxes with the hope that the emperor will often celebrate the *quinquennia*, the Capitoline games instituted by Domitian in AD 86 in honour of Jupiter (62).[66] This wish conveys the hope not only that Domitian will live long enough to celebrate the contests often but that he will continue as an active patron of the arts. The wish thus contains an implied protreptic for the emperor's continuing interest in literature. Statius' own desire for imperial recognition and honour is thus set within a larger appeal for recognition of the value of the arts to the state.

With the mention of the *quinquennia* Statius turns specifically to his own situation. His gratitude for the invitation to the banquet includes a quiet complaint: this honour has come after a long time. The phrase *longo post tempore* (64) brings the poem to its conclusion with yet another Virgilian reminiscence.[67] Statius begins *Silv.* 4. 2 with an allusion to the *Aeneid*; he ends the poem with an echo of *Eclogue* 1, a poem in which Virgil first began his meditation on the social function of poetry. In *Eclogue* 1 the phrase *longo post tempore* occurs in the course of the speech of Tityrus, in which he tells Meliboeus that his freedom came late to him (29). Thanks to a god-like *iuvenis* (42) in Rome, who is generally identified with Octavian, Tityrus has been granted freedom to compose poetry as he wishes. As Unglaub has claimed, 'this is the ultimate admission of dependency upon the larger political world for the maintenance of the pastoral mode of life'.[68] In *Eclogue* 1 Tityrus is given the freedom to

---

[66] On Domitian's institution of Greek games see Coleman (1986) 3097–100; Darwall-Smith (1996) 223–6.

[67] This is noted by Hardie (1983) 65.   [68] Unglaub (1997) 68.

remain in his pastoral pleasance, singing as he pleases of Amaryllis. His freedom, then, while dependent on the larger political world, amounts to disengagement from it in his poetry.

Statius here plays Tityrus to Domitian's Octavian. Yet even as he recalls Virgil's Tityrus, Statius suggests the greater constraints upon the Flavian writer who, moreover, has left the pastoral pleasance for Rome. In Domitian's court, it seems, the ambitious poet should sing of Domitian's deeds, for Statius first won the emperor's favour with a poem on Domitian's German wars sung at the Alban palace (66–7). Here then the poet subtly acknowledges that the relationship between poet and emperor has shifted its balance within the hierarchical structure of Domitian's court. If the aspiring poet wishes social advancement and, indeed, a wider audience, then, it seems, the authority of the present *deus* necessitates that he no longer remain outside the emperor's domain, like Tityrus, and that he no longer choose the poetry of withdrawal.

In *Silv.* 4. 2 Statius uses an intimidating occasion to try to negotiate delicately a new relationship with the emperor that includes acknowledgment of the poet's authority and time-honoured place within society. Despite his hint of liberties lost, Statius endows with dignity the role of praise poet. The fragility of monarchical power that his panegyric has hinted at is closely connected here with the nuanced reminder of the poet's power to grant the ruler immortality through his verse. Indeed, the reference to Statius' former poetic victory carries with it the poet's implicit appeal for further imperial support through which both emperor and poet will benefit, for the poet alone can immortalise Domitian's deeds with song. The gold that glittered on the palace (31) is transmuted here to the gold of the victorious poet's crown (67). The poem thus ends, as it began, with a reminder for Domitian of the value of panegyrical poetry to the state.

Statius constructs himself in this poem not merely as an awe-struck guest but as a major poet who subtly contests the emperor's superiority by stressing his own poetic powers. Through poetry, then, Statius attempts to bridge the gap between himself and the emperor, to create an equality that the social structuring of Domitian's feast denies.

In *Silv.* 4. 2 Statius uses the imperial banquet not only as an index of a magnificent but autocratic regime but also as a vehicle for his subtle negotiation with a remote and powerful ruler. In *Silv.* 1. 5 he seized the Pindaric lyre to assert the importance of private life. Here again he models himself on Pindar but in a civic context that honours Domitian as a victorious ruler and that develops a particularly Pindaric theme, the wealth and magnificence of Domitian's dwelling. But although Statius puts high value on the Pindaric task of praising the ruler, he indicates the obstacles in the way of doing so for the imperial poet. There is of course a wide cultural divide between the poetry of Pindar and the poetry of Statius. Although Statius imitates a performative context, he does not describe himself standing to deliver a speech in front of the emperor; what he offers us, his readers, resembles rather the inner musings of a poet who finds himself one among a thousand at Domitian's huge banquet. It is only by committing a fictionalised performance to writing and circulating it among friends that the poet's voice can be truly heard. For the emperor, this poem makes clear, is a majestic and remote figure with whom communication is difficult. Writing about the emperor, then, requires a new lavish and also allusive poetics.

Ahl has argued that the Romans made an important distinction between speech that was understood *aperte* ('openly') and speech that was understood *palam* ('indirectly').[69] The second kind of speech meant one thing on the surface but implied another, hidden meaning, and was generally, according to Ahl, subversive in its intent. In *Silv.* 4. 2, however, it is the inscrutable face of power itself, rather than tyranny and fear, that requires the poet to speak *palam* rather than *aperte*. For how else could a poet attempt even to negotiate with the complexity of imperial majesty except through the effulgence of richly allusive language?

In *Silv.* 4. 2 Statius offers a conception of imperial panegyric as a new, demanding form of literary expression closely linked with epic and ancient lyric and complex in its social function. As his comparisons with Homer, Virgil and Pindar show, he writes panegyric at least in part on his own terms, as Rome's premier poet of the Flavian age. He does not passively reflect imperial ideology; rather, albeit in an oblique style, he explores its implications for the relationship between the ruler and his subjects, in particular the poet. And he suggests the important role the poet plays in the construction of the imperial image. If Domitian wishes to construct himself as a second Augustus, then, the poem implies, he needs a second Virgil, and he must treat him appropriately. And if the examples of the singers at the feasts of Dido and Alcinous carry any weight, poets have their own dangerous power, and it is well for rulers to pay heed to them.

---

[69] Ahl (1984b). See also Quint. *Inst.* 9. 2. 65–8.

CHAPTER 9

Building the imperial highway: Silvae 4. 3

> He was not bad, as emperors go, not really –
> Not like Tiberius cruel, or poor Nero silly.
> The trouble was only that omens said he would die,
> So what could he, mortal, do?
>
> Robert Penn Warren, Apology for Domitian

Silv. 4. 3, the last poem addressed to Domitian in the *Silvae*, celebrates the emperor's building of a new road, the Via Domitiana. By branching off the Via Appia at Sinuessa, this road formed a significant shortcut for travellers journeying between Rome and Naples.[1] The Romans put road building on a par with triumphal success. It was an amazing technological achievement; it was a civic act that brought social and economic benefit to Rome's citizens; above all, the building of roads created the Empire by imposing on foreign, often inhospitable territory a visible sign of Roman mastery over both nature and alien peoples.[2] As Nicolet comments, 'the ineluctable necessities of conquest and government are to understand (or to believe that one understands) the physical space that one occupies or that one hopes to dominate, to overcome the obstacle of distance and to establish regular contact with the peoples and their territories'.[3] Road building linked Rome to the world and the world to Rome – as indeed, an inscription from the Via Domitiana attests. Erected by the citizens of Puteoli, and then erased but still legible after Domitian's assassination, it expresses thanks to the emperor for moving them closer to Rome.[4]

---

[1] See Coleman (1988) 102–3, with map.
[2] On the importance of road building to the Romans see Chevallier (1976) 85–6. Chevallier claims that the Via Appia earned Appius Claudius Caecus as much fame as military exploits. During the Empire emperors took a personal interest in the road system. They commemorated road building by striking special issues of coins that displayed milestones or bridges decorated with triumphal quadrigae or trophies. The value of the Via Domitiana lay in its fulfilment of three goals, according to Coleman (1988) 102: 'transport, drainage, and propaganda'.
[3] Nicolet (1991) 2.   [4] See Flower (2000) 60–1

Of all Statius' poems of imperial praise, this one alone celebrates the emperor's public works and the marvellous technology that made it possible to build a road through harsh, resistant terrain. Indeed, this poem is an important source for ancient road building, for Statius situates himself at the side of the road and provides a detailed, technical description of the process of laying down a surface (40–55).[5] Since *Silv.* 4. 3 concerns the alteration and domination of nature, in an area close to Naples, moreover, it brings openly into the public realm an important theme of *Silv.* 2. 2. In that poem, I have argued, Statius represents Pollius as 'playing emperor' on his estate. What happens when it is the emperor himself who is involved in the actual act of building, of reshaping nature close, moreover, to Pollius' own terrain? In both *Silv.* 2. 2 and 4. 3 military imagery informs the subjugation of the land. The emperor however is represented as achieving the seemingly impossible in defiance of human and natural laws; he approaches the land as a conquering general with superhuman abilities, creating shock waves throughout nature. He is not, like Pollius, an Orpheus or an Arion, taming the land with magical ease. Rather, he is a better Xerxes or Hannibal, an overreacher whose enormous, expansive capacity for power is given violent as well as wondrous expression. Domination of nature is thus linked here specifically to the implied threat as well as the benefits that the emperor brings. Like his statue, the emperor in action inspires a range of emotions from admiration and awe to fear. In *Silv.* 4. 3 Statius represents the building of the imperial highway as a trope for the exercise of imperial power, here artfully and anxiously investigated and applied.

Yet this poem is not only about the building of Empire, it is also about the poetics of Empire. The topic of road building was a new subject for a poem, and again Statius finds new poetic means in order to do justice to the topic. Praise of the emperor and his technological triumphs require the high style, the grand sweep of energetic, lavish verse. Statius provocatively applies to his theme, however, two Callimachean poetic metaphors, that of the broad, well-travelled highway and that of the pure stream. The former, from Callimachus' prologue to the *Aetia* (25–8), describes poetry that is inflated, unoriginal, and easy of access; the latter, from the end of Callimachus' *Hymn to Apollo* (108–12), describes by contrast refined, exclusive verse.[6] The road-building of the emperor,

---

[5] On the passage's importance for an understanding of the different stages of road building, see Chevallier (1976) 82–3; also Cancik (1965) 110, who emphasises that the poem provides a unique literary source for Roman road construction.

[6] For the interweaving of these two metaphors see also Callim. *Epigr.* 28. 3–4 and F. Williams

an activity that includes the channelling of a river, interacts closely with the ambitious and sophisticated stylistic play of the poet, inviting reflection upon the relationship between emperor and poet in their individual aspirations for fame. Here Statius offers his fullest, perhaps wittiest reflection on the nature and themes of the poetry of imperial praise as he brings the emperor's road within the compass of his own powers of expression and creativity.

The opening lines of the poem situate the poet here as a listener as well as a viewer. Statius positions himself at the side of the road, overwhelmed more by the deafening noise of the construction than by what he sees: 'what terrible din of harsh flint and heavy iron has filled the side of the paved Appian way?' (1–3). As Coleman observes, a road has less visual impact than a monument such as a building or an arch.[7] Yet this emphasis on sound at the beginning, on the aural overload of the poet, suggests too that in the description of the building of the imperial highway, the nature of speech itself, the poet's sound, will play a greater role than the verbal interpretation of sight.

Silv. 4. 3 falls into three distinct parts that celebrate the imperial building project. First the poet himself speaks (1–66), then the river god Volturnus (67–94), and finally the Sibyl (114–64). My discussion of this poem will focus on two major features: first, the intersection of the physical act of road-building with the act of writing poetry; secondly, the poet's use of focalised speech as a way of providing different perspectives upon encomiastic, courtly speech and the poet's acts of commemoration.

THE WELL-TRAVELLED HIGHWAY

In the opening lines of the poem, the building of the road is placed firmly within the context of Domitian's other important civic achievements, specifically his building programme within the capital, and his social legislation (1–26):

> Quis duri silicis gravisque ferri
> immanis sonus aequori propinquum
> saxosae latus Appiae replevit?
> certe non Libycae sonant catervae
> nec dux advena peierante bello
> Campanos quatit inquietus agros

(1978) 85–9. On the development of these metaphors in Roman poetry see Lateiner (1978) 191–2; Thomas (1993) 199–205.

[7] Coleman (1988) 104.

nec frangit vada montibusque caesis
inducit Nero sordidas paludes,
sed qui limina bellicosa Iani
iustis legibus et foro coronat,   10
quis castae Cereri diu negata
reddit iugera sobriasque terras,
quis fortem vetat interire sexum
et censor prohibet mares adultos
pulchrae supplicium timere formae,
qui reddit Capitolio Tonantem
et Pacem propria domo reponit,
qui genti patriae futura semper
sancit limina Flaviumque caelum,
hic segnes populi vias gravatus   20
et campos iter omne detinentes
longos eximit ambitus novoque
iniectu solidat graves harenas,
gaudens Euboicae domum Sibyllae
Gauranosque sinus et aestuantes
septem montibus admovere Baias.

What is the meaning of this terrible din of harsh flint and heavy iron that has
filled the paved Appian Way where it neighbours the sea? I know that no troops
of Libyan warriors are making this din, no foreign leader, restless, is shaking
the Campanian fields with treacherous war, nor does Nero violently drain the
lagoons and channel the swampy water, gouging out mountains. Rather, it is
he who crowns the warlike thresholds of Janus with a forum and with just laws
by which he restores the vine-free land and arable acres long denied chaste
Ceres; by which too he forbids virility to be destroyed and as censor prevents
adolescent males from fearing punishment for their physical beauty; it is he who
restores the Thunderer to the Capitol and replaces Peace in her own home; it
is he who sanctifies for his family line a temple that will last for ever and a
Flavian heaven. He, vexed at the people's slow roads and at the stretches of land
that make every journey cumbersome, removes the lengthy detours and firms
up the water-logged sand with a new surface, rejoicing in moving closer to the
seven hills the home of the Euboean Sibyl, the lakes below Mount Gaurus, and
seething Baiae.

Like *Silv.* 1. 1, *Silv.* 4. 3 opens with a question that is a grand outburst of
wonder (1–3).[8] Each noun has an adjective in a stylistic mirroring of the
'repletion' of sound with which the construction of the road has filled the
Appian Way. This is a grand, an amazing technological achievement, and

---

[8] See Coleman (1988) 105 on the subtle differences, however, between the two openings, the first
in *Silv.* 1. 1 relating the emperor to the divine sphere, the second in *Silv.* 4. 3 relating him to the
historic past.

it demands a correspondingly high-flown style. Only excess of adjectives can convey the full effect of such technological audacity, the work of domination. Yet the path of Empire is also well ordered and controlled, like this opening eulogy which neatly arranges the building of the road as a frame to Domitian's other wonderful achievements. First the acclamation of the road; then praise of Domitian's major building projects in the capital (9–10, 16–19), with his social legislation positioned between (10–15); and once again the road and the tangible benefits it brings – swifter travel and the economic benefits implied by bringing popular resorts like Baiae closer to Rome (20–6).

The grand list of Domitian's achievements ends with a surprisingly bathetic touch in the description of Baiae as *aestuantes* ('steamy', 25), a humorous reference not only to its hot springs but to the heightened emotional temperature of a resort well known for its moral decadence.[9] In the centre of the opening eulogy Domitian has been praised for his actions as censor (13–15). The ironising intervention of the poet's voice here subtly adumbrates a different perspective on the building of the road. Does bringing Baiae closer to Rome mean that the capital will have greater control over the resort, or that Baiae's morals will infiltrate Rome? With an adjective such as *aestuantes*, Statius plays upon the slippage of meaning within the imperial rhetoric of praise. As Montrose points out, 'play can be serious and . . . jest can be earnest; . . . the seeming gratuitousness of play masks its instrumentality'.[10] The function of humour (*iocus*, *praef.* 4. 29) is to engage in an elaborate play with language and positions. Such a departure from the unifying order of the opening encomiastic list delicately suggests then that any reading of panegyric as unified and univocal can overlook the nuanced richness of the text – a point that will be made more explicit at the end of the poem in the Sibyl's speech.

However, the idea that the road has moved the Campanian cities closer to Rome in fact hints at the threat of cultural eclipse. For here at the poem's beginning the insertion of the construction of the road into the larger context of Domitian's civic benefactions expands and defines the imperial mission through the building projects that signified to the

---

[9] *Aestuosus* generally means unpleasantly, excessively hot. *TLL* i. 1115. 58–60 notes the metaphorical use of *aestuosus* and cites Plaut. *Bacch.* 470–1 and *Truc.* 350, both used in an erotic context. Quinn (1973) 113 notes that the *aestuosi* . . . *Iovis* at line 5 of poem 7 of Catullus is probably to be understood as both 'sweltering' and 'lusty', the latter a reference to Jupiter's amorous reputation. The same double meaning, I argue, is in play here with Statius.

[10] Montrose (1996) 43.

world Rome's dominance. Domitian's global and divine ambitions are marked by the list of building projects within Rome, all of which were closely linked to the dynastic ambitions of the Flavians. First, the innovatory temple of Janus Quadrifrons in Domitian's new forum, the Forum Transitorium (9–10), which topographically linked Domitian closely to both Augustus and Vespasian.[11] Appropriately then, Statius begins the list of Domitian's building achievements with Janus, god of beginnings and now, as we see in *Silv.* 4. 1, co-opted for imperial service within the new imperial forum.[12] Next Statius lists the temple of Capitoline Jupiter (16), which had been destroyed twice in Domitian's lifetime, in AD 69 in the civil war between the Flavians and the Vitellians, and subsequently in the great fire of AD 80.[13] The association between Domitian and Jupiter was cultivated by Domitian in order to provide his rulership with divine legitimacy. Jupiter was special to him not just as the head deity, but because it was believed that Jupiter had protected Domitian during the storming of the Capitol by Vitellian troops in 69.[14] Then follows the temple of Pax which Vespasian had begun and which adjoined the Forum Transitorium (17); and then, the climax of the list, the temple dedicated to the deified members of the Flavian family (18–19).[15] The emperor's encompassing power is expressed in the striking phrase *Flaviumque caelum* (19).[16] All the world and the heavens too, it seems, have become the property of the Flavian family. Domitian's expanding conception of the imperial office is expressed here in a vision of Empire that extends under Flavian control to the heavens themselves.

The list of buildings expresses the close relationship cultivated by the emperor with the gods, who thus legitimise Domitian's right to rule. Indeed, as Coleman notes, Domitian's relationship with the gods is presented here as an inversion.[17] Instead of the gods doing favours for Domitian, he does favours for them. Thus he restores Ceres her fields (11–12); he returns Capitoline Jupiter to his temple (16); he replaces Peace

---

[11] Anderson (1984) 119–39; D'Ambra (1993) 19–36; Coleman (1988) 69–71 for discussion and plan of the imperial fora.

[12] Most of *Silv.* 4. 1 is taken up by a speech of Janus honouring Domitian's entry into his seventeenth consulship at the start of the year. On the symbolic nature of the new forum and Janus' location within it see Turcan (1981) 385–7.

[13] Tac. *Hist.* 3. 72; Ash (1999) 47–9.

[14] Tac. *Hist.* 3. 74. 6–8. In thanks, Domitian had built first a shrine of Jupiter Conservator, then a temple of Jupiter Custos on the Capitol.

[15] On this temple and its association with the birthplace of Domitian on the Quirinal see Coarelli (1984) 151–3; Darwall-Smith (1996) 159–65.

[16] On the wordplay upon *caelum*, 'temple roof' or 'heaven's roof' see Coleman (1988) 109–10.

[17] Coleman (1988) 106.

in a new home (17); and, in a sense, with the bold expression *Flaviumque caelum*, he appropriates heaven itself, making it Flavian (19). Is such an inversion of the normal relationship between man and gods simply flattery, as has been suggested?[18] With such an inversion, the language of praise attempts to convey in the most striking terms the scope of the emperor's power, conterminous with Empire itself. At the same time, the eulogy encompasses other discourses that resist any monolithic view of such power. As we have seen, a common feature of court panegyric is the similarity between god and ruler. Here in the last poem of imperial praise, Domitian's superiority to the gods is given particular emphasis. We might remember that the visual reliefs displayed on the pyramidion that surmounted Domitian's obelisk showed the Egyptian deities making obeisance to Domitian.[19] This at least was portrayed at a distance, placed up high on top of the obelisk. The idea of Domitian's superiority to the gods may form a terrific compliment to the emperor, but it is also a very bold reformulation of the ancient concept of hubris.[20] How bold this was can be seen from the reaction expressed in Pliny's *Panegyricus*, which argues forcefully for self-restraint as a key imperial virtue.[21]

Indeed, anxiety is built into the eulogy as well as celebration. Important to Domitian's self-representation was the image of the just ruler who, as censor, promoted traditional Roman moral values.[22] The specific reference to two of Domitian's 'just laws', the edicts against castration and against the growing of vines, may seem an odd choice.[23] Both certainly are connected with Statius' dominant theme in *Silv.* 4. 3, the alteration of nature. The edict against castration was part of Domitian's extensive moral reforms and can be seen as an instance of Domitian's intervention against the alteration of nature.[24] At the same time, it also serves as a reminder of *Silv.* 3. 4 and the exotic nature of the court; it reinforces the portrayal of contemporary Rome through its buildings as a city controlled by and for the Flavians. The vine edict is perhaps a stranger choice, for it was controversial, a radical, sweeping attempt on the part of Domitian some four years before this poem was composed to solve famine in Asia Minor by forbidding further vine growing in Italy. It aroused a lot of

---

[18] Coleman (1988) 108.   [19] See chapter 1 above, 13.

[20] Geyssen (1996) 56 argues that *Silv.* 1. 1 establishes the motif of Domitian's superiority to the gods as a way of demonstrating Domitian's right to belong to their number. See however Goldhill (1991) 138–40 on the motif of divine *phthonos* (envy) in Pindar's poetry and Pindar's concern to develop a necessary 'rhetoric of limits'.

[21] See Plin. *Pan.* 2–4; Wallace-Hadrill (1981) 312–18.   [22] See D'Ambra (1993) 47–77.

[23] See Suet. *Dom.* 8. 3–5 for a far more extensive list of Domitian's actions as censor.

[24] On the edict against castration see chapter 3 above, 112 n. 85.

opposition and ultimately failed.[25] In the midst of enthusiastic claims for limitless power, the reference to the failed or controversial vine edict functions quietly as a cautionary reminder of the actual limits to Domitian's authority.

Otherwise, however, Domitian is presented as a leader who is larger than life and who alters nature on a grand scale. The initial question over who was responsible for this terrible din is answered through a priamel, an elaborate form of comparison. The fields are not shaken by Hannibal (4–6), the mountains are not gouged out by Nero (7–8); rather Domitian the law-giver is doing these very same things – but not because of hostile intent. In these opening lines Statius constructs a picture of Domitian as a ruler who stands outside and above mortal boundaries. His relationship with nature as well as with the gods vividly portrays his challenging – and surpassing – of the limits to human endeavour, for Domitian succeeds in conquering a landscape that had ultimately defeated Hannibal and Nero.

All the same, the comparison with Hannibal and Nero is odd. Traditionally in praise literature rivals in fame are depicted in the most derogatory fashion in order to make the strongest possible contrast with the person being praised.[26] Here in *Silv.* 4. 3 the contrast is blurred. Domitian does the same things as Hannibal and Nero, only more successfully. Domitian's construction of the road is inserted here into a traditional discourse that associated the transgression of nature with the hubris of a tyrant. Domitian is a lawgiver. He is thus different in character from Hannibal or Nero, figures traditionally conceived of as tyrants, yet the presence of these negative comparisons reminds the reader that Domitian's exercise of extensive powers has a potentially dangerous side. Later in the poem Domitian is compared to Xerxes as well as to Nero (56–60), both of whom he far outdoes in his challenging of nature. Unlike Xerxes, we are told, Domitian could build a proper bridge, not a pontoon one; unlike Nero, Domitian could build a canal on the Isthmus.[27] Technological expertise is not the only issue here. The bridging of the

---

[25] On the vine edict see Suet. *Dom.* 7. 2. This edict forbade further planting of vines in Italy, and half of those growing in the provinces were to be cut down, the object being to encourage grain production at a time of severe famine in Asia Minor. The edict is most plausibly dated to AD 90 or 91–2, but it was so controversial that it was probably never put into effect. See Levick (1982) 66–3; Syme (1988) 265–6.

[26] Nixon and Rogers (1994) 25.

[27] On Xerxes as the stereotype of the tyrant, see Hdt. 7. 24 where Xerxes is criticised for digging a canal through Mount Athos out of pride. On Nero's activities in Campania see Suet. *Ner.* 31. 3; D'Arms (1970) 94–9. See also Hdt. 3. 80 on hubris as the defining feature of the tyrant.

Hellespont, the cutting of canals, were projects traditionally associated with the behaviour of tyrannical rulers in a vainglorious rush for fame. The extravagant comparisons elevate Domitian in his extraordinary success to a superhuman level, yet they are also an important part of the protreptic of praise. They serve as an uneasy reminder that the challenging of nature is a risky business, one that indeed brings great glory to those who succeed, but always carrying the possibility of divine retribution for subjects as well as for ruler.[28] Fowler's comments on a different set of comparisons involving the Augustan poets and the emperor is also apt here: 'an "alert" reader cannot in good faith escape making the connections we are told to avoid'.[29]

In *Silv.* 4. 3, the building of the imperial highway is represented as a triumphant project that particularly demonstrates Domitian's military prowess. At the same time, the technical description of the road-building (40–60) suggests that the act of altering nature is a harmonious one as regards the workers.[30] Groups of men labour together (*pariter*, 49) in a collective, national endeavour that is suggestive of the cohesion of Domitian's subjects with the larger imperatives of the national state. Yet the alteration of nature was also seen by the Romans as a morally ambiguous activity; in addition, it could be used as a trope for change in the social and political order. Trees and groves were sacred to the Romans.[31] The cutting down of trees was a hazardous activity for the Romans, to be approached with reverential care. In the *Thebaid* the cutting down of the grove for Opheltes' funeral pyre is presented in the epic as an extension of the violence done to the child – not just change but violation (*Theb.* 6. 84–117). The wood groans in sympathy as trees fall and its inhabitants flee in distress (114). Indeed, the act of cutting down the grove is compared to a predatory act of war (*Theb.* 6. 110–13), a violent sacking of nature that gives affective expression to the chaos in time and human order caused by the premature death of an innocent child and heir. Cutting down trees in this passage is represented as a violation of nature that mirrors the disruption of the ancient order of

---

[28] Imperial literature is similarly ambivalent about the great leaders of the past who challenged their mortal limits. Alexander was a case in point. Seneca admires Alexander, but views his ambitions for glory as seriously misguided and fruitless. See Sen. *Ben.* 1. 13. 2; also Sen. *Suas.* 1. 5. 10.

[29] Fowler (1995a) 254.

[30] Probably slaves or local labourers, since there were no legions permanently stationed in Italy at this time. See Coleman (1988) 116.

[31] On the sacredness of the grove to the Romans see *OLD* 1 on *lucus*. On the prominence of tree-cutting as a motif in the *Aeneid* see Thomas (1988).

kings. When Domitian's road-builders then 'cut down a grove and gouge out mountains' (*hi caedunt nemus exuuntque montes*, 50), they are involved in an activity that automatically involved some ambiguity for the Romans, wonderful though the road itself may have been.[32]

Curiously, the building of the road recalls the building of the temple to Hercules in *Silv.* 3. 1 (117–33). There is a similar use of declamatory pronouns to suggest the even, orderly distribution of the work, a similar emphasis on the overcoming of an obdurate nature; in both passages too echoes suggest the impact of the work upon the surrounding land.[33] Yet the point of comparison between the builders is different. In *Silv.* 3. 1 Pollius is compared to Hercules who, according to the poem's mythological fantasy, helps build the temple as an extra labour (123, 166). The divine cooperation of Hercules, the great civiliser, sanctions work that in other contexts could be seen as desecration. Indeed, Herendeen has argued that Hercules provides a positive paradigm of a relationship with nature that is not marked by animosity.[34] In his own voice Hercules explicitly compares himself to Pollius at the poem's end (*meos imitate labores*, 166), who thus receives divine authorisation for the alteration of nature. In *Silv.* 4. 3 however, the points of comparison for Domitian are negative ones: Hannibal, Nero, and Xerxes. Domitian, it is true, is engaged in a safer enterprise than these other more rash rulers. Yet we are made aware that the gods draw limits even to Roman endeavour. Workers such as Domitian's could, we are told, have bridged the Hellespont, but the gods forbade the attempt (59–60). The great military enterprise of altering nature is hedged around by cautionary examples. Superhuman power, even if it is benevolently exercised or expresses glorious aspirations, is also dangerous power.

Road building undoubtedly brought the builder popularity.[35] But right from the start of this poem we are made aware that building the imperial highway is a powerful project that involves a violent disturbance of nature. There may be harmony among the workers, but not, it seems, between nature and man. Domitian is first of all compared to Hannibal, who 'shook' the Campanian fields with his invading force (4–6). Domitian in effect engages in an act not of colonisation, as in *Silv.* 2. 2, but of war.

---

[32] The interference with nature and its violation is also a major theme of Silius Italicus' *Punica*. See Santini (1991) 63–113.

[33] On the similarities between the two passages see Laguna (1992) 167.

[34] Herendeen (1986) 38 suggests that Hercules provides a 'basic paradigm for humanity's strenuous but creative relationship to the environment'.

[35] Wiseman (1970) 150.

Whereas in *Silv.* 2. 2 the land was represented as docile, pleased and ready to be taught, here the land is represented as physically agitated, its peace disturbed (61–6):

> fervent litora mobilesque silvae,
> it longus medias fragor per urbes
> atque echo simul hinc et inde fractam
> Gauro Massicus uvifer remittit.
> miratur sonitum quieta Cyme
> et Literna palus pigerque Safon.

The shores are simmering and the woods astir; a drawn out crash goes through the heart of cities, and vine-bearing Massicus at once relays to Gaurus the echo split on this side and that. Quiet Cumae wonders at the noise and the Liternian marsh and slowly flowing Savo.

The opening image of the seething shores, *fervent litora*, alludes to the scene in *Aeneid* 4, where the shores of Carthage are described in the same way as 'seething' (409) with the departing Trojans. There the scene is imprinted with Dido's sorrow as the ant-like Trojans take away her prized possessions, and ultimately her life. Here Statius rewrites Virgil's epic scene. The woods move in agitation at the military work of the Trojans' descendants who are not departing predators but are bringing the benefits of Rome to the land. All the same, the text does not mute the violence involved in the alteration of the land. In *Silv.* 2. 2, the expression *gaudet humus* ('the land rejoices', 58), articulates the joy and gratitude of the land at its transformation. In *Silv.* 3. 1 likewise we are told that Pollius' acts of building and landscaping have brought joy to the land.[36] In *Silv.* 4. 3, on the other hand, images of breaking (*fragor* | *fractam*, 62 and 63), stirring, *mobiles* (61), and simmering (*fervent*, 61) give vehement expression both to the enormous effort required in road-building, and to the unsettling impact of such activity not only upon nature but also upon the cities of the region (*urbes*, 62).

---

[36] See particularly *Silv.* 3. 1. 96–7 where in the context of a list of Pollius' improvements to the land Hercules asks *quid enim ista domus, quid terra, priusquam* | *te gauderet, erant?* ('what indeed was that house, what was the land before it rejoiced in you?') Cf. also *Silv.* 3. 1. 78, where the countryside rejoices at the homes settled upon it, *gaudentia rura*. Admittedly, in *Silv.* 3. 1 Statius describes the building of Pollius' new temple to Hercules in terms of awesome sound (128–33) and, in part, as a violent war against nature (112–13, 117–33, 166–70). But such violence is displaced through the central, mythological fantasy of the poem that Hercules is performing another of his labours with the help of the Cyclopes; unlike the building of the road, this work takes place largely within the realm of the imagination. At the same time the poet makes clear not only that nature is benefited by the change to its landscape but is made joyful. Indeed, joy is the only emotion ascribed to nature in this poem. The land is described as partially resistant, but not as suffering.

In particular, Domitian's victory over nature is expressed not only through the cutting, hewing and reshaping of the landscape but through the unpleasant as well as excessive noise that accompanies these activities. The poem for instance opens with the poet overwhelmed by the deafening noise (*immanis sonus*, 2). As Coleman says, *immanis* ('terrible', 2) 'is commonly used of very loud noises, especially if harsh and unpleasant'.[37] The adjectives *duri* ('harsh') and *gravis* ('heavy') used to describe the flint and the iron suggest also the violence as well as the noise involved in the transformation of the landscape; *replevit* ('filled', 3) suggests the excessive effort required in the contest against harsh and resistant terrain as well as the poet's aural and stylistic overload.

The quality of sound, as we have seen, is very important in the ideal poetic landscape. In *Silv.* 1. 3, indeed, silence itself is the appropriate backdrop for poetic composition. Imperial building projects, on the other hand, are consistently associated with deafening noise. Thus as with the road, in *Silv.* 1. 1 the building of the equestrian statue of Domitian creates a terrific din (63–5):

> strepit ardua pulsu
> machina; continuus septem per culmina Martis
> it fragor et magnae uincit uaga murmura Romae.

The towering crane grates with the vibration; the relentless crashing pervades the seven hills of Mars and overwhelms the wandering murmurs of Rome.

The drowsy 'm's of the last line suggest the soothing hum of a great city heard from a distance. By contrast, *strepit* and *fragor* suggest unpleasant, deafening noise. Indeed, this noise dominates every other sound in Rome, conquering the casual interaction (*uaga murmura*) of the capital city and imposing a new hierarchical structure upon it.

Dominating sound functions as a potent and ambivalent expression of imperial power – commanding, awe-inspiring, and terrifying. In *Silv.* 4. 3 the building of the road creates an echo that splits into sounds that go in all directions, between mountains and through the heart of cities (62–4) in an eerie reminiscence of the passage in the *Thebaid* where the fractured echo of lament for the infant Opheltes circulates throughout the land (*Theb.* 6. 28–30):

> iam plangore viae, gemitu iam regia mugit
> flebilis, acceptos longe nemora avia frangunt
> multiplicantque sonos.

[37] Coleman (1988) 105.

Already the roads groan with grief, the sorrowful palace with wailing; the path-
less groves accept the sounds from afar and shatter and multiply them in echoes.

The breakdown of order in nature and in a society overwhelmed by
grief is expressed through the motif of the fractured echo. The violent
disturbance of nature at Opheltes' untimely death is a reflection of the
social and political confusion of the rival city-states. Significantly, in the
settled villa landscapes of the *Silvae*, these models of natural and social
order, there is no echo at all. This absence of echo and of any harsh sounds
reflects the philosophical calm of the owners who cultivated leisure as
a way of life. Here in the *Thebaid*, however, the harsh echo, split into
separate sounds, links the social with the natural realm in a grim, perverse
image of reciprocity. Sound provides a model for social relations here
constructed as hierarchical and unstable.

In Statius' poems of imperial praise the boundaries between the mythical world of the *Thebaid* and the contemporary world of the *Silvae* are
less clearly cut than they are in the private poems to friends. Here in *Silv.*
4. 3 the impact of the echo – and by extension of the road – is left ambiguous. The poet, so often in the position of expressing his own wonder,
displaces this complex emotion upon the quiet region which 'wonders'
at the sound (*miratur sonitum quieta Cyme*, 65). Wonder, as we have seen,
can encompass joy, amazement, and apprehension. As an expression of
the aural rather than the visual imagination, wonder here is a particularly elusive emotion. The ambiguous quality of the land's wonder and
sound, another facet of a nature disturbed by an 'invader', invites the
reader not just to admire the grand effort involved in the building of the
road; it also draws attention to the possibly mixed reaction of the land's
inhabitants.

We should not forget, as Statius comments in the following poem written from Campania, that the entire region had not long ago experienced
a massive disturbance in nature from the eruption of Vesuvius. At lines
79–86 of *Silv.* 4. 4 Statius tells Vitorius Marcellus that the land has not
yet completely recovered from that terrible event. The crops have not
yet returned, the mountain still spews forth its wrath, so many cities have
disappeared beneath the lava. In *Silv.* 4. 3 also Statius positions himself
in Campania, a spectator at the side of the new road. Domitian, who
'shakes' the fields like Hannibal (5–6), and creates a crashing sound that
echoes through the cities as well as the countryside, reproduces the sen-
sations of the earthquakes that accompanied the eruption of Vesuvius.[38]

---

[38] See Plin. *Ep.* 6. 20. 6–9. Time spent in California has taught me that the noise of an earthquake

Of course, the new road may well help this still economically troubled region, but the memory of that disaster resonates through the violent descriptive terminology of Domitian's road-building and surely introduces apprehension into the celebration of the Via Domitiana, at least for Statius' Campanian readers.[39]

According to Coleman, however, with the new road Domitian is bringing nothing but benefit to Statius' Campania. He makes the region of the Bay of Naples easier of access from Rome; in Coleman's words, 'the sleepy backwaters of Campania are woken by Domitian, who flings open a route to action and prosperity'.[40] True, the particular area where the road runs was relatively unpromising terrain, but if we consider *Silv.* 4. 3 within the context of the *Silvae* as a whole, then we need no reminder that Campania has been treated in other poems as far from a sleepy backwater. In *Silv.* 2. 2 Pollius' Campanian villa provides a model of the sophisticated intellectual life and of harmonious social order. In *Silv.* 3. 5 Naples is represented as a 'better' Rome – a cultured city without the dirt, noise, and fractious disorder of the Forum (81–112). Cumae, it is true, is here called 'quiet' (*quieta*, 65), but this adjective need not be construed in simply a negative sense. In the aftermath of the eruption of Vesuvius, 'quiet' is an attractive quality and suggests the peacefulness of the place. *Quies* moreover is given decidedly positive valuation elsewhere in the *Silvae* as a sign of philosophical calm and beatitude.[41] The impact of the road upon a region described here as a peaceful and even sleepy region – quiet Cumae, slow-flowing Savo (65–6) – is expressed through the imperial echo whose harsh, fractured resonance symbolically announces the march of time, Rome, and the emperor upon this ancient Greek region.

The building of roads provided an important means of fighting wars and making a hostile land accessible. In the *Punica* of Silius Italicus, for instance, Vespasian is praised for his penetration of forests and his pacification of the Rhine (*Pun.* 3. 598–9), an act that incorporates the pacification both of the river and of the tribes in the Rhine region. The Via Domitiana, however, is being constructed on long-pacified territory.

comes not only from the shattering and breaking of buildings and objects but also from the long drawn-out roar underground as the faultline violently shifts.

[39] Perhaps it is significant that the inscription erected by the citizens of Puteoli in thanks for the new road was entirely erased after Domitian's assassination (see note 4 above); keeping in the emperor's good graces mattered more to the citizens of Puteoli than the road itself.

[40] Coleman (1988) 119.

[41] See for instance *praef.* 3. 2 where Pollius Felix is honoured as *quiete dignissime*, 'most worthy of tranquillity'.

Hence, as Kleiner argues, *Silv.* 4. 3 emphasises Domitian's role as conqueror of nature.[42] Nature here substitutes for the conquered enemy; the exercise of imperial authority is represented as an act of war intent on subjugation. All the same, this Roman road is not being built through the wilds of Germany or North Britain, for instance, but through the settled region of Campania, which was moreover associated with a very different culture. The negative precedent of Nero, of which Statius reminds the reader, provides another worrying precedent for Domitian's 'invasion'. Indeed, according to Pliny, that emperor's engineering works in Campania led to the decline of a significant section of the wine economy, even before the further disruption caused by the eruption of Vesuvius.[43]

Poetry of praise is, in a sense, always partial, and has to be considered along with the full range of historical, aesthetic, philosophical and political positions that are articulated throughout the collection as a whole. Thus the advantages of Empire which the new road brings depend on point of view. Domitian is coming as conqueror to a land that has its own ancient, even, some would say, superior culture. For those cultivating their professional gardens in the Bay of Naples the coming of the din of Rome could indeed seem an act of aggression. In the context of the *Silvae*, the forging of a closer link between the two separate regions is ambivalently represented as both a triumphal and a hostile act, as the violent penetration of land which Statius had fashioned as special to him and sequestered from political life but which now, it seems, is being brought more firmly under Roman control. As D'Arms has argued, it was not love of leisure that drew the emperors to Campania so much as the concern of imperial policy to secure the allegiance of this important part of Italy and ensure acceptance of the new Flavian dynasty.[44]

Of course the imperial highway has also brought substantial benefits to the Roman world. It has made travel easier and faster, and it has put more people on the road. Indeed, the marvel of Roman technology is expressed in Statius' hortatory vision of the nations of the world now streaming along the imperial highway (107–10):

---

[42] Kleiner (1991).

[43] Plin. *HN* 14. 8. 61. Indeed, it is possible that Domitian's controversial legislation forbidding the further planting of vines in Italy, referred to at line 12, would have had immense impact on the major grape growing area of Campania. Even if it was never put into effect, it may well have been taken as a sign that greater imperial control over this region was not necessarily to the entire benefit of the region, particularly at a time when it was trying to recover economically.

[44] D'Arms (1970) 84, 115.

Ergo omnes, age, quae sub axe primo
Romani colitis fidem parentis,
prono limite commeate, gentes,
Eoae, citius venite, laurus:

So come all you races who beneath the dawn sky pledge worship of the Roman emperor, flock here by the easy route of the road, come more quickly than before, Eastern laurels.

The imperial vision is realised graphically here on the road, which is opened up to the entire world. The traffic of Empire flows in both directions. Such are the wonders of modern communications and travel that a Roman can leave the city at dawn and be boating on the Lucrine lake in the evening (111–13); correspondence, such as Statius' letter to Vitorius Marcellus which forms the text of *Silv.* 4. 4, now has speedy delivery in Rome.[45]

Yet the well-travelled road, open to all and sundry – the dregs of Empire as well as the élite – has an ambiguous function within the poetic strategies of *Silv.* 4. 3. Domitian's road-building is an anti-Callimachean project. He has constructed a broad, well-travelled highway along which stream all the peoples of Empire, high and low. By writing a poem of praise upon the road, Statius boldly rejects Callimachean derision of the highroad or (to use another Callimachean metaphor) mainstream style of poetry. In the prologue to the *Aetia* (25–8) Callimachus used the metaphor of the wide, well-travelled road to articulate his objection to poetry that was bombastic and lacking in artistry.[46] Indeed, Krevans has suggested that Callimachus' objection to Antimachus, a main target of his poetic criticism, was based particularly on the bombastic nature of Antimachus' language and its harshness of sound, exactly the features of Statius' poetry that Domitian's road requires and indeed flaunts.[47] The building of this grand road summons from Statius a correspondingly lavish outburst of enthusiastic praise. Moreover, the cutting down of trees for human construction is an established motif of epic poetry; Masters has shown that Lucan, for instance, employs this act as a metaphor for writing epic poetry.[48] Domitian carves out the landscape in epic style; Statius responds to the building of the imperial highway likewise in heightened fashion, drawing upon the prophetic Sibyl herself to conclude the poem.

[45] See *Silv.* 4. 4. 1–5; *praef.* 4. 7–10. On the exaggeration of travelling speeds here see Coleman (1988) 129.
[46] Cameron (1995) 358.   [47] Krevans (1993) 159–60.
[48] See Masters (1992) 25–9; also Laguna (1992) 168 who traces the motif back to Homer.

On the other hand, in employing the hendecasyllabic metre for a poem of imperial praise, Statius simultaneously follows Callimachus in severing the connection between the formal requirements of a genre and subject and style.[49] Hendecasyllables are short and swift.[50] As readers we move quickly through the poem as travellers move quickly along the road. The virtue of speed made possible by technology finds positive reflection in Statius' swiftly composed poetry. At the same time, in using hendecasyllables instead of hexameters to describe the broad, well-travelled highway, the poem in contrast makes, as can be seen from the text printed above, a narrow track upon the page.[51] Characteristically, Statius plays with Callimachean poetic metaphors in an independent way. The narrow track of his poem asserts his independence from the emperor's needs. Indeed, his play with Callimachean poetic categories is more than a clever poetic game; rather, it represents the poet's struggle to find and articulate his own bold public voice within an increasingly autocratic society.

In *Silv.* 4. 3 the chief justification for the improvement of nature and the expressions of joy and gratitude come not directly in the poet's voice but through the two alternative voices that are introduced in this poem: those of Volturnus, the river god, and, at the poem's climax, the Sibyl. Unlike the poet, who stands at the side of the road and addresses the emperor only in the third person, both these figures physically occupy its centre and address the emperor directly. These two speeches provide different models of 'courtly' praise found within the *Silvae*: the 'bound,' restricted speech of the courtier Volturnus, and the exuberant speech of the Sibyl. In *Silv.* 4. 3 this strategy of distancing from the poetic self moves the poem definitively beyond the description of the road-building; it invites from the reader an evaluative response to the exercise of the emperor's power and its impact upon the poetics of Empire.

As we turn, then, to the two eulogisers who conclude Statius' final poem of imperial praise, we should keep in mind that focalised speech is based upon the practice of selective reading and invites analysis of the political processes involved in such choices. Volturnus and the Sibyl provide instances of what Fowler has called 'deviant focalisation', that is, instances where narrator and focaliser, contrary to expectation, do

---

[49] See Zetzel (1983) 99–100.

[50] Hendecasyllables are for Statius the metre of closure. Hendecasyllabic poems end Books 1, 2, and 4; here the metre marks the end of Statius' poems of imperial praise. See Van Dam (1984) 453.

[51] A point made now by Morgan (2000) 114–15.

not coincide.[52] As he reminds us, 'nothing could be more political than the question of whose point of view language embodies'.[53] By testing the limits of imperial panegyric, Statius can explore here through different voices the relationship between the emperor's and the poet's power.

VOLTURNUS

Out of the poem's 163 lines a total of 63 – over a third of the poem – are ascribed to two internal dramatic narrators, Volturnus (72–94) and the Sibyl (124–63), who are thus distanced from the poetic self. The river Volturnus was the major river of Southern Italy; it provided a serious obstacle for the builders of the Via Domitiana as it had to be bridged, channelled, and drained.[54] Like roads, bridges were monuments to the triumphs of Roman engineering and military prowess.[55] Bridges were frequently adorned with trophies and triumphal statuary, as may have been the case with Volturnus' bridge, despite its situation in long-pacified territory. Certainly an arch close by to where the god speaks bears triumphal imagery, trophies that probably commemorated Domitian's triumphs over the Dacians and Chatti, *arcus belligeris ducis tropaeis | et totis Ligurum nitens metallis* ('an arch adorned with the triumphal trophies of our warlike leader and shining with all the marbles from the Ligurian mines', 98–9).[56] Domitian's triumph, however, is represented as not over hostile tribes but over nature itself, here in the personified form of Volturnus who delivers a speech of praise from the vantage point of the new bridge which has been built over his waters (70).[57]

Dominated nature itself is here in Statius' last poem of imperial praise finally given a voice. But Volturnus, newly bridged and channelled, speaks from a position of subservience. He is no longer a free agent. The speech put in the mouth of the river god expresses his gratitude to the emperor for the marvels of Roman engineering that have brought his waters under control. Like his waters, his words have been restrained. From being a boldly rushing river, Volturnus has become a purified and bridled stream.

---

[52] Fowler (1990) 42–3. [53] Fowler (1990) 47.
[54] Coleman (1988) 120; Wiseman (1970) 130–1. [55] Chevallier (1976) 93–104.
[56] Kleiner (1991) 186–8 argues that triumphal trophies and statuary adorn the bridge; Coleman (1988) 127–8 assumes that Statius at line 98 refers not to the bridge but to one of the three triumphal arches known to span the road. On the Dacian victory see Coleman (1988) 127.
[57] Coleman (1988) 122.

As Herendeen has argued, the river, with its combination of beneficent, fructifying and also destructive powers, has traditionally provided an important focus for the relation between art and nature.[58] By choosing a river god, a traditionally powerful deity, to voice the eulogy of Domitian, Statius draws particular attention to the theme of subjugation. The Volturnus was an important river historically. It played a major role in the wars against Hannibal, forming the crucial dividing line between the Carthaginians in Campania and the Romans.[59] In ancient Roman cult, moreover, Volturnus was an important deity; according to Ennius, Numa instituted a priesthood of Volturnus.[60] In literature and in art also, river gods in general were traditionally seen as powerful figures. Indeed, the Flavian age produced several important sculptures of river gods; the most famous is probably that of the river Nile which, Pliny tells us, was displayed in Vespasian's Temple of Peace and provides our earliest known description of this type.[61] Along with the Nile, the Tiber inspired important sculptural representations at this time.[62] Indeed, it is on Flavian coins that the Tiber first appears in numismatic representation. A sestertius minted in AD 71 under Vespasian depicts the reclining river god, who subsequently appears on Domitian's coins.[63] River gods too appear on the frieze of the Forum Transitorium. Klementa suggests that one of them is Volturnus himself.[64] Statius' Flavian readers would then have been familiar with the standard iconographical representation of the river god as a colossal reclining figure with abundant hair and holding a cornucopia or rudder.[65] The sculptures express the fructifying force of the river and its civilising power. River gods too importantly feature in epic poetry. Statius' Volturnus is to some extent modelled on Virgil's Tiber, who in Book 8 of the *Aeneid* (36–65) plays an important role in counselling Aeneas with his prophetic speech and offering him protection in a new country.[66] As

---

[58] Herendeen (1986) 7, 23–4.

[59] See Livy 22–4. At 23. 19 we are told that the Volturnus served a useful, heroic purpose by being in spate: Gracchus was able to send jars of spelt by night down the river to aid those besieged at Casilinium.

[60] Enn. *Ann.* 116 (Sk.). See also Skutsch (1985) 268–70.

[61] Plin. *HN* 36. 11. 58. On imperial sculptures of the Nile see Klementa (1993) 9–51.

[62] Klementa (1993) 52–72.

[63] Santini (1991) 111. On Domitian's coins, struck in association with his Secular Games, see Le Gall (1953) 28–9. On Roman numismatic representations of river gods see Imhoof-Blumer (1920) 384–97.

[64] Klementa (1993) 60–1.

[65] Le Gall (1953) 31 notes the persistence and uniformity of the type.

[66] Coleman (1988) 120–2; Herendeen (1986) 54–8.

Herendeen comments, here in the *Aeneid* 'the river flows with the national purpose'; it 'is the *genius loci*; it is associated with a heroic, moral or civic *virtu*'.[67]

Statius' Volturnus, however, provides a striking contrast with the noble, powerful river god of history and art. He has had his substantial powers curtailed by imperial laws. When Domitian built a bridge across the Volturnus and channelled the river to prevent it overflowing, he took away the river's vital force and reduced the god to slavery (76–84):

> et nunc ille ego turbidus minaxque
> vix passus dubias prius carinas,
> iam pontem fero perviusque calcor;
> qui terras rapere et rotare silvas
> adsueram (pudet!) amnis esse coepi.
> sed grates ago servitusque tanti est
> quod sub te duce, te iubente, cessi,
> quod tu maximus arbiter meaeque
> victor perpetuus legere ripae.

And now I, who was once turbid and threatening and could scarcely put up with fragile ships, now I support a bridge and am trampled upon by passers by; I who was accustomed to snatch away land and whirl away woods (the shame of it!) have begun to be a stream. But I am grateful and my slavery is worth it because I have submitted under your leadership and at your command, and because people will read of you as the greatest controller of my bank and victor over it in perpetuity.

In losing its violent nature, the river god has become a slave, as *calcor* ('I am trampled upon', 78) and *servitus* ('slavery', 81) emphasise. *Calcor* indeed, as Coleman points out, is paradoxical for a river; the word carries here particular associations of 'humiliation and defeat'.[68] Volturnus too makes the droll comment to Domitian that he has been 'bound by your laws governing the correct riverbed' (*recti legibus alvei ligasti*, 75). *Ligare* is a word associated with the notions of constriction and imprisonment.[69] The river god speaks from the point of view of a slave captured in war. There is no sense of a reciprocal relationship between nature and emperor here. Yet the river god is not resentful. Rather, he frankly and gratefully acknowledges his complete subjugation to the emperor's will. He offers the emperor a meekly subservient voice of imperial praise.

---

[67] Herendeen (1986) 58.
[68] Coleman (1988) 124. The imperial Janus too is described as 'bound by the Temple of Peace' (*vicina Pace ligatum, Silv.* 4. 1. 13).
[69] See *OLD* 4.

The bridging of a river, the home of divine powers, required contending with major forces of nature; it was an act inherently connected with the sanctity of nature and fears of transgression.[70] As O'Connor has remarked, 'to build a bridge, therefore, could be seen as a possible cause of offence to the river-god, and a matter to be approached with fear'.[71] Hence the Latin word for priest, *pontifex*, suggests the close link between the construction of a bridge and religious ritual.[72] Volturnus' speech however presents Domitian's bridging of his waters as a civilising, not a transgressive act, one that meets with his full approval. As in the opening section of the poem, then, the relationship of Domitian to the gods is presented as an inverted one. Domitian, not the river, appears as the civilising force. This is made explicit in the opening of the river god's speech where he addresses Domitian as *camporum bone conditor meorum* ('beneficent civiliser of my land', 72). As Coleman points out, *conditor* is an important title that was particularly associated with Roman deities and heroes who were founders.[73] Volturnus' address implies that Domitian has exercised a civilising influence over previously untamed nature. From the river god's point of view, Domitian has brought nothing but good to Campania. But the poem makes clear that Volturnus speaks from a position of subjugation. What, moreover, does it mean for the Volturnus to have become 'civilised'?

In addition to being bridged and channelled, the river, as a second improvement upon nature, is artificially clean. Domitian dredged the river to prevent it silting up at the harbour mouth and thus hindering traffic.[74] The river's speech, however, says nothing of the technical reasons behind its dredging. Indeed, the climactic portion of Volturnus' tribute to Domitian humorously presents the issue of its cleanliness as a matter of personal hygiene and appearance (85–94):

> et nunc limite me colis beato
> nec sordere sinis malumque late
> deterges sterilis soli pudorem,
> nec me pulvereum gravemque caeno
> Tyrrheni sinus obruat profundi
> (qualis Cinyphius tacente ripa
> Poenos Bagrada serpit inter agros)
> sed talis ferar ut nitente cursu
> tranquillum mare proximumque possim
> puro gurgite provocare Lirim.

[70] O'Connor (1993) 188.   [71] O'Connor (1993) 2.   [72] See Hallett (1970).
[73] Coleman (1988) 123 on line 72.   [74] Coleman (1988) 125 on lines 86–7.

And now you honour me with a splendid embankment, and you do not allow
me to be dirty, and you scrub completely away the foul embarrassment of sterile
soil so that the bay of the Tyrrhenian sea does not wash over me when I am
dusty and sluggish with mud (like the Cinyphian Bagrada which winds between
its silent banks through the Carthaginian fields); but such will be my appearance
as I flow along that with shining current I can challenge the tranquil sea and
my neighbour Liris with my pure waters.

The river god emphasises his 'new look' and the importance Domitian
attaches to his cleanliness – 'you do not allow me to be dirty', he says
(86). Statius departs here from the traditional iconography of the river
god as a mature, paternal figure.[75] This ancient river god has had his
image 'made over' for Rome's new Silicon Valley. Volturnus therefore fits
perfectly into court society where the mastery of appearances was crucial.
Silv. 3. 4 represents physical beauty as both an aspect of divinity and an
important key to acceptance and success in imperial Rome. Sparklingly
clean, with the unusual feature of blonde hair (67), the river god has
been refashioned into an appropriate member of the imperial retinue of
slaves.[76] Volturnus is one of several courtiers or imperial slaves within
the *Silvae* whose speech and movement is curtailed. Earinus is confined
within the physical space of the palace; Janus, who speaks an encomium
in *Silv.* 4. 1, is bound (*ligatum*) to the Flavian temple of Peace (13); Volturnus
has been bound (*ligasti*) within his banks (75). Their physical constriction
is tied to their verbal constriction. Volturnus' speech provides a witty
perspective on the meaning of civilisation – in his case, his revamped
appearance has made him fit for the cultured sophistication of courtly
Rome.[77]

The river god here expresses a different position from the river that
flows through Vopiscus' estate in *Silv.* 1. 3. In that poem the river Anio is
not so much subjugated as cooperative with human needs. Thus, though
an impressive torrent above and below Vopiscus' estate, it temporarily
checks its natural turbulence to flow quietly past the great house (*Silv.* 1. 3.
20–3). The river god is presented as a beneficiary of Roman technology who actively enjoys the technological amenities of Vopiscus' estate.

---

[75] Although river gods conform to two main types, that of the bearded, mature male, and that of
the youth, the latter type is less common and may not even have been known at this time. In fact,
its first, disputed appearance may be on the frieze of the Forum Transitorium. See Klementa
(1993) 7, 204.

[76] Coleman (1988) 120 on line 67 notes that *flavum* represents the colour of sand, appropriate to
the silt-bearing Volturnus and also suggestive of youthfulness and vigour.

[77] Since Volturnus calls himself *amnis* (80), Isidore's definition of *amnis* as a 'prettified river' may be
appropriate here: *amnis fluvius est nemore ac frondibus redimitus et ex ipsa amoenitate amnis vocatur (amnis
is a river fringed by a leafy grove and called *amnis* from its pleasant character, *Etym.* 13. 21. 30).

Joined to the baths, the river laughs (*ridet*, 46) at the nymphs gasping in amazement. Indeed, the river god Anio loves to bathe in the waters of this estate (70–4). In Vopiscus' grounds the river is tamed but not enslaved, and it takes joyful advantage of man's works without losing its essential identity as forceful, fructifying stream. Volturnus on the other hand expresses gratitude but not delight – he is after all a slave.

Yet is there not perhaps a hint of ambivalence in the river god's attitude to his loss of dignity and majesty? *Pudet* ('the shame of it', 80) is ambiguously placed in his description of his former self as a force 'who was accustomed to snatch away lands and whirl away woods but has now become a stream' (*qui terras rapere et rotare silvas | adsueram (pudet!) amnis esse coepi*, 79–80). *Pudet* could modify either *rapere et rotare . . . adsueram*, or *amnis esse coepi*. That is, either the river god is ashamed of his violent behaviour, or he is ashamed of becoming a subjugated stream. The ambiguous positioning of *pudet* raises the possibility then of another point of view as regards the river's servitude, one that suggests that the cultivated image comes at the expense of autonomy. Indeed as we have seen, courtly service situates a person within an unpredictable world that may bring bring fame and status – or disaster.

Although the river god expresses gratitude and adulation then, we need to take into account the fact that as a slave of Domitian, tightly bound by his laws and his personal appearance carefully controlled by the emperor, he has no right of free speech. For the first of his eulogistic singers, Statius has provided a river whose speech is necessarily compromised.

There is therefore an important literary dimension to Volturnus' speech, for the river god offers one possible way of composing imperial eulogy. Indeed, through Volturnus Statius continues the metapoetic discourse of this poem. Relations of dominance and subordination are here translated into aesthetic terms. Callimachus' influential poetic image of the great, muddy Euphrates river carrying lots of refuse passed into Roman poetry as a common symbol of epic poetry.[78] In *Silv.* 4. 3 technological appropriation is linked with generic appropriation. In taming Volturnus, Domitian has stripped the river of its epic force and given it instead the cultivation and polish associated with Callimachean poetry. Domitian has carved out a broad highway, but Volturnus as his subject has become a safe, narrow stream. Statius here imaginatively plays with Callimachus' metaphors of the refuse-laden Euphrates and the undefiled

[78] On the extensive literary-critical play with the Callimachean image of the swollen river in Ov. *Met.* 8 and *Am.* 3. 6 see Barchiesi (1989) 57–64; also Suter (1989).

spring provocatively inserting, for instance, Callimachean categories of refinement and purity into the decorum of public encomium. Through Volturnus he steps back from his poem to take a humorous look at one possible model for encomiastic speech.

The speech of the river god is introduced with a joke that plays upon his former passionate, epic self. He overflows (*redundat*, 71) with words. The verb *redundare* refers not only to the physical overflowing of a river, for *redundatio* was a rhetorical term for the verbal fluency and vigour associated with a high, passionate style.[79] The only kind of overflowing that the river god does nowadays is in theme rather than in style, for he is physically constrained within his wonderful new banks. But the joke goes further, for the short hendecasyllabic lines provide the perfect metre for a river god whose speech is constrained. The reference to the river god's 'overflow' wittily draws attention to the opposite – the metaphorical as well as physical constriction upon the river god and his speech.

Although the ancestry of this river god lies in epic poetry, Volturnus is no longer an epic stream. The initial reference to his epic voice, or harsh-sounding throat – *raucis ... faucibus* (71) – and to his verbal 'over-flow' points to the contrast between the river god's rhetorical pretensions and his actual state – a stream deprived of epic force and voice.[80] If he overflows at all, it is in excessive gratitude to his master. Volturnus is no longer an epic river god, for he speaks in hendecasyllables, not hexameters; he is neither *turbidus* ('turbid') nor *minax* ('threatening', 76); and he is too sparklingly clean to convey any refuse.

Indeed, he contrasts himself with the muddy Bagrada (90–1), an important feature of the epic landscape of Lucan and, even more so, of Silius Italicus.[81] Indeed, the comparison with the river Bagrada – how glad the Volturnus is that he no longer dirty like that notoriously muddy river – provides a final allusion to the dangers of human interference with nature. In an extended passage of Silius' *Punica*, Regulus and his men fight on the banks of the Bagrada a terrible snake-like monster that is closely identified with the river itself.[82] Their victory over this monster is depicted as a violation over nature for which, in the long run, they will have to atone with terrible losses.[83] The Bagrada therefore provides a powerful reminder of the river's role in epic poetry as a heroic and indeed moral

---

[79] Cic. *Orat.* 30. 108.
[80] Virgil's Tiber likewise speaks with 'harsh voice' (*rauca sonans, Aen.* 9. 125).
[81] Luc. 4. 587–8; Sil. *Pun.* 6. 140–293.　　[82] See Santini (1991) 286–90.
[83] Thus see the sorrowful, appalled reaction of the river and landscape at *Pun.* 6. 283–6; soothsayers identify the slaying of the monster specifically as violation (288–90). In *Silv.* 4. 3 the adjective *Poenos* (91) perhaps helps activate the allusion.

force. The Volturnus, by contrast, cares only about cleanliness. It shines and is pure (92–4), metaphorical features of Callimachean poetry.[84] *Provocare* (94), a word of epic challenge, is applied with comic bathos to competition only with a placid sea and a river, the Liris, which was the byword for tranquillity.[85] Thus the river god's appearance and character suggest his abandonment of an epic model, his assumption of a new, less ambitious poetics that lacks a moral or political voice, and his binding by a more restrictive metre. Untrammelled by silt, the river moves quickly within the strict bounds of its banks; correspondingly, the hendecasyllabic metre propels the poem swiftly along, bound by an inflexible eleven-syllable line that marks the text with the patterning of a narrow river.

The Volturnus represents the Callimachean pure stream provocatively reformulated for the Roman Empire. For attractive though the river may now be to look at, it is 'trodden upon' (*calcor*, 78) in the sense that a bridge now lets a road pass over it, and this road is very well-travelled. The river may be purified, but it is no longer exclusive. The aesthetic qualities of Callimacheanism have paradoxically made the river much more accessible to all.

The poetics of Volturnus should not be identified exclusively with those of Callimachus or of Statius in the *Silvae*. Volturnus' speech is subjugated speech. He speaks from the point of view of an attractive slave, whose gratitude is a necessary part of his condition. Themes of transgression, of suffering in nature, cannot be expected in his speech. The transparency of the river's waters is reflected in the (virtual) transparency of the god's words. Volturnus represents safe courtly speech. Indeed, although he speaks in a public place, how much authority do this god's words carry when stripped of epic majesty? In *Aeneid* 8 the river Tiber, by contrast, used speech in order to propel further the Trojan destiny. In *Silv.* 4. 3 the pure stream of Callimachean poetics has been reformulated to define the adulatory language of imperial, courtly service – though even here, there are faultlines within the river's safe speech.

The poetics of the *Silvae* as a whole are far more variegated, sophisticated and nuanced than those of the river's subjugated speech, and their aspirations are greater. Such aspirations slip into the river's comment that people will read about Domitian as the 'victor' over its bank 'in perpetuity' (84): *victor perpetuus legere ripae*. These words probably refer directly to an inscription recording Domitian's achievement as builder of

---

[84] See F. Williams (1978) 85–9.
[85] On the known tranquillity of the Liris see Coleman (1988) 126.

the bridge and the road.[86] But there is surely another reference in play for the readers of this poem, particularly those – the majority in fact – who have never travelled the Via Domitiana or seen the inscription. Subtly suggested here is the idea that Domitian's road- and bridge-building will also be remembered, and indeed be even more widely celebrated, through the poet's recording of it.[87] Thus even in the representation of a flattering, subservient speech, the power of the poet who crafts that speech is diplomatically acknowledged through the slippage between speech and reception. We know of Domitian's road chiefly because of Statius' poem.[88] The swift-moving metre of this poem, appropriate perhaps to the swift construction of the road, provides a medium through which Statius, who claims his own poems were swiftly constructed, can challenge the emperor on his own terms and produce a hendecasyllabic tour de force, the longest poem in that metre in Latin literature. The Volturnus has played here into Statius' ongoing concern with the social function of poetry. Court poetry can be more than safe, carefully conned speech; it can enact skilled, meaningful negotiations between the power of an emperor and that of the poet.

THE SIBYL

Cancik has argued that the speech of the poem's last speaker, the Sibyl, represents the highpoint of *Silv.* 4. 3, the climax to which the poem has been building in its ascending sequence of speeches of imperial praise.[89] Even more so than Volturnus, the Sibyl is a figure of clearly epic lineage. The Virgilian Sibyl, priestess of Apollo at Cumae, provided the literary prototype for the figure of the inspired prophetess. As Parke points out, 'the sixth book of the *Aeneid* became the model for descriptions of oracular consultations and served to establish the Cumaean Sibyl as a familiar figure in Roman literature'.[90] Thus Lucan's Pythia in Book 5 of *De Bello Civili* copies the frenzy of Virgil's Sibyl, thereby influencing in turn Statius' Sibyl in *Silv.* 4. 3.[91] She appears standing on the road near its end in Cumae, a place elevated by its Virgilian and religious

---

[86] Coleman (1988) 125. O'Connor (1993) 38–9 notes that the inscriptions on Roman bridges generally recorded the name of the emperor rather than that of the actual builder.

[87] A point emphasised by the fate of the Puteoli inscription.

[88] Thus Henderson (1998) 111 points out that the equestrian statue of *Silv.* 1. 1 'forms both his [sc. Statius'] own work of representation and the work that symbolizes the rei(g)ning Caesar'.

[89] Cancik (1965) 113–15.   [90] Parke (1988) 147.

[91] Luc. 5. 114–97. See Coleman (1988) 130 on *Silv.* 4. 3. 120.

associations, and, as prophetess, her words are divinely inspired.[92] Hers is the last speech of imperial praise not just in *Silv.* 4. 3 but in Book 4 of the *Silvae*. She is therefore an important figure of closure as well as climax.

Despite the Virgilian legacy, however, Statius' Sibyl is also very much a Flavian Sibyl, the vigorous spokesperson of Empire. As the region's most famous figure, she forms the appropriate welcoming committee for Domitian as his road forges towards the coast and the Bay of Naples. She occupies the well-travelled road as a highly public figure, not an elusive one sequestered in the darkness of a hidden cave. Indeed, she 'fills' the road with her presence (122), as the emperor 'fills' the palace with his (*Silv.* 4. 2. 25–6). She belongs to a culture of display. And instead of warning her imperial visitor of the dangers ahead, as she does Aeneas, she can forecast only blessings for Domitian. Her prophecy forms the ultimate compliment to Domitian, and she takes his eulogy in this poem to another level. Indeed, the subject is no longer the road but the divinity of the emperor as manifested in his mastery and indeed surpassing of nature. This is a challenging, new theme in a society still deeply resistant to claims of monarchical or divine powers, and Statius cleverly assigns it to the Cumaean Sibyl who, like Volturnus, is in Domitian's debt. The new road links Cumae to the Via Appia and will undoubtedly facilitate commerce and, perhaps, increase the tourist trade to the Sibyl's grotto. The Sibyl therefore is no Pollius; she speaks from the point of view of a grateful recipient of the economic and social benefits brought by Rome. Hers is not slavish speech however, for it is focussed on Empire, not, as in Volturnus' case, on her own person. Indeed her speech, which is extravagant in thought and expression, represents encomium taken to an extreme of hyperbole. As 'epicising' climax, Statius' Sibyl is over the top.

Significantly, although Statius introduces the Sibyl by deferring to her as a 'more venerable seer' (*vates sanctior*, 120), he marks his separation from her by falling silent: 'let us yield: lyre, put aside your song, we must be silent' (*cedamus: chely, iam repone cantus . . . tacendum est*, 119–20). Does this remark indicate the triumph of the imperial Sibyl, or, as perhaps in *Silv.* 1. 6, a release from compromised song?

We cannot, for one thing, take the Sibyl herself too seriously. Statius humorously reworks Virgil's Sibyl, as indeed did Ovid in *Metamorphoses* 14, and he establishes a comic distance from her. She is above all a figure of

---

[92] Cancik (1965) 114.

excess, and in this regard at least, the very opposite of the well-groomed Volturnus, who is a figure of restraint. First of all, she is very, very old. As Parke observes, the 'longevity of the Sibyl becomes a favourite motif, often with a touch of exaggeration or humour'.[93] In her speech here she recalls meeting Aeneas (130–3); she was already an old woman then, for in Ovid's *Metamorphoses* 14. 130–53 she explains when she meets Aeneas that she is 700 years old and that she has 300 more to go out of a thousand-year allotted life span. Ovid's Sibyl predicts that she will linger on only as a voice; hence the story in Petronius' *Satyricon* (48) that the Sibyl, though invisible, was preserved in a bottle where a voice could be heard endlessly repeating 'I want to die'. According to the chronology established by literary tradition, then, the Sibyl should have been a handful of dust, a bodiless voice, well before the time of Domitian's imperial highway. Furthermore, according to what we know of the history of the Sibyl at Cumae, no Sibyl had been there since the fifth century BCE.[94] Yet Statius presents the Sibyl as still alive; we must therefore imagine her as quite ancient, a Virgilian reconstruction existing in a time warp. And we are not allowed to forget her great age; even in her prophecy to Domitian she draws attention to it (149–52), wishing for the emperor the same number of years which Apollo granted her – but with youth this time added in. In age alone, she is a figure of excess.

Secondly, the Sibyl is extravagant in gesture and in speech. Indeed, Statius' Sibyl raves on the road as she raves in speech: *en! et colla rotat novisque late | bacchatur spatiis viamque replet* ('look, she whirls her neck and raves far and wide along the new spaces of the road and fills it', 121–2).[95] The new broad highway gives her new scope for her powers. Not enclosed in a cave like Virgil's Sibyl, nor constricted by Apollo like Lucan's Pythia, this Sibyl provides an image of fullness (*replet*) in speech as well as gesture, for she is not restricted in expression by the hendecasyllabic metre. A Sibyl traditionally spoke in hexameter verse.[96] This obviously posed no problem for Virgil, but when Tibullus introduces a Sibyl into his elegies he draws attention to the fact that he has to employ her in the wrong metre. He thus describes her as the Sibyl 'who sings hidden fates in six feet' (*abdita quae senis fata canit pedibus*).[97] The hendecasyllable does not have the dignity, the solemnity, one expects of prophetic or even

---

[93] Parke (1988) 147.

[94] Parke (1988) 71–99, especially 81. Paus. 10. 12. 8 records his visit to Cumae where he was shown the urn in which the Sibyl's bones had been placed.

[95] Cf. Verg. *Aen.* 6. 77–9: Luc. 5. 169–74.　　　[96] See Parke (1988) 6.　　　[97] Tib. 2. 5. 16.

encomiastic speech. Instead, it is characterised by speed.[98] But again, this makes Statius' Sibyl particularly appropriate for a road that provides speedier travel. Hendecasyllables here convey the aged Sibyl's frenzied speech, her rush of words, her verbal excess, for she compensates for the restrictive metre with a speech that explodes with apostrophes, dramatic repetitions, mythical allusions, grand comparatives, and bold styles of address. Indeed, even the metre provides an image of excess, for two of the lines of her speech end in a highly unusual way, with six syllable words (*Quindecimuirorum*, 142, and *abnepotibusque*, 148).[99] The Sibyl is a figure of both physical and linguistic extravagance. Unlike Volturnus, then, there is nothing neat or tidy about her appearance or style of expression. She is 'unCallimachean' in her expansiveness. The 'new spaces of the road' can be understood to refer metaphorically to the novel material that the building of the road has offered the Sibyl, material that inspires her to lavish behaviour and speech.

Yet the particular attraction of the Sibyl as a final vehicle for imperial praise lies, I believe, in her well-known association with obscure and riddling speech.[100] In *Aeneid* 6 the Sibyl's prophecies are called 'fear-inspiring riddles' (*horrendas..ambages*, 99); she weaves the true with the false (100).[101] Typically the Sibylline verses employed acrostics, and they were so inexplicit that they were open to multiple interpretation. As Potter comments, 'oracular texts were encoded with a wide range of meanings by their readers, and there was an enormous fluctuation in what an individual text could signify'.[102] Hence the Romans appointed a special priestly body, the *quindecimviri*, to decipher the Sibylline texts and confine their interpretation to one authoritative version.[103] The position of these priests was one of the most cherished in the Roman state.[104] Statius' Sibyl

---

[98] True, Statius also uses the hendecasyllabic metre in *Silv.* 2. 7, a poem commemorating Lucan's birthday and a solemn occasion. Perhaps he did not wish to compete with Lucan's hexameters. But the metre also conveys the quick passing of Lucan's life, a theme of this poem. See Van Dam (1984) 453.

[99] I am grateful to J. McKeown for pointing out these unusual endings to me.

[100] I disagree here with Morgan (2000) 116–17 who characterises the Sibyl's speech as 'direct' like the metre.

[101] O'Hara (1990) argues that deception is the main characteristic of prophecies in the *Aeneid*. See especially 118: 'the content of prophecies in the poem is often determined more by what the speaker wants or needs to hear than by what the truth of the situation is'.

[102] Potter (1990) 102.   [103] Potter (1990) 112.

[104] The openness of the Sibylline prophecies to political manipulation is well illustrated by an example provided by Cicero, *Div.* 2. 54. 110–12. At the end of the Republic, without order of the Senate, some Sibylline verses circulated which claimed that the salvation of the Roman people depended on their leader being made king; these were popularly interpreted as calling for the crowning of Julius Caesar. Cicero points out that, as is typical of Sibylline prophecy, the

openly dispenses with the *quindecimviri* (141–4). Her encomiastic speech
is addressed orally and directly to her recipient, Domitian himself. But
as unmediated praise, it therefore lies open to interpretation not only by
the emperor but also by a multiple readership unrestrained by priestly
authority. The lifting of sacred restraints releases her speech from state
control.

Indeed, the speech of Statius' Sibyl is riddled with 'faultlines'. For the
more capacious the discourse, the more possibility there is for slippage.
The Sibyl's physical demeanour suggests that her words, like her appearance, may not be not entirely in her control. Embedded in the shared
discourses of literary history and state power, her words lie open for the
reader's interpretation. The Sibyl's rich and complex speech provides the
final parade of imperial praise in the *Silvae*. It should therefore be read
not simply as a discrete part, a separate encomium for the emperor's
ears alone, but as part of a larger, dynamic whole, Statius' collected
Silvae.

The extravagance that the Sibyl demonstrates in age, gesture and style
of speech spills over into the content of her encomium. Characteristically,
she goes further in encomiastic expression than elsewhere in the *Silvae*
and develops boldly the earlier themes of 4. 3: Domitian's divine status
and ability to alter nature. For instance, at the start of *Silv.* 4. 3, as we
have seen, Domitian is represented in the inverted role of benefactor to
the gods. The Sibyl begins her speech with the startling direct address of
Domitian as a god: *en hic est deus, hunc iubet beatis | pro se Iuppiter imperare terris*
('look, he is a god, Jupiter orders him to command the fortunate earth
on his behalf', 128–9). Moreover, Domitian is in a sense even superior to
other deities, for he has been commissioned by Jupiter to rule the earth in
his stead. The Jovian ideology is further developed in his nomenclature
as *dux hominum et parens deorum* ('leader of men and parent of gods', 139).
As Coleman points out, this form of address is an adaptation of Ennius'
formula for Jupiter, *divum pater atque hominum rex* (*Ann.* 203 [Sk.]).[105] In
the Sibyl's bold address, Domitian assumes the titles of the chief deity
himself. Virgil too paraphrases the Ennian style of address when Apollo
addresses Ascanius as 'descendant and progenitor of gods', *dis genite et
geniture deos* (*Aen.* 9. 642), a clear reference to the founding of the Julian

---

verses lacked name and date and therefore could in fact be applied to other people and times.
What particularly militates against the authenticity of this prophecy for Cicero, however, is the
fact that it was not authorised by the Senate and therefore was not given official scrutiny and
interpretation by the *quindecimviri*.
[105] Coleman (1988) 132.

dynasty.[106] Virgil, however, does not go so far as to say that Ascanius is a god himself. The Sibyl is bolder and more direct: Domitian is both a god and the parent of gods. Domitian's identification with Jupiter was a political concept well suited to the autocratic character of Domitian's rule, though not without its dangers, as we have seen.[107]

Yet the acclamation *en hic est deus* also has a very different resonance in Roman literature. The phrase is reminiscent of Lucretius' endorsement of Epicurus at the start of Book 5 of *De Rerum Natura*, *deus ille fuit, deus* ('he was a god, a god', 8). The reader is reminded here of other *Silvae* set in Campania where friends, notably Pollius Felix and his wife, followed the teachings of the 'divine' Epicurus – godlike in the sense that he taught human beings true wisdom. Statius' Sibyl goes further in asserting that Domitian is a god now, in the present, and he is a god in a very different sense from Lucretius' 'god'.[108] He has made war upon nature as well as upon hostile nations; towards the end of the Sibyl's speech he is described as *belliger* ('wager of war', 159). His ambitions are located within a Roman literary genealogy that defines Roman identity through expansion and conquest and that drive him well beyond the boundaries set by a philosophical creed of temperance. The bold acclamation of Domitian as a god is subtly suggestive of a tension between the two cultures of Rome and Naples; the wide-travelled road threatens the philosophical garden.

Then again, the emperor's supremacy is vividly expressed by a very bold statement of his transgressive relationship with nature: he is better and more powerful than nature itself. If he were to drive the chariot of the sun he could even alter the climate, making Africa wet, the North warm (136–8):[109]

> hic si flammigeros teneret axes,
> Natura melior potentiorque,
> largis, India, nubibus maderes,
> undaret Libye, teperet Haemus.

[106] Coleman (1988) 132. This is further demonstrated by Silius Italicus, who adapts this formula to Domitian, addressed as *nate deum divosque dature* ('son of gods and about to give us gods', *Pun.* 3. 625). Again, the parenting of gods is delicately put in the future, and the direct comparison with Jupiter is avoided.

[107] Pivotal to the representation of imperial power in Domitian's Rome was the evolution of a Jovian theology. See Fears (1981) 74–80.

[108] Cf. also Verg. *Ecl.* 5. 64, *deus, deus ille*, generally taken to refer to the apotheosis of Julius Caesar. As military commanders Caesar and Domitian are alike; yet Julius Caesar was by contrast the founder of a long and powerful dynasty. See Leach (1974) 188–9.

[109] I have followed Courtney's ordering of these lines. On the numbering and arrangement of these lines see however Coleman (1988) 132 on 134–6.

If he, better and more powerful than nature, were to possess the sun's flame-bearing chariot you, India, would be drenched by abundant showers of rain, Libya would be wet, Haemus would grow warm.

In myth only one person ever usurped the chariot of the Sun – Phaethon – with disastrous results. The implied comparison between Domitian and Phaethon in *Silv.* 4. 3 inextricably associates the concept of imperial majesty with transgressive power and the fear such power provokes in those subject to it. Statius' Sibyl of course implies that Domitian would do better than Ovid's Phaethon: he would improve the earth's climate, making India and Africa wet, and the North temperate.

Despite the contrary-to-fact conditional here, the very allusion to Phaethon, like the earlier mention of Hannibal and Nero, is unsettling. In the preceding poem, *Silv.* 4. 2, Domitian was compared to the god of the sun. Lucan, moreover, provides a troubling and immediate political precedent for the comparison between an emperor and Phaethon here. The adjective *flammigeros* ('fiery', 136) was first used by Lucan in the eulogy of Nero at the start of *De Bello Civili*, where he compared that emperor to Phaethon (48–50) and described the chariot of the Sun god as *flammigeros* (48). Beginning with the ancient scholiasts, there has been considerable debate over whether Lucan's comparison was panegyrical or ironic.[110] Historical circumstances, however, surely affected the reception of this passage. How could any reader after AD 68, the year of Nero's fall from power, not recognise how apt Lucan's comparison between Nero and Phaethon was? Both overreached themselves and suffered a spectacular fall from power – with devastating consequences for the world and, specifically in Rome's case, civil war. For a post-Neronian reader then, the usurpation of the Sun's chariot must surely have linked the concept of imperial majesty with transgressive power and fear of civic dissolution.

Moreover, there was a long political tradition stemming from Hellenistic treatises on kingship in which Phaethon figured as a symbol of the bad king.[111] In the first oration of Dio Chrysostom, for instance, which was written in the early years of Trajan's reign, the king who is wicked and undisciplined, setting his own desires ahead of the interests of his subjects, will meet the terrible end of Phaethon.[112] The

---

[110] See Hinds (1987) 26–9 and Dewar (1994) for an overview of this debate; also Hinds (1998) 88.
[111] For a detailed discussion of the Hellenistic tradition of Phaethon as the bad king see Goodenough (1928), especially 76–83; for discussion of the application of the Phaethon image in the imperial age see Fears (1977) 153–7.
[112] Dio Chrys. *Or.* 1. 46.

Sibyl, then, compares Domitian to a figure that readers would recognise had a long heritage as a sign of bad rulership. Phaethon is an unstable sign which, applied here to Domitian, can be read as having an admonitory and troubling function, as a subtle reminder of the dangers of a power raised so high above its subjects that it disregards safe limits and the public good. The comparison with Phaethon is suggestive of both wonder and fear. It marks the emperor's godlike separation from common humanity, and it also suggests the dangers inherent in autocratic power that styles itself as omnipotent, 'better and more powerful than nature'.

The Sibyl is also extravagant in the expression of her wish for the emperor's long life, a conventional feature of panegyric. But the Sibyl gives this trope particular emphasis and elevation by drawing on the prophetic language of Virgil's fourth *Eclogue* – wittily so, since that poem too is her song. For instance, she predicts that a great order of ages awaits Domitian, that he will outlive his children and grandchildren, and that he will enjoy perpetual youth (147–52):

> magnus te manet ordo saeculorum,
> natis longior abnepotibusque
> annos perpetua geres iuventa
> quos fertur placidos adisse Nestor,
> quos Tithonia computat senectus
> et quantos ego Delium poposci!

A great order of ages awaits you. You will pass your years in perpetual youth, and outliving your sons and grandsons you will reach the mellow years which Nestor is said to have reached, which old Tithonus counts, in number as many as I demanded from the Delian god!

The solemn phrase *magnus..ordo saeculorum* is drawn directly from the opening of the *Eclogue*, where Sibylline song predicts the birth of a miraculous child who will restore peace and prosperity to earth (4. 4–5):

> ultima Cumaei venit iam carminis aetas;
> magnus ab integro saeculorum nascitur ordo.

The last age predicted by Sibylline song has arrived:
a great order of centuries is born anew.

With this particular Virgilian allusion Statius' Sibyl is cast in the elevated role of the prophetess who predicts a new, wonderful Golden Age. Yet she 'corrects' her earlier prophecy with an extravagant compliment to Domitian: it is in his reign that the Golden Age will come about.

However, there is a striking difference between the Virgilian concept of the Golden Age and the Sibyl's here. In *Eclogue* 4 the new Golden Age is derived from human fertility – in particular the birth of a child – and the principle of dynastic succession. The different historical situation of Domitian's world is dramatised by a startling inversion of the normative generative order on which *Eclogue* 4 is based, for the Sibyl predicts that Domitian will live longer than his children and grandchildren (148). This can be read as a startling compliment on the one hand, on the other as a worrying allusion to the fact that Domitian's only child had died in infancy some twenty years earlier.[113] The phrase *natis longior abnepotibusque*, marked by its striking six-syllable ending, opens up a rather undiplomatic faultline in the text. If we look back too to the Sibyl's opening acclamation of Domitian as *parens deorum* ('parent of gods', 139), we see that her characteristic exaggeration in fact opens up to question the basis of her praise.

The problem of dynastic succession and of the civil war that can erupt when there is a disputed heir or no clear heir at all was essentially a theme that had occupied the poet of the *Thebaid* for twelve years, and, as we have seen, it is a highly topical preoccupation of the *Silvae*. The future of the Flavian dynasty was in a particularly critical state in the middle of AD 95 when Statius wrote *Silv.* 4. 3. After fourteen years of rule Domitian still had no biological heirs.[114] As Syme dryly comments, Vespasian 'presided over a large family, to be thinned and reduced by the course of nature or by actions of Domitian'.[115] The problem of the emperor's childlessness was exacerbated by Domitian's notorious mistrust of his own relatives, with whom he was reluctant to share power.[116] At the same time, perhaps bowing to popular pressure, he had remarried the wife of over twenty years who had failed to bear him an heir; the likelihood that she would do so must have become remote by this time.[117] The relatively early death of Titus too must have set an unsettling precedent for Domitian himself.

Finally, at the start of AD 95 Domitian made his cousin, Flavius Clemens, consul with him, probably as a way of bringing recognition

---

[113] The date of this child's birth is disputed, but it fell between AD 74 and 80. See Suet. *Dom.* 3. 1 on the birth and early death of Domitian's only son; and Southern (1997) 28. Also chapter 2 above, 67–9.
[114] On the chronology of the composition and publication of Book 4 of the *Silvae* see Coleman (1988) xix–xx.
[115] Syme (1988) 262.
[116] On the hostility between Titus and Domitian see Jones (1992) 18–21. Flavius Sabinus, heir-apparent on Domitian's accession to power, was executed early in Domitian's reign. On his fate and that of other members of Domitian's family see Jones (1992) 42–49.
[117] See Vinson (1989) 447–9.

to Clemens' two very young sons, whom he had recently adopted as heirs.[118] *Silv.* 4. 1 celebrates Domitian's seventeenth consulship, an office that he initially shared with the unfortunate Flavius Clemens. But any dynastic hopes roused by these actions quickly foundered, and the hopes for continuity and stability of the regime expressed in that poem and in *Silv.* 4. 2 and 4. 3 must have been read in an ironic light after their publication. In May of that year Clemens was executed on the charge of atheism, and Clemens' wife was sent into exile.[119] The fate of the boys is unknown. Even if they survived the disgrace of their parents, they were very young, the sole survivors of seven children.[120] As Syme comments, 'the fate of mortality at Rome, especially among the young, deterred hopes for a long perpetuation of the dynasty – or, at the best, prudent men might be moved to exclaim, *dii avertant principes pueros*'.[121] Besides, adoption was an expedient that did not have a good precedent. In the civil war of AD 68–9, Galba's attempt to secure an heir by adopting Piso did not win him the throne.[122] The trouble with adoption, as Waters points out, is that it does not impose the same general acceptance on others as does the principle of hereditary succession, for there may indeed be other candidates whose merits are considered superior.[123] Suetonius tells us that Domitian made a terrible mistake in executing his cousin Flavius Clemens, and that it was this event that determined Domitian's assassination: *quo maxime facto maturavit sibi exitium (Dom.* 15. 1). There were many alive in Rome who remembered the civil war of AD 68–9, and must have worried that chaos would resume if Domitian died without resolving the incipient dynastic crisis.

Silv. 4. 3 was probably composed shortly after the dramatic events of the spring.[124] Seen in the light of contemporary political circumstances, the direct allusion in *Silv.* 4. 3 to the Sibylline prophecy of *Eclogue* 4 invites troubling reflection on the different dynastic conditions of the Flavian age. The building of the road and the execution of Flavius Clemens are linked as the notable events of AD 95 in the epitome of Dio Cassius.[125] These two events are also related in *Silv.* 4. 3 in that dynastic instability forms a faultline below the surface of the Sibyl's enthusiastic praise.

Indeed, Domitian's childlessness and his lack of an heir ironically give particular point to the Sibyl's prediction of a long life for him, for in

[118] Suet. *Dom.* 15. 1; Dio Cass 67. 14. 1; Coleman (1988) 62–3.   [119] See Syme (1988) 262–77.
[120] Suet. *Dom.* 15. 1 refers to the two boys as *parvulos*, very young.   [121] Syme (1988) 264.
[122] Tac. *Hist.* 1. 15ff. Indeed, Syme (1958) 207 views the adoption of Piso 'as an act of despair'.
[123] Waters (1963) 207.   [124] See Coleman (1988) xx–xxi.   [125] Dio Cass. 67. 14. 1

Domitian's longevity lies the only current hope of stability for the state. Wisely she wishes for Domitian not perpetual life but perpetual youth (149).[126] With this boon, presumably, he will stave off the problems of succession that seem to lurk beneath her prophetic discourse. The Sibyl's enthusiastic prophecy of long life and a glorious future for Domitian and his heirs, then, also encompasses anxieties about that future, for it rests on the unstable basis of his failing dynastic ambitions. The Sibyl is a particularly appropriate vehicle for the prediction of longevity, since she herself enjoys extraordinarily long life. But at the same time, this extravagant, legendary spokesperson also dramatises the fictionality of such imperial claims.

There is another inversion in the prediction of Statius' Sibyl that, if referred to the particular historical situation of AD 95, further unsettles the enthusiastic discourse of praise. The great order of ages will usher in not an era of universal peace, a new Golden Age, but a period of imperial conquest (153–9):

> iuravit tibi iam nivalis Arctus,
> nunc magnos Oriens dabit triumphos.
> ibis qua vagus Hercules et Euhan
> ultra sidera flammeumque solem
> et Nili caput et nives Atlantis,
> et laudum cumulo beatus omni
> scandes belliger abnuesque currus.

Already the snowy North has pledged itself to you, now the East will grant you great triumphs. You will travel in the same direction as pioneering Hercules and Bacchus, beyond the stars and the flaming sun and the source of the Nile and the snows of Atlas, and blessed on every pinnacle of praise, you will mount and refuse triumphal chariots, bringer of war.

The Sibyl reinterprets 'the great order of ages' as a dream of imperial conquest, of an empire beyond the stars. There is Virgilian precedent for this too. In *Aeneid* 6. 795–805 Anchises prophesies Augustus' glorious career as world conqueror in terms very similar to those that Statius' Sibyl employs in lines 153–7.[127] *Eclogue* 4 prophesied a ruler who would put an end to all war. Here in this rewriting of literary tradition two different Virgilian views of a ruler's function are juxtaposed together with two different notions of Roman *virtus*. Statius' Sibyl forecloses Virgil's dream of pastoral peace in Italy and substitutes a vision that is in keeping with

---

[126] In asking for perpetual youth, she seems to have learned from her own failure to ask Apollo for such a boon. See Ov. *Met.* 14. 130–53.
[127] On this passage in the *Aeneid* see Romm (1992) 160–2.

Domitian's close association between himself and Jupiter; he is *belliger* (159), wager of war who can conquer earth and even heaven.

The pastoral dream of a life lived in harmony with friends and with nature is of course also an important theme of the *Silvae*. The boldest expression of this vision is located in Campania, on the villa estate of Pollius Felix where the intellectual life in pursuit of philosophy and poetry is fully developed. Indeed, in *Silv.* 2. 2 military imagery offers a new version of cultural identity in which civic virtue and martial prowess are redescribed within a peaceful environment that is self-contained and set apart from Rome. Yet, despite her encomiastic froth, the vision of the Sibyl on the road that links Naples to Rome expresses the Roman drive for expansion, for glory earned from war, and for conquest beyond the boundaries of the known world. Underlying this dream of world-encompassing Empire was a long tradition going back to the Hellenistic mythology involving Alexander the Great. In Roman tradition beginning with Augustus, global or even extra-global expansion was seen as the natural concomitant of autocratic rule.[128] This vision of universal domination challenged the pastoral enclave. Here in *Silv.* 4. 3 Hercules is not domesticated or tamed as he was in *Silv.* 2. 2 and 3. 1; he too is perceived as *vagus* (155), the pioneer.

But even here this expansive vision of Roman imperialism is underwritten by anxiety. Indeed, the gap between the Sibyl's dream and present reality is particularly wide. As we have seen, the ideology of Domitian as successful warrior was crucial to his public image. But although Domitian capitalised publicly on military conquests in order to bolster his authority among the people and the army, in practice Domitian ranged no further than Germany; imperial explorations in North Britain led to prudent withdrawal. Indeed, his martial policy was essentially defensive; Jones argues that Domitian's military policy was based on a rejection of the idea of expansionist warfare.[129] The Sibyl's vision is essentially anachronistic.

Complicating the reader's reception of this passage, moreover, lies the knowledge that between Virgil and Statius lay other versions of territorial expansion, in particular that of Seneca who confronted the imperial ideal with a despairing vision of moral and cosmic dissolution brought about by human audacity.[130] The tradition of territorial expansion was ultimately an ambivalent one associated with either reckless or glorious ambition. As

---

[128] On this tradition see Romm (1992) 121–71, especially 136–7; Nicolet (1991) 21–56, especially 21–4.

[129] Jones (1992) 127. On Domitian's wars in general see Jones (1992) 126–59.

[130] See Romm (1992) 165–71.

with the Phaethon myth, here too Domitian is praised within an ideology of rulership that rested on a tradition of mixed response. The Sibyl's imperialistic vision points to the stressed dualism within Empire itself.

This passage too, moreover, is underwritten by dynastic anxiety. In *Aeneid* 6 the idea of the great imperial mission is unfolded by Anchises in his speech to Aeneas, father talking to son. Together, moreover, they are looking at the great line of their descendants: *hanc aspice gentem | Romanosque tuos. hic Caesar et omnis | progenies magnum caeli ventura sub axem* ('look at this race and your Romans. Here is Caesar and all the successors of Iulus who will come beneath the great axle of the sky', 788–90). But Statius' Sibyl speaks to Domitian alone; she can point to no great line of descendants as a spur to virtue. The Roman vision of imperial conquest depended on successors who would emulate and sustain their father's deeds: who would emulate Domitian's?

An important precedent for *Silv.* 4. 3 lies with Tibullus as well as with Virgil, specifically the two highly innovative elegies of Tibullus, 1. 7 and 2. 5. In the former Tibullus praises his patron Messalla for, among other things, his rebuilding of the Via Latina (57–60).[131] The later poem, which honours the appointment of Messalla's son Messalinus to the board of *quindecimviri*, contains a long prophecy by the Cumaean Sibyl to Aeneas (15–70).[132] These two poems together provide Statius with a precedent for including the topics of road-building and Sibylline verse in poems that stand outside epic tradition. But there is a closer link. Tibullus' two poems are connected to one another through the relationship of the father and the son, of Messalla and Messalinus, a relationship that Tibullus stresses in both poems. In *Elegy* 1. 7 Tibullus prays for offspring to rival Messalla's achievements (55–6).[133] *Elegy* 2. 5 acknowledges the success of this prayer with its praise of Messalinus' accomplishments. The elegy concludes with the picture of Messalla the proud father applauding the successes of his son (119–20). These two connected poems, then, provide a normative view of Roman parentage, whereby sons carry on the father's name and achievements. Tibullus' two poems underlie *Silv.* 4. 3, providing a precedent for Domitian's deeds and at the same time underscoring the dynastic problem faced by the last of the Flavians.

The Sibyl's obsession with age and fertility points to the gap between imperial fictions of invincible power and contemporary reality. Her large

---

[131] On Messalla's road-building see McCracken (1932).
[132] On Tibullus' treatment of the Sibyl see Cardauns (1961); Ball (1975); Murgatroyd (1994) 176–8, 205–11.
[133] Messalla seems to have had three children. See Murgatroyd (1980) 229 on lines 55–6.

dreams for Domitian's continuing life and glory are unsettled by their embedding within a world of flux and instability. Like *Silv.* 1.6, the poem ends with reference to Domitian's rebuilding of the temple of Jupiter Capitolinus, here described significantly as *renatae* ('reborn' or 'restored', 160). This is Domitian's true offspring, the building honouring the god with whom he sees himself closely identified. But the phrase *renatae* also conjures up a final reminder of Domitian's failure to provide an heir; thus the poem is opened up at its end to the notion of mutability that the Sibyl attempts to deny. Of course, *renatae* with its suggestions of wonderful rebirth is appropriate to Domitian's second rebuilding in the Flavian age, which was particularly magnificent; Plutarch criticises him later for his extravagance.[134] It was, moreover, conventional to associate longevity or immortality with the perpetuity of Rome and her buildings.[135] But even as the Sibyl wishes extraordinarily long life for Domitian, her words remind the reader that nothing remains fixed or unchanged in this imperial city, for even the temple of Jupiter Optimus Maximus Capitolinus, the sacred, ancient heart of Rome, has been rebuilt – indeed by AD 95 the temple of Capitoline Jupiter had been destroyed and rebuilt three times.[136] *Renatae* also reminds the reader of these restorations, of the temple's instability as a monument of stability.

The Sibyl's prophecies were traditionally associated with times of national crisis, not celebration. Her forecasts, Parke tells us, were characteristically grim: war, famine, pestilence, earthquakes, floods, volcanic eruptions had to be staved off by sometimes extraordinary measures on the part of the Roman people.[137] Parke comments that the Sibyl's production 'was not a tragedy but a horror film'.[138] Virgil's Sibyl conforms to this historic mould. Her prophecy to Aeneas begins with the vision of *bella, horrida bella,* | *et Thybrim multo spumantem sanguine* ('wars, horrid wars and the Tiber foaming with much blood', *Aen.* 6. 86–7). Statius' new, eulogistic Sibyl may seem to depart from tradition.[139] Indeed, this is a

---

[134] Plut. *Publ.* 15. 3–4.

[135] The classic example of course is provided by the ending of Hor. *Carm.* 3. 30.

[136] It was destroyed in 83 BCE in civil war; in AD 69 again in civil war; and in AD 80 after a fire. Domitian completed the restoration begun by Titus after the fire of AD 80. See Suet. *Tit.* 8. 3–4; *Dom.* 5. 1. See also chapter 7 above, 250.

[137] When Hannibal first invaded Italy, the Sibylline books were consulted after all kinds of bizarre prodigies were observed – shields sweating blood, soldiers' javelins on fire, ears of corn dripping with gore falling into the baskets of harvesters, roosters and hens undergoing sex changes. Livy 22. 1. 8–13; also 21. 62. 6–11; 22. 9. 7–11.

[138] Parke (1988) 13.

[139] We should perhaps take into account the major exception to the rule, Virgil's fourth *Eclogue*, where the Sibyl's prophecy is associated with an age of universal peace (4). Yet when she appears

rewriting of epic tradition in the interests of Empire – the Sibyl made
accessible for Domitian. But she is also made accessible to us, for she
is given a highly public voice. She is on the well-travelled highway, not
closeted in a cave. And if the reader sets the Sibyl's speech within the
historical context of AD 95, a turbulent year of severe dynastic setback,
then we can see a certain topicality in her appearance. For panegyric, as I
have suggested, flourishes particularly in times of political crisis when the
need to look towards a glorious future and assert continuity and stability
is particularly strong.[140] A figure of extraordinarily long life, the Sibyl
dramatises in her person the boldness and the weakness of Domitian's
imperial ideology. Her multivalent speech celebrates not only the marvellous technological achievement of the road but also draws attention
to two major contemporary issues; Domitian's divinity, which staves off
the problem of succession, and the problem of dynastic succession itself.

The Sibyl's fulsome speech provides an example of encomium that
is extravagant in praise almost to the point of ridicule. Yet, as a result,
her speech is multivalent, and the poet's distance from her invites the
reader's evaluative response. Her encomiastic vision is clearly out of
touch with the political realities of AD 95 and stretches the conditions of
belief. The gap between fiction and reality in her speech is so wide as to
activate doubts and anxieties in the reader. Although the Sibyl's speech
celebrates the majesty of Domitian's rule, it invites a reception alert to
the intimations of that rule's vulnerability and its uncertain future. Her
speech makes an important ending to Statius' final poem of imperial
praise, suggesting that the *Silvae* are important contemporary witnesses
not so much to facts about the Flavian age as to the ways in which
people thought and felt at the time. They celebrate the new splendours
of imperial culture and they express the doubts at its heart.

CONCLUSION

The building of the road, like the construction of the villa, can be viewed
as a metaphor for the exercise of imperial power. Domitian is compared
to other rulers who challenged or dominated nature in extraordinary
ways. Now this may just suggest his extraordinary powers; nonetheless,
we as readers are invited in various ways to consider his acts as potentially
dangerous or threatening to the social order. The varying perspective

first in Statius' poem her lineage is firmly epic; she is associated with the Sibyl who prophesied
civil war to Aeneas, the Pythia who prophesied likewise to Lucan's Appius.
[140] See chapter 1 above, 21; also chapter 7 above, 251–2.

of three figures on the road to Naples invites the reader to scrutinise the ideology behind the imperial drive for domination. Indeed, many of the contemporary readers of Book 4 of the *Silvae* would have been readers of Statius' newly published *Thebaid*. Certainly Vitorius Marcellus, to whom Book 4 is dedicated and *Silv.* 4. 4 is addressed, was closely involved with the progress of both Statius' epics (49–55, 87–100). Readers like Marcellus would have been alert to the disastrous consequences of overreaching that are so tragically and sometimes gruesomely depicted in the *Thebaid*.

Domitian is no Capaneus or Tydeus. He is, as the opening lines of *Silv.* 4. 3 tell us, a lawgiver who reveres the gods, albeit with an inverted piety. *Silv.* 4. 3 translates the transgressive ambitions of the *Thebaid* into encomiastic terms. Nonetheless, in the building of the road, and even more so in the Sibyl's song, the emperor's powers are represented as superhuman and therefore inherently precarious. In Domitian's challenging and surpassing of the limits of mortal endeavour the boundaries between the mythic world of the *Thebaid* and the contemporary world of the *Silvae* become blurred.

The emperor's separation from common humanity suggests the dangers inherent in autocratic power and the necessity perhaps of acknowledging limits and change, given the mutable nature of the world – and of Roman society and its political structuring. Such acknowledgement is perhaps particularly necessary with an emperor dangerously sustained by the fiction of invincibility and lacking the necessary infrastructure of dynastic stability. I am not suggesting that Statius is subversive of Domitian; the word subversive does not do justice to the capacious, playful, equivocal, and indeed anxious discourse of the *Silvae*. *Silv.* 4. 3 is humorous as well as encomiastic, critical as well as celebratory. It attempts, perhaps, to foster good conduct and also self-awareness in the emperor and his subjects. Through different voices, moreover, the poem invites resistance to the universalising claims of an imperial mission that could threaten regional and personal autonomy.

Silv. 4. 3 also explores the function of praise poetry within imperial society. In particular, Volturnus and the Sibyl, Statius' poets of Empire, offer different strategies for imperial praise: the safe, bound speech of the river god with his subservient Callimacheanism, the ebullient, capacious, and multivalent speech of the Sibyl. Then there is Statius himself, both adroitly Callimachean and epicising, a poet of anxiety as well as praise, for whom the expansive capacities of encomium dynamically engage him with competing visions of Empire. Indeed, through play with the familiar Callimachean metaphors of river and road Statius has in fact skilfully appropriated the imperial building project and made the road his own. Thus in *Silv.* 4. 3 he forges a swift but elegant and *new* path through Latin literature.

The Sibyl ends the road and Statius' sequence of poems addressed to Domitian. What better figure for imperial praise and closure could Statius have found than a figure whose speech's reception cannot ultimately be bound and who leaves the poet and the reader on the road between Naples and Rome?

References

The following reference works are cited in the notes as follows: *Dictionnaire étymologique de la langue latine, histoire des mots* (4th ed.) A. Ernout and A. Meillet, Paris 1959 (Ernout-Meillet); *Oxford Latin Dictionary*, P. G. Glare (ed.) Oxford 1968–82 (*OLD*); *Prosopographia Imperii Romani Saeculi I, II, III* (2nd ed.) E. Groag, A. Stein, L. Petersen, and K. Wachtel, Berlin 1933– (*PIR*); and *Thesaurus Linguae Latinae*, Leipzig 1900– (*TLL*). Classical texts follow the standard abbreviations used in *OLD*.

Ackerman, J. (1985) *The Villa: Form and Ideology of Country Houses*. Princeton
Ahl, F. (1984a) 'The Rider and the Horse: Politics and Power in Roman Poetry from Horace to Statius', *ANRW* 2. 1: 40–124
 (1984b) 'The Art of Safe Criticism in Greece and Rome', *AJP* 105: 174–208
 (1985) *Metaformations*. Ithaca, NY
 (1986) 'The *Thebaid*: A Reconsideration', *ANRW* 2. 32. 4: 2803–912
Alexandropoulos, J. (1994) 'La Propagande impériale par les monnaies de Claude á Domitien: quelques aspects d'une évolution', in Pailler and Sablayrolles (1994): 79–89
Almeida, E. R. (1995) '*Domus*: L. Arruntius Stella', *LTUR* 2: 37–8
Alpers, P. (1996) *What is Pastoral?* Chicago
Anderson, J. C. (1984) *The Historical Topography of the Imperial Fora*. Collection Latomus 182. Brussels
André, J. (1966) *L'Otium dans la Vie Morale et Intellectuelle Romaine*. Paris
Andreae, B. (1977) *The Art of Rome*, trans. R. E. Wolf. New York
Ascan, K., Fischer-Hansen, T., Johansen, F., Stovgaard-Jensen, S. and Skydsgaard, J. E. (eds.) (1976) *Studia Romana in Honorem Petri Krarup Septuagenarii*. Odense
Ash, R. (1999) *Ordering Anarchy: Armies and Leaders in Tacitus' Histories*. London
Asmis, E. (Forthcoming) 'Epicurean Economics', in Fitzgerald, Holland and Obbink. Leiden
Babcock, B. (ed.) (1978) *The Reversible World: Symbolic Inversion in Art and Society*. Ithaca, NY
Bailey, C. (1947) *De rerum natura libri sex Titi Lucreti Cari*. Oxford
Bakhtin, M. (1968) *Rabelais and his World*, trans. H. Iswolsky. Cambridge, MA
Ball, R. (1975) 'Tibullus 2. 5 and Virgil's *Aeneid*', *Vergilius* 21: 33–50

Barchiesi, A. (1989) 'Voci e istanze narrative nelle Metamorfosi di Ovidio', *MD* 23: 55–97
  (1996) 'La guerra di Troia non avrà luogo: il proemio dell' Achilleide di Stazio', *AION* 18: 45–62
  (1997) 'Virgilian Narrative: Ecphrasis', in Martindale (1997): 271–81
  (1998) 'Otto punti su una mappa dei naufragi', *MD* 39: 209–26
Barkan, L. (1999) *Unearthing the Past: Archaeology and Aesthetics in the Making of Renaissance Culture*. New Haven, CT
Barthes, R. (1992) *S/Z*, trans. R. Miller. New York
Bartsch, S. (1994) *Actors in the Audience: Theatricality and Doublespeak from Nero to Hadrian*. Cambridge, MA
Beagon, M. (1992) *Roman Nature: The Thought of Pliny the Elder*. Oxford
Becker, A. (1992) 'Reading Poetry through a Distant Lens: Ecphrasis, Ancient Greek Rhetoricians, and the Pseudo-Hesiodic Shield of Herakles', *AJP* 113: 5–24
  (1995) *The Shield of Achilles and the Poetics of Ekphrasis*. Lanham, MD
Bek, L. (1976) 'Antithesis', in Ascan, Fischer-Hansen, Johansen, Stovgaard-Jensen and Skydsgaard (1976): 154–66
  (1983) 'Questiones Conviviales: The Idea of the Triclinium and the Staging of Convivial Ceremony from Rome to Byzantium', *ARID* 12: 81–107
Bergmann, B. (1991) 'Painted Perspectives of a Villa Visit', in Gazda (1991): 49–70
Bernstein, M. (1992) *Bitter Carnival*. Princeton
Bing, P. (1995) 'Ergänzungsspiel in the Epigrams of Callimachus', *A & A* 41: 115–31
Birley, A. (ed.) (1988) *Roman papers JV*. Oxford
Bishop, T. G. (1996) *Shakespeare and the Theatre of Wonder*. Cambridge
Bodel, J. (1997) 'Monumental Villas and Villa Monuments', *JRA* 10: 5–35
Bömer, F. (1958) *Ovid: Die Fasten*, vol. II. Heidelberg
Bouchard, D. (ed.) (1978) *Language, Counter-Memory, Practice: Selected Essays and Interviews*. Oxford
Bourdieu, P. (1977) *Outline of a Theory of Practice*, trans. R. Nice. Cambridge
Boyle, A. J. (1986) *The Chaonian Dove: Studies in the Eclogues, Georgics, and Aeneid of Virgil*. Leiden
Boyle, A. J. (ed.) (1990) *The Imperial Muse: Ramus Essays on Roman Literature of the Empire. Flavian Epicist to Claudian*. Victoria, Australia
Boyle, A. J. (ed.) (1993) *Roman Epic*. London and New York
Boyle, A. J. (ed.) (1995) *Roman Literature and Ideology: Ramus Essays for J. P. Sullivan*. Berwick, Australia
Bradley, A. (1969) 'Augustan Culture and a Radical Alternative: Vergil's *Georgics*', *Arion* 8: 347–58
Braund, S. M. (1996) 'The Solitary Feast: A Contradiction in Terms?' *BICS* 41: 37–52
  (1998) 'Praise and Protreptic in Early Imperial Panegyric: Cicero, Seneca, Pliny', in Whitby (1998): 53–76

Bright, D. (1980) *Elaborate Disarray: The Nature of Statius' 'Silvae'*. Meisenheim am Glan

Buchner, E. (1982) *Die Sonnenuhr des Augustus*. Mainz

Bulloch, A., Gruen, E. S., Long, A. A. and Stewart, A. (eds.) (1993) *Images and Ideologies: Self-definition in the Hellenistic World*. Berkeley and Los Angeles

Busch, S. (1999) *Versus Balnearum: Die antike Dichtung über Bäder und Baden im römischen Reich*. Stuttgart and Leipzig

Cairns, F. and Heath, M. (eds.) (1998) *Greek Poetry, Drama, Prose and Roman Poetry. Papers of the Leeds International Seminar 1996*. Leeds

Cameron, A. (1995) *Callimachus and his Critics*. Princeton

Cancik, H. (1965) *Untersuchungen des lyrischen Kunst des P. Papinius Statius*. Hildesheim
 (1968) 'Eine epikureische Villa', *AU* 11: 62–75
 (1978) 'Tibur Vopisci', *Boreas* 1: 116–34

Cannadine, D. (1987) 'Introduction: Divine Rites of Kings', in Cannadine and Price (1987): 1–19

Cannadine, D. and Price, S. (eds.) (1987) *Rituals of Royalty: Power and Ceremonial in Traditional Societies*. Cambridge

Cardauns, B. (1961) 'Zu den Sibyllen bei Tibull 2, 5', *Hermes* 89: 357–66

Carradice, I. (1979) 'The Banishment of the Father of Claudius Etruscus: Numismatic Evidence', *LCM* 4. 5: 101–3
 (1983) *Coinage and Finances in the Reign of Domitian, AD 81–96*. Oxford

Champlin, E. (1978) 'The Life and Times of Calpurnius Siculus', *JRS* 68: 95–110

Chevallier, R. (1976) *Roman Roads*. London

Cima, M. and La Rocca, E. (eds.) (1998) *Horti Romani*. Rome.

Clinton, K. (1972) 'Publius Papinius St [---] at Eleusis', *TAPA* 103: 79–82

Coarelli, F. (1984) 'La Casa di Flavio Sabino e il Tempio della Gente Flavia', in *Roma Sepolta*: 147–55. Rome

Coleman, K. (1986) 'The Emperor Domitian and Literature', *ANRW* 2. 32. 5: 3087–115
 (1988) *Statius Silvae IV*. Oxford
 (1990) 'Fatal Charades: Roman Executions Staged as Mythological Enactments', *JRS* 80: 44–73
 (1998) 'Martial Book 8 and the Politics of AD 93', in Cairns and Heath (1998): 337–57
 (1999) 'Mythological Figures as Spokespersons in Statius' Silvae', in De Angelis and Muth (1999): 67–80

Collini, S. (2000) 'Is this the end of the world as we know it?', *Guardian Weekly* (January 2000): 11–12

Connors, C. (2000) 'Imperial Space and Time: The Literature of Leisure', in Taplin (2000): 492–58

Conte, G. B. (1994) *Latin Literature: A History*, trans. J. Solodow. Baltimore and London

Courtney, E. (1984) 'Criticisms and Elucidations of the *Silvae* of Statius', *TAPA* 114: 327–41

Courtney, E. (ed.) (1992) *P. Papini Stati Silvae*. Oxford

Cubeta, P. M. (1963) 'A Jonsonian Ideal: *To Penshurst*', *PQ* 42: 14–24

Curtius, E. R. (1973) *European Literature and the Latin Middle Ages*, trans. W. R. Trask. Princeton

D'Ambra, E. (1993) *Private Lives, Imperial Virtues: the Frieze of the Forum Transitorium in Rome*. Princeton

Damon, C. (1992) 'Statius *Silvae* 4. 9: *Libertas Decembris?*', *ICS* 17. 2: 301–8

D'Arms, J. (1970) *Romans on the Bay of Naples*. Cambridge, MA

(1974) 'Puteoli in the Second Century', *JRS* 64: 104–24

Darwall-Smith, R. (1996) *Emperors and Architecture: A Study of Flavian Rome*. Collection Latomus 231. Brussels

De Angelis, F. and Muth, S. (1999) *Im Spiegel des Mythos, Bilderwelt und Lebenswelt; Lo specchio del Mito, Immaginario e Realtà*. Wiesbaden

Degrassi, A. (1963) *Inscriptiones Italiae*, vol. XIII: 2. Rome

Dewar, M. (1994) 'Laying it on with a Trowel: The Proem to Lucan and Related Texts', *CQ* 44: 199–211

Dominik, W. J. (1990) 'Monarchical Power and Imperial Politics in Statius' *Thebaid*', in Boyle (1990): 74–97

(1994) *The Mythic Voice of Statius: Power and Politics in the Thebaid*. Leiden

Dunbabin, K. (1989) '*Baiarum grata voluptas*: Pleasures and Dangers of the Baths', *PBSR* 57: 7–46

Dunkle, J. R. (1967) 'The Greek Tyrant and Roman Political Invective of the Late Republic', *TAPA* 98: 151–71

Durry, M. (1938) *Pline le Jeune. Panégyrique de Trajan*. Paris

(1950) *Éloge Funèbre d'une Matrone Romaine*. Paris

Eck, W. (1997a) '*Cum dignitate otium*: Senatorial *Domus* in Imperial Rome', *Studia Classica Israelica* 16: 162–90.

(1997b) 'Rome and the Outside World: Senatorial Families and the World They Lived In', in Rawson and Weaver (1997): 73–99

Edwards, C. (1993) *The Politics of Immorality in Rome*. Cambridge

(1994) 'Beware of Imitations: Theater and the Subversion of Imperial Identity', in Elsner and Masters (1994) 83–97

Edwards, M. J. (1994) 'Callimachus, Roman Poetry and the Impotence of Song', Collection Latomus 53: 806–23

Elias, N. (1983) *The Court Society*, trans. E. Jephcott. Oxford

Elsner, J. and Masters J. (eds.) (1994) *Reflections of Nero*. Chapel Hill and London

Elsner, J. (ed.) (1996a) *Art and Text in Roman Culture*. Cambridge

(1996b) 'Inventing Imperium: Texts and the Propaganda of Monuments in Augustan Rome', in Elsner (1996a): 32–53

Empson, W. (1935) *Some Versions of Pastoral*. London

Evans, E. (1969) 'Physiognomics in the Ancient World', *TAPS* 59: 5–101

Evans, H. B. (1978) 'Horace, Satires 2. 7 : Saturnalia and Satire', *CJ* 73: 307–12

(1994) *Water Distribution in Ancient Rome: The Evidence of Frontinus*. Ann Arbor, MI

Evans, J. (1978) 'The Role of *Suffragium* in Imperial Political Decision-Making: a Flavian Example', *Historia* 27: 102–28

Fagan, G. (1999) *Bathing in Public in the Roman World*. Ann Arbor, MI

Fant, J. C. (1988) 'The Roman Emperor in the Marble Business: Capitalists, Middlemen or Philanthropists?', in Herz and Waelkens (1988): 147–58

Fantham, E. (1996) *Roman Literary Culture: From Cicero to Apuleius*. Baltimore and London

Farrar, L. (1998) *Gardens of Italy and the Western Provinces of the Roman Empire: From the 4th Century BC to the 4th Century AD*. Rome

Fears, J. R. (1977) '*Princeps a Diis Electus*': *The Divine Election of the Emperor as a Political Concept at Rome*. Rome

  (1981) 'Jupiter and Roman Imperial Ideology', *ANRW* 2. 17. 1: 3–141.

Feeney, D. (1993) *The Gods in Epic*. Oxford

Feldherr, A. (1995) 'Ships of State: *Aeneid* 5 and Augustan Circus Spectacle', *CA* 14: 245–65

Fitzgerald, W. (2000) *Slavery and the Roman Literary Imagination*. Cambridge

Flower, H. (2000) 'Damnatio Memoriae and Epigraphy', in Varner (2000a): 58–69

Fontenrose, J. (1981) *Orion: The Myth of the Hunter and the Huntress*. Berkeley

Foucault, M. (1978) 'A Preface to Transgression', in Bouchard (1978): 29–52

Fowler, A. (1982) 'The Silva Tradition in Jonson's *The Forrest*', in Mack and Lord (1982): 163–80.

Fowler, D. (1990) 'Deviant Focalization in Virgil's *Aeneid*', *PCPS* 36: 42–63

  (1991) 'Narrate and Describe: The Problem of Ekphrasis', *JRS* 81: 25–35

  (1995a) 'Horace and the Aesthetics of Politics', in Harrison (1995a): 248–66

  (1995b) 'Martial and the Book', in Boyle (1995): 199–26

  (2000) 'The Ruins of Time', in *Roman Constructions: Readings in Postmodern Latin*. Oxford: 193–217

Friedländer, P. (1912) *Johannes von Gaza und Paulus Silentarius – Kunstbeschreibungen Justinianischer Zeit*. Leipzig and Berlin

Friedman, A. (1989) *House and Household in Elizabethan England*. Chicago

Garnsey, P. and Saller, R. (1987) *The Roman Empire: Economy, Society and Culture*. Berkeley and Los Angeles

Garthwaite, J. (1984) 'Politics and Power in Roman Poetry. Appendix: Statius, *Silvae* 3. 4: On the Fate of Earinus', *ANRW* 2. 32. 1: 111–24

Gazda, E. K. (ed.) (1991)*Roman Art in the Private Sphere*. Ann Arbor, MI

Genette, G. (1980) *Narrative Discourse*, trans. J. E. Lewin. Oxford

  (1987) *Seuils*. Paris

  (1988) *Narrative Discourse Revisited*, trans. J. E. Lewin. Ithaca, NY

Geyssen, J. (1996) *Imperial Panegyric in Statius: A Literary Commentary on Silvae 1. 1*. New York

Gleason, M. (1995) *Making Men: Sophists and Self-Presentation in Ancient Rome*. Princeton

Goddard, J. (1994) 'The Tyrant at Table', in Elsner and Masters (1994): 67–82

Gold, B. K. (ed.) (1982) *Literary and Artistic Patronage in Ancient Rome*. Austin, TX

Goldhill, S. (1991) *The Poet's Voice*. Cambridge

Goldthwaite, R. A. (1993) *Wealth and the Demand for Art in Italy, 1300–1600.* Baltimore and London

Goodenough, E. R. (1928) 'The Political Philosophy of Hellenistic Kingship', *YCIS* 1: 55–102

Gordon, R. L. (1979) 'The Real and the Imaginary: Production and Religion in the Graeco-Roman World', *Art History* 2: 5–34

Gowers, E. (1993) *The Loaded Table: Representations of Food in Roman Literature.* Oxford

Gransden, K. W. (1970) 'The Pastoral Alternative', *Arethusa* 3: 103–21

Greenblatt, S. (1988) *Shakespearean Negotiations.* Berkeley and Los Angeles

Greene, T. (1982) *The Light in Troy.* New Haven, CT

Grénier, J.-C. (1987) 'L'Obélisque Pamphili: un témoignage méconnu sur l'avènement de Domitien', *MEFRA* 99: 937–61

(1996) 'Obeliscus Domitiani', *LTUR* 3: 357–8

Griffin, J. (1984) 'Augustus and the Poets: *Caesar qui cogere posset*', in Millar and Segal (1984): 189–218

Griffin, M. (1976) *Seneca: A Philosopher in Politics.* Oxford

Griffith, R. D. (1995) 'Catullus' *Coma Berenices* and Aeneas' Farewell to Dido', *TAPA* 125: 47–59

Grimal, P. (1969) *Les Jardins Romains,* 2nd. ed. Paris

Gros, P. (1996) 'Iuppiter Tonans, Aedes', *LTUR* 3: 159–60

Gsell, S. (1894) *Essai sur le règne de l'empereur Domitien.* Paris

Guiliani, C. F. (1995) 'Equus: Domitianus', *LTUR* 2: 228–9

Gunn, T. (1982) *The Occasions of Poetry.* London

Gutzwiller, K. (1991) *Theocritus' Pastoral Analogies.* Madison, WI

(1998) *Poetic Garlands: Hellenistic Epigram in Context.* Berkeley and Los Angeles

Habinek, T. N. (1990) 'Towards a History of Friendly Advice: The Politics of Candor in Cicero's *de Amicitia*', *Apeiron* 23: 165–85

(1998) *The Politics of Latin Literature: Writing, Identity, and Empire in Ancient Rome.* Princeton

Hallett, J. (1970) 'Over Troubled Waters: The Meaning of the Title *Pontifex*', *TAPA* 101: 219–27

Hannestad, N. (1988) *Roman Art and Imperial Policy.* Aarhus

Harder, M. A., Regtuit, R. F. and Wakker, G. C. (eds.) (1993) *Callimachus.* Groningen

Hardie, A. (1983) *Statius and the Silvae: Poets, Patrons and Epideixis in the Graeco-Roman World.* Liverpool

Hardie, P. (1993a) *The Epic Successors of Virgil.* Cambridge

(1993b) 'Ut pictura poesis? Horace and the Visual Arts', in Rudd (1993): 120–39

Hariman, R. (1995) *Political Style: The Artistry of Power.* Chicago

Harrison, S. J. (1985) '*Fronde Verecundo*: Statius, *Silvae* 1, 5, 14', *PLLS* 5: 337–40

(1995a) *Homage to Horace.* Oxford

(1995b) 'Horace, Pindar, Iullus Antonius, and Augustus: Odes 4. 2', in Harrison (1995a): 108–27

References

Haslam, M. (1993) 'Callimachus' Hymns', in Harder, Regtuit, and Wakker (1993): 111–25

Heffernan, J. (1993) *Museum of Words: Poetics of Ekphrasis from Homer to Ashbery.* Chicago and London

Henderson, J. (1991) 'Statius' *Thebaid*/Form Premade', *PCPS* 37: 30–80
(1993) 'Form Remade/Statius' *Thebaid*', in Boyle (1993): 162–91
(1998) *A Roman Life: Rutilius Gallicus on Paper & in Stone.* Exeter

Herendeen, W. H. (1986) *From Landscape to Literature: The River and the Myth of Geography.* Pittsburgh

Herescu, N. (1958) *Ovidiana.* Paris

Herford, C. E., Simpson, P. and Simpson, E. (1952) *Ben Jonson*, vol. XI. Oxford

Hershkowitz, D. (1998) *The Madness of Epic: Reading Insanity from Homer to Statius.* Oxford

Herz, N. and Waelkens, M. (1988) (eds.) *Classical Marble: Geochemistry, Technology, Trade.* Dordrecht, Boston, and London

Hinds, S. (1987) 'Generalising about Ovid', *Ramus* 16: 4–31
(1998) *Allusion and Intertext.* Cambridge
(Forthcoming) 'Cinna, Statius, and "Immanent Literary History"' in the Cultural Economy', *Entretiens 2000, Fondation Hardt: Immanente Literaturgeschichte in römischen Dichtungen*

Hofmann, W. (1990) 'Motivvariatonen bei Martial: die Mucius-Scaevola – und die Earinus-Gedichte', *Philologus* 134: 37–49

Hollander, J. (1988) 'The Poetics of Ekphrasis', *Word and Image* 4: 209–19
(1995) *The Gazer's Spirit: Poems Speaking to Silent Works of Art.* Chicago and London

Hopkins, K. (1965) 'Élite Mobility in the Later Roman Empire', *Past and Present* 32: 12–26
(1983) *Death and Renewal.* Cambridge

Hubbard, T. K. (1996) 'Calpurnius Siculus and the Unbearable Weight of Tradition', *Helios* 23: 67–89

Hunter, R. (1996) *Theocritus and the Archaeology of Greek Poetry.* Cambridge
(1997) 'Defining Pastoral', *CR* 47: 320–2

Imhoof-Blumer, F. (1920) 'Fluss- und Meergötter auf Griechischen und Römischen Münzen (Personifikationen der Gewässer)', *RSN* 23: 173–442

Jakobson, R. (1987) 'The Statue in Pûskin's Poetic Mythology', in *Language in Literature.* Cambridge, MA: 318–67

Jones, B. (1992) *The Emperor Domitian.* London and New York
(1994) 'Domitian and the Court', in Pailler and Sablayrolles (1994): 329–35
(1996) *Suetonius: Domitian.* Bristol

Keene, C. H. (1887, 1996) *Calpurnius Siculus: The Eclogues.* Bristol

Kenney, E. J. (1958) 'Nequitiae Poeta', in Herescu (1958): 201–9

Kerenyi, C. (1962) *The Religion of the Greeks and Romans*, trans. C. Holme. London

Kleiner, D. E. (1992) *Roman Sculpture.* New Haven, CT

Kleiner, F. S. (1991) 'The Trophy on the Bridge and the Roman Triumph over Nature', *L'Antiquité Classique* 60: 182–92

Klementa, S. (1993) *Gelagerte Flussgötter des Späthellenismus und der Römischen Kaiserzeit*. Cologne, Weimar, and Vienna

Koenen, L. (1993) 'The Ptolemaic King as a Religious Figure', in Bulloch, Gruen, Long, and Stewart (1993): 25–115

Konstan, D. (1973) *Some Aspects of Epicurean Psychology*. Leiden
(1997) *Friendship in the Classical World*. Cambridge

Kraus, C. (ed.) (1994) *Livy: Ab Urbe Condita Book VI*. Cambridge

Krevans, N. (1993) 'Fighting against Antimachus: The *Lyde* and the *Aetia* Reconsidered', in Harder, Regtuit, and Wakker (1993): 149–60

Kuhrt, A. (1987) 'Usurpation, Conquest and Ceremonial: From Babylon to Persia', in Cannadine and Price (1987): 20–55

Kurke, L. (1991) *The Traffic in Praise*. Ithaca, NY

Kuttner, A. (1999) 'Looking Outside Inside: Ancient Roman Garden Rooms', *Studies in the History of Gardens and Designed Landscapes* 1: 7–35

Laguna, G. (1992) *Estacio, Silvas III. Introducción, Edición Crítica, Traducción y Comentario*. Madrid

Laird, A. (1996) '*Ut figura poesis*: Writing Art and the Art of Writing in Augustan Poetry', in Elsner (1996a): 75–102

Last, H. (1948) 'On the Flavian Reliefs from the Palazzo della Cancellaria', *JRS* 38: 9–14

Lateiner, D. (1978) 'Ovid's Homage to Callimachus and Alexandrian Poetic Theory (*Am.* 2, 19)', *Hermes* 106: 188–96

Leach, E. W. (1974) *Vergil's 'Eclogues': Landscapes of Experience*. Ithaca, NY

Le Gall, J. (1953) *Recherches sur le Culte du Tibre*. Paris

Leiwo, M. (1994) *Neapolitana. Commentationes Humanarum Litterarum* 102. Helsinki

Lengrand, D. (1994) 'L'Essai sur le règne de l'empereur Domitien de S. Gsell et la réévaluation du règne de Domitien', in Pailler and Sablayrolles (1994): 57–67

Levene, D. S. (1997) 'God and Man in the Classical Latin Panegyric', *PCPS* 43: 66–103

Levick, B. (1982) 'Domitian and the Provinces', Collection Latomus 36: 50–73

Lomas, K. (1993) *Rome and the Western Greeks 350 BC–AD 200: Conquest and Acculturation in Southern Italy*. London and New York

Lorenz, S. (1997) 'Kaiserpanegyrik bei Martial', MA thesis, University of Munich
(2000) 'The Swimming Pool Library', *CR* 50: 67–8

MacCormack, S. (1981) *Art and Ceremony in Late Antiquity*. Berkeley and Los Angeles

Macdonald, W. (1982) *The Architecture of the Roman Empire*, vol. 1. New Haven, CT

MacDougall, E. B. (ed.) (1987) *Ancient Roman Villa Gardens. Dumbarton Oaks Colloquium on the History of Landscape Architecture 10*. Washington, DC

Mack, M. and Lord, G. de F. (eds.) (1982) *Poetic Traditions of the English Renaissance*. New Haven, CT

Maclean, G., Landry, D. and Ward, J. P. (eds.) (1999) *The Country and the City Revisited: England and the Politics of Culture, 1550–1850*. Cambridge

Macrides, R. and Magdalino, P. (1988) 'The Architecture of Ekphrasis: Construction and Context of Paul the Silentiary's Poem on Hagia Sophia', *BMGS* 12: 47–82

Malaise, M. (1972) *Les Conditions de Pénétration et de Diffusion des Cultes Egyptiens en Italie*. Leiden

Malamud, M. (1995) 'Happy Birthday, Dead Lucan: (P)raising the Dead in Silvae 2. 7', in Boyle (1995): 169–98

Mannspergo, D. (1974) 'ROM ET AUG. Die Selbstdarstellung des Kaisertums in der Römischen Reichsprägung', *ANRW* 2. 1: 919–96

Markus, D. (2000) 'Performing the Book: The Recital of Epic in First-Century C.E. Rome', *CA* 19: 138–79

Martindale, C. (ed.) (1997) *The Cambridge Companion to Virgil*. Cambridge

Marx, L. (1964) *The Machine in the Garden*. Oxford

Masters, J. (1992) *Poetry and Civil War in Lucan's Bellum Civile*. Cambridge

Mattingly, H. (1926) *The Roman Imperial Coinage*. London

Mauss, M. (1967) *The Gift*, trans. I. Cunnison. New York

Mayer, R. (1980) 'Calpurnius Siculus. Technique and Date', *JRS* 70: 175–6
    (1994) *Horace: Epistles Book 1*. Cambridge

Mayor, J. E. B. (1878, 1966) *Thirteen Satires of Juvenal*, vol. II. Hildesheim

McClung, W. A. (1977) *The Country House in English Renaissance Poetry*. Berkeley and Los Angeles

McCracken, G. (1932) 'Tibullus, Messalla, and the Via Latina', *AJP* 53: 344–52

McGuire, D. (1997) *Acts of Silence: Civil War, Tyranny, and Suicide in the Flavian Epics*. Hildesheim

McKay, A. G. (1975) *Houses, Villas and Palaces in the Roman World*. Ithaca, NY

McKeown, J. C. (1989) *Ovid 'Amores'. A Commentary on Book 1*, vol. II. Leeds

McNelis C. (2000) 'Reflexive Narratives, Poetics and Civil War in Statius' Thebaid', Ph.D. dissertation, University of California, Los Angeles

Melchiori, G. (1956) *The Tightrope Walkers: Studies of Mannerism in Modern English Literature*. London

Miles, R. (ed.) (1999) *Constructing Identities in Late Antiquity*. London and New York

Millar, F. (1965) 'Epictetus and the Imperial Court', *JRS* 55: 141–8
    (1977) *The Emperor in the Roman World 31 BC–AD 317*. Ithaca, NY

Millar, F. and Segal, E. (eds.) (1984) *Caesar Augustus: Seven Aspects*. Oxford

Molesworth, C. (1968) 'In More Decent Order Tame': Marvell, History, and the Country-House Poem*. Buffalo, NY

Montrose, L. (1983) 'Of Gentlemen and Shepherds: The Politics of Elizabethan Pastoral Form', *ELH* 10: 415–59
    (1986) 'The Elizabethan Subject and the Spenserian Text', in Parker and Quint (1986): 304–40. Baltimore and London
    (1996) *The Purpose of Playing*. Chicago

Morgan, L. (1997) 'Achilleae Comae: Hair and Heroism according to Domitian', *CQ* 47: 209–14
    (2000) 'Metre Matters: Some Higher-Level Metrical Play in Latin Poetry', *PCPS* 46: 99–120

Mumford, L. (1938) *The Culture of Cities*. New York

Murgatroyd, P. (1980) *Tibullus I: A Commentary on the First Book of the Elegies of Albius Tibullus*. Natal

(1994) *Tibullus: Elegies II*. Oxford

Murray, O. (1990) 'Sympotic History', in *Sympotica: A Symposium on the 'Symposion'*. Oxford: 3–13

Myerhoff, B. (1978) 'Return to Wirikuta: Ritual Reversal and Symbolic Continuity on the Peyote Hunt of the Huichol Indians', in Babcock (1978): 225–30

Myers, K. S. (1994) *Ovid's Causes: Cosmogony and Aetiology in the Metamorphoses*. Ann Arbor, MI.

(1996) 'The Poet and the Procuress: The *Lena* in Latin Love Elegy', *JRS* 86: 1–21

(2000) '*Miranda fides*: Poet and Patrons in Paradoxographical Landscapes in Statius' *Silvae*', *MD* 44: 103–38

Newlands, C. E. (1987) 'Urban Pastoral: The Seventh Eclogue of Calpurnius Siculus ', *CA* 6: 218–31

(1988) 'Statius' Villa Poems and Ben Jonson's *To Penshurst*: The Shaping of a Tradition', *Classical and Modern Literature* 8: 291–300

(1991) '*Silvae* 3. 1 and Statius' Poetic Temple', *CQ* 41: 438–52

(1995) *Playing with Time: Ovid and the Fasti*. Ithaca, NY

Newmyer, S. (1979) *The Silvae of Statius: Structure and Theme*. Leiden

(1984) 'The Triumph of Art over Nature; Martial and Statius on Flavian Aesthetics', *Helios* 11: 1–7

Nicolet, C. (1991) *Space, Geography, and Politics in the Early Roman Empire*. Ann Arbor, MI

Nisbet, R. G. M. (1978) '*Felicitas* at Surrentum', *JRS* 68: 1–11

Nisbet, R. G. M. and Hubbard, M. (1970) *A Commentary on Horace: Odes, Book I*. Oxford

(1978) *A Commentary on Horace: Odes, Book II*. Oxford

Nixon, C. E. V. and Rogers, B. S. (eds.) (1994) *In Praise of Later Roman Emperors: The Panegyrici Latini*. Berkeley and Los Angeles

North, M. (1985) *The Final Sculpture: Public Monuments and Modern Poets*. Ithaca, NY

Nugent, S. G. (1992) 'Vergil's "Voice of the Women" in *Aeneid* V', *Arethusa* 25: 255–92

O'Connor, C. (1993) *Roman Bridges*. Cambridge

O'Hara, J. J. (1990) *Death and the Optimistic Prophecy in Vergil's Aeneid*. Princeton

Oliensis, E. (1998) *Horace and the Rhetoric of Authority*. Cambridge

Pagán, V. (1999) 'Beyond Teutoburg: Transgression and Transformation in Tacitus *Annales* 1. 61–62', *CP* 94: 302–20

(2000) 'Distant Voices of Freedom in the *Annales* of Tacitus', *Collection Latomus* 254: *Studies in Latin Literature and Roman History X*: 358–69

Pailler, J. M. and Sablayrolles, R. (eds.) (1994) *Les Années Domitien*. Toulouse-Le Mirail

Parke, H. W. (1988) *Sibyls and Sibylline Prophecy in Classical Antiquity*. London and
    New York
Parker, P. and Quint, D. (eds.) (1986) *Literary Theory / Renaissance Texts*. Baltimore
    and London
Parry, H. (1964) 'Ovid's *Metamorphoses*: Violence in a Pastoral Landscape', *TAPA*
    95: 268–82
Parsons, P. (1977) 'Callimachus' *Victoria Berenices*', *ZPE* 25: 1–50
Patterson, A. (1984) *Censorship and Interpretation: The Conditions of Writing and Reading
    in Early Modern England*. Madison, WI
    (1987) *Pastoral and Ideology: Virgil to Valéry*. Berkeley and Los Angeles
Pavlovskis, Z. (1965) 'Statius and the Late Latin Epithalamia', *CP* 60: 164–77
    (1973) *Man in an Artificial Landscape*. Mnemosyne, Suppl. 25. Leiden
Pearcy, L. T. Jr. (1977) 'Horace's Architectural Imagery', *Collection Latomus*
    36: 772–81
Pederzani, O. (1991) 'L'Epos Privato e Quotidiano di Stazio', *Maia* 43: 21–31
    (1992) 'L'Imperatore e l'Eunuco', *Athenaeum* 80: 79–95
Poggioli, R. (1975) *The Oaten Flute: Essays on Pastoral Poetry and the Pastoral Ideal*.
    Cambridge, MA
Potter, D. (1990) *Prophecy and History in the Crisis of the Roman Empire: A Historical
    Commentary on the 'Thirteenth Sibylline Oracle'*, Oxford
Purcell, N. (1987) 'Town in Country and Country in Town', in MacDougall
    (1987): 185–203
Putnam, M. (1986) *Artifices of Eternity: Horace's Fourth Book of Odes*. Ithaca, NY
    (1998) *Virgil's Epic Designs: Ekphrasis in the Aeneid*. New Haven, CT
Quinn, K. (1973) *Catullus: The Poems*. London
Rawson B. and Weaver, P. (eds.) (1997) *The Roman Family in Italy: Status, Sentiment,
    Space*. Oxford
Reynolds, L. D. (ed.) (1983) *Texts and Transmission*. Oxford
Richmond, I. (1969) 'Two Flavian Monuments', in Salway (1969): 218–28
Roberts, M. (1989a) 'The Use of Myth in Latin Epithalamia from Statius to
    Venantius Fortunatus', *TAPA* 119: 321–48
    (1989b) *The Jeweled Style: Poetry and Poetics in Late Antiquity*. Ithaca, NY
Rogers, R. S. (1960) 'A Group of Domitianic Treason-Trials', *CP* 55: 19–23
Roller, L. E. (1998) 'The Ideology of the Eunuch Priest', in Wyke (1998): 118–35
Romm, J. (1992) *The Edges of the Earth in Ancient Thought*. Princeton
Rosand, D. (1990) 'Ekphrasis and the Generation of Images', *Arion* 1: 61–105
Rose, C. B. (1997) *Dynastic Commemoration and Imperial Portraiture in the Julio-Claudian
    Period*. Cambridge
Rosenmeyer, T. G. (1969) *The Green Cabinet*. Berkeley and Los Angeles
Rudd, N. (ed.) (1993) *Horace 2000: A Celebration*. Ann Arbor, MI
Russell, D. (1998) 'The Panegyrists and their Teachers', in Whitby (1998): 17–50
Sablayrolles, R. (1994) 'Domitien, l'Auguste Ridicule', in Pailler and Sablayrolles
    (1994): 113–44
Saller, R. (1984) '*Familia, Domus*, and the Roman Conception of the Family',
    Phoenix 38: 336–55

(1994) *Patriarchy, Property and Death in the Roman Family*. Cambridge
(1999) '*Pater Familias, Mater Familias*, and the Gendered Semantics of the Roman House', *CP* 94: 182–97
Salway, P. (ed.) (1969) *Roman Archaeology and Art: Essays and Studies by Sir Ian Richmond*. London
Santini, C. (1991) *Silius Italicus and his View of the Past*. Amsterdam
Sauter, F. (1934) *Der Römische Kaiserkult bei Martial und Statius*. Stuttgart and Berlin
Schmidt, E. (1997) *Sabinum*. Heidelberg
Scott, G. F. (1991) 'The Rhetoric of Dilation: Ekphrasis and Ideology', *Word and Image* 7: 301–10
Scott, K. (1936) *The Imperial Cult under the Flavians*. Stuttgart and Berlin
Scullard, H. H. (1981) *Festivals and Ceremonies of the Roman Republic*. Ithaca, NY
Segal, C. P. (1969a) *Landscape in Ovid's Metamorphoses: A Study in the Transformation of a Literary Symbol*. Hermes Einzelschriften 23. Wiesbaden
(1969b) 'Horace Odes 2. 6', *Philologus* 113: 235–53
Simon, E. (1960) 'Zu den Flavischen Reliefs von der Cancellaria', *JDAI* 75: 1134–56
Sinfield, A. (1992) *Faultlines*. Oxford
Skutsch, O. (ed.) (1985) *The 'Annals' of Quintus Ennius*. Oxford
Southern, P. (1997) *Domitian: Tragic Tyrant*. London and New York
Stallybrass, P. and White, A. (1986) *The Politics and Poetics of Transgression*. Ithaca, NY
Stewart, P. (1999) 'The Destruction of Statues in Late Antiquity', in Miles (1999): 159–89
Strobel, K. (1994) 'Domitian – Kaiser und Politik im Spannungsfeld des Überganges zur Monarchie des 2. Jh. N. Chr.', in Pailler and Sablayrolles (1994): 359–95
Suter, A. (1989) 'Ovid, From Image to Narrative: *Amores* 1. 8 and 3. 6', *CW* 83: 15–22
Syme, R. (1958) *Tacitus*, vol. I. Oxford
(1988) 'Domitian: The Last Years', in Birley (1988): 252–77
Szelest, H. (1966) 'Die Originalität der Sog. Beschreibenden *Silvae* des Statius', *Eos* 56: 186–97
(1972) 'Mythologie und ihre Rolle in den *Silvae* des Statius', *Eos* 60: 309–17
Taisne, A.-M. (1994) *L'Esthétique de Stace*. Paris
Tanner, R. G. (1986) 'Epic Tradition and Epigram in Statius', *ANRW* 2. 32. 5: 3020–46
Taplin, O. (ed.) (2000) *Literature in the Greek and Roman Worlds: A New Perspective*. Oxford
Thébert, Y. (1987) 'Private Life and Domestic Architecture in Roman Africa', in Veyne (1987): 313–409
Thomas, R. (1983) 'Callimachus, the *Victoria Berenices*, and Roman Poetry', *CQ* 33: 92–113
(1988) 'Tree Violation and Ambivalence in Virgil', *TAPA* 118: 261–73

(1993) 'Callimachus Back in Rome,' in Harder, Regtuit, and Wakker (1993): 197–215

Toner, J. P. (1995) *Leisure and Ancient Rome*. Cambridge, MA

Townend, G. B. (1980) 'Calpurnius Siculus and the Munus Neronis', *JRS* 70: 166–74

Troxler-Keller, I. (1964) *Die Dichterlandschaft des Horaz*. Heidelberg

Turcan, R. (1981) 'Janus à l'époque impériale', *ANRW* 2. 17. 1: 374–402

Turner, V. (1969) *The Ritual Process: Structure and Anti-Structure*. Ithaca, NY

Unglaub, J. (1997) "The Concert Champêtre': The Crises of History and the Limits of the Pastoral', *Arion* 5: 46–90

Van Dam, H.-J. (1984) *P. Papinius Statius, Silvae Book II: A Commentary*. Mnemosyne, Suppl. 82, Leiden

Van Sickle, J. (1978) *The Design of Virgil's 'Bucolics'*. Rome

Varner, E. (ed.) (2000a) *From Caligula to Constantine. Tyranny and Transformation in Roman Portraiture*. Atlanta

(2000b) 'Tyranny and the Transformation of the Roman Visual Landscape', in Varner (2000a): 9–26.

Verstraete, B. C. (1989) 'Panegyric and Candour in Statius, *Silvae* 3, 4', *Collection Latomus* 206: 405–13

Vessey, D. W. T. C. (1971) 'Review of Hakanson, *Silvae*', *CP* 66: 273–6

(1972) 'Aspects of Statius' Epithalamion', *Mnemosyne* 25: 172–87.

(1973) *Statius and the Thebaid*. Cambridge

(1981) 'Atedius Melior's Tree: Statius *Silvae* 2. 3', *CP* 76: 46–52

(1983) 'Mediis Discumbere in Astris: Statius, *Silvae* IV, 2', *AC* 52: 206–20

(1986) 'Transience Preserved: Style and Theme in Statius' *Silvae*', *ANRW* 2. 32. 5: 2754–802

Veyne, P. (ed.) (1987) *A History of Private Life*, vol. 1. Cambridge, MA

(1990) *Bread and Circuses*, trans. B. Pearce. London

Vinson, M. (1989) 'Domitia Longina, Julia Titi, and the Literary Tradition', *Historia* 38: 431–50

Vismara, C. (1994) 'Domitien, Spectacles, Supplices et Cruauté', in Pailler and Sablayrolles (1994): 413–20

Vollmer, F. (ed.) (1898) *P. Papinii Statii Silvarum Libri*. Leipzig

Wallace-Hadrill, A. (1970) 'The Imperial Court', *CAH* 2. 10: 283–308

(1981) 'The Emperor and his Virtues', *Historia* 30: 298–323

(1987) 'Time for Augustus: Ovid, Augustus, and the Fasti', in Whitby, Hardie, and Whitby (1987): 221–30

(1988) 'The Social Structure of the Roman House', *PBSR* 56: 43–97

(1989) 'Patronage in Roman Society: from Republic to Empire', in *Patronage in Ancient Society* (1989): 63–87. London

(1990) 'Pliny the Elder and Man's Unnatural History', *G&R* 37: 80–96

(1994) *Houses and Society in Pompeii and Herculaneum*. Princeton

(1995) 'Horti and Hellenization', in Cima and La Rocca (1998): 1–12

Ward-Perkins, J. B. (1992) *Marble in Antiquity: Collected Papers of J. B. Ward-Perkins*, eds. H. Dodge and B. Ward-Perkins. London

Waters, K. H. (1963) 'The Second Dynasty of Rome', *Phoenix* 17: 198–218
(1964) 'The Character of Domitian', *Phoenix* 18: 49–77

Wayne, D. E. (1984) *Penshurst: the Semiotics of Place and the Poetics of History*. Madison, WI

Weaver, P. R. C. (1965) 'The Father of Claudius Etruscus: Statius, *Silvae* 3. 3', *CQ* 15: 145–54

Webb, R. and James, L. (1991) '"To Understand Ultimate Things and Enter Secret Places": Ekphrasis and Art in Byzantium', *Art History* 14: 1–17

Webb, R. (1999) '*Ekphrasis* Ancient and Modern: The Invention of a Genre', *Word and Image* 15: 7–18

Weisman, L. K. (1992) *Discrimination by Design*. Urbana and Chicago

Whitby, M., Hardie, P. and Whitby, M. (eds.) (1987) *Homo Viator: Classical Essays for John Bramble*. Bristol

Whitby, M. (ed.) (1998) *The Propaganda of Power: The Role of Panegyric in Late Antiquity*. Leiden

White, P. (1974) 'The Presentation and Dedication of the *Silvae* and the Epigrams', *JRS* 64: 40–61
(1975) 'The Friends of Martial, Statius, and Pliny, and the Dispersal of Patronage', *HSCP* 79: 265–300
(1978) 'Amicitia and the Profession of Poetry in early Imperial Rome', *JRS* 68: 74–92
(1993) *Promised Verse*. Cambridge, MA

Whitehorne, J. E. G. (1969) 'The Ambitious Builder', *AUMLA* 31: 28–39

Wiedemann, T. (1992) *Emperors and Gladiators*. London and New York

Williams, F. (1978) *Callimachus. Hymn to Apollo: A Commentary*. Oxford

Williams, G. (1978) *Change and Decline: Roman Literature in the Early Empire*. Berkeley and Los Angeles

Williams, R. (1973) *The Country and the City*. New York and Oxford
(1981) *The Sociology of Culture*. Chicago

Wilson, R. (1987) '"Is This a Holiday?": Shakespeare's Roman Carnival', *ELH* 54: 31–44

Wirszubski, C. (1950) *Libertas as a Political Idea at Rome during the Late and Early Principate*. Cambridge

Wiseman, T. P. (1970) 'Roman Republican Road-Building', *PBSR* 38: 122–52
(1978) 'Flavians on the Capitol', *AJAH* 3: 163–78
(1982a) 'Calpurnius Siculus and the Claudian Civil War', *JRS* 72: 57–67
(1982b) '*Pete Nobiles Amicos*: Poets and Patrons in Late Republican Rome', in Gold (1982): 28–49
(1987) '*Conspicui postes tectaque digna deo:* The Public Image of Aristocratic and Imperial Houses in the Late Republic and Early Empire', in *L'Urbs: Espace Urbain et Histoire*. Rome: 393–413

Wyke, M. (ed.) (1998) *Gender and the Body in the Ancient Mediterranean*. Oxford

Yegül, F. (1979) 'The Small City Bath in Classical Antiquity and a Reconstruction Study of Lucian's Baths of Hippias', *Arch Cl* 31: 108–31

(1992)*Baths and Bathing in Classical Antiquity.* Cambridge, MA

Zanker, P. (1998) *Pompeii: Public and Private Life.* Cambridge, MA

Zetzel, J. (1983) 'Recreating the Canon: Augustan Poetry and the Alexandrian Past', *Critical Inquiry* 10: 83–105

Index locorum

341

Index of subjects and proper names